JAVA™
Complete Course
in Programming & Problem Solving

Dr. Kenneth A. Lambert
Washington & Lee University

Dr. Martin Osborne
Western Washington University

VISIT US ON THE INTERNET
www.swep.com

South-Western Educational Publishing
an International Thomson Publishing company I(T)P®

www.thomson.com

Cincinnati • Albany, NY • Belmont, CA • Bonn • Boston • Detroit • Johannesburg • London • Madrid
Melbourne • Mexico City • New York • Paris • Singapore • Tokyo • Toronto • Washington

To Nathaniel—Ken
To Tess—Martin

Library of Congress Cataloging-in-Publication Data
Lambert, Kenneth (Kenneth A.)
   Java: complete course in programming and problem solving /
Kenneth A. Lambert, Martin Osborne.
     p.   cm.
   Includes index.
   ISBN 0-538-68707-X (hardbound). — ISBN 0-538-68711-8 (softcover)
   1. Java (Computer program language)   I. Osborne, Martin
QA76.J38L355   2000
005.13'3—dc21   98-35332
                                      CIP

Managing Editor:	Carol Volz
Project Manager:	Dave Lafferty
Consulting Editor::	Custom Editorial Productions, Inc.
Marketing Manager:	Steve Wright & Larry Qualls
Design Coordinator:	Mike Broussard
Production:	Custom Editorial Productions, Inc.

ISBN: 0-538-68707-X (hard cover)
0-538-68771-8 (soft cover)

1 2 3 4 5 D 02 01 00 99 98

Printed in the United States of America

I(T)P®

International Thomson Publishing

South-Western Educational Publishing is a division of International Thomson Publishing, Inc. The ITP registered trademark is used under license.

BreezyGUI® is a registered trademark of Brooks/Cole Publishing, a division of International Thomson Publishing, Inc.

PREFACE

This text is intended for a first course in programming and problem solving. We want students to focus on traditional topics in computer science, while writing object-oriented programs with graphical user interfaces in Java. Thus, the text covers seven major aspects of computing:

1. **Programming Basics.** This deals with the basic ideas of problem solving with computers, primitive data types, control structures, and methods.

2. **Data and Information Processing.** Fundamental data structures are discussed. These include strings, arrays, and files.

3. **Object-Oriented Programming.** OOP is today's dominant programming paradigm. All the essentials of this subject are covered.

4. **Graphical User Interfaces and Event-Driven Programming.** Many texts at this level cling to what has now become an antiquated mode of programming—character-based terminal I/O. The reason is simple. GUIs and event-driven programming are too complex for beginning students. In this text, we overcome the barrier of complexity in the manner explained below.

5. **Software Development Life Cycle.** Rather than isolate software development techniques in separate lessons, our text deals with them throughout in the context of numerous case studies.

6. **Graphics.** Our text explores problem solving with simple graphics. This includes drawing simple shapes, representing data graphically, and implementing a rudimentary sketching program.

7. **Networking.** We introduce the programming of Web pages and applets.

Early, Easy GUIs with BreezyGUI®

Every CS1 Java text faces a dilemma: either do terminal I/O and look like a C++ text, or do graphical user interfaces and overwhelm the reader with the details of Java's Abstract Windowing Toolkit. To overcome this dilemma, our text comes with a software package, **BreezyGUI**, which simplifies the programming of graphical user interfaces. **BreezyGUI** insulates students from the complex details of setting up window objects and managing interface events. Thus, students can use GUIs without being overwhelmed and distracted from the basic business of software development—algorithm design and factoring code into classes. Every example program in the first 12 lessons is GUI-based and uses **BreezyGUI**. The mystery behind the **BreezyGUI** package is removed in the final lesson of the text, where we introduce the details of Java's Abstract Windowing Toolkit and delegation event model.

Focus on Traditional Computer Science Topics

Many introductory Java books succumb to the temptation to focus on the popular features of Java for Web-based programs, such as applets, threads, client/server network applications, and multimedia. We believe that these are actually advanced topics, which presuppose a principled introduction to the field. The example programs in the first 11 lessons of our book are stand-alone Java applications. Lesson 12 introduces HTML programming and applets, which allow Java programs to run in Web browsers. Because all of our applications are GUI-based, the transition from applications to applets is straightforward.

Just-in-Time, Multiparadigm Approach to Problem Solving

At one time there was a movement in computer science texts to introduce user-defined procedures as early as possible. Many texts are now supplanting this approach with another one: introduce user-defined classes as early as possible. Both approaches overlook the fact that procedures and classes are mechanisms for structuring code, and as such they are best introduced when students start working with problems that call for these organizational tools. Thus, the early lessons of our book (2 through 4) emphasize calculations, control constructs, and algorithms. User-defined methods arrive in Lesson 5 and user-defined classes in Lesson 7. There they are needed, and their benefits are appreciated.

Case Studies and the Software Life Cycle

This text contains numerous case studies. These are complete Java programs, ranging from the simple to the substantial. To emphasize the importance and reality of the software development life cycle, case studies are always presented in the framework of a user request, analysis, design, and implementation, with well-defined tasks performed at each stage. Some case studies are carried through several lessons or extended in end-of-lesson programming projects.

Alternative Paths Through the Text

We have organized the text to satisfy different time frames and topic preferences. We recommend starting with the first three lessons, which provide CS background; explain how to run a first Java program; and explore the basics of syntax, semantics, and debugging. After the first three lessons have been covered, the following alternatives suggest themselves:

1. Those who cannot resist doing applets should skip to Lesson 12 and then return to Lesson 4.

2. Those who cannot resist doing graphics should do Lessons 4 and 5, then skip to Lesson 10, and return to Lesson 6.

3. Those who cannot resist doing files should do Lessons 4–6 then skip to Lesson 11, and return to Lesson 7.

4. Those who want to cover user-defined classes but omit inheritance should skip Lesson 9.

   Of course, the best way to use this text is simply to go through it.

Reports of Errors and Updates

We have made every effort to produce an error-free text, although this cannot be guaranteed with certainty. We assume full responsibility for all errors or omissions. Readers are encouraged to report errors to **klambert@wlu.edu**. A listing of errata, should they be discovered, and other information about the book will be posted on the author's Web site, **http://www.wlu.edu/~lambertk/hsjava/index.html**.

Acknowledgments

We would like to take this opportunity to thank those who in some way contributed to the completion of this text. Several reviewers offered constructive comments during various phases of this project. They include:

Mark Ciampa, Volunteer State Community College, Gallatin, TN

Fred Bartels, Rye Country Day School, Rye, NY

Derek Hodgkins, New Hampshire Community Technical College, Manchester, NH

Lily Hou, Carnegie-Mellon University, Pittsburgh, PA

Tsang-Ming Jiang, University of Alaska, Fairbanks, AK

Gail Miles, Lenoir-Rhyne College, Hickory, NC

Arland J. Richmond, Computer Learning Center, Somerville, MA

Christopher Starr, College of Charleston, Charleston, SC

Hoyt D. Warner, Western New England College, Springfield, MA

Lee Wittenberg, Kean University, Union, NJ

Winnie Yu, Southern Connecticut State University, New Haven, CT

John Zelle, Drake University, Des Moines, IA

Several other people deserve mention because, without their expertise, this text would not exist:

Cat Skintik of Custom Editorial Productions, Inc., Developmental Editor. Cat worked through not only the text but also all of the ancillaries and program code, testing all of the programs, taking the quizzes, and offering helpful commentary.

Jim Reidel, Valerie Brandenburg, and Cindy Lanning of Custom Editorial Productions, Inc., for the production and layout of this book.

John Wills, Partnerships Manager. Among other things, John negotiated the agreement that resulted in the compiler that is bundled with the text.

Dave Lafferty, Project Manager. Dave drew up the blueprints for a complete teaching package, from text to workbook to instructor's CD, and kept the project on target.

Carol Volz, Managing Editor. Carol focused our eyes on the need for this text and worked out the arrangements for placing it in South-Western's computer education listing.

Finally, we are grateful to our wives and children for giving us the time and support to develop this text.

Kenneth A. Lambert
Martin Osborne

v

How to Use this Text

What makes a good computer programming text? Sound pedagogy and the most current, complete materials. That is what you will find in the new *Java: Complete Course in Programming and Problem Solving*. Not only will you find an inviting layout, but also many features to enhance learning.

Objectives— Objectives are listed at the beginning of each lesson, along with a suggested time for completion of the lesson. This allows you to look ahead to what you will be learning and to pace your work.

Enhanced Screen Shots—Screen shots now come to life on each page.

Program Code Examples—Many examples of program code are included in the text to illustrate concepts under discussion.

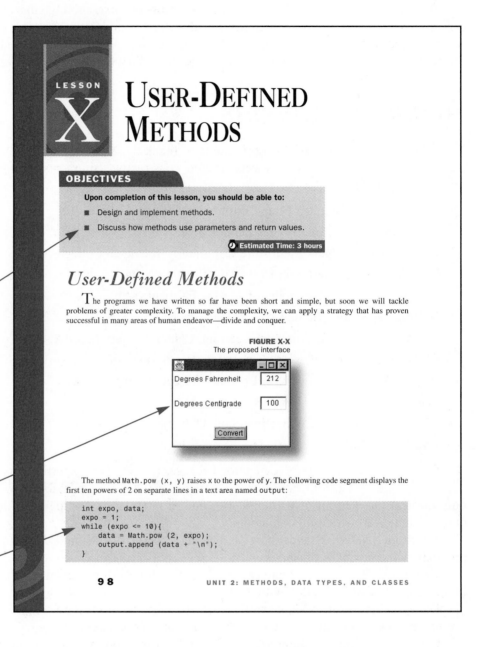

LESSON X

USER-DEFINED METHODS

OBJECTIVES

Upon completion of this lesson, you should be able to:

■ Design and implement methods.

■ Discuss how methods use parameters and return values.

⏱ **Estimated Time: 3 hours**

User-Defined Methods

The programs we have written so far have been short and simple, but soon we will tackle problems of greater complexity. To manage the complexity, we can apply a strategy that has proven successful in many areas of human endeavor—divide and conquer.

FIGURE X-X
The proposed interface

| Degrees Fahrenheit | 212 |
| Degrees Centigrade | 100 |

Convert

The method `Math.pow (x, y)` raises x to the power of y. The following code segment displays the first ten powers of 2 on separate lines in a text area named `output`:

```
int expo, data;
expo = 1;
while (expo <= 10){
    data = Math.pow (2, expo);
    output.append (data + "\n");
}
```

98   UNIT 2: METHODS, DATA TYPES, AND CLASSES

How to Use this Text

Case Studies—Case studies present Java program solutions to specific user requests and show the analysis, design, and implementation stages of the software development life cycle.

SCANS (Secretary's Commission on Achieving Necessary Skills)—The U.S. Department of Labor has identified the school-to-careers competencies. The five workplace competencies (resources, interpersonal skills, information, systems, and technology) and foundation skills (basic skills, thinking skills, and personal qualities) are identified in Case Studies and Projects throughout the text. More information on SCANS can be found on the *Electronic Instructor.*

Summary—At the end of each lesson, you will find a summary to help you complete the end-of-lesson activities.

Review Questions—Review material at the end of each lesson and each unit enables you to prepare for assessment of the content presented.

CASE STUDY 5 : A Sales Table

Request

Write a program that allows the user to enter the names and annual sales figures for any number of salespeople. The program should display a formatted table of salespeople, their sales, and their commissions (at 10% of the sales amount).

Summary

In this lesson, you learned:

■ The modern computer age began in the late 1940s with the development of ENIAC. Business computing became practical in the 1950s, and time-sharing computers advanced computing in large organizations in the 1960s.

LESSON 1 REVIEW QUESTIONS

WRITTEN QUESTIONS

Write your answers to the following questions.

1. What are the three major hardware components of a computer?
2. Name three input devices.

LESSON ? PROJECT

1. Java's `Integer` class defines public constants, `MIN_VALUE` and `MAX_VALUE`, that name the minimum and maximum `int` values supported by the language. Thus, the expression `Integer.MAX_VALUE` returns the maximum `int` value. The `Double` class defines similar constants. Write a program that displays the values of these four constants.

CRITICAL THINKING ACTIVITY

You have an idea for a program that will help the local pizza shop handle take-out orders. Your friend suggests an interview with the shop's owner to discuss her user requirements before you get started on the program. Explain why this is a good suggestion, and list the questions you would ask the owner to help you determine the user requirements.

UNIT 1 APPLICATIONS

1. Light travels at $3 * 10^8$ meters per second. A light-year is the distance a light beam would travel in 1 year. Write a program that calculates and displays the value of a light-year.

9 9

Lesson Projects—End-of-lesson hands-on application of what has been learned in the lesson allows you to actually apply the techniques covered.

Critical Thinking Activity—Each lesson and each unit review gives you an opportunity to apply creative analysis to situations presented.

End-of-Unit Applications—End-of-unit hands-on applications of concepts learned in the unit provides opportunity for a comprehensive review.

CONTENTS

UNIT 3   ARRAYS, INHERITANCE, AND GRAPHICS   189

Explore the Flavor of Java!

With these exciting new products from South-Western!

Our new Java programming books offer everything from beginning, to intermediate, to advanced courses to meet your programming needs.

- *NEW! Java Complete Course in Programming and Problem Solving* by Lambert and Osborne is the most comprehensive instructional text available for learning Java. It contains 75+ hours of instruction on the most widely used beginning-through-advanced features of Java. Covers Java for both Windows and Macintosh.

Student book, hard cover	0-538-68707-X
Student text-workbook/data CD-ROM package, soft cover	0-538-68708-8
Activities Workbook	0-538-68710-X
Electronic Instructor CD-ROM package	0-538-68709-6

- *NEW! Java: Introduction to Programming* by Knowlton covers the beginning-through-intermediate features of Java in 35+ hours of instruction. The text is available in hard or soft cover and is for the Windows version of Java only.

Student book, hard cover	0-538-68565-4
Student book/3.5″ template disk package, soft cover	0-538-68772-X
Activities Workbook	0-538-68571-9
Electronic Instructor CD-ROM package	0-538-68557-3
Student book, hard cover/Microsoft Visual J++ package	0-538-68774-6
Student book/3.5″ template disk package, soft cover with Microsoft Visual J++ package	0-538-68773-8

- *NEW! Java: Programming Basics for the Internet* by Barksdale and Knowlton, et al., gives the user a quick introduction to the beginning-through-advanced features of Java. It contains 15+ hours of instruction; the emphasis is on applets and activities.

Student Text-Workbook	0-538-68012-1
Student Text-Workbook/Microsoft Visual J++ package	0-538-68564-6
Instructor's Manual (online)	0-538-68013-X

A new feature available for these products is the *Electronic Instructor*, which includes a printed Instructor's manual and a CD-ROM. The CD-ROM contains tests, lesson plans, all data solutions files, and more! Also, ask about our ProgramPaks for compiler software bundles!

For information call 1-800-354-9706.

South-Western
Educational Publishing

Join Us On the Internet
www.swep.com

GETTING STARTED WITH JAVA

UNIT 1

A BRIEF HISTORY OF COMPUTER PROGRAMMING

OBJECTIVES

Upon completion of this lesson, you will be able to:

■ Give a brief history of computers.

■ Describe how hardware and software make up computer architecture.

■ Discuss the evolution of programming languages.

■ Describe the software development process.

■ Discuss the fundamental concepts of object-oriented programming.

⏱ **Estimated Time: 2 hours**

History of Computers

ENIAC, built in the late 1940s, was one of the world's first computers. It was a large, stand-alone machine that filled a room and used more electricity than all the houses on an average city block. ENIAC contained hundreds of miles of wire and thousands of heat-producing vacuum tubes. The mean time between failures was less than an hour, yet because of its fantastic speed, when compared to hand-operated electro-mechanical calculators, it was immensely useful. To read more about the ENIAC and see photos of early computers, contact the following site by using your Web browser: **http://ftp.arl.mil/ftp/historic-computers.**

In the early 1950s, IBM sold its first business computer. At the time, analysts estimated that the world would never need more than ten such machines, yet its awesome computational power was a mere 1/200 of the typical 200-megahertz Pentium personal computer purchased for about $1000 in 1998.

The first computers could perform only a single task at a time. Input and output were handled by such primitive means as switches, punch cards, and paper tape.

In the 1960s, time-sharing computers, costing hundreds of thousands and even millions of dollars, became popular at organizations large enough to afford them. Even back then, computers were so much faster that 30 people could work on such a computer simultaneously without loss of computing power. Each person sat at a Teletype console connected by wire to the computer. By making a connection through the telephone system, Teletype consoles could be placed at a great distance from the computer. The Teletype was a primitive device by today's standards. It looked like an electric typewriter with a large roll of paper attached. Keystrokes entered at the keyboard were transmitted to the computer, which then echoed them back on the roll of paper. Output from the computer's programs was also printed on this roll.

In the 1970s, people began to see the advantage of connecting computers in networks, and the wonders of e-mail and file transfers were born.

In the 1980s, personal computers (PCs) appeared in great numbers. Soon thereafter, local area networks of interconnected PCs became popular. These networks allowed a local group of PCs to communicate and share such resources as disk drives and printers with each other and with large, centralized multiuser computers.

The 1990s have seen an explosion in computer use, and the hundreds of millions of computers now appearing on every desktop and in almost every home can be connected through the Internet (Figure 1-1), a fact known by every hacker and feared by every bank and government installation.

And the common language of all these computers is fast becoming Java.

FIGURE 1-1
Computers are interconnected
through the Internet

Computer Architecture

Modern computers can be viewed as machines that process information. Information processors consist of two primary components: *hardware* and *software*. Hardware consists of the physical devices that you see on your desktop. Software consists of the programs that enable human beings to use the hardware.

Computer Hardware

A general-purpose computer consists of many interconnected and interacting parts. Figure 1-2 shows the hardware components of a typical PC.

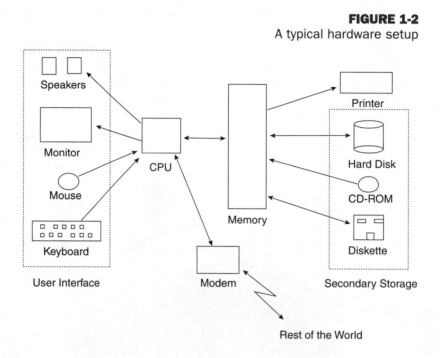

FIGURE 1-2
A typical hardware setup

Input devices send information to the computer for processing. Examples of input devices include:

- A keyboard for entering text.

- A microphone for entering sound.

- A mouse for direct manipulation of images on the monitor screen.

- A *modem* for entering information from other computers.

Output devices display information in a form that people can understand. Examples of output devices include:

- A monitor for displaying text and images on a screen.

- Speakers for emitting sound.

- A printer for producing hard copies of text and images.

Secondary storage devices store information that must be retained on a permanent or semipermanent basis. Examples are disks and CD-ROMs.

A computer uses two devices to process information: *memory* and a *central processing unit* (CPU). The memory (sometimes also called *main memory* or *primary memory*) consists of a large number of cells that can contain information. Each cell is an electronic device that can be in one of two states, either on or off. A given pattern of these states can be used to represent any information whatsoever, such as numbers, text, images, and sound.

Some of the information stored in memory represents *data,* or the information to be processed. The rest of the information stored in memory represents instructions, which tell the computer how to process the data. In other words, both the *program* (the instructions) and the information to be processed (the data) are stored as patterns of electronic states in memory.

The CPU consists of circuitry that transforms given patterns of information into new patterns of information. The basic operations of the CPU are those of arithmetic, logic, and the rearrangement of information in memory. The appropriate combination of these simple operations is all that a computer needs to achieve the amazing range of applications that we now take for granted.

To process information, the computer begins with the first instruction in memory. This instruction is sent to the CPU, where it is decoded and executed. As a result, information in memory may be rearranged. The computer then repeats this process with the remaining instructions in memory, until a special "halt" instruction is reached. We return to the representation of information, the organization of computer memory, and the way in which a machine executes programs in later lessons.

Computer Software

Computer hardware processes complex patterns of electronic states. Computer software hides these patterns from human users, enabling them to view this information as text, images, and so forth.

System software provides basic facilities that allow users to interact with a computer. This software includes:

- The *operating system,* especially the file system for transferring information to and from disk and schedulers for running multiple programs concurrently.

- Communications software for connecting to other computers.

- Compilers for translating user programs into executable form.

- Desktop managers for visualizing tasks and data.

Application software lets human users accomplish a specialized task. Common application software includes word processing and spreadsheet programs, database systems, and other programs designed to complete specific tasks.

Programming Languages

Question: "If a program is just some very long pattern of electronic states in computer memory, then what is the best way to write a program?" The history of computing provides several answers to this question, in the form of generations of *programming languages.*

Generation 1 (Late 1940s to Early 1950s)—Machine Language

Computers were new and very expensive, and programs were short. The programmer viewed the states *off* and *on* as the numbers 0 and 1, respectively. The programmer toggled switches on the front of the computer to enter 0s and 1s directly into memory. Later, a machine read the 0s and 1s from punched cards or paper tape into memory. There were several problems with this *machine language* coding technique:

1. Coding was prone to error (make just one mistake and the program no longer worked correctly).

2. Coding was tedious and slow.

3. Programs were extremely difficult to modify.

4. It was nearly impossible for one person to decipher another person's program.

5. A program was not portable to a different type of computer, because each type had its own unique machine language.

Needless to say, this technique is no longer used!

Generation 2 (Early 1950s to the Present)—Assembly Language

Instead of the binary notation of machine language, *assembly language* uses mnemonic symbols to represent instructions and data. For instance, here is a machine language instruction followed by its assembly language equivalent:

```
0011 1001 / 1111 0110 / 1111 1000 / 1111 1010
ADD            A,           B,          C
```

meaning

1. Take the number at location 246, which we refer to as A.

2. Add that number to the number at location 248, which we refer to as B.

3. Store the result at location 250, which we refer to as C.

Each assembly language instruction corresponds to exactly one machine language instruction. The standard procedure for using assembly language consists of several steps:

1. Write the program in assembly language.

2. Translate the program into a machine language program. This is done by a computer program called an *assembler.*

3. Load and run the machine language program. This is done by another program called a *loader.*

When compared to machine language, assembly language is more programmer friendly. But assembly language is still tedious to use and difficult to modify. And it is no more portable than machine language, because each type of computer still has its own unique assembly language.

Assembly language is used as little as possible, although sometimes it is used when memory or processing speed are at a premium. Thus, every computer science major probably learns at least one assembly language.

Generation 3 (Middle 1950s to the Present)—High-Level Language

Early examples of *high-level languages* are FORTRAN and COBOL, which are still in widespread use. Later examples are BASIC and Pascal. Recent examples are Smalltalk, C++, and Java. These languages are designed to be human friendly—easy to write, easy to read, and easy to understand—at least when compared to assembly language. For example, all high-level languages support the use of algebraic notation, such as the expression $x + y * z$.

Each instruction in a high-level language corresponds to many instructions in machine language. Translation is done by a program called a *compiler.* Generally, a program written in a high-level language is portable, but it must be recompiled for each type of computer on which it is going to run. The vast majority of software is written in high-level languages.

Software Development Process

The use of a high-level programming language helps programmers write high-quality software, but more help is needed. To this end, computer scientists have developed a view of the software development process, known as the *software life cycle.* We now present a particular version of this life cycle, called the *waterfall model.*

The software life cycle consists of several phases:

1. **Customer request.** In this phase, the programmers receive a broad statement of a problem that is potentially amenable to a computerized solution. This step is also called the *user requirements* phase.

2. **Analysis.** The programmers determine what the program will do. This is sometimes viewed as a process of clarifying the specifications for the problem.

3. **Design.** The programmers determine how the program will do its task.

4. **Implementation.** They write the program. This step is also called *coding* phase.

5. **Integration.** Large programs have many parts. These parts must be brought together into a smoothly functioning product, usually not an easy task.

6. **Maintenance.** Programs usually have a long life; 5 to 15 years is common. During this time, requirements change and minor or major changes must be made.

The interaction between the phases is shown in Figure 1-3. Note that the figure resembles a waterfall, in which the results of each step trickle down to the next phase. A mistake detected in one phase often requires the developer to back up and redo some of the work in the previous phase. Modifications made during maintenance also require backing up to an earlier phase.

FIGURE 1-3
The waterfall model of software development

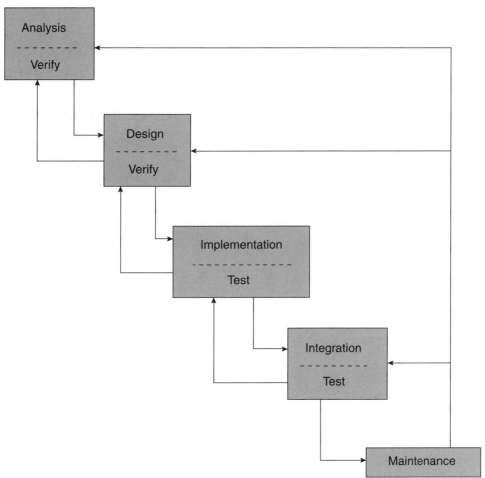

Programs rarely work as hoped the first time they are run. Thus, they should be subjected to extensive and careful testing. Many people think that testing is an activity that applies to only the implementation and integration phases. However, the outputs of each phase should be scrutinized carefully. In fact, mistakes found early are much less expensive to correct than those found later. Figure 1-4 illustrates some relative costs of repairing such mistakes.

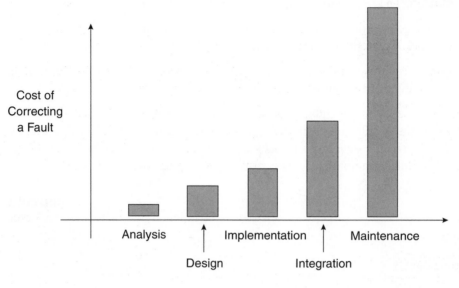

FIGURE 1-4
Costs of repairing a fault rise as the development process proceeds

Finally, the cost of developing software is not spread equally over the phases. Figure 1-5 shows typical percentages.

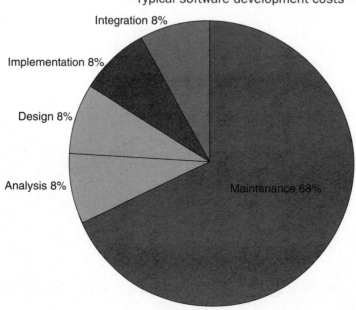

FIGURE 1-5
Typical software development costs

Most people would probably think that implementation takes the most time and therefore costs the most. However, maintenance is in fact the most expensive aspect of software development.

As you read this book and begin to sharpen your programming skills, you should therefore remember two things:

1. There is more to software development than writing code.

2. If you want to reduce the overall cost of software development, write programs that are easy to maintain. This requires thorough analysis, careful design, and good coding style. We will have more to say about coding style throughout the book.

For a thorough introduction to software engineering, see Stephen R. Schach, *Software Engineering with Java* (Chicago: Irwin, 1997).

Object-Oriented Programming

Object-oriented programming (OOP) is a style of programming that can also lead to better quality software. Introductory programming courses are now frequently taught using object-oriented languages. C++ and Java are the most popular.

Large programs contain many thousands of lines of code. Writing a large program is a highly complex task in any language. The job is best handled by breaking code into many smaller communicating components. There are various strategies for doing this, depending on the type of programming language being used. We now attempt to give an overview of this process in the context of OOP. Along the way, we illustrate some fundamental concepts of OOP: class, object, message, method, attribute, encapsulation, inheritance, and polymorphism. At the end of this section, you will have a broad understanding of the programming process.

We proceed by way of an extended analogy, in an attempt to associate something already familiar with something new. Like all analogies, this one is imperfect but hopefully useful. Imagine that it is your task to plan an expedition in search of the lost treasure of Balbor. How familiar can this be, you ask? Well, that depends on your taste in books, movies, and video games. Your overall approach might consist of the following components.

Planning

You determine the types of team members needed: leaders, pathfinders, porters, trail engineers. You then define the responsibilities of each type of team member. For example, what materials will each type carry? What special knowledge must each type of team member have? You must also specify rules governing the behavior of each type of team member in various situations. Finally, you decide how many of each type of team member will be needed.

Execution

You assemble the team at the starting point, send the team on its way, and sit back and wait for the outcome. No sense in endangering your own life, too.

Outcome

If the planning was done well, you will be rich. Otherwise, prepare for a disappointment.

The World of OOP

How does this analogy relate to OOP? Table 1-1 gives the details. We explore the concepts in the rest of the book.

TABLE 1-1
Understanding object-oriented programming

THE WORLD OF THE EXPEDITION	THE WORLD OF OOP
Planning the trip.	Programming.
Going on the trip.	Running the program.
Different types of team members.	Different types of software components, called *classes*.
Individual team members.	*Objects*.
A team member is classified according to a particular type—porter, pathfinder, etc.	An object is an *instance* of a class.
During planning, we specify the types needed and their rules of behavior.	During programming, we define the classes needed and their *methods* (rules of behavior).
The actual expedition involves individuals, not types of team members.	The running program involves objects, not classes.
During the trip, team members ask each other to do things.	When the program is running, objects send each other *messages*.
When a team member receives a request, he follows the instructions in a corresponding rule.	When an object receives a message, it refers to its class to find a corresponding method to execute.
A pathfinder knows the route and has a compass.	An object contains data resources, also called *attributes*.
If someone wants to know where north is, he or she asks a pathfinder rather than grabbing a pathfinder's compass. This is because a pathfinder not only owns basic resources such as a compass, but also knows the procedures and techniques needed to use it correctly.	If object A needs information, then A sends a message to some object B that is responsible for managing that type of information. The object B contains not only data resources but also the methods needed to manage and manipulate the data. The combining of data and related methods into a single software entity is called *encapsulation*.
The expedition might include different types of trail engineers. All trail engineers share some common skills, but some specialize in bridge building and others in clearing landslides. Thus, there is a hierarchy of engineers:	Classes can be organized in a hierarchy also. The class at the root of the hierarchy defines methods and attributes shared by its subclasses. Each subclass defines additional methods and attributes. This process is called *inheritance*.

TABLE 1-1
(continued)

Lesson ① A Brief History of Computer Programming

THE WORLD OF THE EXPEDITION	THE WORLD OF OOP
At the end of the day, the leader tells each member to set up camp. All members understand this request, but their responses depend on their specialties.	Different types of objects also can understand the same message. This is referred to as *polymorphism*. However, an object's response depends on which class it belongs to.
During the trip, everyone is careful not to ask an individual to do something for which he or she is not trained, i.e., for which he or she does not have a rule of behavior.	When writing a program, do not send a message to an object unless its class has a corresponding method.
One can rely on team members to improvise and resolve ambiguities and contradictions in rules.	A computer does exactly what the program specifies—neither more nor less—thus, programming errors and oversights, no matter how small, are usually disastrous. Therefore, programmers need to be excruciatingly thorough and exact.

CS CAPSULE:
The ACM Code of Ethics and Intellectual Property

The ACM Code of Ethics

The Association for Computing Machinery (ACM) is the flagship organization for computing professionals. The ACM supports publications of research results and new trends in computer science, sponsors conferences and professional meetings, and provides standards for computer scientists as professionals. The standards concerning the conduct and professional responsibility of computer scientists have been published in the ACM Code of Ethics. The code is intended as a basis for ethical decision making and for judging the merits of complaints about violations of professional ethical standards.

The code lists several general moral imperatives for computer professionals:

■ Contribute to society and human well-being.

■ Avoid harm to others.

■ Be honest and trustworthy.

■ Be fair and take action not to discriminate.

■ Honor property rights including copyrights and patents.

■ Give proper credit for intellectual property.

■ Respect the privacy of others.

■ Honor confidentiality.

11

The code also lists several more specific professional responsibilities:

- Strive to achieve the highest quality, effectiveness, and dignity in both the process and products of professional work.

- Acquire and maintain professional competence.

- Know and respect existing laws pertaining to professional work.

- Accept and provide appropriate professional review.

- Give comprehensive and thorough evaluations of computer systems and their impacts, including analysis of possible risks.

- Honor contracts, agreements, and assigned responsibilities.

- Improve public understanding of computing and its consequences.

- Access computing and communication resources only when authorized to do so.

In addition to these principles, the code offers a set of guidelines to provide professionals with explanations of various issues contained in the principles.

The complete text of the ACM Code of Ethics is available at the ACM's World Wide Web site, **http://www.acm.org.**

Copyright, Intellectual Property, and Digital Information

For hundreds of years, copyright law has existed to regulate the use of intellectual property. At stake are the rights of authors and publishers to a return on their investment in works of the intellect, which include printed matter (books, articles, etc.), recorded music, film, and video. More recently, copyright law has been extended to include software and other forms of digital information. For example, the software on the disk included with this book is protected by copyright law. This prohibits the purchaser from reproducing the software for sale or free distribution to others. If the software is stolen or "pirated" in this way, the perpetrator can be prosecuted and punished by law. However, copyright law also allows for "fair use"—the purchaser may make backup copies of the software for personal use. When the purchaser sells the software to another user, the seller thereby relinquishes the right to use it and the new purchaser acquires this right.

When governments design copyright legislation, they try to balance the rights of authors and publishers to a return on their work against the rights of the public to fair use. In the case of printed matter and other works that have a physical embodiment, the meaning of fair use is fairly clear. Without fair use, borrowing a book from a library or playing a CD at a high school dance would be unlawful.

With the rapid rise of digital information and its easy transmission on networks, different interest groups—authors, publishers, users, and computer professionals—are beginning to question the traditional balance of ownership rights and fair use. For example, is browsing a copyrighted manuscript on a network service an instance of fair use? Or does it involve a reproduction of the manuscript that violates the rights of the author or publisher? Is the manuscript a physical piece of intellectual property when browsed, or just a temporary pattern of bits in a computer's memory? Users and technical experts tend to favor free access to any information placed on a network. Publishers and, to a lesser extent, authors tend to worry that their work, when placed on a network, will be resold for profit.

Legislators struggling with the adjustment of copyright law to a digital environment face many of these questions and concerns. Providers and users of digital information should also be aware of the issues. For a detailed discussion, see Pamela Samuelson, "Regulation of Technologies to Protect Copyrighted Works," *Communications of the ACM,* Volume 39, Number 7 (July 1996): 17–22.

Summary

In this lesson, you learned:

■ The modern computer age began in the late 1940s with the development of ENIAC. Business computing became practical in the 1950s, and time-sharing computers advanced computing in large organizations in the 1960s. The 1980s saw the development and widespread sales of personal computers. The 1990s have seen an explosion in computer use in business and in the home.

■ Modern computers consist of two primary components: hardware and software. Computer hardware is the physical component of the system. Computer software consists of programs that enable us to use the hardware.

■ Programming languages have been developed in the course of three generations. Generation 1 is machine language. Generation 2 is assembly language. Generation 3 is high-level language.

■ The software development process consists of several standard phases: customer request, analysis, design, implementation, integration, and maintenance.

■ Object-oriented programming is a style of programming that can lead to better quality software. By breaking code into easily handled components, you simplify the job of writing a large program.

LESSON 1 REVIEW QUESTIONS

WRITTEN QUESTIONS

Write your answers to the following questions.

1. What are the three major hardware components of a computer?

2. Name three input devices.

3. Name two output devices.

4. What is the difference between application software and system software?

5. Name a first-generation programming language, a second-generation programming language, and a third-generation programming language.

FILL IN THE BLANKS

Complete each of the following statements by writing your answer in the blank provided.

6. In the _____ phase of the software life cycle, the programmer describes what the software system will do to solve a problem.

7. The _____ phase of the software life cycle is also called the coding phase.

8. More than half of the cost of developing software goes to the _____ phase of the software life cycle.

9. ACM stands for _____.

10. Copyright law is designed to give fair use to the public and to protect the rights of _____ and _____.

LESSON 1 PROJECT

Take some time to become familiar with the architecture of the computer you will use for this course. On a separate piece of paper, describe your hardware and software, using the following guidelines:

■ What hardware components make up your system?

■ How much memory does your system have?

■ What are the specifications of your CPU? (Do you know its speed and what kind of microprocessor it has?)

■ What operating system are you using? What version of that operating system is your computer currently running?

■ What major software applications are loaded on your system?

CRITICAL THINKING ACTIVITY

You have just written some software that you would like to sell. Your friend suggests that you copyright your software. Discuss why this might be a good suggestion.

A FIRST JAVA
PROGRAM

OBJECTIVES

Upon completion of this lesson, you will be able to:

■ Discuss why Java is an important programming language.

■ Explain the Java virtual machine and byte code.

■ Describe the structure of a simple Java program.

■ Use Java syntax and semantics to write a simple program.

■ Edit, compile, and run a program.

■ Format a program to give a pleasing, consistent appearance.

■ Discuss syntax, run-time, and logic errors and debug a simple program.

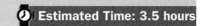 **Estimated Time: 3.5 hours**

In this lesson we will take you through the steps for developing a Java program, from the initial customer request to debugging the final program. But first, let us discuss why Java is an important and appropriate programming language.

Why Java?

Java is the fastest growing programming language in the world. Companies such as IBM and Sun have adopted Java as their major application development language. There are several reasons for this.

First, Java is a modern object-oriented programming language. The designers of Java spent much time studying the features of classical object-oriented languages such as Smalltalk and C++ and made a successful effort to incorporate the good features and omit the less desirable ones.

Second, Java is secure, robust, and portable. That is, the Java language

■ Enables the construction of virus-free, tamper-free systems (secure).

■ Supports the development of programs that do not overwrite memory (robust).

■ Yields programs that can be run on different types of computers without change (portable).

These features make Java ideally suited to develop distributed, network-based applications, an area of ever-increasing importance.

Third, Java supports the use of advanced programming concepts such as threads. A *thread* is a process that can run concurrently with other processes. For example, a single Java application might consist of two threads. One thread transfers an image from one machine to another across a network, while the other thread simultaneously interacts with the user.

Fourth and finally, Java bears a superficial resemblance to C++, which is currently the world's most popular industrial-strength programming language. Thus, it is easy for a C++ programmer to learn Java and for a Java programmer to learn C++. However, compared with C++, Java is easier to use and to learn. It is also less error prone, more portable, and better suited to the Internet.

On the negative side, Java runs more slowly than most modern programming languages because it is interpreted. To understand this last point, we must now turn our attention to the Java virtual machine and byte code.

The Java Virtual Machine and Byte Code

Compilers usually translate a higher-level language into the machine language of a particular type of computer. However, the Java compiler translates Java not into machine language, but into a pseudo–machine language called Java *byte code*. Byte code is the machine language for an imaginary Java computer. To run Java byte code on a particular computer, you must install a Java *virtual machine* (JVM) on that computer.

A JVM is a program that behaves like a computer. Such a program is called an *interpreter*. An interpreter has advantages and disadvantages. The main disadvantage of an interpreter is that a program pretending to be a computer runs programs more slowly than an actual computer. However, JVMs are getting faster every day. For instance, some can translate byte code into machine language as they go—called just-in-time (JIT) compilation. Also, new computer chips are being developed that implement a JVM directly in hardware so that there is no performance penalty.

The main advantage of an interpreter is that any computer can run it. Thus, Java byte code is highly portable. For instance, many of the pages you download from the Web contain small Java programs already translated into byte code. These are called *applets* and are run in a JVM that is incorporated into your Web browser. These applets can be decorative (display an animated character on the Web page) or practical (display a continuous stream of stock market quotes).

Because Java programs run inside a virtual machine, it is possible to limit their capabilities. Thus, ideally, you never have to worry about a Java applet infecting your computer with a virus, erasing the files on your computer, or stealing sensitive information and sending it across the Internet to a competitor. In practice, however, computer hackers have successfully penetrated Java's security mechanisms in the past and may succeed again in the future. But all things considered, Java applets really are very secure, and security weaknesses are repaired as soon as they become known.

For a discussion of the current impact of Java, see "The Java Factor," *Communications of the ACM,* Volume 41, No. 6 (June 1998): 34–76.

CASE STUDY:
Request, Analysis, and Design for the First Program

We now present our first Java program. In this example and many of the examples that follow, we walk through the life cycle discussed in Lesson 1. The use of this technique might seem overblown for our early examples, but you will soon appreciate how it scales up when the examples become more complex.

Request

We start with a customer request: Deliver a program that converts degrees Fahrenheit to degrees centigrade. That's all. Such requests are usually simple, and we must then apply analysis to spell out more precisely what the program will do.

Analysis

The program accepts user input that consists of a number representing degrees Fahrenheit. The program then converts degrees Fahrenheit to degrees centigrade. Finally, the program displays the results. The program allows this process to be repeated as frequently as desired. As part of our analysis, we provide a snapshot of the proposed interface in Figure 2-1.

FIGURE 2-1
The proposed interface

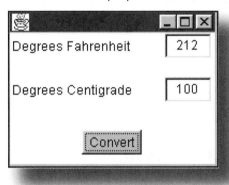

The interface consists of the following components:

1. A data field labeled **Degrees Fahrenheit.**

2. A data field labeled **Degrees Centigrade.**

3. A command button labeled **Convert.**

4. A window bar containing sizing and close controls.

The inclusion of an interface at this point is a good idea because it allows the customer and the programmer to discuss the intended program's behavior in a context understandable to both. In this and other examples, we use a *graphical user interface* (GUI).

The last part of analysis is instructions for use of the interface. These instructions might be enumerated as follows:

1. The user enters the Fahrenheit temperature in the first data field.

2. The user clicks the **Convert** button.

3. The program computes and displays the centigrade temperature in the second data field.

4. The user repeats the process or clicks the **X** to close the window.

Design

In this part of the process, we describe how the program accomplishes its task. This involves describing the *algorithm* that the program will use. Like a recipe, an algorithm is a sequence of steps that describes how to solve a problem in much the same way a recipe in a cookbook describes how to bake a cake. Algorithms are often written in a somewhat stylized version of English called *pseudocode*.

The following pseudocode describes what happens when the **Convert** button is clicked:

```
get fahrenheit
compute centigrade = (fahrenheit - 32) * 5 / 9
display centigrade
```

In this algorithm,

■ `fahrenheit` indicates a variable quantity whose value depends on the actual number entered by the user.

■ `centigrade` indicates a variable quantity whose value depends on the outcome of the calculation.

■ = means assign the value of the expression on the right to the variable on the left.

■ * indicates multiplication.

■ / indicates division.

Pseudocode usually ignores details concerning the behavior of the user interface.

Writing the Program

Given the above GUI and pseudocode, an experienced programmer would now find it easy to write the needed Java program. For a beginner, on the other hand, writing the code is the most difficult part of the process. Here is the Java program. Except for lines that have been boldfaced, the code is going to seem rather mysterious. However, by the end of the lesson we dispel much of the mystery.

```
import java.awt.*;
import BreezyGUI.*;

public class FahrenheitToCentigrade extends GBFrame{

    Label degreesFahrenheitLabel = addLabel ("Degrees Fahrenheit",1,1,1,1);
    IntegerField degreesFahrenheitField = addIntegerField (0,1,2,1,1);
    Label degreesCentigradeLabel = addLabel ("Degrees Centigrade",2,1,1,1);
    IntegerField degreesCentigradeField = addIntegerField (0,2,2,1,1);
    Button convertButton = addButton ("Convert",3,1,2,1);

    int fahrenheit;
    int centigrade;
```

```
    public void buttonClicked (Button buttonObj){
        fahrenheit = degreesFahrenheitField.getNumber();
        centigrade = (fahrenheit - 32) * 5 / 9;
        degreesCentigradeField.setNumber (centigrade);
    }

    public static void main (String[] args){
        Frame frm = new FahrenheitToCentigrade();
        frm.setSize (200, 150);
        frm.setVisible (true);
    }
}
```

If you are feeling intimidated by the fact that three lines of pseudocode translate into 21 lines of Java code, take heart from the fact that all the programs discussed in the first several lessons of the book have more or less the same structure, as illustrated next. The words in bold italic indicate portions of the structure that change from one program to the next.

```
import java.awt.*;
import BreezyGUI.*;

public class <name of program> extends GBFrame{

    <define window objects>

    <declare variables>

    public void buttonClicked (Button buttonObj){
        <do what needs to be done when a button
        is clicked>
    }

    public static void main (String[] args){
        Frame frm = new <name of program>();
        frm.setSize (<width of window>, <height of window>);
        frm.setVisible (true);
    }
}
```

Language Elements

Before writing code in a programming language, you need to be aware of some basic language elements. Every natural language, such as English, Japanese, or German, has its own vocabulary, syntax, and semantics. Programming languages also have these three elements.

Vocabulary

The vocabulary is the set of all of the words in the language. Here are examples taken from Java:

arithmetic operators	+ – * /
assignment	=
numeric literals	5 9
programmer-defined variable names	fahrenheit centigrade

Syntax

The *syntax* contains the rules for combining words into sentences. Here are two typical syntax rules:

1. In an expression, two arithmetic operators must not be adjacent. Thus, (f - 32) * / 9 is invalid.

2. In an expression, left and right parentheses must occur in pairs (…). Thus,)f - 32(* 5 / 9 is invalid, and f - 32) * 5 / 9 is invalid.

Semantics

The *semantics* contains the rules for interpreting the meaning of the sentences. For example, the expression (f - 32) * 5 / 9 means "Subtract 32 from the variable quantity indicated by f; multiply the result by 5; and finally divide the whole thing by 9."

Programming and Natural Languages

Despite their similarities, programming languages and natural languages have important differences. First, programming languages have limited vocabularies, syntax, and semantics. Thus, their basic elements are not hard to learn. Second, in a programming language one must get the syntax absolutely correct, whereas an ungrammatical English sentence is usually comprehensible. This strictness of expression often makes writing programs difficult for beginners, although no more so than writing good sentences in English. Third, when we give a friend instructions in English, we can be a little vague, relying on the friend to fill in the details. In a programming language, we must be exhaustively thorough. Computers do exactly what they are told, neither more nor less. When people blame problems on computer error, they should more accurately blame sloppy programming. This difference is the one that makes programming difficult even for competent programmers.

Although programming languages are simpler than human languages, the task of writing programs is challenging, because it is difficult to express complex ideas using the limited syntax and semantics of a programming language.

Interpreting the Program

The discussion that follows introduces enough of Java's syntax and semantics to help you understand our program. Later lessons will explore all topics in greater detail.

Variables

A *variable* is an item whose value may change during the execution of a program. A variable can be thought of as a named box that exists in the computer's memory, as illustrated in Figure 2-2. Changing the value of a variable is equivalent to replacing the number that was in the box with another number.

For instance, if our program were used to convert first 212 and then 95 from Fahrenheit to centigrade, then the variable fahrenheit would first have a value of 212 and then a value of 95.

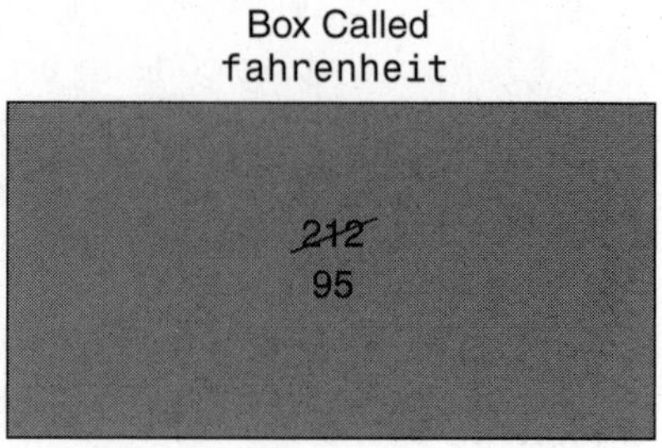

A Variable's Type

During the course of a program, a specific variable can hold only one type of data. Some common *data types* include integer, floating point, character, and string. Before using a variable for the first time, the programmer must declare its type. For instance,

FIGURE 2-2
Changing the value of a variable

Box Called
fahrenheit

212
95

in our program `fahrenheit` and `centigrade` are of type `int`, as shown in the code below, meaning that they can hold integers in the approximate range of minus two billion to plus two billion.

```
int fahrenheit;
int centigrade;
```

Note that the semicolon (;) must follow the data type declaration.

Literals

A *literal* is an item whose value does not change. For instance, the numbers 5, 9, and 32 are literals.

Declaration and Assignment Statements

In Java, as in many programming languages, programs are comprised of *statements*. A statement is the programming equivalent of a sentence in English. Whereas English sentences end with a period, Java statements end with a semicolon. There are many types of statements in Java. We have just seen examples of *declaration statements*. Another common example is an *assignment statement*. It has the following form:

```
<variable> = <expression>;
```

where the value of the expression on the right is assigned to the variable on the left. For instance,

```
centigrade = (fahrenheit - 32) * 5 / 9;
```

Arithmetic Expressions

An *arithmetic expression* consists of operands and binary operators combined in a manner familiar from algebra. The following rules of precedence apply to arithmetic expressions:

- Multiplication and division are evaluated before addition and subtraction.

- Operations of equal precedence are evaluated from left to right.

- Parentheses can be used to change the order of evaluation.

  Unlike in algebra, multiplication must be indicated explicitly. Thus, `a * b` cannot be written as `ab`.

Import Statements

A Java program often needs to refer to *libraries* of code written by other people. This is done by using import statements:

```
import java.awt.*;
import BreezyGUI.*;
```

java.awt is the name of a *package* of code, provided by Java, that must be imported to write GUI programs. **BreezyGUI** is the name of a package that is provided by the authors of this book. This package makes it easy to write GUI programs. Packages are discussed in more detail in Appendix G.

Program Name

Every program must have a name. The name of our first example is `FahrenheitToCentigrade`. The name is embedded in a line that for now must go unexplained:

```
public class FahrenheitToCentigrade extends GBFrame{
```

Window Objects and the User Interface

The user interface is defined in the following lines:

```
Label degreesFahrenheitLabel = addLabel ("Degrees Fahrenheit",1,1,1,1);
IntegerField degreesFahrenheitField = addIntegerField (0,1,2,1,1);
Label degreesCentigradeLabel = addLabel ("Degrees Centigrade",2,1,1,1);
IntegerField degreesCentigradeField = addIntegerField (0,2,2,1,1);
Button convertButton = addButton ("Convert",3,1,2,1);
```

A user interface consists of *window objects*. The program contains two label objects, two integer field objects, and a button object. The objects are positioned in an imaginary grid such as the one shown in Figure 2-3.

FIGURE 2-3
Window objects are positioned
according to an imaginary grid

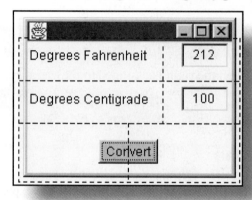

The purpose of a label object is to display text in the window. This text is normally used to label some other window object, such as an integer field. An integer field object can accept user input and/or display program output. A button object triggers some action in the program when clicked by the user.

Java is one of the few programming languages that provide standard features for programming window objects. Because these features are difficult for beginning programmers to use, we provide a framework that simplifies them. In this framework, the syntax for defining a window object is:

```
<type of object> <name> = <addType> (<initial value>, <row #>, <column #>,
                                      <width>, <height>)
```

More will be said about window objects and their use in the next lesson.

Messages

Programs manipulate window objects by sending them *messages*. For instance, in the line of code

```
fahrenheit = degreesFahrenheitField.getNumber();
```

the program sends the `getNumber()` message to the object `degreesFahrenheitField`. The object responds to the message by returning the number entered by the user. This number is then assigned to the variable `fahrenheit`.

In the line of code

```
degreesCentigradeField.setNumber (centigrade);
```

the program sends the setNumber (centigrade) message to the object degreesCentigradeField. The object responds by displaying the value of centigrade on the screen.

Methods

When an object receives and responds to a message, it does so by executing a block of code called a *method*. A method is thus a block of code that is activated as a unit to accomplish a particular task. There are two methods in our program: main and buttonClicked.

Method main

At this stage, you should not expect to understand the following explanation fully. However, it will make complete sense eventually. Here is the code that defines method main:

```
public static void main (String[] args){
    Frame frm = new FahrenheitToCentigrade();
    frm.setSize (200, 150);
    frm.setVisible (true);
}
```

When the Java virtual machine runs the program, it treats the program as a whole as if it were an object. The first thing the JVM does is to send the message main to this program object. Execution of the method main proceeds as follows:

■ In the line

```
Frame frm = new FahrenheitToCentigrade();
```

the method creates a FahrenheitToCentigrade object called frm, which is a frame object capable of displaying a window on the screen

■ In the line

```
frm.setSize (200, 150);
```

the object frm is told the height and width, expressed in pixels, of the window to be displayed. (Your computer screen is considered to be a certain number of pixels high and wide. The exact number depends on the screen's resolution. Values such as 640×480 and 800×600 are typical.)

■ The line

```
frm.setVisible (true);
```

instructs the object frm to display its window on the screen.

Every method must begin with a line similar to the following:

```
public static void main (String[] args){
```

The meaning of words such as public and static will be explained later.

Method `buttonClicked`

Once the object `frm` has been created and has displayed its window, it just sits passively in the computer waiting for the user to click the **Convert** button, at which point the JVM sends object `frm` the `buttonClicked` message. The response to the message is implemented in the `buttonClicked` method:

```
public void buttonClicked (Button buttonObj){
    fahrenheit = degreesFahrenheitField.getNumber();
    centigrade = (fahrenheit - 32) * 5 / 9;
    degreesCentigradeField.setNumber (centigrade);
}
```

The method retrieves the number entered by the user, converts it, and displays the result. The object `frm` then goes back to sleep until the user clicks the **Convert** button again.

Stopping the Program

The user stops the program by clicking the close box in the window, at which point the window closes.

Overview of Editing, Compiling, and Running a Program

Almost every modern programming language requires the programmer to perform the following steps during coding:

1. **Edit.** In this step, the programmer uses some sort of text editor to enter the program into the computer and to store it in a file. In our example, the program would be saved in a file named `FahrenheitToCentigrade.java`. Note that the name of the file must be the same as the name of the program and the extension must be `.java`.

2. **Compile.** The next step is to invoke the Java language compiler to translate the Java program into Java byte code. In our example program, the compiler would translate the code in `FahrenheitToCentigrade.java` to byte code in `FahrenheitToCentigrade.class`. Note that the byte code file always has the same name as the Java file, but with the extension `.class`.

3. **Run.** In the final step, the programmer loads the byte code file into the JVM and runs it.

The details of this process will vary depending on the actual development environment being used. For example, some companies provide software packages that integrate an editor for entering and editing a Java program, the Java compiler, a debugger, and a run-time system (a JVM) for testing programs. Compiling and running a program require that a Java environment be installed properly on your computer. The installation and use of some of the major packages are discussed in Appendix A.

All Java development environments come with program libraries. A library contains useful code that implements many common programming tasks. When we write new Java programs, we usually combine our own new code with code extracted from these libraries. To facilitate the process of extraction, the Java compiler and the JVM must access the libraries.

Figure 2-4 summarizes our discussion.

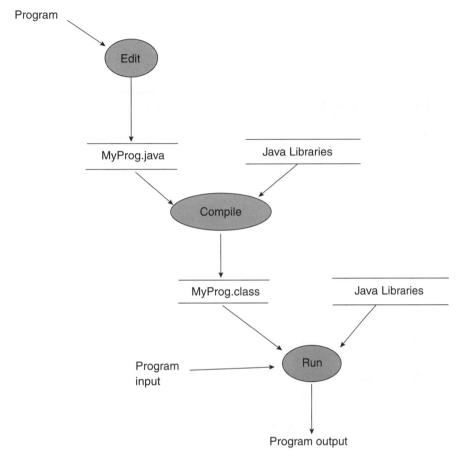

FIGURE 2-4
The tools and resources used in Java programming

Creating and Running the First Program

Now we are ready to code and run the program. As already mentioned, the details of this process depend on the development environment being used. Some common development environments are

- UNIX using a standard text editor and the command line.
- Windows 95 or 98 using Notepad for the editor and the command line inside the MS-DOS Prompt window.
- Windows 95 or 98 using an integrated development environment such as Microsoft's Visual J++.
- Macintosh using an integrated development environment such as Symantec's Visual Café.

For the sake of simplicity, our program examples throughout this book are based on the second environment.

Run-Time Tip

To create and run a program in other development environments, see Appendix A.

Step 1. Use Windows Explorer to create a folder to store your Java programs. Place the BreezyGUI folder in your new folder.

Step 2. Open Notepad by clicking the **Start** button, then **Programs,** then **Accessories,** and finally **Notepad.** Notepad opens a new, blank document, as shown in Figure 2-5.

FIGURE 2-5
A new Notepad document

Step 3. Type the program in Notepad. After you have finished, save the program by clicking **File,** then **Save.** In the Save As dialog box, locate the folder you created in Step 1 and open it. Click the Save as type drop-down list and choose the **All Files (*.*)** option. Then type the file name `FahrenheitToCentigrade.java` in the File name box. The file name should always be the same as the program name, with the `.java` extension. See Figure 2-6.

FIGURE 2-6
The Save As dialog box

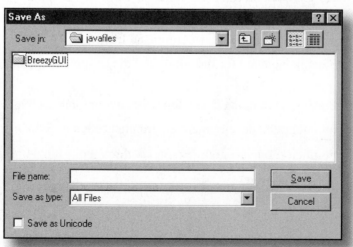

Your Notepad window should now look like that shown in Figure 2-7. You can leave the window open while you compile and run the program or close it.

FIGURE 2-7
The completed program

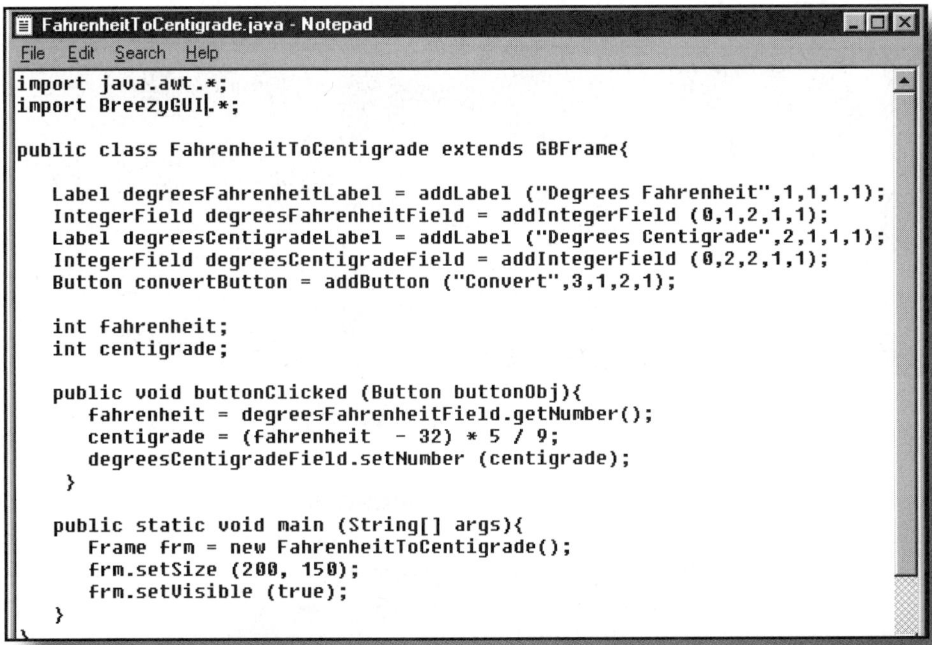

```
FahrenheitToCentigrade.java - Notepad
File  Edit  Search  Help
import java.awt.*;
import BreezyGUI.*;

public class FahrenheitToCentigrade extends GBFrame{

    Label degreesFahrenheitLabel = addLabel ("Degrees Fahrenheit",1,1,1,1);
    IntegerField degreesFahrenheitField = addIntegerField (0,1,2,1,1);
    Label degreesCentigradeLabel = addLabel ("Degrees Centigrade",2,1,1,1);
    IntegerField degreesCentigradeField = addIntegerField (0,2,2,1,1);
    Button convertButton = addButton ("Convert",3,1,2,1);

    int fahrenheit;
    int centigrade;

    public void buttonClicked (Button buttonObj){
        fahrenheit = degreesFahrenheitField.getNumber();
        centigrade = (fahrenheit  - 32) * 5 / 9;
        degreesCentigradeField.setNumber (centigrade);
     }

    public static void main (String[] args){
        Frame frm = new FahrenheitToCentigrade();
        frm.setSize (200, 150);
        frm.setVisible (true);
     }
}
```

Step 4. To compile the program, you must open the MS-DOS window and use the DOS command line. Click the **Start** button, then **Programs,** and then **MS-DOS Prompt.** The MS-DOS Prompt window opens. To change to the folder containing your Java files, type cd\, then cd\ and the name of your folder, as shown in Figure 2-8.

Step 5. Compile the program by typing javac FahrenheitToCentigrade.java. If there are no errors in your program, the DOS prompt reappears in a moment or two. Java creates the FahrenheitToCentigrade class file in your current folder.

FIGURE 2-8
Change to the folder
containing your Java files

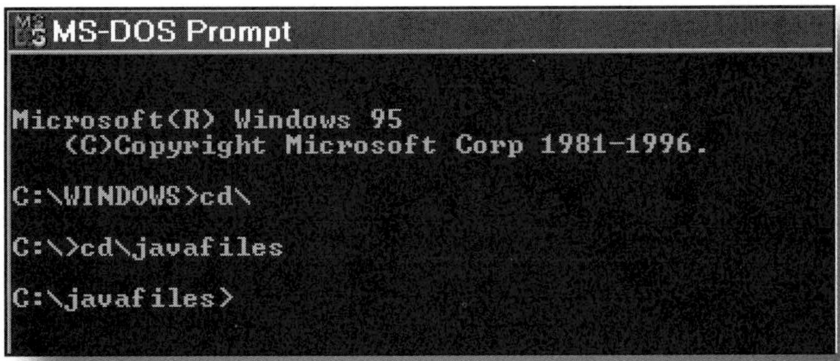

```
MS-DOS Prompt

Microsoft(R) Windows 95
    (C)Copyright Microsoft Corp 1981-1996.

C:\WINDOWS>cd\

C:\>cd\javafiles

C:\javafiles>
```

2 7

Step 6. Run the program by typing java FahrenheitToCentigrade, as shown in Figure 2-9. Figure 2-10 shows the resulting window.

FIGURE 2-9
The compile (javac) and run (java) commands

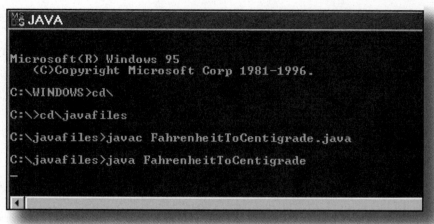

FIGURE 2-10
The completed program window

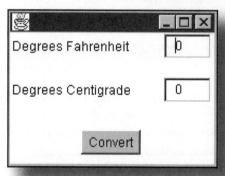

Formatting a Program and Comments

The layout of a program greatly affects its readability. Indentation, the inclusion of blank lines and spaces, and other typographic considerations make the difference between an intelligible program and an incomprehensible program. Actually, the computer could not care less about a program's format, provided that you do not break a line in the middle of a word. Throughout the book, we will attempt to give the example programs a pleasing and consistent appearance, and you should strive for the same goal in your programs. Here for your enjoyment is a highly unreadable rendering of the FahrenheitToCentigrade program:

```
import
    java.
      awt

      .
     *;
```

```
import BreezyGUI.*;public class FahrenheitToCentigrade extends
GBFrame{Label degreesFahrenheitLabel = addLabel ("Degrees Fahrenheit",
1,1,1,1);IntegerField degreesFahrenheitField = addIntegerField (0,1,2,1,1);
Label degreesCentigradeLabel = addLabel ("Degrees Centigrade",2,1,1,1);
IntegerField degreesCentigradeField = addIntegerField (0,2,2,1,1);
Button convertButton = addButton("Convert",3,1,2,1);int fahrenheit;
int centigrade;public void buttonClicked (Button buttonObj
){fahrenheit = degreesFahrenheitField.getNumber();centigrade = (fahrenheit
-32)*5/9;degreesCentigradeField.setNumber(centigrade);}public static void
main (String[] args){Frame frm = new FahrenheitToCentigrade();
frm.setSize (200, 150);frm.setVisible(true);}}
```

Programmers can improve the readability of a complex program by including *comments*. A comment gives you additional information about a line of code. The computer ignores these comments when it runs a program. There are two styles for indicating comments:

1. **End-of-line comments.** These include all of the text following two forward slashes (/ /) on one line.

2. **Multiline comments.** These include all of the text between an opening / * and a closing * / .

The following code segment illustrates the use of both kinds of comments:

```
/* This code segment illustrates the
use of assignment statements and comments */

a = 3;        // assign 3 to variable a
b = 4;        // assign 4 to variable b
c = a + b;    // add the number in variable a
              //    to the number in variable b
              //    and assign the result, 7, to variable c
c = c * 3;    // multiply the number in variable c by 3
              //    and assign the result, 21, to variable c
```

Programming Errors

According to an old saying, we learn from our mistakes. Most people find it impossible to write a program without making numerous mistakes. These mistakes, or errors, are of three types: syntax errors, run-time errors, and logic errors.

Syntax Errors

Syntax errors occur when you violate a syntax rule, no matter how minor. These errors are detected at compile time. For instance, if a semicolon is missing at the end of a statement or if a variable is undeclared, the compiler will be unable to translate the program into byte code. The good news is that when the Java compiler finds a syntax error, it displays an error message, and the programmer can make the needed correction. The bad news is that the error messages are often quite cryptic. However, just knowing that there is a syntax error at a particular point in the program is usually enough of a clue for most programmers.

Run-Time Errors

Run-time errors occur when you ask the computer to do something that it considers illegal, such as dividing by zero. For example, suppose that the symbols x and y are variables. Then the expression x/y is syntactically correct, so the compiler cannot complain. However, when the expression is run, the meaning of this expression depends on the values contained in the variables. If the variable y picks up the value 0 at run time, then the expression is meaningless and cannot be interpreted. The good news is that the Java run-time environment will display a message telling you the nature of the error and where it was encountered. Once again, the bad news is that the error message might be hard to understand.

Logic Errors

Logic errors, also called design errors or bugs, occur when you fail to express yourself accurately. For instance, in everyday life, you might tell someone to go left when you really meant to tell them to go right. In this example,

■ The instruction is phrased properly. Thus, the syntax is correct.

■ The instruction is meaningful. Thus, the semantics are valid.

■ But the instruction does not do what the programmer thought it would do. Thus, its logic is incorrect.

The bad news is that programming environments do not detect logic errors and respond with error messages. However, we offer many tips on how to prevent logic errors and how to detect them.

Illustration of Syntax Errors

To illustrate the effect of syntax errors, two errors are introduced into the `buttonClicked` method:

```
public void buttonClicked (Button buttonObj){
    farenheit  = degreesFahrenheitField.getNumber();
    centigrade = (fahrenheit  - 32) * 5 / 9
    degreesCentigradeField.setNumber (centigrade);
}
```

The errors in this code are that `fahrenheit` has been changed to `farenheit` and the semicolon after 9 has been omitted. When the program is compiled the command window looks like that shown in Figure 2-11.

FIGURE 2-11
Java lists syntax errors

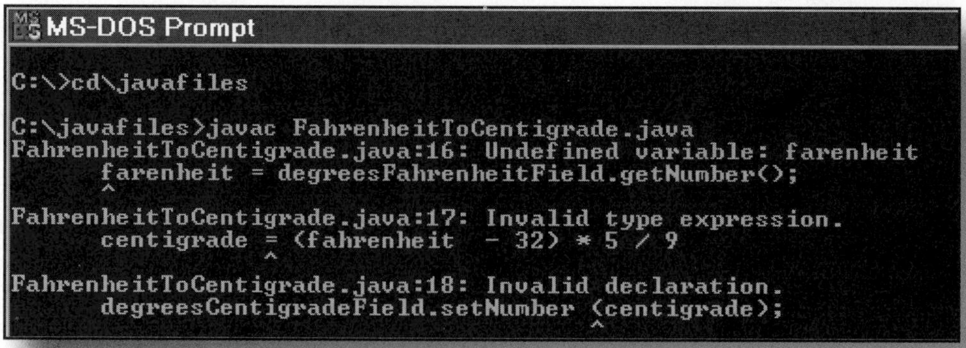

Three errors are listed, despite the fact that there are only two:

Error 1. The compiler says that line 16 contains an undefined variable called `farenheit`. This is just what we expected. Notice that a copy of line 16 is displayed for our further edification with a ^ marker immediately under the word that contains the error. The line number 16 refers to the fact that this is the 16th line from the top of the program, a fact that is easily verified by examining the program in Notepad and counting down lines from the top.

Error 2. The compiler says that line 17 contains an invalid type expression. This message makes no sense, and the ^ marker is under an equal sign. However, when we look at the line, we notice that a semicolon is missing. At least the compiler realizes something is wrong with this line.

Error 3. The compiler says that line 18 contains an invalid declaration. Sorry, this is not so. This line is fine. However, when the compiler is thrown off balance by a syntax error, it often spits out pointless error messages for several lines thereafter.

The corrective action is to go back into Notepad, fix all the errors that make sense, save the file, and compile again. You repeat this process until the compiler stops complaining.

Illustration of Run-Time Errors

To experiment with run-time errors, we modify the program so that it attempts to divide by 0. We cannot be too obvious about this. For example, if we attempt to divide by a literal zero (0), the compiler will notice and flag a syntax error, as shown in Figure 2-12.

FIGURE 2-12
Java flags a syntax error

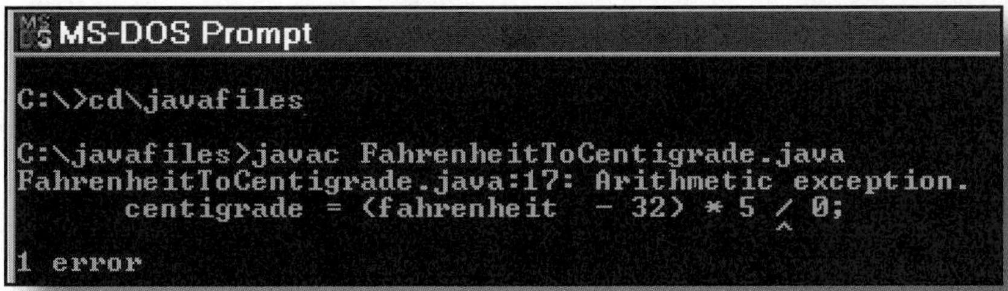

Thus, we need to be a little more devious, as follows:

```
public void buttonClicked (Button buttonObj){
    fahrenheit = degreesFahrenheitField.getNumber();
    centigrade = (fahrenheit - 32) * 5 / fahrenheit;
    degreesCentigradeField.setNumber (centigrade);
}
```

Instead of dividing by 9, we divide by `fahrenheit`. Now we compile and run the program again. The program's window opens, we enter a temperature of 0, and click the **Convert** button. Figure 2-13 shows the resulting screen.

FIGURE 2-13
A temperature of 0 is entered

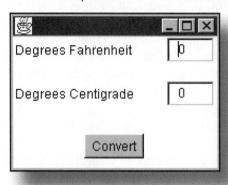

The computer reacts as shown in Figure 2-14.

FIGURE 2-14
Java throws an exception

```
C:\WINDOWS>cd\

C:\>cd\javafiles

C:\javafiles>javac FahrenheitToCentigrade.java

C:\javafiles>java FahrenheitToCentigrade
Exception occurred during event dispatching:
java.lang.ArithmeticException: / by zero
        at FahrenheitToCentigrade.buttonClicked(FahrenheitToCentigrade.java:17)
        at JavaQuickWindows.GBFrameButtonListener.actionPerformed(GBFrame.java:2
26)
        at java.awt.Button.processActionEvent(Button.java:257)
        at java.awt.Button.processEvent(Button.java:230)
        at java.awt.Component.dispatchEventImpl(Compiled Code)
        at java.awt.EventDispatchThread.run(Compiled Code)
```

Although you cannot expect to understand all of this now, you can comprehend enough to locate the offending line of code. When a run-time error occurs in a Java program, Java throws an *exception*. Thus, the phrase "java.lang.ArithmeticException: / by zero" should ring a bell. Next, look at the collection of lines that begins with the word at. These lines provide information about the location of the error. For now, we focus on the top line. In a later lesson, we will talk about the other lines as well. The top line indicates that the error occurred in line 17 of our program, which we can easily determine to be

```
centigrade = (fahrenheit - 32) * 5 / fahrenheit;
```

Looking at this line, we know for a fact that somehow fahrenheit has managed to take on the value 0. The present situation is highly contrived, so we know exactly what is wrong. However, in general, we may have to think long and hard to deduce the cause of a problem.

Programming with Java exceptions is a topic in its own right. We explore Java exceptions in more detail in Lesson 11 and in Appendix F.

Illustration of Logic Errors

Incorrect output is often the only indication of a logic error in a program. For instance, suppose that the program converts 212 degrees Fahrenheit to 101 degrees centigrade, as illustrated in Figure 2-15.

FIGURE 2-15
The conversion is slightly incorrect

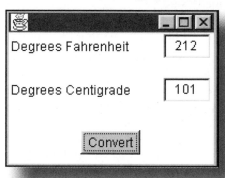

The error is small, but we notice it. And, if we do not notice the error, our customers surely will. In the following statement, the number 30 should have been 32:

```
centigrade = (fahrenheit - 30) * 5 / 9;
```

This simple example illustrates the necessity for testing programs extensively, after they are finally free of syntax and run-time errors. But how many tests must we make before we can feel confident that this program contains no more logic errors? Sometimes, the fundamental nature of a program provides an answer. Perhaps your mathematical skills are sufficiently fresh to recognize that the statement

```
centigrade = (fahrenheit -- 30) * 5 / 9;
```

is actually the equation of a line. Because two points determine a line, if the program works correctly for two temperatures, it should work correctly for all.

Usually, however, we are never certain that our programs are error free. Thus, after making a reasonable number of tests, we launch our program upon the world and wait for the angry complaints.

We can reduce the number of logic errors in a program by rereading the code carefully after we have written it. This is best done when the mind is fresh. It is even possible by using mathematical techniques to prove that a program or segment of a program is free of logic errors. We will return to this topic later. Because programming requires an exhausting and excruciating attention to detail, avoid programming when tired or for long stretches, a rule you will break frequently unless you manage your time well.

Another way to reduce logic errors is with carefully planned testing. For example, when testing a program that expects integer inputs, run it with several values in the range of expected inputs. For instance, if a program expects a positive integer as input, run it with the values 1, 10, and 1000. Then note the outputs and make sure that they are the expected ones also. If any of these outputs is unexpected, reexamine the logic of your program to find where it is not doing what it is supposed to do.

Debugging

After we have established that a program contains a logic error (bug), we still have the problem of finding it. Sometimes the nature of a bug suggests its general location in the program. We can then read this section of the program carefully with the hope of spotting the error. Unfortunately, the bug often is not located where we expect to find it, and even if it is, we will probably miss it. After all, we thought we were writing the program correctly the first time, so when we reread it, we tend to see what we were trying to say rather than what we actually said.

Thus, programmers are frequently forced to resort to a rather tedious, but powerful, technique for finding bugs. We add to the program extra lines of code that display the values of variables. Of course, we add these lines where we anticipate they will do the most good, that is, preceding and perhaps following the places in the program where we think the bug is most likely located. We then run the program again, and from the extra output we can determine if any of the variables deviate from their expected values. If one does, then we know the bug is close by, but if none do, we must try again. Variables are displayed in the Command Prompt window as follows:

```
System.out.println ("<some message>" + <variable name>);
```

Now let us try to find a bug in our program. Suppose the program behaves as shown in Figure 2-16. Something is seriously wrong. Perhaps we should check the value of fahrenheit just before centigrade is calculated. The needed code looks like this:

```
System.out.println ("fahrenheit = " + fahrenheit);
centigrade = (fahrenheit - 32) * 5 / 9;
```

FIGURE 2-16
An incorrect conversion

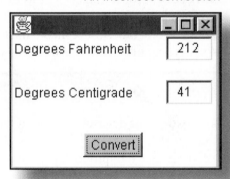

Now let us recompile and run the program again using the same numbers. When we click the **Convert** button, the message shown in Figure 2-17 appears.

FIGURE 2-17

```
C:\javafiles>java FahrenheitToCentigrade
fahrenheit = 106
```

Interesting! We entered 212 but for some reason the program says the value is 106. Perhaps we should look at the surrounding code and see if we can spot the cause.

```java
public void buttonClicked (Button buttonObj){
    fahrenheit = degreesFahrenheitField.getNumber();
    fahrenheit = fahrenheit / 2;
    System.out.println ("fahrenheit = " + fahrenheit);
    centigrade = (fahrenheit - 32) * 5 / 9;
    degreesCentigradeField.setNumber (centigrade);
}
```

There is the problem. It seems as if someone has divided `fahrenheit` by 2.

Applets and Stand-alone Programs

The program `FahrenheitToCentigrade` runs on the computer in the same manner as any other window-based application. It is what we will call a *stand-alone program.* Java also supports another type of program called an applet. An applet runs inside a Web browser or an applet viewer such as the one provided by JDK. For most of the book, we restrict our attention to stand-alone programs. In Lesson 12, we show you how to create Web pages containing Java applets.

In most regards, stand-alone programs and applets are similar. However, for security reasons, the scope of applets is restricted in various ways, which we explain near the end of the book. Applets cannot, for instance, manipulate the computer's file system. Fortunately, the skills you will learn while writing stand-alone programs transfer to writing applets.

C S   C A P S U L E : Intrusive Hacking and Viruses

Hacking

Hacking is a term whose use goes back to the early computer programmers. In its original sense, a "hack" is a program that exhibits rare problem-solving ability and commands the respect of other programmers. The hacker culture began in the late 1950s at the MIT computer science labs. These programmers, many of them students and later professionals and teachers in the field, regarded hacking as an accomplishment along the lines of Olympic gymnastics. These programmers even advocated a "hacker ethic," which stated, among other things, that hackers should respect the privacy of others and distribute their software for free. For a narrative of the early tradition of hacking, see Steven Levy, *Hackers: Heroes of the Computer Revolution* (Garden City, NY: Anchor Press/Doubleday, 1984).

Unfortunately, the practice of hacking has evolved through the years, and the term has acquired darker connotations. Programmers who break into computer systems in an unauthorized way are called hackers, whether their intent is just to impress their peers or to cause actual harm. Students and professionals who lack a disciplined approach to programming are also called hackers. An excellent account of the most famous case of intrusive hacking can be found in Clifford Stoll, *The Cuckoo's Egg: Tracking Through the Maze of Computer Espionage* (New York: Doubleday, 1989).

Viruses

A *virus* is a computer program that can replicate itself and move from computer to computer. Some programmers of viruses intend no harm. They just want to demonstrate their prowess by creating viruses that go undetected. Other programmers of viruses intend harm, by causing system crashes, corruption of data, or hardware failures.

Viruses migrate by attaching themselves to normal programs and then become active again when these programs are launched. Early viruses were easily detected, if one had detection software. This software examined portions of each program on the suspect computer and could repair infected programs.

However, viruses and virus detectors have coevolved through the years, and both kinds of software have become very sophisticated. Viruses now hide themselves better than they used to. Virus detectors can no longer just examine pieces of data stored in memory to reveal the presence or absence of a virus. Researchers have recently developed a method of running a program that might contain a virus to see whether the virus becomes active. The suspect program runs in a "safe" environment that protects the computer from any potential harm. As you can imagine, this process takes time and costs money. For an overview of the history of viruses and the new detection technology, see Carey Nactenberg, "Computer Virus–Antivirus Coevolution," *Communications of the ACM*, Volume 40, No. 1 (January 1997): 46–51.

Summary

In this lesson, you learned:

- Java is the fastest growing programming language in the world. It is secure, robust, and portable. It supports the use of threads. And it is similar to C++, the world's most popular programming language.

- The Java compiler translates Java into a pseudo–machine language called Java byte code. Byte code can be run on any computer that has a JVM installed. The JVM is a program that behaves like a computer—an interpreter.

- Like any natural language, programming languages have specific vocabulary, syntax, and semantics. Java programs include variables, arithmetic expression, statements, objects, messages, and methods.

- Three basic steps in the coding process are editing, compiling, and running a program. Programmers should pay attention to a program's format to ensure readability.

- You must guard against three types of errors: syntax errors, run-time errors, and logic errors. Debugging is the process of locating and fixing errors.

LESSON 2 REVIEW QUESTIONS

WRITTEN QUESTIONS

Write your answers to the following questions.

1. List three reasons why Java is an important programming language.

2. What is byte code?

3. What is a pseudocode algorithm?

4. List three window objects.

5. State the differences between syntax errors, run-time errors, and logic errors, and give an example of each.

6. Why go to the trouble of analysis and design before coding a program?

7. State the purpose of a program comment.

8. What is the purpose of an `import` statement in a Java program?

FILL IN THE BLANKS

Complete each of the following statements by writing your answer in the blank provided.

9. GUI stands for _____.

10. The set of all of the words in a language is called its _____.

11. The _____ of a language contains rules for combining words into sentences.

12. _____ contain rules for interpreting the meaning of sentences.

13. A(n) _____ stores the value of the expression in the variable.

14. Programs manipulate window objects by sending them _____.

LESSON 2 PROJECTS

Beginning with this lesson, we conclude with a set of programming problems and activities. We want to emphasize that programming is not just coding. Ideally, a complete solution to each exercise in this section would include not just a set of .java and .class files for the program, but also a report that covers the analysis, design, and results of testing the program. In any case, you should go through the analysis and design steps before coding and running each program. We take you through these steps for the first problem.

1. The surface area of a cube can be known if we know the length of an edge. Write a program that takes the length of an edge as input and displays the cube's surface area as output.

   Analysis

   The user's input is an integer representing the length of the cube's edge. The program's output is an integer representing the surface area of the cube. Important information:

   - A cube has six faces.

   - Each face is a square.

   - The area of each square = edge * edge.

   The proposed interface is shown in Figure 2-18.

   FIGURE 2-18

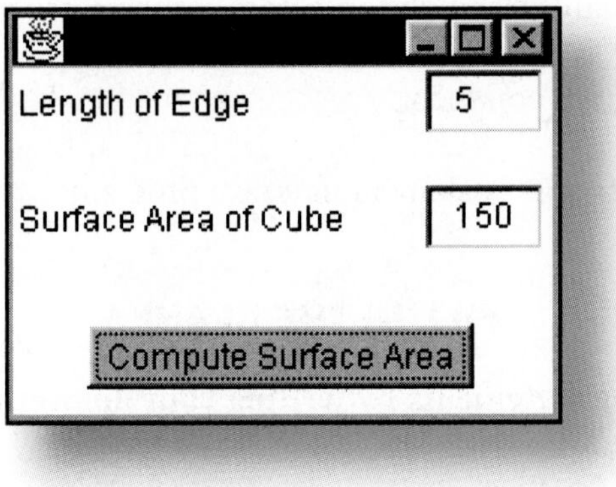

   The user enters an integer in the field labeled **Length of Edge** and clicks the **Compute Surface Area** button. The surface area then appears in the field labeled **Surface Area of Cube.**

   Design

   Using the information from analysis, a pseudocode algorithm for the `buttonClicked` method would be

   ```
   get edge
   set surface area to edge * edge * 6
   output surface area
   ```

2. Write a program that takes as input a number of kilometers, and displays the corresponding number of nautical miles. You may rely on the following items of information:

   - A kilometer represents 1/10,000 of the distance between the North Pole and the equator.

   - There are 90 degrees, containing 60 minutes of arc each, between the North Pole and the equator.

   - A nautical mile is 1 minute of arc.

3. Write a program that calculates and displays the number of minutes in a year.

4. An object's momentum is its mass multiplied by its velocity. Write a program that expects an object's mass (in kilograms) and velocity (in meters per second) as inputs, and displays its momentum.

5. The kinetic energy of a moving object is given by the formula $KE = (1/2)mv^2$, where m is the object's mass and v is the object's velocity. Modify the program of Problem 4 so that it displays the object's kinetic energy as well as its momentum.

CRITICAL THINKING ACTIVITY

You have an idea for a program that will help the local pizza shop handle take-out orders. Your friend suggests an interview with the shop's owner to discuss her user requirements before you get started on the program. Explain why this is a good suggestion, and list the questions you would ask the owner to help you determine the user requirements.

JAVA BASICS

Upon completion of this lesson, you will be able to:

■ Name and use variables.

■ Create arithmetic expressions.

■ Lay out window objects.

■ Display messages using strings.

Estimated Time: 4 hours

We begin this lesson by presenting two programs built on the structure introduced in Lesson 2. These programs contain some new features of Java that will be explained in the discussion that follows the programs. These features include the basic structure of GUIs; elements of syntax and semantics; and the use of integers, floating-point numbers, and strings.

C A S E   S T U D Y   1 : Area of a Circle

Request

Write a program that computes the area of a circle.

Analysis

The program

■ Uses the formula area = πr^2.

■ Accepts input representing the radius of a circle, expressed as a floating-point number.

■ Computes and displays the area of the corresponding circle.

Figure 3-1 shows the proposed interface.

FIGURE 3-1

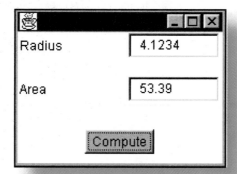

Design

Our estimate for π is 3.14. Obviously, more accurate estimates yield better results. Soon we will see how Java itself can provide an excellent estimate. Because our estimate of π is accurate to only two places, and because the user is probably estimating the radius, it is misleading to include a large number of digits after the decimal point when we display the area. Let's set the limit at 2.

Here is pseudocode for computing the area (the buttonClicked method):

```
get radius
area = 3.14 * radius * radius
display area with two digits after the decimal point
```

Implementation

```java
import java.awt.*;
import BreezyGUI.*;

public class CircleArea extends GBFrame{

    Label radiusLabel = addLabel ("Radius",1,1,1,1);
    DoubleField radiusField = addDoubleField (0,1,2,1,1);
    Label areaLabel = addLabel ("Area",2,1,1,1);
    DoubleField areaField = addDoubleField (0,2,2,1,1);
    Button computeButton = addButton ("Compute",3,1,2,1);

    double radius, area;

    public void buttonClicked (Button buttonObj){
        radius = radiusField.getNumber();
        area = 3.14 * radius * radius;
        areaField.setNumber (area);
        areaField.setPrecision (2);
    }

    public static void main (String[] args){
        Frame frm = new CircleArea();
        frm.setSize (200, 150);
        frm.setVisible (true);
    }
}
```

4 1

Request

Write a program that computes a person's income tax.

Analysis

Here is the relevant tax law (mythical in nature):

■   Flat tax rate of 20%.

■ $10,000 standard deduction.

■ $2,000 additional deduction for each dependent.

■   Gross income expressed in whole dollars.

■   Income tax rounded off to the nearest dollar.

The user inputs are the gross income and number of dependents, expressed as integers. The program calculates the income tax based on the inputs and the tax law and displays the income tax, rounded to the nearest whole number.

Figure 3-2 shows the proposed interface:

FIGURE 3-2

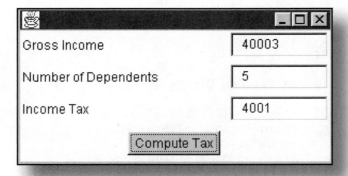

Design

We treat the following quantities as integers: gross income, number of dependents, standard deduction, and dependent deduction. We treat the following quantity as floating point: tax rate.

Here is the pseudocode for computing the income tax (the buttonClicked method):

```
get grossIncome
get numberOfDependents
taxableIncome = grossIncome - 10000 -
               numberOfDependents * 2000
incomeTax = taxableIncome * 0.20
display incomeTax rounded to a whole number
```

Implementation

```java
import java.awt.*;
import BreezyGUI.*;

public class IncomeTaxCalculator extends GBFrame{

    Label grossIncomeLabel = addLabel ("Gross Income",1,1,1,1);
    IntegerField grossIncomeField = addIntegerField (0,1,2,1,1);

    Label numberOfDependentsLabel = addLabel("Number of Dependents",
                                             2,1,1,1);
    IntegerField numberOfDependentsField = addIntegerField (0,2,2,1,1);

    Label incomeTaxLabel = addLabel ("Income Tax",3,1,1,1);
    DoubleField incomeTaxField = addDoubleField (0,3,2,1,1);

    Button computeButton = addButton ("Compute Tax",4,1,2,1);

    int grossIncome;
    int numberOfDependents;
    double taxableIncome;
    double incomeTax;

    public void buttonClicked (Button buttonObj){
        grossIncome = grossIncomeField.getNumber();
        numberOfDependents = numberOfDependentsField.getNumber();
        taxableIncome = grossIncome - 10000 - numberOfDependents * 2000;
        incomeTax = taxableIncome * 0.20;
        incomeTaxField.setNumber (incomeTax);
        incomeTaxField.setPrecision (0);
    }

    public static void main (String[] args){
        Frame frm = new IncomeTaxCalculator();
        frm.setSize (300, 150);
        frm.setVisible (true);
    }
}
```

When the method `setPrecision` receives zero digits, the number in the double field is rounded to the nearest whole number before display.

CS CAPSULE:
Binary Representation of Information and Computer Memory

As we saw in Lesson 1, computer memory stores patterns of electronic signals, which the CPU manipulates and transforms into other patterns. These patterns in turn can be viewed as representing strings of *binary digits,* or *bits.* Because programs and data are stored in memory, there is no discernible difference between program instructions and data. We see only 0s and 1s. To determine what these strings of bits might represent, we must use context. We now examine how data of different types are represented in binary notation.

Binary Representation of Information

The number system we use in mathematics is the decimal (base 10) system. Decimal notation is a natural product of our physiology (we have ten fingers to count on). A computer, however, uses binary (base 2) notation, because a computer circuit has only two states: on or off.

In the decimal system, each "place" in a number represents a power of 10. Suppose we want to represent the number 5403 in decimal notation. Then 5403 is equivalent to

$$5 \times 10^3 + 4 \times 10^2 + 0 \times 10^1 + 3 \times 10^0 \text{ or } 5000 + 400 + 0 + 3$$

In the binary system, each place in a number represents a power of 2. The powers of 2 are 1, 2, 4, 8, 16, 32, and so on. Suppose we want to represent the integer 19 in binary notation. Using binary notation, this number becomes 10011, which is equivalent to

$$1 \times 2^4 + 0 \times 2^3 + 0 \times 2^2 + 1 \times 2^1 + 1 \times 2^0 \text{ or } 16 + 0 + 0 + 2 + 1$$

Table 3-1 shows some sample base 10 numbers and their equivalents in base 2.

TABLE 3-1
Numbers in base 10 and base 2

BASE 10	BASE 2
0	0
1	1
2	10
3	11
4	100
5	101
6	110
7	111
43	101011

All types of data that you input into a computer are represented by binary notation. The notation differs, however, depending on the type of information. The sections below describe some of the kinds of information you commonly input into a computer.

Integers

An *integer* is a positive or negative whole number, such as 19 or −35. Java allows you to select from several different integer data types. In this book, you will most often use the int data type to represent integers. You will learn more about data types later in this lesson.

Floating-Point Numbers

Numbers with a fractional part, such as 354.98, are called *floating-point numbers.* They are a bit trickier to represent in binary than integers. One way is to use *mantissa/exponent notation.* For example,

$$354.98_{10} = .35498_{10} * 10^3$$

The fractional part or mantissa is represented by the digits 35498. The exponent is represented by 3. Similarly,

$$10001.001_2 = .10001001_2 * 2^5$$

The fractional part is represented by 10001001, and the exponent is represented by $5_{10} = 101_2$. Thus, we can represent a floating-point number by two separate sequences of bits, one sequence for the fractional part and the other sequence for the exponent.

Java has two common data types you can use to indicate floating-point numbers. In this book, you will most often use the `double` data type for these numbers.

Characters and Strings

To process text, computers must represent characters, such as letters, digits, and other symbols on a keyboard. There are many encoding schemes for characters. One popular scheme is called *ASCII* (American Standard Code for Information Interchange). In this scheme, each character is represented as a pattern of 8 bits called a *byte.* In binary notation, byte values can range from 0000 0000 to 1111 1111, allowing for 256 possibilities. These are more than enough for

- A..Z

- a..z

- 0..9

- + — * / and other such characters.

- Various unprintable characters such as carriage return, line feed, bell, and command sequences.

Table 3-2 shows some characters and the corresponding ASCII bit patterns.

TABLE 3-2
Bit patterns for ASCII characters

CHARACTER	BIT PATTERN	CHARACTER	BIT PATTERN	CHARACTER	BIT PATTERN
A	0100 0001	a	0110 0001	0	0011 0000
B	0100 0010	b	0110 0010	1	0011 0001
Z	0101 1010	z	0111 1010	9	0011 1001

Java uses a scheme called *Unicode.* In this scheme, each character is represented by a pattern of 16 bits, ranging from 0000 0000 0000 0000 to 1111 1111 1111 1111. Unicode allows for 65,535 possibilities and can represent different alphabets (such as Greek, Japanese, and Chinese dialects). Within Unicode, the patterns 0000 0000 0000 0000 to 0000 0000 1111 1111 duplicate the ASCII encoding scheme.

Strings are another type of data used in text processing. Strings are collections of characters, such as "The cat sat on the mat." The computer encodes each character in ASCII or Unicode and strings them together.

Pictures

Representing images in a computer is a little more complicated than representing other kinds of data. For example, consider a black and white picture. To represent this image in black and white, we superimpose a fine grid on the screen. If a grid cell should contain black, we encode this cell as 1. Otherwise, we encode the cell as 0. Color images require several bits to represent the color value in each cell in the grid.

Sound

We might digitize sound as follows:

1. For each stereo channel, every 1/44,000 seconds measure the amplitude of the sound on a scale of 0 to 65,535.

2. Convert this number to binary using 16 bits.

Thus, 1 hour of music requires 60 * 60 * 88,000 * 16 = 5,068,800,000 bits, which fits just fine on a CD.

Program Instructions

The computer represents program instructions as bit strings. The following example shows the translation of the assembly language instruction ADD A, B, C to binary notation:

```
0000 1001 / 0100 0000 / 0100 0100 / 0100 0010
ADD         A,          B,          C
```

Note that each symbol (except the comma) in the assembly language instruction translates to an 8-bit part of the 32-bit instruction. The leftmost 8 bits of the instruction represent the *opcode,* or machine-language operation (in this case, addition). The remaining 8-bit parts represent the locations of cells in memory where the computer can locate or store data for the values of A, B, and C.

Computer Memory

We can envision computer memory as a giant sequence of bytes. A byte's location in memory is called its *address.* Addresses are numbered from 0 to one less than the number of bytes of memory installed on that computer. For example, 32M–1, where M stands for *megabyte,* that is, $2^{20} = 1,048,576$, which is approximately a million bytes.

A group of contiguous bytes can represent a number, a string, a picture, a chunk of sound, a program instruction, or whatever, as determined by context. For example, let us consider the meaning of the two bytes starting at location 3 in Figure 3-3.

FIGURE 3-3

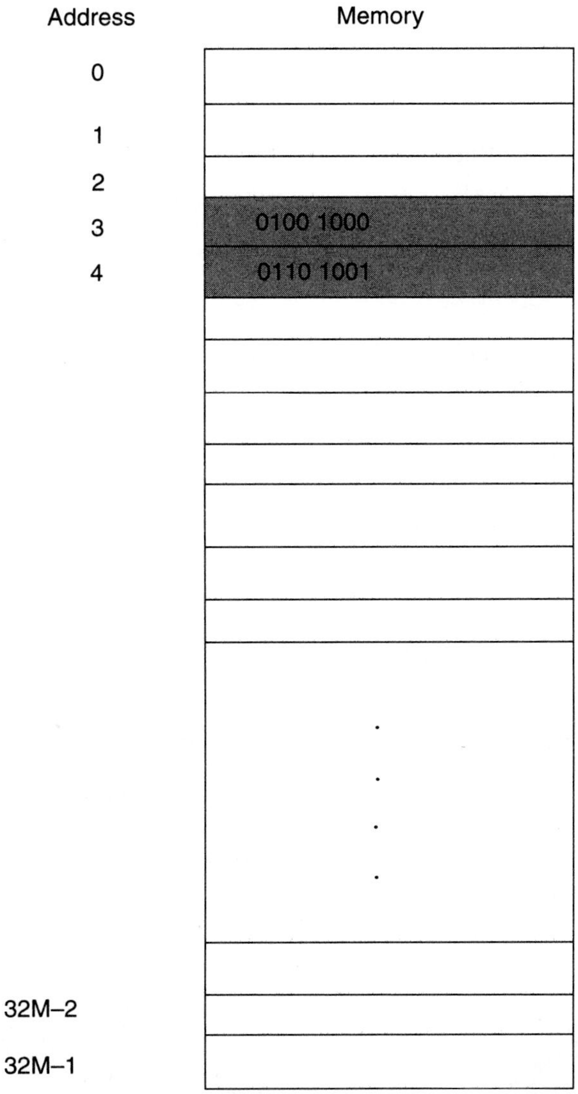

Address   Memory

Address	Memory
0	
1	
2	
3	0100 1000
4	0110 1001
	.
	.
	.
	.
32M–2	
32M–1	

The several possible meanings include these:

1. If it's an ASCII encoded string, then the meaning is "Hi".

2. If it's a binary encoded integer, then the meaning is 18537_{10}.

3. If it's a program instruction, then it might mean ADD, depending on the type of computer.

Numeric Data Types and Numeric Literals

Java programs can manipulate different types of numeric data, but in this and the next few lessons, we use just int (for integers) and double (for floating-point numbers). The storage requirements and ranges of these types are shown in the following table:

TYPE	STORAGE REQUIREMENTS	RANGE
int	4 bytes	−2,147,483,648 to 2,147,483,647
double	8 bytes	−1.79769313486231570E+308 to 1.79769313486231570E+308

Below are some examples of numeric literals of types `int` and `double`:

51	int
−31444843	int
3.14	double
5.301E-10	double

Note that numeric literals must not contain commas.

Variables

We have already learned that a variable is a name or label for a quantity that can change. Variable names must consist of a letter followed by a sequence of letters and/or digits. Letters are defined to be

- A..Z
- a..z
- _ and $
- Symbols that denote letters in several languages other than English.

Digits are the characters 0..9. Variable names are case sensitive. Thus, `radius` and `Radius` are different variable names.

Some words cannot be used as variable names in Java. These words are called *keywords* or *reserved words*. They have special meaning in Java, as we shall see throughout the book. Table 3-3 lists Java's keywords.

TABLE 3-3
Java's keywords

abstract	double	import	private	throws
boolean	else	inner	protected	transient
break	extends	instanceof	public	try
byte	final	int	rest	var
case	finally	interface	return	void
catch	float	long	short	volatile
char	for	native	static	while
class	future	new	super	
const	generic	null	switch	
continue	goto	operator	synchronized	
default	if	outer	this	
do	implements	package	throw	

The next table shows examples of valid and invalid names:

VALID VARIABLE NAMES	INVALID VARIABLE NAMES
surfaceArea3	3rdPayment
_$_$$$	pay.rate

It is considered good programming style to give variables meaningful names such as `radius` rather than `r` and `taxableIncome` rather than `ti`.

Java programmers usually capitalize the first letter of each word except the first word when compound names are used. For example, `taxableIncome` rather than `taxableincome`, `TAXABLEINCOME`, or `TaxableIncome`.

The goal of these rules and of all stylistic rules is to produce programs that are easier to understand and maintain.

It is possible to declare several variables of the same type by listing them.

```
int a, b, c;
```

It is possible to declare a variable and give it an initial value at the same time.

```
int age = 21;
double weight = 162.5; height = 62.5;
```

The declaration of a variable can be postponed until the moment of use.

```
<bunch of statements>
.
.
int age = 21;
<use age in other statements>
```

It is good programming practice to initialize variables before using them in an expression.

Naming Other User-Defined Symbols

We have just discussed the rules for naming variables. Variables are just one example of user-defined symbols. A program's name is another, and we will encounter further examples later in the book. The rules for naming user-defined symbols of all types are similar.

Expressions

There are several types of expressions. For now, we limit our attention to arithmetic expressions. As previously stated, an arithmetic expression consists of operands and binary operators combined in a manner familiar from algebra classes. Unlike in algebra, multiplication must be expressed explicitly. Thus, `a * b` cannot be written as `ab`. Table 3-4 shows some operands.

Some common operators are shown in Table 3-5.

TABLE 3-4
Common operands

TYPE	EXAMPLE
Literals	3.14 6
Variables	radius taxableIncome
Parenthesized expressions	(3 + 4)

TABLE 3-5
Common operators

OPERATION	SYMBOL	PRECEDENCE (HIGHEST TO LOWEST)	ASSOCIATION
Grouping	( )	1	Not applicable
Method selector	.		Left to right
Multiplication	*	3	Left to right
Division	/		
Remainder	%		
Addition	+	4	Left to right
Subtraction	–		

The semantics of division are different for integer and floating-point operands. Thus,

```
5.0 / 2.0    yields  2.5
5 / 2        yields  2    (the fractional portion of the answer is dropped,
                              yielding a quotient)
```

The operation % yields the remainder when one number is divided by another. Thus

```
9 % 5        yields  4
9.3 % 5.1    yields  4.2
```

When evaluating an expression, Java performs operations of higher *precedence* before those of lower precedence, unless overridden by parentheses. The highest precedence is 1.

```
3 + 5 * 3    yields  18
3 + 5 * -3   yields  -12
(3 + 5) * 3  yields  24
3 + 5 % 3    yields  5
(3 + 5) % 3  yields  2
```

The column labeled *Association* in Table 3-5 indicates the order in which to perform operations of equal precedence. Thus,

```
18 - 3 - 4   yields  11
18 / 3 * 4   yields  24
18 % 3 * 4   yields  0
```

Some more examples of expressions and their values are shown in Table 3-6.

TABLE 3-6
Example expressions

EXPRESSION	SAME AS	VALUE
3 + 4 − 5	7 − 5	2
3 + (4 − 5)	3 + (−1)	2
3 + 4 * 5	3 + 20	23
(3 + 4) * 5	7 * 5	35
8 / 2 + 6	4 + 6	10
8 / (2 + 6)	8 / 8	1
10 − 3 − 4 − 1	7 − 4 − 1	2
10 − (3 − 4 − 1)	10 − (−2)	12
(15 + 9) / (3 + 1)	24 / 4	6
15 + 9 / 3 + 1	15 + 3 + 1	19
(15 + 9) / ((3 + 1) * 2)	24 / (4 * 2) 24 / 8	3
(15 + 9) / (3 + 1) * 2	24 / 4 * 2 6 * 2	12

Two fairly obvious rules apply with regard to the use of parentheses:

1. Parentheses must occur in matching pairs.

2. Parenthetical expressions may be nested. In nested parenthetical expressions, the innermost expressions are evaluated first, proceeding to the outermost parenthesized expressions.

Mixed-Mode Arithmetic

When working with a hand-held calculator, we do not give much thought to the fact that we intermix integers and floating-point numbers. This is called *mixed-mode arithmetic*. For instance, if a circle has radius 3, we compute the area as follows:

```
3.14 * 3 * 3
```

In Java, when there is a binary operation on operands of different numeric types, the less inclusive type (int) is temporarily and automatically converted to the more inclusive type (double) before the operation is performed. Thus,

```
double d;
d = 5.0 / 2;  // same as 5.0 / 2.0, yields 2.5
```

Mixed-mode assignments are allowed, provided the variable on the left is of a more inclusive type than the expression on the right. Otherwise, a syntax error occurs, as shown in the following code segment:

```
double d;
int i;

i = 45;        // OK, because we assign an int to an int.

d = i;         // OK, because left is more inclusive than right.
               // 45.0 is stored in d.
i = d;         // Syntax error, because left is less inclusive than
               // right.
```

In Lesson 6, we show how to overcome this restriction on assignment statements.

Tester Programs

Suppose you are unsure of the results of some proposed computation, such as 31.4 * 21 + 5. A quick way to examine the results is to write a short tester program that performs the computation and displays the results in the terminal window. The following code does this:

```
import BreezyGUI.*;

public class Tester{
    public static void main (String[] args){
        double a = 31.4;
        int b = 21;
        int c = 5;

        System.out.println (a * b + c);
        GBFrame.pause();
    }
}
```

The program was saved in a file called **Tester.java.** Figure 3-4 shows the compilation and execution of the Tester program.

Next time you are unsure of how some aspect of Java works, embed the appropriate test code in the Tester program and see what happens. The only restrictions on this kind of Tester program are that all variables should be declared in the main method and no other methods should be defined. The method GBFrame.pause() prevents a "fly-by" terminal window.

FIGURE 3-4
The program is compiled and run

```
JAVA

Microsoft(R) Windows 95
    (C)Copyright Microsoft Corp 1981-1996.

C:\WINDOWS>cd\

C:\>cd\javafiles

C:\javafiles>javac Tester.java

C:\javafiles>java Tester
664.4

Hit Enter to continue: _
```

BreezyGUI: Layout, Objects, and Methods

As mentioned in Lesson 2, BreezyGUI is a Java package that makes GUIs easy. We now describe the general rules for laying out window objects in a GUI and discuss some messages that can be sent to window objects.

Laying out Window Objects

Consider again the temperature conversion program described in Lesson 2. Figure 3-5 shows its window with a superimposed grid. The code that defines the window is listed below.

FIGURE 3-5
Layout grid for the window

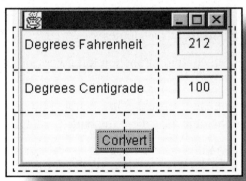

```
Label degreesFahrenheitLabel = addLabel ("Degrees Fahrenheit",1,1,1,1);
IntegerField degreesFahrenheitField = addIntegerField (0,1,2,1,1);
Label degreesCentigradeLabel = addLabel ("Degrees Centigrade",2,1,1,1);
IntegerField degreesCentigradeField = addIntegerField (0,2,2,1,1);
Button convertButton = addButton ("Convert",3,1,2,1);
```

5 3

The grid has six cells arranged in three rows and two columns. The width of a cell is adjusted automatically by the computer as appropriate. A cell's location is given as an ordered pair—(row number, column number)—thus, the phrase "Degrees Centigrade" is in cell (2,1) and the number "100" is in cell (2,2). The cells of the grid contain the window objects. Each object has the following attributes:

■ Type.

■ Variable name.

■ Value.

■ Location.

■ Extent.

Table 3-7 lists the window objects for the temperature conversion project.

TABLE 3-7
Window objects

TYPE OF WINDOW OBJECT	VARIABLE NAME FOR OBJECT IN PROGRAM	INITIAL VALUE	LOCATION	EXTENT
Label	degreesFahrenheitLabel	"Degrees Fahrenheit"	(1,1)	(1,1)
Label	degreesCentigradeLabel	"Degrees Centigrade"	(2,1)	(1,1)
Integer Field	degreesFahrenheitField	0	(1,2)	(1,1)
Integer Field	degreesCentigradeField	0	(2,2)	(1,1)
Button	convertButton	"Convert"	(3,1)	(2,1)

We now further explain a window object's attributes:

■ **Location.** The location of the cell containing the top left corner of the object. Thus, the location of the **Convert** button is (3,1).

■ **Extent.** The number of horizontal and vertical cells occupied by the object, expressed as (width, height). Thus, the extent of all the objects, except the button, is (1,1). The button's extent is (2,1).

■ **Type.** The programs in this lesson illustrate the use of several types of objects. There are several other types, which will be introduced when needed. The types used in the temperature conversion program are

• Label type—Used to explain the purpose of a window object.

• IntegerField type—Used for a data entry or display field of integer values. If the user enters nonnumeric or floating-point data in an integer field, the program automatically converts it to 0 before use.

- DoubleField type—Used for a data entry or display field of floating-point values. If the user enters nonnumeric data in a double field, the program automatically converts it to 0 before use. (See the CircleArea program for an example.)

- Button type—Used to tell the program to perform some processing.

To lay out a window, simply indicate the position and extent of the objects you want to use. The grid automatically adjusts itself to the needed number of rows and columns.

Again, the syntax for defining a window object is:

```
<type of object> <name> = <addType> (<initial value>, <row #>,
                                      <column #>, <width>, <height>)
```

Table 3-8 lists all the window objects encountered so far and shows how to add them to a program.

TABLE 3-8
Adding window objects

```
HOW TO ADD THE VARIOUS WINDOW OBJECTS

IntegerField <name> = addIntegerField (<integer>,r,c,w,h);

DoubleField  <name> = addDoubleField  (<double> ,r,c,w,h);

Label        <name> = addLabel        ("..."    ,r,c,w,h);

Button       <name> = addButton       ("..."    ,r,c,w,h);
```

Messages and Methods for Window Objects

Let us quickly review some of the terminology introduced in Lessons 1 and 2. Programs manipulate window objects by sending them messages. For instance,

```
fahrenheit = degreesFahrenheitField.getNumber();
```

and

```
degreesCentigradeField.setNumber (centigrade);
```

Asking an object for information or telling it what to do is called sending the object a message. Sending an object a message activates in the object a method that accomplishes the desired task. Methods are implemented by Java code. Thus, with respect to the statement

```
fahrenheit = degreesFahrenheitField.getNumber();
```

we can say that

■ The getNumber message is sent to the degreesFahrenheitField object.

■ The degreesFahrenheitField object implements a getNumber method.

■ The degreesFahrenheitField object understands the getNumber message.

■ The getNumber method returns an integer, which in this example is assigned to the variable fahrenheit.

Notice that the message and the method have the same name (getNumber). An object may—or may not—return a value in response to a message. For example, getNumber returns a value, whereas setNumber returns nothing (also called void).

When an object is sent a message, sometimes additional information is required as part of the message. Each piece of additional information is called a *parameter*. Thus, the variable centigrade is a parameter in the following message:

```
degreesCentigradeField.setNumber (centigrade);
```

In general, several parameters may be included or passed at once. For instance:

```
someObject.someMethod (parm1, parm2, . . ., parmn);
```

Sometimes no parameters are needed. For instance:

```
fahrenheit = degreesFahrenheitField.getNumber();
```

If a method expects parameters, they must always be included and must always appear in the same order.

Table 3-9 lists the most useful methods implemented by the window objects.

TABLE 3-9
Common Java methods

TYPE OF OBJECT	NAME OF METHOD	WHAT THE METHOD DOES
IntegerField	setNumber(anInteger) returns void	Displays anInteger on the screen. Nothing is returned.
	getNumber() returns anInteger	If the number on the screen is a valid integer, then reads the number and returns it. If the number is not a valid integer, then sets it to 0 and returns 0.
	isValid() returns aBoolean	Determines if the number entered on the screen is a valid integer. More about Booleans later.
DoubleField	setNumber(aDouble) returns void	Displays aDouble on the screen. Nothing is returned.
	getNumber() returns aDouble	If the number on the screen is a valid double, then reads the number and returns it. If the number is not a valid double, then sets it to 0 and returns 0.
	isValid() returns aBoolean	Determines if the number entered on the screen is a valid double.
	setPrecision(anInteger) returns void	• Sets the object's precision to the specified number.

TABLE 3-9
(continued)

Lesson ③ Java Basics

TYPE OF OBJECT	NAME OF METHOD	WHAT THE METHOD DOES
		• When a double is displayed on the screen, the number of digits after the decimal point is equal to the precision. • If the precision is never set or if it is set to –1, then the format of the number on the screen varies and depends on the size of the number; however, at most six digits will be displayed.
	getPrecision() returns anInteger	Returns the value of the precision.
Label	getText() returns aString	Returns the text of the label. Such text is called a string.
	setText(aString) returns void	Sets the text of the label to the specified string.
Button	setLabel(aString) returns void	Sets the text written on the button to the specified string.
	getLabel() returns aString	Returns the text written on the button.
All Window Objects	setVisible(true/false) returns void	If false, then hides the object so that the user can no longer see it on the screen. If true, then makes the object visible again.
	setEnabled (true/false) returns void	If false, then disable the object for user input. If true, then enable the object for user input. Default is enabled.
	requestFocus() returns void	Moves the focus to the object.

Strings

Strings are not data types in the same sense as integers and floating-point numbers. The latter are examples of what are called *primitive data types,* whereas strings are objects. The distinction is a consequence of how Java's originators decided to implement the language and is not due to theoretical considerations concerning the nature of object-oriented programming. Fortunately, we do not need to go more deeply into this subject and now turn our attention to practical issues concerning strings.

String Literals

We have already used string literals several times. For instance, we use a string to place a label in a window or on a button:

```
Label degreesCentigradeLabel = addLabel ("Degrees Centigrade",2,1,1,1);
IntegerField degreesCentigradeField = addIntegerField (0,2,2,1,1);
Button convertButton = addButton ("Convert",3,1,2,1);
```

Unlike integers and floating-point numbers, the characters in a string literal are enclosed by double quotation marks. Thus, 453 is an `int`, whereas "453" is a string. Occasionally, a programmer needs to use the empty string, represented as `""`. The empty string contains no characters. You might use an empty string for a field in which someone will later type text data.

String Variables and String Concatenation

String variables are declared and initialized in much the same way as integer variables. The following code declares four strings and initializes three of them:

```
String firstName;
String middleInitial;
String lastName;
String fullName;

firstName = "Bill";
middleInitial = "J";
lastName = "Smith";
```

The next line of code uses the *concatenation operator,* +. Concatenation hooks strings together to form a new string:

```
fullName = firstName + " " + middleInitial + ". " + lastName;
```

Notice that in order to insert spaces between the various parts of the name, we concatenate a string containing a single space.

Strings can be concatenated with other data types. When this happens, the other data type is automatically converted to its string representation first. In the next code segment, the numeric values a, b, and a * b are converted to strings and concatenated with the strings " times " and " is ".

```
int a, b;
String result;

a = 5;
b = 6;
result = a + " times " + b + " is " + a * b;     // "5 times 6 is 30"
```

Notice that the expression a * b is evaluated in the last example *before* the concatenation, so that the two numbers are multiplied. Some care must be exercised, because plus (+) can be interpreted as an arithmetic operation or as concatenation. The order in which the operations are performed is the determining factor. In the next example, the first expression concatenates the string "5 plus 6 " to the number 5, whereas the second expression adds the two numbers before concatenating this string to the sum.

```
int a, b;
String result;

a = 5;
```

```
b = 6;
result = a + " plus " + b + " is " + a + b;      // "5 plus 6 is 5 + 6"
result = a + " plus " + b + " is " + (a + b);    // "5 plus 6 is 11"
```

Message Boxes

A *Message box* is a simple device for displaying messages on the screen. When executed, the following line of code pops up a message box like the one shown in Figure 3-6.

```
messageBox ("Hello world!");
```

FIGURE 3-6
A Message box

To dismiss the Message box, click the **OK** button or the close box in the window. The method `messageBox` can also accept a `double` or an `int` as a parameter.

 **IMPORTANT:**

If you take a second look at all of our applications, you will see that in the first line, they include the phrase `extends GBFrame`. The use of message boxes is restricted to such applications and cannot, for instance, be used in the `Tester` program introduced earlier in this chapter.

Adding Newline Characters to Strings

Occasionally, you will want to display more than one line of text in a message box. You can embed *newline characters* in a string to accomplish this. In Java, the newline character is expressed as \n. For example, the following code segment constructs a multiline message and displays it in a message box. Figure 3-7 shows the message output.

```
String name = "Mary Roe\n";
String address = "Lexington, Virginia\n"
int age = 19;
String message = name + address + age + "\n";
messageBox (message);
```

5 9

FIGURE 3-7
The output in the Message box

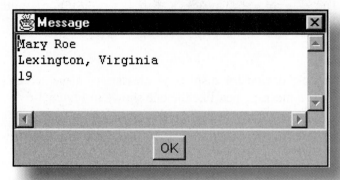

Be careful to distinguish the backslash (\) and the slash (/) characters. Java uses the slash character as a division operator or uses two slash characters to precede a program comment. The backslash character should precede the symbol for a nonprinting character. Several other nonprinting characters are discussed in Lesson 6.

Text Fields

A *text field* is an input/output region on the screen that holds one line of string data. A text field is useful for entering or displaying such things as a person's name. Text fields are declared in much the same manner as other window objects:

```
TextField <name of field> = addTextField ("<initial string>",
                                    <row>, <col>, <width>, <height>);
```

Table 3-10 shows the three most commonly used text field methods.

TABLE 3-10
Text field methods

NAME OF METHOD	WHAT THE METHOD DOES
setText(aString) returns void	Displays aString on the screen. Nothing is returned.
getText() returns aString	Returns the string entered on the screen.
setEditable(true/false) returns void	Enables or disables editing of the field.

Text fields usually open with no initial display of data. For example, the following code displays a label and an empty text field for entering a person's name:

```
Label nameLabel = addLabel ("Name",1,1,1,1);
TextField nameField = addTextField ("",1,2,1,1);
```

CASE STUDY 3 : Vital Statistics

Request

Write a program that displays the user's name, height, and weight.

Analysis

The program accepts input representing the user's name, the user's height in inches, and the user's weight in pounds. When the user selects the **Display** button, the program displays this information, appropriately labeled, in a message box.

Figure 3-8 illustrates the proposed interface. Figure 3-9 shows the resulting message box.

FIGURE 3-8

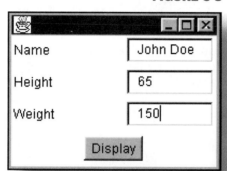

FIGURE 3-9

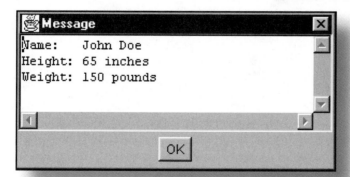

Design

Here is pseudocode for accepting the inputs and displaying the output (the `buttonClicked` method):

```
get name
get height
get weight
```

```
set output string to "Name:    " + name + "\n" +
                     "Height: " + height + " inches\n" +
                     "Weight: " + weight + " pounds\n"
display output string
```

The method `setEditable` can also be used with `IntegerField` and `DoubleField`. This method is useful for making a field read-only. For example, `nameField.setEditable(false)` makes `nameField` a read-only field.

Implementation

```
import java.awt.*;
import BreezyGUI.*;

public class VitalStatistics extends GBFrame{

    Label nameLabel = addLabel ("Name",1,1,1,1);
    TextField nameField = addTextField ("",1,2,1,1);
    Label heightLabel = addLabel ("Height",2,1,1,1);
    IntegerField heightField = addIntegerField (0,2,2,1,1);
    Label weightLabel = addLabel ("Weight",3,1,1,1);
    IntegerField weightField = addIntegerField (0,3,2,1,1);
    Button displayButton = addButton ("Display",4,1,2,1);

    String name, outputString;
    int height, weight;

    public void buttonClicked (Button buttonObj){
        name = nameField.getText();
        height = heightField.getNumber();
        weight = weightField.getNumber();
        outputString = "Name:    " + name + "\n" +
                       "Height: " + height + " inches\n" +
                       "Weight: " + weight + " pounds\n";
        messageBox (outputString);
    }

    public static void main (String[] args){
        Frame frm = new VitalStatistics();
        frm.setSize (200, 150);
        frm.setVisible (true);
    }
}
```

Design, Testing, and Debugging Hints

- When testing programs that use floating-point numbers, be sure that the outputs are displayed with the correct precision (number of digits to the right of the decimal point).

- A good way to track down logic errors is to examine the values of critical variables during the computation. To do this, insert calls to `System.out.println(<critical variable>)` at the appropriate places in the program.

- Another way to debug a difficult chunk of code is to include it in a tester program that just displays the values of the variables in a terminal window. This method allows you to focus on the logic of an algorithm without being distracted by its interaction with a GUI.

Summary

In this lesson, you learned:

- Computer memory stores patterns of electronic signals. Because electric current is either on or off, computer data are represented using the binary system. Data can include whole numbers, decimal numbers, characters and strings of characters, pictures, and sound.

- Java programs use the `int` data type for whole numbers (integers) and `double` for floating-point numbers (numbers with decimals).

- Java variable names consist of a letter followed by additional letters or digits. Java keywords cannot be used as variable names.

- Arithmetic expressions are evaluated according to precedence. Some expressions yield different results for integer and floating-point operands.

- Window objects are positioned according to a grid. Each object has attributes of type, variable name, value, location, and extent. Programs manipulate window objects by sending them messages, which then activate methods to accomplish a task.

- Strings are objects. They can be either literals or variables. Strings may be concatenated to create a new string.

LESSON 3 REVIEW QUESTIONS

WRITTEN QUESTIONS

Write your answers to the following questions.

1. Write a pseudocode algorithm that determines the batting average of a baseball player. *Hint:* To compute a batting average, divide number of hits by number of at-bats. Batting averages have three decimal places.

2. How is all information represented in the memory of a computer?

3. What translation steps must be taken to store a character (such as the letter *A*) in the memory of a computer?

4. What is an opcode?

5. Is it possible to assign a value of type `int` to a variable of type `double`? Why or why not?

6. State which of the following are valid Java identifiers. For those that are not valid, explain why.
   a. `length`
   b. `import`
   c. `6months`
   d. `hello-and-goodbye`
   e. `HERE_AND_THERE`

FILL IN THE BLANKS

Complete each of the following statements by writing your answer in the blank provided.

7. In mixed-mode arithmetic with operand types `int` and `double`, the result type is always _____.

8. The precision of a number displayed in a `DoubleField` can be set with the method _____.

9. The operation that joins two strings together is called _____.

10. The arithmetic operators for multiplication have a higher _____ than those for addition.

11. A quotient results when the _____ operator is used with two operands of type _____.

LESSON 3 PROJECTS

SCANS

1. Java's `Integer` class defines public constants, `MIN_VALUE` and `MAX_VALUE`, that name the minimum and maximum `int` values supported by the language. Thus, the expression `Integer.MAX_VALUE` returns the maximum `int` value. The `Double` class defines similar constants. Write a program that displays the values of these four constants.

2. Write a program that takes a number of seconds as input. The program converts this value to the corresponding number of hours, minutes, and seconds and displays these values.

3. One method to calculate the height of an object is to read a barometer at ground level and then get another reading at the top. The height in feet is then equal to

   ```
   25,000 * ln(ground pressure / top pressure)
   ```

   where `ln` means natural log. The method `Math.log(n)` returns this value. Write a program that accepts two barometric pressures as inputs (the values 30.25 and 29.50 are examples) and displays the height of the object in feet.

4. The arithmetic mean of two numbers is the result of dividing their sum by 2. The geometric mean of two numbers is the square root of their product. The harmonic mean of two numbers is the arithmetic mean of their reciprocals. Write a program that takes two floating-point numbers as inputs and displays these three means.

5. A baseball team's winning percentage is equal to the number of wins divided by the number of games played, rounded to three decimal places. Write a program that takes a team's wins and losses as inputs and displays its winning percentage. *Hint:* Multiply by 1.0 before dividing, and use `setPrecision(3)` before output.

6. A baseball player's batting average is equal to

   number of hits / (number of appearances at the plate – number of walks)

   Write a program that takes the number of plate appearances, hits, and walks as inputs and displays a batting average, rounded to three decimal places.

7. The StoneWood Construction Company pours concrete for the basement floors of the houses it builds. The cement is poured to a uniform depth of 6 inches. Write a program that takes as inputs the dimensions of the house (assumed to be rectangular) and the price per yard and displays the number of cubic yards of cement needed and the total cost of the cement. Contact a local cement company to obtain the current price per cubic yard. *Hint:* Use appropriate precision for the output values.

8. A student's GPA is equal to the sum of the student's grades divided by the number of grades entered. Write a program that allows the user to enter a grade as input and to click a button to display the current GPA. Typical inputs are 3.5, 2.75, and 4.0. The output should be rounded to the nearest hundredth. The user should be able to enter any number of grades. *Hint:* To keep a running sum, initialize sum to 0 and add to it every time the button is clicked.

9. Most real estate agencies charge a 6% commission for the sale of a house. Write a program that keeps track of the commissions for these sales. The input should be the sale price of a house. When the user clicks a button, the output should be the total commission thus far, rounded to the nearest hundredth. The user should be able to enter any number of sales.

10. Modify the program of Project 9 so that it also displays the commission amount and the amount left after deducting the commission for each sale.

11. Many people calculate their mileage when they fill their cars up with gasoline. Write a program that takes as inputs the odometer reading the first time a tank is filled, the odometer reading at the second fill-up, and the number of gallons of gasoline used at the second fill-up. The program should display the number of miles traveled and the mileage (equal to miles traveled divided by gallons used).

12. Write a tester program that allows you to experiment with the function `Math.sqrt`. The program should compute and display the square root of 100, 2, and –6. The output should look like this:

```
Square root of 2  : 1.4142135623730951
Square root of 100: 10.0
Square root of -6 : NaN
```

The result "NaN" is Java's way of telling you that the square root of a negative number is not a number. Actually, the square root of –6 is a complex number, but Java does not know about these. *Hint:* The first line of output was produced using the statement

```
System.out.println ("Square root of 2  : " + Math.sqrt(2));
```

13. Write a tester program that illustrates the manner in which arithmetic expressions are evaluated. The output should look like this:

```
3 + 5 * 3   yields : 18
3 + 5 * -3  yields : -12
(3 + 5) * 3 yields : 24
18 - 3 - 4  yields : 11
18 / 3 * 4  yields : 24
18 % 3 * 4  yields : 0
```

CRITICAL THINKING ACTIVITY

During the summer before the academic year, the registrar's office must enter new data for incoming freshmen. Design and implement a program that displays a data entry form with the following labeled fields:

Last name
First name
Middle initial
Class year (an integer)
Campus phone

When the user selects the **Display** button, the program should display this information on several lines in a message box.

CONTROL STATEMENTS

Upon completion of this lesson, you will be able to:

- Make choices with `if` and `if-else` statements.

- Construct conditions with relational operators.

- Build loops with `while` statements.

- Validate data with different control statements.

- Display formatted output in text areas.

🕐 **Estimated Time: 4 hours**

A Visit to the Farm

Once upon a time in a faraway land, Jack visited his cousin Jill in the country and offered to milk the cow. Jill gave him a list of instructions:

```
fetch the cow from the field;
tie her in the stall;
milk her into the bucket;
pour the milk into the bottles;
drive her back into the field;
clean the bucket;
```

Although Jack was a little taken aback by Jill's liberal use of semicolons, he had no trouble following the instructions. A year later Jack visited again. In the meantime Jill had acquired a herd of cows, some red and some black. This time, when Jack offered to help, Jill gave him a more complex list of instructions:

```
herd the cows from the field into the west paddock;
while (there are any cows left in the west paddock){
   fetch a cow from the west paddock;
   tie her in the stall;
   if (she is red){
      milk her into the red bucket;
      put the milk into red bottles;
   }
   else{
      milk her into the black bucket;
```

```
        put the milk into black bottles;
    }
    put her into the east paddock;
}
herd the cows from the east paddock back into the field;
clean the buckets;
```

These instructions threw Jack for a loop (pun intended) until Jill explained

```
while (some condition){
    do stuff;
}
```

means do the stuff repeatedly as long as the condition holds true and

```
if (some condition){
    do stuff one;
}
else{
    do stuff two;
}
```

means if some condition is true do stuff one, and if it is false, do stuff two.

"And what about all the semicolons and braces?" asked Jack.

"Those," said Jill, "are just a habit I picked up from programming in Java, where `while` and `if-else` are called control statements."

The *if and* *if-else Statements*

In Java, the `if` and `if-else` statements allow for the conditional execution of statements. These statements are called *selection statements*. For instance:

```
if (condition){
    statement;
    statement;
}
if (condition){
    statement;
    statement;
}
else{
    statement;
    statement;
}
```

The indicated semicolons and braces are required. However, the exact format of the text, including the indentation, depends on the aesthetic sensibilities of the programmer, who should be guided by a desire to make the program as readable as possible. Notice that braces always occur in pairs and that there is no semicolon immediately following a closing brace.

The braces can be dropped if only a single statement follows the word `if` or `else`, for instance:

```
if (condition)
    statement;
if (condition)
    statement;
else
    statement;
if (condition){
    statement;
       ...
    statement;
}
else
    statement;
if (condition)
    statement;
else{
    statement;
       ...
    statement;
}
```

In general, it is better to overuse than underuse braces. Likewise, in expressions it is better to overuse parentheses. The extra braces or parentheses can never do any harm, and their presence helps to eliminate logic errors.

Figure 4-1 shows a diagram called a *flowchart* that illustrates the behavior of `if` statements. When the statements are executed, either the left or the right branch is executed, depending on whether the condition is true or false.

FIGURE 4-1
Flowchart of `if` statements

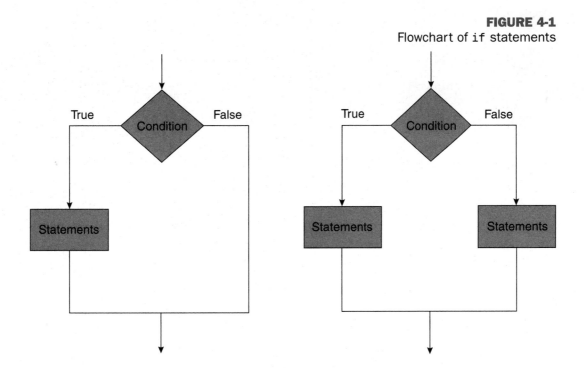

Here are some examples of if statements:

```
//Increase a salesman's commission by 10% if his sales are over $5000
if (sales > 5000)
   commission = commission * 1.1;
//Pay a worker $14.5 per hour plus time and a half for overtime
pay = hoursWorked * 14.5;
if (hoursWorked > 40){
   overtime = hoursWorked - 40;
   pay = pay + overtime * 7.25;
}
//Let c equal the larger of a and b
if (a > b)
   c = a;
else
   c = b;
```

Relational Operators and Their Precedence

The symbol > is called a *relational operator*. Relational operators are used to compare data items of the same type. There are six relational operators. Table 4-1 shows the precedence of the relational operators, as compared with the arithmetic operators and the parentheses.

TABLE 4-1
Precedence of relational operators

OPERATION	SYMBOL	PRECEDENCE (HIGHEST TO LOWEST)	ASSOCIATION
Grouping	( )	1	Not applicable
Method selector	.		Left to right
Multiplication	*	3	Left to right
Division	/		
Remainder	%		
Addition	+	4	Left to right
Subtraction	–		
Less than	<	5	Not applicable
Less than or equal	<=		
Greater than	>		
Greater than or equal	>=		
Equal	==	6	Not applicable
Not equal	!=		

Table 4-2 shows some examples of the use of relational operators.

TABLE 4-2
Examples of relational operators

EXPRESSION	MEANING
a < b	a less than b
a <= b	a less than or equal to b
a == b	a equal to b
a != b	a not equal to b
a – b > c + d	a – b greater than c + d (precedence of > is lower than + or –)
a < b < c	INVALID (we soon show how to deal with this situation)
a == b == c	INVALID (we soon show how to deal with this situation)

C A S E   S T U D Y   1 : Circle Area and Radius

Request

Modify the CircleArea program so that it has the additional capability of computing the radius from the area.

Analysis, Design, and Implementation

The program uses radius = $\sqrt{area/\pi}$ to compute the radius. The program uses Math.sqrt (aDouble) to compute and return the square root of a number. We discuss the Math class methods in Lesson 6. The program uses Math.PI to estimate π. PI is a constant defined in the Math class. We discuss how to define constants in Lesson 6. User input is either a radius or an area. The input is determined by selecting either a **Compute Radius** button or a **Compute Area** button.

Figure 4-2 shows the proposed interface. The code for this program is:

```
import java.awt.*;
import BreezyGUI.*;

public class CircleAreaAndRadius extends GBFrame{

    Label radiusLabel = addLabel ("Radius",1,1,1,1);
    DoubleField radiusField = addDoubleField (0,1,2,1,1);
    Label areaLabel = addLabel ("Area",2,1,1,1);
    DoubleField areaField = addDoubleField (0,2,2,1,1);
    Button radiusButton = addButton ("Compute Radius",3,1,1,1);
    Button areaButton = addButton ("Compute Area",3,2,1,1);

    double radius, area;

    public void buttonClicked (Button buttonObj){
        if (buttonObj == areaButton){
```

```
            radius = radiusField.getNumber();
            area = Math.PI * radius * radius;
            areaField.setNumber (area);
        }
        else{
            area = areaField.getNumber();
            radius = Math.sqrt (area / Math.PI);
            radiusField.setNumber (radius);
        }
    }

    public static void main (String[] args){
        Frame frm = new CircleAreaAndRadius();
        frm.setSize (200, 150);
        frm.setVisible (true);
    }
}
```

FIGURE 4-2

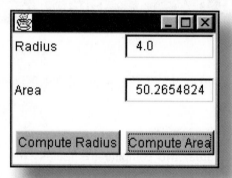

Commentary

As an experiment, enter a negative value for the area and click the **Compute Radius** button. Notice the entry in the Radius field box, as shown in Figure 4-3. "NaN" is Java's way of indicating that it cannot take the square root of a negative number.

FIGURE 4-3
Java cannot calculate the
square root of a negative number

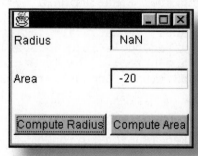

The while *Statement*

The while statement implements a *control loop*. It allows the statement or group of statements inside the loop to execute repeatedly while the condition remains true. Here is the while statement's format:

```
while (condition)          // loop test
    statement;             // inside the loop
while (condition){         // loop test
    statement;             // inside
    statement;             // the
    ...                    // loop
}
```

If the condition is false from the outset, the statement or statements inside the loop never execute. The diagram in Figure 4-4 illustrates the behavior of a while statement.

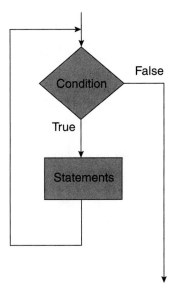

FIGURE 4-4
Flowchart of the
while statement

Three Short Examples

Here is a trivial example of a while statement:

```
//Compute the sum of the integers from 1 to 100
sum = 0;
i = 1;
while (i <= 100){
    sum = sum + i;     // point p (we will refer to this later)
    i = i + 1;
}
```

The behavior of the above snippet is obvious. The variable sum starts at 0 and i starts at 1. The code inside the loop executes 100 times, and each time through the loop, sum is incremented by increasing values of i.

To understand a loop fully, one must think about the way in which the variables change on each pass through the loop. Table 4-3 can help in this endeavor. On the 100th iteration, i is increased to 101, so there is never a 101st iteration, and the sum is computed correctly.

TABLE 4-3
Behavior of variables in the loop

ITERATION NUMBER	VALUE OF i AT POINT P	VALUE OF sum AT POINT P
1	1	1
2	2	1+2
...	...	...
100	100	1+2+...+100

Here are two more examples in the same vein:

```
//Compute the product of the even integers from 2 to 100
product = 1;
i = 2;
while (i <= 100){
   product = product * i;
   i = i + 2;
}
//Compute the sum of all the integers from 1 to 100 that are
//divisors of 100, excluding 1 and 100
sum = 0;
i = 2;
while (i <= 99){
   if (100 % i == 0)
      sum = sum + i;
   i = i + 1;
}
```

A Common Loop Structure

The loops in the three previous examples share a structure that is both common and useful:

```
initialize an accumulator;
initialize a counter;
while (some condition is true about the counter){
   make a calculation;
   store the result in the accumulator;
   increment the counter;
}
```

Logic Errors in Loops, Including Infinite Loops

It is easy to make logic errors when coding loops. A loop typically has four component parts:

1. **Initializing statements.** These statements initialize variables used within the loop.

2. **Terminating condition.** This condition is tested before each pass through the loop to determine if another iteration is needed.

3. **Body statements.** These statements execute on each iteration and implement the calculation in question.

4. **Update statements.** These statements, which usually occur at the bottom of the loop, change the values of the variables tested in the terminating condition.

A careless programmer can introduce logic errors into any one of these parts. To demonstrate, we first present a simple but correct `while` loop, and then show several revised versions, each with a different logic error. The correct version:

```
//Compute the product of the odd integers from 1 to 100
//Outcome - product will equal 3*5*...*99
product = 1;
i = 3;
while (i <= 100){
   product = product * i;
   i = i + 2;
}
```

This code shows an error in the initializing statements:

```
//Error - failure to initialize the variable product
//Outcome - the compiler detects the problem
i = 1;
while (i <= 100){
   product = product * i;
   i = i + 2;
}
```

This error is detected by the compiler, which detects attempts to use variables that may not have been initialized. Figure 4-5 shows the error on the screen.

FIGURE 4-5
Java flags the error

```
Tester.java:12: Variable product may not have been initialized.
         product = product * i;
                   ^
1 error
```

The remaining loops contain logic errors that are detected only after the program is running. Here is another error in the initializing statements:

```
//Error - initialization of product to 0
//Outcome - product will equal 0
product = 0;
```

```
i = 3;
while (i <= 100){
   product = product * i;
   i = i + 2;
}
```

Here is an error in the terminating condition:

```
//Error - use of "< 99" rather than "<= 100" in the
//        terminating condition
//Outcome - product will equal 3*5...*97
product = 1;
i = 3;
while (i < 99){
   product = product * i;
   i = i + 2;
}
```

This is called an *off-by-one error* and occurs whenever a loop goes around one too many or one too few times. Here is an error in the terminating condition:

```
//Error - use of != rather than <= in the terminating condition
//Outcome - the program will never stop
product = 1;
i = 3;
while (i != 100){
   product = product * i;
   i = i + 2;
}
```

The variable i takes on the values 3, 5, . . . , 99, 101, . . . and never equals 100. This is called an *infinite loop*. Anytime a program responds more slowly than expected, it is reasonable to assume that it is stuck in an infinite loop. Do not pull the plug. Instead, reactivate the prompt window and type Ctrl-C, that is, hold down the Ctrl key and C simultaneously. (On a Macintosh, press Command, Option, Control, and Esc simultaneously.) This will stop the program. An error in the body looks like this:

```
//Error - use of + rather than * when computing product
//Outcome - product will equal 3+5+...+99
product = 1;
i = 3;
while (i <= 100){
   product = product + i;
   i = i + 2;
}
```

Here is an error in the update statements:

```
//Error - placement of the update statement in the wrong place
//Outcome - product will equal 5*7*...*99*101
product = 1;
i = 3;
while (i <= 100){
   i = i + 2;
   product = product * i;
}
```

Debugging Loops

If you suspect that you have written a loop that contains a logic error, inspect the code and make sure the following are true:

■ Variables are initialized correctly before entering the loop.

■ The terminating condition stops the iterations when the test variables have reached the intended limit.

■ The statements in the body are correct.

■ The update statements are positioned correctly and modify the test variables in such a manner that they eventually pass the limits tested in the terminating condition.

When writing terminating conditions, it is usually safer to use <, <=, >, and >= than == and !=, as was demonstrated earlier.

If you cannot find the error by inspection, then use the System.out.println statement to print key variables to the prompt window. Good places for these statements are

■ Immediately after the initialization statements.

■ Inside the loop, at the top.

■ Inside the loop, at the bottom.

You will then discover that some of the variables have values different from those you expected, and this will provide clues that reveal the nature and location of the logic error.

C A S E   S T U D Y   2 : Count the Divisors

Request

Write a program that computes the number of divisors of an integer.

FIGURE 4-6

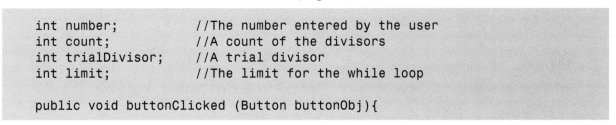

Analysis, Design, and Implementation

The program considers only positive numbers and positive divisors. We do not include 1 or the number itself when counting the divisors. If the user enters a negative number, the program computes the answer for the corresponding positive number.

Figure 4-6 shows the proposed interface.

A number *A* is a divisor of a number *B* if the remainder produced by dividing *B* by *A* is equal to zero. Thus, the test for this condition in Java is B % A == 0. Here is code for the core of the program:

```
int number;        //The number entered by the user
int count;         //A count of the divisors
int trialDivisor;  //A trial divisor
int limit;         //The limit for the while loop

public void buttonClicked (Button buttonObj){
```

```
        number = numberField.getNumber();
        if (number < 0)
            number = -number;
        count = 0;
        trialDivisor = 2;
        limit = number / 2 + 1;
        while (trialDivisor < limit){
            if (number % trialDivisor == 0)
                count = count + 1;
            trialDivisor = trialDivisor + 1;
        }
        countField.setNumber (count);
}
```

Note that if `trialDivisor` is greater than or equal to `limit`, then it is too large to be a divisor of `number`. For example:

IF number IS: **THEN limit IS:**

100   51

101   51

Obviously, 51 is too large to be a divisor of 100 or 101.

C A S E   S T U D Y   3 : Fibonacci Numbers

There is a famous sequence of numbers that occurs frequently in nature. In 1202, the Italian mathematician Leonardo Fibonacci presented the following problem:

■ Assume that each pair of rabbits in a population produces a new pair of rabbits each month.

■ Rabbits become fertile after one month.

■ Rabbits do not die.

■ If a single pair of rabbits is introduced into an environment, how many pairs of rabbits will exist after *N* months?

The numbers in this sequence are called the *Fibonacci numbers.* The first and second numbers in the sequence are 1. Thereafter each number is the sum of its two immediate predecessors, as follows:

   1 1 2 3 5 8 13 21 34 55 89 144 233 ...

Request

Write a program that can compute the *n*th Fibonacci number on demand, where *n* is a positive integer.

Analysis, Design, and Implementation

The user input is a positive integer. If the user enters anything less than 1, the program will replace it by 1.

Figure 4-7 shows the proposed interface.

FIGURE 4-7

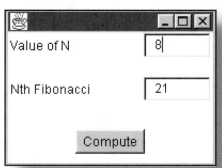

Here is code for the core of the program:

```
int n;          //The number entered by the user
int fib;        //The nth Fibonacci number
int a,b,count;  //Variables that facilitate the computation

public void buttonClicked (Button buttonObj){
   n = nField.getNumber();
   if (n <= 0) n = 1;
   if (n == 1) fib = 1;
   if (n == 2) fib = 1;
   if (n > 2){
      a = 1;
      b = 1;
      count = 3;
      while (count <= n){
         fib = a + b;       //Point p. Referred to later.
         a = b;
         b = fib;
         count = count + 1;
      }
   }
   nthFibField.setNumber (fib);
}
```

Commentary

The workings of the above loop are not obvious at first glance, so to clarify what is happening, we again construct a table (Table 4-4) that traces the changes to key variables on each pass through the loop.

TABLE 4-4
Changes to variables in the loop

Count AT POINT P	a AT POINT P	b AT POINT P	fib AT POINT P
3	1	1	2
4	1	2	3
5	2	3	5
6	3	5	8
...	...	...	...
n	(n–2)th Fibonacci number	(n–1)th Fibonacci number	nth Fibonacci number

As an experiment, use this program to compute the 80th Fibonacci number. You will be surprised by the program's answer, shown in Figure 4-8.

FIGURE 4-8
A surprising result

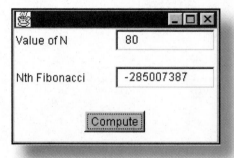

The problem is due to *arithmetic overflow*. Remember that integers have a limited range and exceeding that range leads to strange results.

Nested if *Statements*

The complexities of programming sometimes require if and if-else statements to be nested in various combinations.

Everyday Examples

Here is an everyday example written in a mixture of Java and English called Javish (Javish, anyone?):

```
if (the time is after 7 PM){
    if (you have a book)
        read the book;
    else
        watch TV;
}
else
    go for a walk;
```

A *truth table* helps to clarify the meaning. The truth table shows the four possible combinations of the two conditions and the outcome for each combination.

AFTER 7 PM	HAVE A BOOK	OUTCOME
true	true	read book
true	false	watch TV
false	true	walk
false	false	walk

One can also diagram the code as shown in Figure 4-9.

FIGURE 4-9
Flowchart of nested `if` statements

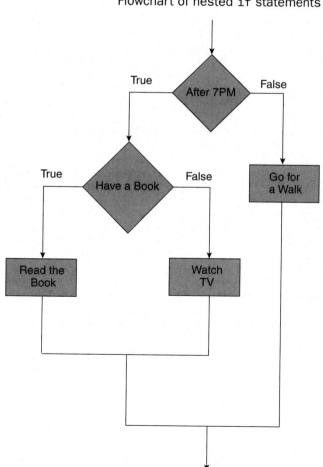

Determining a Student's Grade

Here is a final example written in Javish. The code determines a student's grade based on his test average:

```
if (average >= 90)
   grade is A;
else{
   if (average >= 80)
      grade is B;
   else{
      if (average >= 70)
         grade is C;
      else{
         if (average >= 60)
            grade is D;
         else{
            grade is F;
         }
      }
   }
}
```

In the absence of braces, an `else` is associated with the preceding `if`, so one can rewrite the code as follows:

```
if (average >= 90)
   grade is A;
else
   if (average >= 80)
      grade is B;
   else
      if (average >= 70)
         grade is C;
      else
         if (average >= 60)
            grade is D;
         else
            grade is F;
```

or after some reformatting as

```
if (average >= 90)
   grade is A;
else if (average >= 80)
   grade is B;
else if (average >= 70)
   grade is C;
else if (average >= 60)
   grade is D;
else
   grade is F;
```

This is a very common format for a sequence of `if` statements in which a variable must be compared to a sequence of threshold values.

Data Validation and Robust Programs

A *robust program* tolerates errors in user input and recovers gracefully. For example, the `CircleAreaAndRadius` program of Case Study 1 is not robust, because it attempts to compute the radius of a negative area and outputs a strange value in the radius field. A robust version of this program would check the validity of the input value before calculating the results. If the input is valid, the calculation proceeds. Otherwise, the program displays an informative error message.

CASE STUDY 4:
Making `CircleAreaAndRadius` Robust

Request

Revisit the `CircleAreaAndRadius` program and make it robust. That is, modify the program to display an error message if the user tries to derive the radius of a circle from a negative area.

FIGURE 4-10

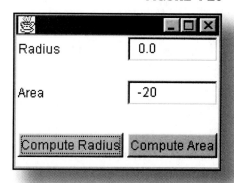

Analysis

When the user selects **Compute Radius** and the area field contains a negative number, the program displays an error message in a message box.

Figure 4-10 shows the proposed interface. Figure 4-11 shows the error message that will display in a message box.

FIGURE 4-11

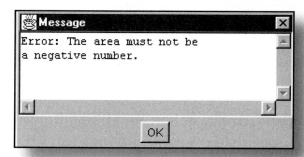

Design and Implementation

Use a nested `if` statement to check the value of the area before computing the radius. The following code contains the relevant changes:

```
public void buttonClicked (Button buttonObj){
   if (buttonObj == areaButton){
```

```
        radius = radiusField.getNumber();
        area = Math.PI * radius * radius;
        areaField.setNumber (area);
    }
    else{
        area = areaField.getNumber();
        if (area >= 0){
            radius = Math.sqrt (area / Math.PI);
            radiusField.setNumber (radius);
        }
        else
            messageBox("Error: The area must not be \na negative number.");
    }
}
```

BreezyGUI: Text Areas and Formatted Output

Thus far, we have used integer fields, double fields, and text fields for the input and output of data. However, some applications call for the output of many lines of data. This requires a larger window object than a field. Moreover, some applications output data that are aligned in columns, such as tables and schedules. In this section, we present some new tools that support the input, output, and formatting of text.

Text Areas

A *text area* is similar to a text field, except that it can handle several lines of text at a time. A text area can be used for entering or displaying an address, table, schedule, or any multiline descriptive information. Text areas are declared as follows:

```
TextArea <name of field> = addTextArea ("<initial string>",
                             <row>, <col>, <width>, <height>);
```

Whereas a text field typically has a width and height of one row, a text area is usually several columns wide and high. Table 4-5 shows some methods that manipulate text areas.

TABLE 4-5
Manipulating text areas

NAME OF METHOD	WHAT THE METHOD DOES
setText(aString) returns void	Displays aString on the screen. Nothing is returned.
append(aString) returns void	Appends aString to the text already displayed on the screen.
getText() returns aString	Returns the string entered on the screen.

The following code would create a text area that allows the display of five rows of text:

```
TextArea output = addTextArea ("", 1, 1, 2, 5);
```

Text areas have scroll bars similar to those used with text editors, to allow the user to view hidden parts of the output data.

Formatted Output

The method `Math.pow (x, y)` raises x to the power of y. The following code segment displays the first ten powers of 2 on separate lines in a text area named `output`:

```
int expo, data;
expo = 1;
while (expo <= 10){
    data = Math.pow (2, expo);
    output.append (data + "\n");
}
```

The output this code produces would be

```
2
4
8
16
32
64
128
256
512
1024
```

Consider the *justification* of this list. These numbers appear to be left justified, that is, aligned to the left. Now suppose we would like them to appear right justified, that is, aligned to the right. To accomplish this, we must somehow insert the correct number of blank spaces as padding in front of each number. The largest number in our data set occupies four columns of output area. Thus, we would want three blanks inserted in front of single-digit numbers, two blanks in front of two-digit numbers, and one blank in front of three-digit numbers, as shown in the following output:

```
   2
   4
   8
  16
  32
  64
 128
 256
 512
1024
```

The **BreezyGUI** package provides a `Format` class that allows the programmer to format output that is left justified, right justified, or centered within a given number of columns. The `Format` class defines four methods to format data, as listed in Table 4-6.

TABLE 4-6

Methods in the Format class

METHOD	WHAT IT DOES
String justify (char alignment, String data, int width)	Returns the string data aligned to the left ('l'), center ('c'), or right ('r') in the columns specified by width.
String justify (char alignment, char data, int width)	Returns the character data aligned to the left ('l'), center ('c'), or right ('r') in the columns specified by width.
String justify (char alignment, long data, int width)	Returns the string representation of data aligned to the left, center, or right in the columns specified by width.
String justify (char alignment, double data, int width, int precision)	Returns the string representation of data aligned to the left, center, or right in the columns specified by width. precision specifies the number of places to the right of the decimal point.

Some example calls of the justify method are shown in Table 4-7.

TABLE 4-7

Example calls of justify

EXAMPLE	WHAT IT DOES
Format.justify('l', "Hello", 7)	Returns the string "Hello ".
Format.justify('c', "Hello", 7)	Returns the string " Hello ".
Format.justify('r', "Hello", 7)	Returns the string " Hello".
Format.justify('r', "Hi", 7)	Returns the string " Hi".
Format.justify('r', "H", 7)	Returns the string " H".
Format.justify('r', 237, 7)	Returns the string " 237".
Format.justify('r', 2.37, 7, 1)	Returns the string " 2.4".

Note that in the last example, the decimal point occupies one column of the string's width, and the number is rounded to the nearest tenth. Thus, the following code segment would output the first ten powers of 2 in right-justified format:

```
int expo, data;
expo = 1;
while (expo <= 10){
    data = Math.pow (2, expo);
    output.append (Format.justify ('r', data, 4) + "\n");
}
```

C A S E   S T U D Y   5 : A Sales Table

Request

Write a program that allows the user to enter the names and annual sales figures for any number of salespeople. The program should display a formatted table of salespeople, their sales, and their commissions (at 10% of the sales amount).

Analysis

User inputs are

- A salesperson's name (no more than ten characters), in a text field.

- The salesperson's annual sales amount (a floating-point number), in a double field.

- An **Accept** button to enter each pair of data values.

The program's output is a table of three columns, appropriately headed, in a text area. The first column is headed **NAME,** the second column is headed **SALES**, and the third column is headed **COMMISSION.** The names are left justified within 12 columns, the sales are right justified within 15 columns, and the commissions are right justified within 15 columns.

Figure 4-12 shows the proposed interface.

FIGURE 4-12

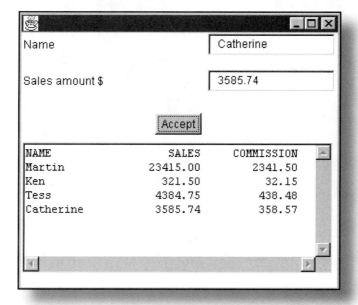

Design

Here is pseudocode for the buttonClicked method:

```
Get the salesperson's name
Get the sales amount
```

Calculate the commission
Create formatted strings for the three data values
Concatenate these strings and append them to the text area

Implementation

```java
import java.awt.*;
import BreezyGUI.*;

public class SalesTable extends GBFrame{

    // Format the header of the table.
    String header = Format.justify ('l', "NAME", 12) +
                    Format.justify ('r', "SALES", 15) +
                    Format.justify ('r', "COMMISSION", 15) + "\n";

    Label nameLabel = addLabel ("Name",1,1,1,1);
    Label salesLabel = addLabel ("Sales amount $",2,1,1,1);
    TextField nameField = addTextField ("",1,2,1,1);
    DoubleField salesField = addDoubleField (0.0,2,2,1,1);
    Button acceptButton = addButton ("Accept",3,1,2,1);
    TextArea output = addTextArea (header,4,1,3,4);

    String name;
    double sales, commission;
    String nameOutput, salesOutput, commissionOutput;

    public void buttonClicked (Button buttonObj){
        // Get the user input.
        name = nameField.getText();
        sales = salesField.getNumber();

        // Calculate the commission.
        commission = sales * 0.10;

        // Format the output data.
        nameOutput = Format.justify ('l', name, 12);
        salesOutput = Format.justify ('r', sales, 15, 2);
        commissionOutput = Format.justify ('r', commission, 15, 2);

        // Output a line of data.
        output.append (nameOutput + salesOutput + commissionOutput +
                       "\n");
    }

    public static void main (String[] args){
        Frame frm = new SalesTable();
        frm.setSize (350, 300);
        frm.setVisible (true);
    }
}
```

CS CAPSULE:
Artificial Intelligence, Robots, and Softbots

You have seen in this chapter that a computer not only can calculate results, but can also respond to conditions in its environment and take the appropriate actions. This additional capability forms the basis of a branch of computer science known as *artificial intelligence*, or AI. AI programmers attempt to construct computational models of intelligent human behavior. These tasks involve, among many others, interacting in English or other natural languages, recognizing objects in the environment, reasoning, creating and carrying out plans of action, and pruning irrelevant information from a sea of detail.

There are many ways to construct AI models. One way is to view intelligent behavior as patterns of *production rules.* Each rule contains a set of conditions and a set of actions. In this model, an intelligent agent, either a computer or a human being, compares conditions in its environment to the conditions of all of its rules. Those rules with matching conditions are scheduled to fire—meaning that their actions are triggered—according to a higher-level scheme of rules. The set of rules is either hand-coded by the AI programmer or "learned" by using a special program known as a *neural net.*

AI systems have been used to control *robots.* While not quite up to the performance of Commander Data in the television series *Star Trek: The Next Generation,* these robots can perform mundane tasks such as assembling cars.

AI systems are also embedded in software agents known as *softbots.* For example, softbots exist to filter information from e-mail systems, to schedule appointments, and to search the World Wide Web for information.

For a detailed discussion of robots and softbots, see Rodney Brooks, "Intelligence Without Representation," in *Mind Design II,* ed. John Haugeland (Cambridge, MA: MIT Press, 1997), and Patti Maes, "Agents that Reduce Work and Information Overload," *Communications of the ACM,* Volume 37, No. 7 (July 1994): 30–40.

Design, Testing, and Debugging Hints

■ Most errors involving selection statements and loops are not syntax errors caught at compile time. Thus, you will detect these errors only after running the program, and perhaps then only with extensive testing.

■ The presence or absence of the {} symbols can seriously affect the logic of a selection statement or loop. For example, the following selection statements have a similar look but a very different logic:

```
if (x > 0){
    y = x;
    z = 1 / x;
}
if (x > 0)
    y = x;
    z = 1 / x;
```

The first selection statement guards against division by 0; the second statement only guards against assigning x to y. The next pair of code segments shows a similar problem with a loop:

```
while (x > 0){
    y = x;
    x = x - 1;
}

while (x > 0)
    y = x;
    x = x - 1;
```

The first loop terminates, because the value of x decreases within the body of the loop. The second loop is infinite, because the value of x decreases below the body of the loop.

■ Variables declared within a block (code enclosed in {}) are local to that block and cannot be used outside of that block. If the same variable name is declared before the block and in the block, references in the block apply to the variable declared in the block.

■ When testing programs that use if or if-else statements, be sure to use test data that force the program to exercise all of the logical branches.

■ Use an if-else statement rather than two if statements when the alternative courses of action are mutually exclusive.

■ When testing a loop, be sure to use limiting values as well as typical values. For example, if a loop should terminate when the control variable equals 0, run it with the values 0, –1, and 1.

■ Be sure to check

• Entry conditions for each loop.

• Exit conditions for each loop.

■ For a loop with errors, use debugging output statements to verify the values of the control variable on each pass through the loop. Check this value

• Before the loop is initially entered.

• After each update.

• After the loop is exited.

■ Test data should include

• Typical data and boundary cases.

• Erroneous cases to check robustness.

Summary

In this lesson, you learned:

■ The if and if-else statements allow for the conditional execution of statements.

■ Relational operators are used to compare data items of the same type.

■ The `while` statement implements a control loop. Although a condition in the loop remains true, the loop executes repeatedly. If the condition is false from the outset, the statement within the loop never executes.

■ It is easy to make logic errors when coding loops. An off-by-one error occurs when a loop goes around one too many or one too few times. An infinite loop occurs when a loop never terminates.

■ `if` and `if-else` statements can be nested to calculate variables that depend on a sequence of values.

■ A robust program tolerates errors in user input and recovers gracefully.

■ Text areas can handle several lines of text at a time to display addresses, tables, schedules, and so on. The `Format` class enables you to justify output in specified column widths.

LESSON 4 REVIEW QUESTIONS

WRITTEN QUESTIONS

Write your answers to the following questions.

1. Assume that the variables x and y contain the values 19 and 2, respectively. Indicate if the Boolean expressions below are true, false, or syntactically incorrect.
   a. `x <= y`
   b. `x * 2 > y`
   c. `x - 1 == y * 9`
   d. `x < y < 25`
   e. `x * 2 != y`

2. For each item below, write a valid Java statement. Assume that data are output with the method `messageBox`.
   a. Display "greater" if the value of variable x is greater than the value of variable y. Otherwise, display "less."
   b. Add 10 to the value of x and display this value if the variable y is negative.
   c. Display the string A if x is greater than 90, B if x is greater than 80, or C otherwise.

3. Indicate whether each loop heading below is syntactically correct. If incorrect, explain why.
   a. `while (x > 0)`
   b. `while (y = 10)`
   c. `while x != 0`

4. Write a valid Java statement for each item below. Assume that data are output with the `TextArea` method `append`.
   a. Output the positive numbers from x up to y.
   b. Output the product of the squares of the numbers from x up to y.
   c. Output the numbers from y down to 0.

5. Use the method `Format.justify` to create the appropriate data for the items below.
   a. The value of the integer variable x, right justified in 10 columns.
   b. The value of the `String` variable `name`, left justified in 20 columns.
   c. The value of the `double` variable d, right justified in 12 columns and with two figures of precision.

LESSON 4 PROJECTS

In the spirit of this lesson, all of the projects that follow require data validation.

1. When you first learned to divide, you expressed answers using a quotient and a remainder rather than a fraction or decimal quotient. For example, if you divided 9 by 2, you gave your answer as 4 r. 1. Write a program that takes two integers as inputs and displays their quotient and remainder as outputs. Do not assume that the integers are entered in any order, but be sure to divide the larger integer by the smaller integer.

2. Write a program that takes the lengths of three sides of a triangle as inputs. The program should display, in a text area, whether or not the triangle is a right triangle. You should assume that the side with the rightmost, lowest field is the longest one. *Data validation:* Make sure both numbers are positive.

3. The German philosopher and mathematician Gottfried Wilhelm Leibnitz developed the following method to approximate the value of π:

   $$\pi/4 = 1 - 1/3 + 1/5 - 1/7 + \ldots$$

   Write a program that allows the user to specify the number of iterations used in this approximation, and displays the resulting value. *Data validation:* Make sure the number of iterations is positive.

4. A local biologist needs a program to predict population growth. The inputs would be the initial number of organisms, the rate of growth (a real number greater than 0), the number of hours it takes to achieve this rate, and a number of hours during which the population grows. For example, one might start with a population of 500 organisms, a rate of growth of 2, and a growth period to achieve this rate of 6 hours. Assuming that none of the organisms die, this would imply that this population would double in size every 6 hours. Thus, after allowing 6 hours for growth, we would have 1000 organisms, and after 12 hours, we would have 2000 organisms. Write a program that takes these inputs and displays a prediction of the total population. *Data validation:* Inputs are positive.

5. Computers use the binary system, which is based on powers of 2. Write a program that displays the first ten powers of 2, beginning with 2^0. The output should be in headed columns in a text area.

6. Modify the program of Project 5 so that the user can specify the number of powers of 2 to be displayed. *Data validation:* Inputs are positive.

7. Modify the program of Project 6 so that the user can specify the base (2 or higher) as well. The header of the output should display which base was entered.

8. The theory of relativity holds that as an object moves, it appears smaller relative to a stationary observer. The formula for determining the new length of the object is

$$\text{Apparent length} = \text{Stationary length} * \sqrt{(1 - B^2)}$$

where B is the fraction of the speed of light at which the object is moving, entered in decimal form. Write a program that takes the length of an object as input, and displays its new length for speeds ranging from 0 to 99 % of the speed of light. The output should be displayed in two columns labeled **Percent of Speed of Light** and **Length of Object**. *Data validation:* Length > 0 and 0 <= speed <= 1.

9. Teachers in most school districts are paid on a schedule that provides a salary based on their number of years of teaching experience. For example, a beginning teacher in the Lexington School District might be paid $20,000 the first year. For each year of experience after this up to 10 years, a 2% increase over the preceding value is received. Write a program that displays a salary schedule for teachers in any district. The inputs are the starting salary, the percentage increase, and the number of years in the schedule. ***Data validation:*** Starting salary > 0, 0 < annual percent increase <= 20, and 0 < number of year <= 40.

10. John has $500 to invest. Sue knows of a mutual fund plan that pays 10% interest, compounded quarterly (that is, every 3 months, the principal is multiplied by the 2.5% and the result is added to the principal). Write a program that will tell John how much money will be in the fund after 20 years. Make the program general. That is, it should take as inputs the interest rate, the initial principal, and the number of years to stay in the fund. The output should be a table whose columns are the year number, the principal at the beginning of the year, the interest earned, and the principal at the end of the year. ***Data validation:*** 0 <= interest rate <= 200, 0 <= initial investment <= 10,000, and 0 < number of years <= 40.

CRITICAL THINKING ACTIVITY

The analysis of a program requires three buttons, labeled **Height, Weight,** and **Age,** in row 3 of the window. The method to handle button clicks should call the methods `enterHeight`, `enterWeight`, and `enterAge`. Assume that these three methods have already been implemented, and write the code to set up the buttons and handle the user's clicks.

UNIT 1 REVIEW QUESTIONS

TRUE/FALSE

On a separate piece of paper, type True if the statement is true or False if it is not.

T F **1.** The first generation of programming language is assembly language.

T F **2.** Java is an example of a high-level language.

T F **3.** Mistakes found early in the coding process are much more expensive to fix than mistakes found later in the process.

T F **4.** Byte code is a program that behaves like a computer.

T F **5.** An arithmetic expression consists of operands and binary operators combined as in algebra.

T F **6.** Programs manipulate window objects by sending them methods.

T F **7.** An integer is a positive or negative whole number.

T F **8.** Strings are objects, not data types.

T F **9.** A relational operator is used to compare data items of the same type.

T F **10.** A robust program can check the validity of input before calculating results.

FILL IN THE BLANKS

On a separate piece of paper, type the information necessary to complete the following statements.

1. OOP stands for _____.

2. The software responsible for translating a program in a high-level language to machine code is called a(n) _____.

3. JVM stands for _____.

4. When an object receives a message, the object responds by running a block of code called a(n) _____.

5. Numbers with a fractional part are called _____.

6. When evaluating an expression, Java performs operations of higher _____ unless overridden by _____.

7. Use the _____ operator to create a new string out of existing strings.

8. The `while` statement implements a _____.

9. A(n) _____ error occurs when a loop goes around one too many or one too few times.

10. A(n) _____ is similar to a text field except that it can handle several lines of text at a time.

WRITTEN QUESTIONS

On a separate piece of paper, type the answers to the following questions or problems.

1. What is the purpose of a variable in a program?

2. What are the three types of programming errors? Give a brief example of each.

3. Describe the differences between the data types `double` and `int`.

4. Assume that the variables x and y contain the values 8 and 4, respectively. What are the values of the expressions listed below?
   a. `x + y * 2`
   b. `(x + y) / 3`
   c. `x - y * 3`
   d. `x + y * 1.5`

5. Write a valid Java statement that adds 5 to the value of variable x if the value of variable y is greater than 10.

6. A program has the following loop heading: `while (3 < x < 10)`. Is the heading syntactically correct? If incorrect, explain why.

7. Use the method `Format.justify` to create a list of numbers from x up to y and their cubes, in two columns that are right justified within ten columns each.

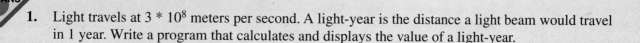

UNIT 1 APPLICATIONS

SCANS

1. Light travels at $3 * 10^8$ meters per second. A light-year is the distance a light beam would travel in 1 year. Write a program that calculates and displays the value of a light-year.

2. Write a program that expects the length and width of a rectangle as inputs. The program should calculate the rectangle's area and perimeter and display these values rounded to the nearest tenth of a foot.

3. A 2-minute telephone call to Lexington, Virginia, costs $1.15. Each additional minute costs $0.50. Write a program that takes the total length of a call in minutes as input and calculates and displays the cost.

4. The local bookstore has a markup of 10% on each book sold. Write a program that takes the sales price of a book as input and displays the following outputs:
   a. The markup amount of the book just sold.
   b. The wholesale amount (to go to the publisher) of the book just sold.
   c. The total sales prices of all of the books sold thus far.
   d. The total markup amount of all of the books sold thus far.

   The output can be displayed either in field or in a message box.

5. The TidBit Computer Store has a credit plan for computer purchases. There is a 10% downpayment and an annual interest rate of 12%. Monthly payments are 5% of (the listed purchase price minus the down payment). Write a program that takes the purchase price as input. The program should display a table, with appropriate headers, of a payment schedule for the lifetime of the loan. Each row of the table should contain the following items:
   a. The month number (beginning with 1).
   b. The current total balance owed.
   c. The interest owed for that month.
   d. The amount of principal owed for that month.
   e. The payment for that month.
   f. The balance remaining after payment.

   The amount of interest for a month is equal to balance * rate / 12. The amount of principal for a month is equal to the monthly payment minus the interest owed.

CRITICAL THINKING ACTIVITY

SCANS

Modify the program of Application 5 so that it displays the total interest paid and the total of the monthly payments at the end of the loan. Then modify the program again so that it allows the user to specify the interest rate and the percentage of the purchase price representing the monthly payment amount.

METHODS, DATA TYPES, AND CLASSES

USER-DEFINED METHODS

User-Defined Methods

The programs we have written so far have been short and simple, but soon we will tackle problems of greater complexity. To manage the complexity, we can apply a strategy that has proven successful in many areas of human endeavor—divide and conquer. Thus, when confronted by the task of writing a long and difficult method, we instead write a number of shorter methods that cooperate to achieve the same result. We will call these *user-defined methods*.

First Look at User-Defined Methods

Let us revisit the CircleAreaAndRadius program and divide the buttonClicked method into three simpler methods. The interface is shown in Figure 5-1.

FIGURE 5-1

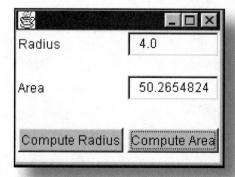

Here is the new code:

```
double radius, area;

public void buttonClicked (Button buttonObj){
   if (buttonObj == areaButton)
      computeArea();
   else
      computeRadius();
}

private void computeArea(){
   radius = radiusField.getNumber();
   area = Math.PI * radius * radius;
   areaField.setNumber (area);
}

private void computeRadius(){
   area = areaField.getNumber();
   radius = Math.sqrt (area / Math.PI);
   radiusField.setNumber (radius);
}
```

In the above code, the `buttonClicked` method does not calculate the area or the radius directly. Instead it *calls* or *activates* the other methods to do so. The relationship among the three methods is illustrated in the diagram called a *structure chart* shown in Figure 5-2. The downward-pointing arrows stand for calls or activates.

FIGURE 5-2
Structure chart of the `buttonClicked` method

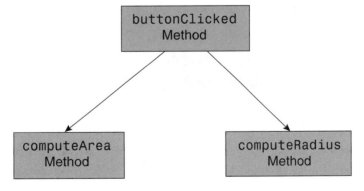

We are not quite ready to discuss the significance of the words `private`, `public`, and `void` in the preceding code. For now, suffice it to say that the `buttonClicked` method must be `public`, while the other two methods should be `private`. By the way, the order of the methods in the program is merely a matter of personal taste. However, from the perspective of someone reading the program, perhaps it is better to list the calling method first. By reading the calling method first, the reader gets an overview of the task at hand and can find the details in the called methods. This top-down order also corresponds to the order in which programmers tend to develop the methods, an approach called *top-down design*. Well-chosen method names help to make a system of cooperating methods easy to understand.

When the computer runs a program, it executes only one instruction at a time, and the point of execution shifts from method to method. Figure 5-3 illustrates how the point of execution (also called the *flow of control*) shifts when the **Compute Area** button is clicked.

Execution starts in the buttonClicked method and remains there until the computeArea method is called. Then, when the computeArea method completes its task, execution returns to the buttonClicked method immediately following the point of departure.

FIGURE 5-3
Shifting control flow

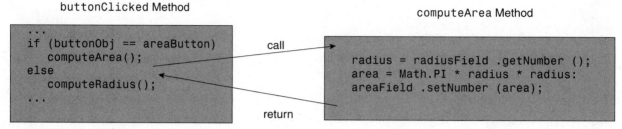

Cohesion of Methods

We now place a user-defined method in the CountDivisors program. The interface for that program is shown in Figure 5-4.

FIGURE 5-4

Here is the code:

```
int number;        //The number entered by the user
int count;         //A count of the divisors
int trialDivisor;  //A trial divisor
int limit;         //The limit for the while loop

public void buttonClicked (Button buttonObj){
    number = numberField.getNumber();
    if (number < 0)
        number = -number;
    computeCount();
    countField.setNumber (count);
}
```

```
private void computeCount(){
   count = 0;
   trialDivisor = 2;
   limit = number / 2 + 1;
   while (trialDivisor < limit){
      if (number % trialDivisor == 0)
         count = count + 1;
      trialDivisor = trialDivisor + 1;
   }
}
```

Whenever we break a task down into cooperating methods, we create what might be called a division of labor. However, all divisions of labor are not equally effective. Imagine you are in charge of organizing a large party with the help of some friends. You could make a list of all the individual tasks involved and assign them at random to your helpers. But random assignments are not a good idea because each person's tasks would be unrelated, making the project difficult to supervise. It would make more sense to give each person a single clearly defined responsibility, which in turn would encompass a set of related tasks. The party would then come off smoothly and easily.

The same principle applies to programming. When a method has a single clearly defined responsibility, we say that it has *high cohesion.* If it implements unrelated or loosely related tasks, it has *low cohesion. Cohesion* is thus a measure of a method's unity of purpose. In writing programs, we strive for methods whose cohesion is as high as possible. In the preceding example, the computeCount method has high cohesion. It has a single clearly defined purpose: to count the number of divisors. The computeArea method, despite being shorter, has low cohesion. Rather than doing a single task, it does three related ones: get data from the screen, perform a computation, and display the result. For now, do not be overly concerned about cohesion, but nonetheless keep it in mind.

Parameters and Return Values

Cooperating methods must be able to communicate. In the examples above, this communication was achieved indirectly by shared access to a common pool of variables, as suggested by the diagram in Figure 5-5.

FIGURE 5-5
Communication takes place through access to common variables

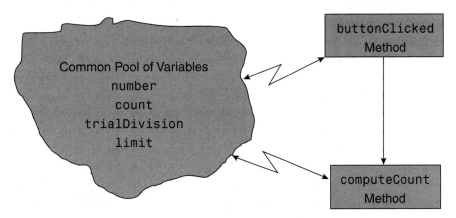

The sharing in the `CountDivisors` program took place as follows:

■ The `buttonClicked` method put a value in `number` and called `computeCount`.

■ The `computeCount` method accessed the value in `number` and put the answer in `count`.

■ The `buttonClicked` method then accessed the value in `count` and displayed it.

Notice in Figure 5-5 that variables `trialDivisor` and `limit` were used only by `computeCount` even though they are in the common pool.

Instead of sharing a common pool of variables, methods can communicate by passing parameters and returning values. A parameter as named in a method declaration is called a *formal parameter*. The value passed to the method in the position of a formal parameter when the method is called is known as an *actual parameter* or *argument*. In addition, each method can declare its own private stash of variables. These we call *local variables*. Figure 5-6 shows some illustrative code. The code in this figure is discussed below.

FIGURE 5-6
How methods use local variables

```
public void buttonClicked (Button buttonObj) {
    int number;                               ←————————— Local Variables
    int count;
    number = numberField.getNumber();         ←— Actual Parameter
    if (number < 0)
        number + -number;
    count = computeCount (number);
    countField.setNumber (count);             Returned Value
                                              Assigned to count
}

    private int computeCount (int nmbr) {     Return Type
    int cnt;                                  Formal Parameter
    int trialDivisor:                         ←————————— Local Variables
    int limit;
    cnt = 0;
    trialDivisor = 2;
    limit = nmbr / 2 + 1;
    while (trialDivisor < limit) {
        if (nmbr % trialDivisor == 0)
            cnt = cnt + 1;
        trialDivisor = trialDivisor + 1;

    }
        return cnt;                           ←————————— Value Returned
}
```

First we discuss the `computeCount` method. The line

```
private int computeCount (int nmbr){
```

indicates that the method returns an integer value and expects an integer parameter, which here is called nmbr. In the line

```
return cnt;
```

the method returns an integer value to the calling method. There can be more than one return statement in a method. However, the first one executed ends the method.

Now consider the buttonClicked method. The line

```
count = computeCount (number);
```

activates the computeCount method, passing it the value of the variable number. This value is then assigned to the variable nmbr in the computeCount method. It is important to understand that the variables number and nmbr are otherwise completely independent of each other. For instance, changing the value of nmbr would have no effect on the value of number. When computeCount has completed its calculations, buttonClicked assigns the returned integer value to the variable count. Figure 5-7 illustrates this process.

Sometimes a method has many parameters, as illustrated in Figure 5-8. In the example in Figure 5-8, notice that the number, type, and order of the actual parameters must match the number, type, and order of the formal parameters.

FIGURE 5-7
How parameters are passed and value is returned

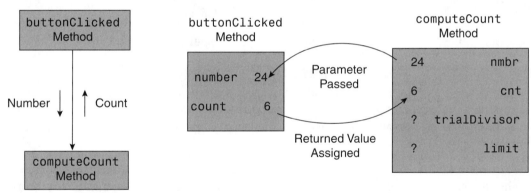

FIGURE 5-8
A method can have many parameters

```
public class ParameterDemo extends GBFrame{
    ...
    public void buttonClicked  (Button buttonObj){
       double x;
        int i;
        ...
       x = myMethod (i*3, 2.4, i);
        ...
    }

    private double myMethod (int parm1, double parm2, int parm3) {
        ...
       return aDouble;
    }
    ...
}
```

A method does not have to use a return type and parameters simultaneously. All four possibilities are allowed: no return type and no parameters, no return type and some parameters, a return type and no parameters, and a return type and some parameters. The preceding examples have illustrated only the first and last of these.

If a method's return type is void, the method can still have a return statement, but no return expression is allowed. If a method's type is not void, then a return expression must be written. Its type must match the method's return type. The rule for matching types of parameters and return values is the same as the rule for matching the operands of an assignment statement. Values of less inclusive types can be used where values of more inclusive types are expected, and Java does automatic type conversion. However, values of more inclusive types cannot be used where values of less inclusive types are expected.

Overloaded Methods

Two methods in a program can have the same name, provided the number and types of their parameters are not identical. Whether the methods have the same return type is immaterial. These methods are said to be *overloaded*. Here is an example:

```
private int doIt (int parm1, double parm2){
   ...
}

private int doIt (int parm1, int parm2){
   ...
}
```

The headers of these two methods differ only in the second parameter's type.

Sharing Variables Versus Passing Parameters

As shown in the previous examples, methods can communicate by sharing a common pool of variables or by the more explicit means of parameters and return values. Years of software development experience have convinced computer scientists that the second approach is preferable. Here are three illustrations:

1. Suppose that several methods share a pool of variables and that one method misuses a variable. Then other methods can be affected, and the resulting error can be difficult to find. For example, if method m1 mistakenly sets the variable x to 0 and if method m2 uses x as a divisor, then when the program is run, the computer will flag an error in m2, despite the fact the source of the error is in m1.

2. It is easier to understand methods and the relationships between them when communications are explicit.

3. Methods that access a pool of shared variables can be used only in their original context, whereas methods that are passed parameters can be reused in many different situations.

Scope and Lifetime of Variables

The *scope* of a variable is that region of the program within which it can be used. We will consider two possibilities: local and global scope. The *lifetime* of a variable is the period during which it can be accessed.

Variables declared inside a method are said to be *local* and can be used only within the declaring method. The compiler would flag as an error any attempt to use these variables outside the method. However, the same variable name can be declared within several different methods without there being a conflict. Thus in the `computeCount` method, we could have named the variables as follows, which duplicates names in the `buttonClicked` method:

```
private int computeCount (int number){
    int count;
    int trialDivisor;
    int limit;
    ...
    return count;
}
```

Whether one declares the same variable name in several different methods is merely a matter of taste.

If a variable is declared outside all methods, then its scope includes all the methods, and it is said to be a *global variable*. For instance, in all the programs we have written, the variables for the window objects are global. Here is an example that illustrates the difference between local and global scope:

```
public class ScopeDemo extends GBFrame{
    int iAmGlobal;

    public void buttonClicked (Button buttonObj){
        int iAmLocalToo;
        ...
    }

    private int userMethod (int parm1, int parm2){
        int iAmLocal;
        ...
    }
    ...
}
```

Table 5-1 shows where each of the variables can be used (i.e., its scope).

TABLE 5-1
Scope of variables

VARIABLE	userMethod	buttonClicked
iAmGlobal	yes	yes
parm1 and parm1	yes	no
iAmLocal	yes	no
iAmLocalToo	no	yes

The lifetime of a variable depends on whether it is local or global. A local variable, one declared in a method, can be accessed only during a single execution of the method, whereas a global variable can be accessed for the duration of the program. Thus, any variable that must outlast any single execution of a method must be global. For instance, the variables for the window objects must be global.

To be precise, we mention a point that might not make much sense yet: A global variable is more commonly called an *instance variable,* and its lifetime is the duration of the object in which it resides.

Preconditions and Postconditions

It is difficult to tell at a glance whether a program that consists of several methods and global variables is correct. This task is made easier by specifying what each method is supposed to do. When the correctness of a method is an issue, the programmer can specify it in terms of *preconditions* and *postconditions*.

One can think of preconditions and postconditions as the subject of a conversation between the user of a method (an application) and the implementer of the method. Here is the general form of this conversation:

```
Implementer: "Here are the things that you must guarantee to be true before
             my method is invoked. They are its preconditions."

User: "Fine. And what do you guarantee will be the case if I do that?"

Implementer: "Here are the things that I guarantee to be true when my method
             finishes execution. They are its postconditions."
```

A precondition of a method is a statement of what must be true before a method is invoked for the method to run correctly. A postcondition of a method is a statement of what must be true after the method has finished execution. In Java programs, preconditions and postconditions appear in program comments, usually placed directly above or below the method heading. Preconditions usually describe the state of any parameters and instance variables that a method is about to access. Postconditions describe the state of any parameters and instance variables that the method has accessed; the value returned, if any; as well as the method's response to any errors that might occur.

The following example adds preconditions and postconditions to the first version of the `compute-Count` method:

```java
// Preconditions: number is an integer >= 0.
// Postconditions: number is unchanged.
//                 limit equals number / 2 + 1.
//                 trialDivisor equals limit.
//                 count equals the number of divisors of number.

private void computeCount(){
    count = 0;
    trialDivisor = 2;
    limit = number / 2 + 1;
    while (trialDivisor < limit){
        if (number % trialDivisor == 0)
            count = count + 1;
        trialDivisor = trialDivisor + 1;
    }
}
```

Note two things about this documentation:

1. When invoked, the method makes an assumption about the state of the instance variable `number`, but not about any of the other instance variables. Thus, there is only one precondition.

2. Because the method can access four instance variables, it must state what is true about each of the four when it terminates execution. Thus, there are four postconditions.

The next example shows the preconditions and postconditions of the second version of `computeCount`:

```
// Preconditions: number is an integer >= 0.
// Postconditions: number of divisors of number is returned.

private int computeCount (int number){
    int count = 0;
    int trialDivisor = 2;
    int limit = number / 2 + 1;
    while (trialDivisor < limit){
        if (number % trialDivisor == 0)
            count = count + 1;
        trialDivisor = trialDivisor + 1;
    return count;
    }
}
```

In the second version of the method, we have made `number` a parameter of the method, and have made `count`, `trialDivisor`, and `limit` local variables instead of instance variables. These changes have the following consequences:

1. The precondition is unchanged, although the user must now pass the number as a parameter.

2. The four earlier postconditions have been dropped. Instead, there is a single postcondition, which guarantees that the method returns the number of divisors.

Our two examples show that the use of local variables and parameters can reduce the number of conditions needed to build our confidence that a method is correct. The examples also show that the use of preconditions and postconditions is especially desirable when a method can access instance variables.

Writing preconditions and postconditions for every method can be tedious. When the focus is not on proving a program to be correct, they can be used with a few critical methods or omitted entirely. We leave it to the reader (student and/or instructor) to decide whether to include this documentation.

CS CAPSULE : Function-Oriented Programming

In 1977, John Backus, the inventor of the programming language FORTRAN, was given the ACM Turing Award for his contributions to computer science at the annual meeting of the Association for Computing Machinery. Each recipient of this annual award presents a lecture. Backus discussed a new discipline in his talk called *function-oriented programming*. This style of programming was developed to address concerns about the reliability and maintainability of large software systems. One of the principal causes of errors in large programs is the presence of side effects and unintentional modifications of variables. These modifications can occur anywhere in a program with assignment statements whose targets are global variables. Backus proposed that function-oriented programming could eliminate side effects by eliminating the assignment statement and keeping global variables to a minimum. Function-oriented programs consist of sets of function declarations and *function applications*. A function application simply evaluates the parameters to a function, applies the function to these values, and returns a result to the caller. No assignment statements to global variables are allowed within a function. No side effects occur.

The philosophy of function-oriented programming has motivated the design of function-oriented languages. These languages do not allow the programmer to perform assignments to global variables within functions. The closest thing in Java to a function is a method. However, Java methods allow this kind of side effect. In fact, as we will see when we introduce object-oriented programming in Lesson 7, many important Java methods exist just for the purpose of modifying global variables within objects. However, by exercising some discipline, Java programmers can still emulate a function-oriented style to guard against unwanted side effects in their programs.

CASE STUDY : Tally Grades

Successful completion of large, complex programs requires the use of a good design and implementation strategy. We now present one in the context of a case study.

Request

Write a program that allows a teacher to tally the grades on a test.

Analysis

The user input consists of student scores on a test. The program calculates the number of As, Bs, and so on, and a running average, and displays the tallies and the running average. We provide a facility to reset the program so that more than one set of scores can be entered.

The program should be robust, meaning that it responds sensibly when invalid scores are entered. (Robust should not be confused with *correct*. A program is correct if it produces correct output when presented with correct inputs.) A score is considered invalid if

- It is outside the range 0 to 100 (for instance, –6 and 105).

- It is nonnumeric (for instance, "cat").

- It is numeric but not an integer (for instance, 3.14).

A message box should be used to display an appropriate error message in response to invalid inputs.

Figure 5-9 shows the proposed interface. The user must click the **Tally Score** button after entering each score, at which point one of the tallies is incremented and the running average is updated. Clicking the **Reset** button reinitializes the program, resetting the variables in preparation for another batch of scores.

FIGURE 5-9

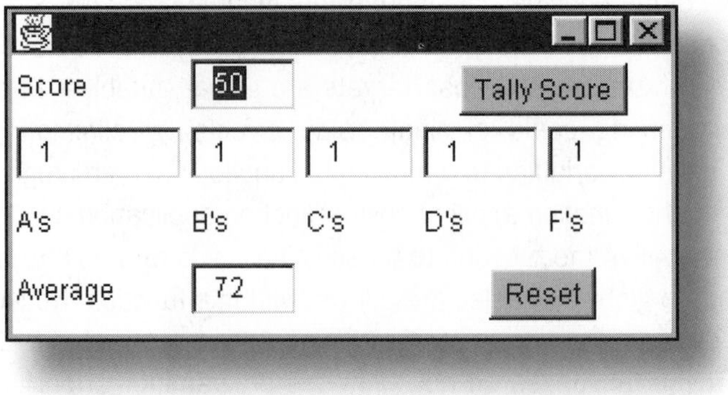

After either button is clicked, the program moves the cursor back to the score field and selects its text. This makes the program easier to use.

Design

Let us begin by determining the variables needed by this program:

- The variables for window objects are fairly routine and can be chosen during implementation.

- The variables to tally the number of As, Bs, and so on, are

  `tallyA, tallyB, tallyC, tallyD, tallyF`

- The variables needed to compute the average are

  `numberOfTests`—the number of test scores entered so far.

  `totalOfTests`—the total of the test scores entered so far.

  `average`—the average of the test scores entered so far.

In developing the pseudocode for the `buttonClicked` method, we illustrate the approach suggested by top-down design; that is, we show how methods can work together to accomplish the overall task of the program. Starting with the top-level method, `buttonClicked`, we write it in terms of subordinate methods that can help it carry out its task. These subordinate methods are then in turn written in the same manner. In this process, we do not worry about fully explaining the lowest-level details; rather, we focus on the logic whereby the methods coordinate their activity. Unfortunately, there is no formula that one can learn for doing this. But with exposure to examples and practice, it begins to come naturally. Here is the pseudocode:

```
buttonClickeMethod
    if (reset button clicked)
       resetGlobalVariables()
    else
       processScore()
    set the focus to the input field for the score

resetGlobalVariables
    set the tallies to zero (tallyA, etc.)
    set the totals to zero (numberOfTests, etc.)
    set the average to zero
    displayTalliesAndAverage()

displayTalliesAndAverage
    display the tallies and the average on the screen

processScores
if (score entered by user is invalid)
   display an error message
else{
   get the score from the screen;
   if (score is out of the range 0 to 100)
      display an error message
   else{
```

```
        updateTallies (score)
        updateAverage (score)
        displayTalliesAndAverage()
    }
}

updateTallies (int score)
    update one of the tallies based on the value of score

updateAverage (int score)
    update the totals based on the score
    compute the average
```

The relationships among the methods are clarified by the structure chart in Figure 5-10.

FIGURE 5-10
Relationships among methods

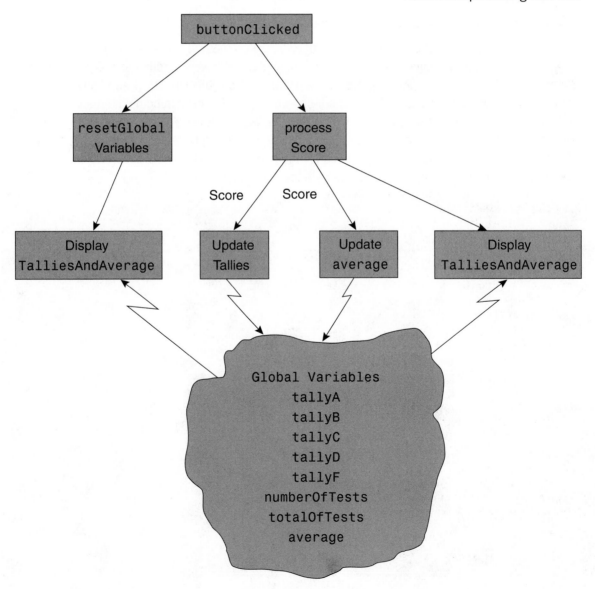

Top-Down Implementation and Testing Strategy

Rather than writing the code for a complex program all at one shot, we can develop it incrementally in a top-down fashion, mirroring the process used during design. In this manner, we can test the validity of our program step by step. At each small step, it is easy to find and remove any errors we may have made and then to proceed from a firm basis to the next step. In contrast, if we go for broke and implement the whole program at one shot, we may never unravel the errors. Here, then, is one possible *top-down implementation* of the program.

In the first step, we implement the interface and the `buttonClicked` method fully. However, the methods called by `buttonClicked` contain only enough code to indicate that they are called appropriately. Such simplified methods are called *stubs*. After making the usual number of programming errors and testing thoroughly, we arrive at the following code:

```java
import java.awt.*;
import BreezyGUI.*;

public class TallyGrades extends GBFrame{

   //Window objects
   Label scoreLabel = addLabel ("Score",1,1,1,1);
   Label AsLabel = addLabel ("A's",3,1,1,1);
   Label BsLabel = addLabel ("B's",3,2,1,1);
   Label CsLabel = addLabel ("C's",3,3,1,1);
   Label DsLabel = addLabel ("D's",3,4,1,1);
   Label FsLabel = addLabel ("F's",3,5,1,1);
   Label averageLabel = addLabel ("Average",4,1,1,1);

   IntegerField scoreField = addIntegerField (0,1,2,1,1);
   IntegerField AsField = addIntegerField (0,2,1,1,1);
   IntegerField BsField = addIntegerField (0,2,2,1,1);
   IntegerField CsField = addIntegerField (0,2,3,1,1);
   IntegerField DsField = addIntegerField (0,2,4,1,1);
   IntegerField FsField = addIntegerField (0,2,5,1,1);
   IntegerField averageField = addIntegerField (0,4,2,1,1);

   Button tallyScoreButton = addButton ("Tally Score",1,4,2,1);
   Button resetButton = addButton ("Reset",4,4,2,1);

   public void buttonClicked (Button buttonObj){
      if (buttonObj == resetButton)
         resetGlobalVariables();
      else
         processScore();
      scoreField.requestFocus();
      scoreField.selectAll();
   }

   private void resetGlobalVariables(){
      System.out.println ("I am resetGlobalVariables");
   }

   private void processScore(){
```

```
      System.out.println ("I am processScore");
   }

   public static void main (String[] args){
      Frame frm = new TallyGrades();
      frm.setSize (300, 150);
      frm.setVisible (true);
   }
}
```

In the second step, we introduce the global variables, expand down one level in the structure chart, and test the logic for detecting invalid user input. We are introducing sufficient complexity in this step to make our job challenging without making it overly difficult:

```
import java.awt.*;
import BreezyGUI.*;

public class TallyGrades extends GBFrame{

   //Window objects
   Label scoreLabel = addLabel ("Score",1,1,1,1);
   Label AsLabel = addLabel ("A's",3,1,1,1);
   Label BsLabel = addLabel ("B's",3,2,1,1);
   Label CsLabel = addLabel ("C's",3,3,1,1);
   Label DsLabel = addLabel ("D's",3,4,1,1);
   Label FsLabel = addLabel ("F's",3,5,1,1);
   Label averageLabel = addLabel ("Average",4,1,1,1);

   IntegerField scoreField = addIntegerField (0,1,2,1,1);
   IntegerField AsField = addIntegerField (0,2,1,1,1);
   IntegerField BsField = addIntegerField (0,2,2,1,1);
   IntegerField CsField = addIntegerField (0,2,3,1,1);
   IntegerField DsField = addIntegerField (0,2,4,1,1);
   IntegerField FsField = addIntegerField (0,2,5,1,1);
   IntegerField averageField = addIntegerField (0,4,2,1,1);

   Button tallyScoreButton = addButton ("Tally Score",1,4,2,1);
   Button resetButton = addButton ("Reset",4,4,2,1);

   //Other global variables
   int tallyA = 0;
   int tallyB = 0;
   int tallyC = 0;
   int tallyD = 0;
   int tallyF = 0;
   int numberOfTests = 0;
   int totalOfTests = 0;
   int average;

   public void buttonClicked (Button buttonObj){
      if (buttonObj == resetButton)
         resetGlobalVariables();
      else
```

```java
            processScore();
        scoreField.requestFocus();
        scoreField.selectAll();
    }

    private void resetGlobalVariables(){
        //on next step reset variables here
        scoreField.setNumber(0);
        displayTalliesAndAverage();
    }

    private void processScore(){
        int score;
        if (!scoreField.isValid()){
            messageBox ("SORRY: The score must be an integer.");
        }
        else{
            score = scoreField.getNumber();
            if (score < 0){
                messageBox
                ("SORRY: Test scores must be between 0 and 100, inclusive.");
            }
            else if (score > 100)
                messageBox
                ("SORRY: Test scores must be between 0 and 100, inclusive. ");
            else{
                updateTallies (score);
                updateAverage (score);
                displayTalliesAndAverage();
            }
        }
    }

    private void updateTallies(int score){
        System.out.println ("I am updateTallies");
    }

    private void updateAverage(int score){
        System.out.println ("I am updateAverage");
    }

    private void displayTalliesAndAverage(){
        System.out.println ("I am displayTalliesAndAverage");
    }

    public static void main (String[] args){
        Frame frm = new TallyGrades();
        frm.setSize (300, 150);
        frm.setVisible (true);
    }
}
```

In the third and final step, we complete the program and the testing:

```java
import java.awt.*;
import BreezyGUI.*;

public class TallyGrades extends GBFrame{

    //Window objects
    Label scoreLabel = addLabel ("Score",1,1,1,1);
    Label AsLabel = addLabel ("A's",3,1,1,1);
    Label BsLabel = addLabel ("B's",3,2,1,1);
    Label CsLabel = addLabel ("C's",3,3,1,1);
    Label DsLabel = addLabel ("D's",3,4,1,1);
    Label FsLabel = addLabel ("F's",3,5,1,1);
    Label averageLabel = addLabel ("Average",4,1,1,1);

    IntegerField scoreField = addIntegerField (0,1,2,1,1);
    IntegerField AsField = addIntegerField (0,2,1,1,1);
    IntegerField BsField = addIntegerField (0,2,2,1,1);
    IntegerField CsField = addIntegerField (0,2,3,1,1);
    IntegerField DsField = addIntegerField (0,2,4,1,1);
    IntegerField FsField = addIntegerField (0,2,5,1,1);
    IntegerField averageField = addIntegerField (0,4,2,1,1);

    Button tallyScoreButton = addButton ("Tally Score",1,4,2,1);
    Button resetButton = addButton ("Reset",4,4,2,1);

    //Other global variables
    int tallyA = 0;
    int tallyB = 0;
    int tallyC = 0;
    int tallyD = 0;
    int tallyF = 0;
    int numberOfTests = 0;
    int totalOfTests = 0;
    int average;

    public void buttonClicked (Button buttonObj){
        if (buttonObj == resetButton)
            resetGlobalVariables();
        else
            processScore();
        scoreField.requestFocus();
        scoreField.selectAll();
    }

    private void resetGlobalVariables(){
        tallyA = 0;
        tallyB = 0;
        tallyC = 0;
        tallyD = 0;
        tallyF = 0;
        numberOfTests = 0;
```

```
         totalOfTests = 0;
         average = 0;
         scoreField.setNumber(0);
         displayTalliesAndAverage();
      }

      private void processScore(){
         int score;
         if (!scoreField.isValid()){
            messageBox("SORRY: The score must be an integer.");
         }
         else{
            score = scoreField.getNumber();
            if (score < 0){
               messageBox
               ("SORRY: Test scores must be between 0 and 100, inclusive.");
            }
            else if (score >100)
               messageBox
               ("SORRY: Test scores must be between 0 and 100, inclusive.");
            else{
               updateTallies (score);
               updateAverage (score);
               displayTalliesAndAverage();
            }
         }
      }

      private void updateTallies (int score){
         if      (score >= 90) tallyA = tallyA + 1;
         else if (score >= 80) tallyB = tallyB + 1;
         else if (score >= 70) tallyC = tallyC + 1;
         else if (score >= 60) tallyD = tallyD + 1;
         else                  tallyF = tallyF + 1;
      }

      private void updateAverage(int score){
         totalOfTests = totalOfTests + score;
         numberOfTests = numberOfTests + 1;
         average = totalOfTests / numberOfTests;
      }

      private void displayTalliesAndAverage(){
         AsField.setNumber (tallyA);
         BsField.setNumber (tallyB);
         CsField.setNumber (tallyC);
         DsField.setNumber (tallyD);
         FsField.setNumber (tallyF);
         averageField.setNumber (average);
      }

      public static void main (String[] args){
```

```
        Frame frm = new TallyGrades();
        frm.setSize (300, 150);
        frm.setVisible (true);
    }
}
```

Finding the Location of Run-Time Errors

We now demonstrate how to find the location of run-time errors. In Lesson 2, we explored the consequences of division by 0. If a program attempts to divide by 0, the Java interpreter generates or *throws* an *arithmetic exception*. When this happens, the Java interpreter writes messages in the prompt window that direct the programmer's attention to the erroneous line of code. Now we see what these messages look like when the error is several levels deep within a stack of user-defined methods. Suppose we introduce a divide-by-zero error into the method updateAverage listed above. Here is the modified code. The error messages that are generated when the user clicks the **Tally Score** button are shown in Figure 5-11.

```
private void updateAverage (int score){
    totalOfTests = totalOfTests + score;

    //numberOfTests = numberOfTests + 1;

    average = totalOfTests / numberOfTests;   // numberOfTests will be 0
}
```

FIGURE 5-11
Arithmetic exceptions to a divide-by-zero error

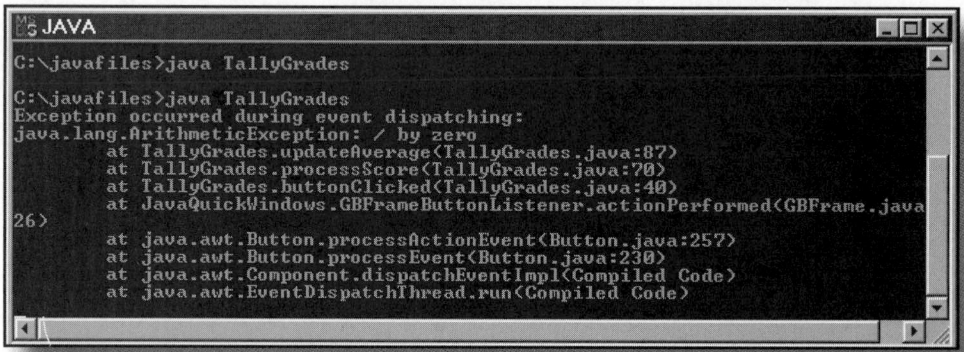

The error messages show the *call stack*—that is, which methods were being called by which other methods—at the time the error occurred. The last method called is listed first. Thus, the error messages say that division by 0 occurred in method updateAverage (line 87), which at the time was being called by method processScore (line 70), which was at the time being called by method buttonClicked (line 40). Below this point, the listed methods belong to parts of the Java virtual machine that are beyond the scope of this book. Here are the contents of lines 87, 70, and 40:

```
line 87 in updateAverage: average = totalOfTests / numberOfTests;
line 70 in processScore : updateAverage (score);
line 40 in buttonClicked: processScore();
```

Other Implementation Strategies

A second implementation strategy worth mentioning is called a *bottom-up implementation.* In this approach, one first implements the methods at the bottom of the structure chart. To test these, one must of course create a context in which they can be run. This context often includes simplified versions of the calling methods, called *drivers.* After the methods at the bottom of the hierarchy are thoroughly tested and known to work correctly, one then moves up a level, and so on until one reaches the top.

A third implementation strategy is called an *expanding capabilities implementation.* Again, we take an incremental approach, but this time it is not top down or bottom up. At the first step, we develop and test a program that fully implements some aspect of the problem. At the second step, we add additional capabilities, and so on until the program fully satisfies the requirements as specified during analysis. When taking this approach, we must avoid painting ourselves into a corner. In other words, at each step we want a program that expands naturally in the direction of the final solution. The best way to ensure that this will be so is to complete the analysis and design before starting the implementation.

Because of the extra work required to write the stubs needed for the top-down approach and drivers for the bottom-up approach, you will probably find yourself using the expanding capabilities strategy most often. In any event, some form of an incremental approach is highly recommended. Nothing more surely spells doom and hours of frustration than trying to debug a large, completely untested program.

Recursion

When asked to add the integers from 1 to *N,* we usually think of the process as iterative. We start with 1, add 2, then 3, then 4, and so forth until we reach *N.* Expressed differently,

```
sum(N) = 1 + 2 + 3 + ... + N, where N >= 1
```

Java's looping constructs make implementing the process easy. There is, however, a completely different way to look at the problem, one that at first seems very strange:

```
sum(1) = 1
sum(N) = N + sum(N - 1) if N > 1
```

At first glance, expressing `sum(N)` in terms of `sum(N - 1)` seems to yield a circular definition. However, it does not. Consider for example what happens when the definition is applied to the problem of calculating `sum(4)`:

```
sum(4) = 4 + sum(3)
       = 4 + 3 + sum(2)
       = 4 + 3 + 2 + sum(1)
       = 4 + 3 + 2 + 1
```

The fact that `sum(1)` is defined to be 1, without making reference to further invocations of `sum`, saves the process from going on forever and the definition from being circular. Such definitions are called *recursive,* and they all follow a similar pattern. Here, for example, are two ways to express the definition of factorial, the first iterative and the second recursive:

```
factorial(N) = 1 * 2 * 3 * ... * N, where N >= 1
factorial(1) = 1
   factorial(N) = N * factorial(N - 1) if N > 1
```

There can be no doubt that in two of the examples just presented the iterative definition is easier to understand than the recursive one. Such is not always the case. Consider the definition of Fibonacci numbers first encountered in Lesson 4. The first and second numbers in the Fibonacci sequence are 1. Thereafter, each number is the sum of its two immediate predecessors, as follows: 1 1 2 3 5 8 13 21 34 55 89 144 233 and so on. This is a recursive definition, as becomes obvious when we rewrite it. In fact, it is hard to imagine how one could express the definition nonrecursively.

```
fibonacci(1) = 1
fibonacci(2) = 1
fibonacci(N) = fibonacci(N - 1) + fibonacci(N - 2) if N > 2
```

From these examples we can see that recursion involves two factors. First, some function $f(N)$ is expressed in terms of $f(N - 1)$, $f(N - 2)$, $f(N - 3)$, and so on. Second, to prevent the definition from being circular, $f(1)$, $f(2)$, and so on, are defined explicitly.

Implementing Recursion

Given a recursive definition of some process, it usually is easy to write a *recursive method* that implements it. A method is said to be recursive if it calls itself. Let us start with a method that computes factorials.

```
int factorial (int N){
    if (N <= 1)
        return 1;
    else
        return N * factorial (N - 1);
}
```

Notice that the method begins with the test N <= 1 rather than N == 1, even though no one should call the method with a value of *N* less than 1. However, it seems prudent to write the method in a robust manner that can withstand accidental abuse. For comparison, here is an iterative version of the method. As you can see, it is longer and more difficult to understand.

```
int factorial (int N){
    int i, product;
    product = 1;
    for (i = 2; i <= N; i++){
        product = product * N;
    }
    return product;
}
```

As a second example of recursion, here is a method that calculates Fibonacci numbers:

```
int fibonacci (int N){
    if (N <= 2)
        return 1;
    else
        return fibonacci (N - 1) + fibonacci (N - 2);
}
```

Turn back to Lesson 4 to see how difficult it would be to write an iterative version of this method. Perhaps recursion is going to be a good thing.

Tracing Recursive Calls

An illustration clarifies the inner workings of recursion. Suppose we want to compute the factorial of 4. We call `factorial(4)`, which in turn calls `factorial(3)`, which in turn calls `factorial(2)`, which in turn calls `factorial(1)`, which returns 1 to `factorial(2)`, which returns 2 to `factorial(3)`, which returns 6 to `factorial(4)`, which returns 24.

```
factorial(4)
          calls factorial(3)
                          calls factorial(2)
                                          calls factorial(1)
                                          which returns 1
                          which returns 2*1 or 2
          which returns 3*2 or 6
which returns 4*6 or 24
```

It seems strange to have all these invocations of the `factorial` method, each in a state of suspended animation, waiting for the completion of the ones further down the line. When the last invocation completes its work, it returns to its predecessor, which completes its work, and so forth up the line, until eventually the original invocation reactivates and finishes the job. Fortunately, one does not have to repeat this dizzying mental exercise every time one uses recursion.

Guidelines for Writing Recursive Methods

Just as we must guard against writing infinite loops, so too we must avoid recursions that never come to an end. First, a recursive method must have a well-defined termination or *stopping state*. For the `factorial` method, this was expressed in the lines:

```
if (N <= 1)
   return 1;
```

Second, the *recursive step,* in which the method calls itself, must lead eventually to the stopping state. For the `factorial` method, the recursive step was expressed in the lines:

```
else
   return N * factorial(N - 1);
```

Because each invocation of the `factorial` method is passed a smaller value, eventually the stopping state must be reached. Had we accidentally written

```
else
   return N * factorial(N+1);
```

the recursion would have run out of control. Eventually, the user would notice and terminate the program or else the Java interpreter would run out of memory, at which point the program would crash.

Here is a subtler example of a malformed recursive method:

```
int badMethod (int N){
   if (N == 1)
      return 1;
   else
      return N * badMethod(N - 2);
}
```

This method works fine if N is odd, but when N is even, the method passes through the stopping state and keeps on going. For instance,

```
badMethod(4)
  calls badMethod(2)
    calls badMethod(0)
      calls badMethod(-2)
        calls badMethod(-4)
          calls badMethod(-6)
            . . .
```

When to Use Recursion

Recursion can always be used in place of iteration and vice versa. Ignoring the fact that arbitrarily substituting one for the other is pointless and sometimes difficult, the question remains, which is it better to use? Recursion involves a function repeatedly calling itself. Executing a function call and corresponding `return` statement usually takes longer than incrementing and testing a loop control variable. In addition, a function call ties up some memory that is not freed until the function completes its task. Some programmers state these facts as an argument against ever using recursion. However, in many situations recursion provides the clearest, shortest, and most elegant solution to a programming task, as we shall soon see. As a beginning programmer, you should not be overly concerned about squeezing the last drop of efficiency out of a computer. Instead, you need to master useful programming techniques, and recursion ranks among the best.

Design, Testing, and Debugging Hints

- Be sure that a method is cohesive, that is, that it performs a single, well-defined task.

- Begin the definition of a method as a stub. When tested, a stub allows you to verify that the method receives and transmits data properly. Then fill in the code for manipulating these data and retest.

- As a rule of thumb, use global variables (declared within a class) only to share data among methods or for storing data that should survive a method call. If the data should not be shared, use local variables (declared within a method).

- Use a parameter when the data transmitted to a method might be sent from more than one variable in a program. For example, `Math.sqrt(data)` can return the square root of many different data variables.

- Write preconditions and postconditions for each method you define. This information will help you during testing and debugging and will help your readers during program maintenance.

- To debug a method, perform the following steps:

  1. Examine the preconditions and postconditions by placing output statements with the appropriate variables before and after the calls of the method. If a precondition is not satisfied, fix it and retest.

  2. Place output statements with the appropriate variables at the beginning and at the end of the method body. Observe the outputs, and move the statements toward the middle of the method, until you discover the source of the error.

  3. If a method invokes another user-defined method, repeat steps 1 and 2 for this method.

Summary

In this lesson, you learned:

- One way to handle a large, complex method is to write a number of shorter methods that cooperate to achieve the same result. These are called user-defined methods.

- Cooperating methods can communicate by sharing a common pool of variables or by passing parameters and returning values. In addition, each method can declare its own local variables.

- The scope of a variable is the region of the program within which it can be used. The lifetime of a variable is the period during which it can be accessed. If a variable is declared outside all methods, its scope includes all methods and it is said to be global.

- A precondition of a method is a statement of what must be true before a method can run correctly. A postcondition of a method is a statement of what must be true after the method has finished execution.

- Recursion is the process of a subprogram calling itself.

LESSON 5 REVIEW QUESTIONS

WRITTEN QUESTIONS

Write your answers to the following questions.

1. Explain the difference between a formal parameter and an actual parameter.

2. Assume that a method has been defined with the header

   ```
   void sampleMethod(int x, int y, double d)
   ```

   the variables `int1` and `int2` are integers, and the variable `double1` is a `double`. Which method calls below are syntactically correct? If a call is incorrect, explain why.
   a. `sampleMethod(3, 4, 5.6);`
   b. `sampleMethod;`
   c. `sampleMethod(int1 + 6, int2, double1);`
   d. `sampleMethod(int1, int2);`
   e. `sampleMethod(int1, int2, 45);`
   f. `sampleMethod(double1, int1, int2);`

3. Write a method `numberSign` that expects an `int` parameter. The method should return the string `"Positive"` if the number is positive, `"Negative"` if the number is negative, or `"Zero"` if the number is 0.

4. Write a method `displayData` that expects a `double` and a `TextArea` as parameters. The method should use a loop that displays the numbers from the parameter down to zero, right justified in 10 columns.

5. Rewrite the method from Question 4 using a recursive strategy.

6. There are two ways to call a method. One way uses the dot notation to send a message to an object, and the other way omits the dot and the reference to an object. Give an example of each and explain why the reference to an object can be omitted in the second case.

LESSON 5 PROJECTS

In each of the projects that follow, structure your solutions with the appropriate Java methods. Be sure to state clearly what each method does by writing preconditions and postconditions in comments. Finally, where appropriate, test your methods using a short tester program before integrating them into a GUI program.

1. Modify the program of Project 1 of Lesson 4 with the following constraints:

- Data validation—make sure both numbers are positive.

- Global variables other than window objects—`quotient, remainder`.

- User-defined methods—

   `private void computeQuotientAndRemainder (int n1, int n2)`

   sets the global variables `quotient` and `remainder`.

2. The tax rate for a mythical state is based on the following table:

INCOME	TAX RATE
$0–5,000	0%
5,001–10,000	5%
$10,001–20,000	10.5%
$20,001–30,000	15%
More than $30,000	25.5%

Note that this is a graduated tax rate. For example, the tax on each dollar up to $10,000 is 5%, whereas the tax on each dollar after that, up to $20,000, is 10.5%, and so on. Write a program that, when given a person's income as input, displays the tax owed rounded to the nearest dollar. The constraints are

- Data validation—make sure income is positive.

- No global variables other than window objects.

- User-defined methods—

   `private double computeTax (double income)`

   returns the amount of tax.

Before writing the complete GUI application, write a tester program that allows you to confirm the correctness of the computeTax method. The program will have the following format:

```
import BreezyGUI.*;

public class Tester{

    static double computeTax (double income){
        . . .
    }

    public static void main (String[] args) {
        System.out.println ("Tax on 4999 = "
                            + computeTax (4999));

        . . .
        GBFrame.pause();
    }
}
```

The output might look like this:

```
Tax on 4999  = 0.0
Tax on 5000  = 0.0
Tax on 5001  = 0.05
Tax on 9999  = 249.95000000000002
Tax on 10000 = 250.0
Tax on 10001 = 250.105
Tax on 19999 = 1299.895
Tax on 20000 = 1300.0
Tax on 20001 = 1300.15
Tax on 29999 = 2799.85
Tax on 30000 = 2800.0
Tax on 30001 = 2800.255
```

Notice that the computeTax method in the tester program is declared to be static, whereas in the GUI program the method is declared to be private. The reason for this difference is discussed in Lesson 7.

3. An object floats in water if its density (mass/volume) is less than 1 gram per cubic centimeter. It sinks if its density is 1 or more. Write a program that takes the mass (in grams) and volume (in cubic centimeters) of an object as inputs and displays whether it will sink or float. The constraints are

■ Data validation—make sure inputs are positive.

■ No global variables other than window objects.

■ User-defined methods—

   private String determineBuoyancy (double m, double v)

   returns "It floats" or "Glug, glug"

4. A quadratic equation has the form

$$ax^2 + bx + c = 0$$

where $a \neq 0$. Solutions to this equation are given by

$$x = \frac{-b \pm \sqrt{b^2 - 4ac}}{2a}$$

where the quantity $(b^2 - 4ac)$ is referred to as the *discriminant* of the equation. Write a program that takes three integer inputs as the respective coefficients (a, b, and c), computes the discriminant, and displays the real number solutions. Use the following rules:

a. Discriminant $= 0 \rightarrow$ single root.

b. Discriminant $< 0 \rightarrow$ no real number solution.

c. Discriminant $> 0 \rightarrow$ two distinct real solutions.

The constraints are

■ Data validation—`a != 0`.

■ No global variables other than window objects.

■ User-defined methods—

```
private int determineNumberOfSolutions (double a, double b, double c)
```

returns 0, 1, or 2 indicating the number of real solutions.

5. Write a program that takes as input a positive integer N and displays as output the Fibonacci numbers from 1 to N. You should define a method that computes the Fibonacci number for any value of N that is greater than 0. The constraints are

■ Data validation—make sure N is positive.

■ No global variables other than window objects.

■ User-defined methods—

```
private int computeFibonacci (int n) -- RECURSIVE
```

returns the nth Fibonacci number.

6. The least common multiple (LCM) of two positive integers X and Y is the positive integer Z, such that Z is the smallest multiple of both X and Y. For example, the LCM of 8 and 12 is 24. Write a program that takes two positive integers as inputs and displays as output the LCM of the two integers. The constraints are

■ Data validation—make sure inputs are positive.

■ No global variables other than window objects.

■ User-defined methods—

```
private int lcm (int x, int y)
```

returns the least common multiple of X and Y.

7. Use a `Tester` program to implement and test a recursive method to compute the greatest common divisor (GCD) of two integers. The recursive definition of GCD is

```
gcd(a, b) = b, when a = 0
gcd(a, b) = a, when b = 0
gcd(a, b) = gcd(b, a % b), when a > 0 and b > 0
```

8. Design and implement a recursive method that raises a given positive integer to a positive power. *Hint*: Both the base and the exponent should be parameters. Test the method with a tester program.

CRITICAL THINKING ACTIVITY

Write a recursive method that displays a string backwards in the terminal window and test the method with a `Tester` program. *Hint*: The string and the index position should be parameters. Recurse to the last index position in the string, and display an individual character after each recursive call.

LESSON 6

More Operators, Control Statements, and Data Types

OBJECTIVES

Upon completion of this lesson, you will be able to:

■ Construct expressions with logical operators.

■ Use additional Java control statements for looping and selection.

■ Make appropriate use of Boolean, character, and other numeric data types.

■ Define and use symbolic constants.

■ Solve problems using the Math class.

■ Manipulate strings using methods from the String class.

⏱ **Estimated Time: 2 hours**

It is rather amazing how many operators, control statements, and data types there are in a typical programming language. So as not to overwhelm you with unnecessary detail, we have presented only a few of these in the first five lessons. We now discuss a few more that are convenient to use in solving problems.

Operators

The operators we have seen thus far are those for standard arithmetic, comparison, and assignment. To these we now add unary operators, increment operators, and logical operators.

Unary Plus and Minus

Unary minus can be used as follows:

```
-3 * 4      yields -12
-3 * -4     yields 12
3 * - -4    yields 12
3 * --4     is to be avoided for now because - - is an operator called decrement (to be discussed shortly)
```

Using the unary + operator is pointless but allowed:

```
3 * +4      yields 12
3 * ++4     is to be avoided for now because ++ is an operator called increment (to be discussed shortly)
```

Increment and Decrement Operators

One of the most common programming tasks is that of incrementing or decrementing numeric variables by 1. This task is easily accomplished through the use of an assignment statement:

```
x = x + 1;
```

However, in imitation of C++, on which it is modeled, Java provides two more operators that make the task even easier. These are ++ (increment) and -- (decrement), as illustrated next:

```
x++;     // Increment x by 1.        Called postfix increment.
++x;     // Also increment x by 1.  Called prefix increment.
x--;     // Decrement x by 1.        Called postfix decrement.
--x;     // Also decrement x by 1.  Called prefix decrement.
```

The difference between the postfix and prefix versions of these operators is illustrated in the next snippet of code:

```
double x = 3.1, y = 3.1, z;
z = 2 * x++;  // z equals 6.2 because x is incremented after it is used.
z = 2 * ++y;  // z equals 8.2 because y is incremented before it is used.
```

Caution is advised when using these operators, because it is easy to interchange the postfix and prefix versions accidentally. In this text, we use just the postfix version in stand-alone statements, such as

```
x++;
```

The most common use of the increment and decrement operators is in `for` statements, which will be discussed soon.

Logical Operators

Nested `if` statements are not the only means of handling logical complexity in programs. Java also provides *logical operators* equivalent to AND, OR, and NOT. These are &&, ¦¦, and !, respectively.

&& (AND)

The && operator means logical AND. The two conditions or expressions on either side of && must both be true for the entire compound expression to be true. If one or both of the conditions is false, the entire compound expression is false. Java evaluates the conditions in order from left to right but does not evaluate the second condition if the first condition is false.

Here is a Javish example that illustrates the use of && (AND):

```
if (the sun shines && you have the time)
    let's go for a walk;
else
    let's stay home;
```

A truth table showing all of the logical possibilities clarifies the example:

p SUN SHINING	q HAVE THE TIME	p && q	OUTCOME
true	true	true	walk
true	false	false	stay home
false	true	false	stay home
false	false	false	stay home

¦¦ (OR)

The ¦¦ operator means logical OR. The two conditions or expressions on either side of ¦¦ must be false for the entire compound expression to be false. If one or both of the conditions is true, the entire compound expression is true. Java evaluates the conditions in order from left to right but does not evaluate the second condition if the first condition is true.

The next example demonstrates the use of ¦¦ (OR):

```
if (the sun shines ¦¦ you have the time)
    let's go for a walk;
else
    let's stay home;
```

p SUN SHINING	q HAVE THE TIME	p ¦¦ q	OUTCOME
true	true	true	walk
true	false	true	walk
false	true	true	walk
false	false	false	stay home

! (NOT)

The ! operator means logical NOT. The single condition or expression to the right of ! must be false for the entire compound expression to be true, or that condition must be true for the entire compound expression to be false.

Here is an example illustrating ! (NOT):

```
if (!the sun shines)
    let's stay home;
else
    let's go for a walk;
```

p SUN SHINING	!p SUN NOT SHINING	OUTCOME
true	false	walk
false	true	stay home

REWRITING NESTED IF STATEMENTS

The use of && allows us to rewrite the code for determining a student's grade:

```
if (90 <= average                 ) grade is A;
if (80 <= average && average < 90) grade is B;
if (70 <= average && average < 80) grade is C;
if (60 <= average && average < 70) grade is D;
if (            average < 60) grade is F;
```

Here we have replaced nested if statements by a number of independent ones. This feat is always possible.

In the above code, the expression

```
(80 <= average && average < 90)
```

has three operators. This causes no confusion because && has lower precedence than either <= or <. Extra parentheses could be included if desired:

```
((80 <= average) && (average < 90))
```

It is natural to ask, "Which is better, nested `if`s or independent ones?" There is no clear-cut answer, but keep in mind that, generally speaking, nested `if` statements execute more quickly, take less time to type, and are more prone to programmer error.

&& AND ¦¦ TOGETHER

The operators && and ¦¦ sometimes appear together, but the result can be difficult to interpret and the probability of making a programming error is high:

```
if ((the sun shines && you have the time) ¦¦ it is Sunday)
    let's go for a walk;
else
    let's stay home;
```

Because && has higher precedence than ¦¦, the parentheses are unnecessary, although they do help to make a complex situation slightly more comprehensible.

To really understand the meaning of the example, we must construct a truth table such as the one shown in Table 6-1. Now the number of possibilities swells to eight, because there are three separate conditions and each can be true or false (2*2*2 yields 8).

TABLE 6-1

p SUN SHINES	q HAVE TIME	r IS SUNDAY	p && q	(p && q) ¦¦ r	OUTCOME
true	true	true	true	true	walk
true	true	false	true	true	walk
true	false	true	false	true	walk
true	false	false	false	false	stay home
false	true	true	false	true	walk
false	true	false	false	false	stay home
false	false	true	false	true	walk
false	false	false	false	false	stay home

Moving the parentheses slightly in the above example yields a radically different meaning, as shown in the code below and in Table 6-2.

```
if (the sun shines && (you have the time ¦¦ it is Sunday))
    let's go for a walk;
else
    let's stay home;
```

TABLE 6-2

p SUN SHINES	q HAVE TIME	r IS SUNDAY	q ¦¦ r	p && (q ¦¦ r)	OUTCOME
true	true	true	true	true	walk
true	true	false	true	true	walk
true	false	true	true	true	walk
true	false	false	false	false	stay home
false	true	true	true	false	stay home
false	true	false	true	false	stay home
false	false	true	true	false	stay home
false	false	false	false	false	stay home

REWRITING COMPLEX CONDITIONS

Because if statements such as

```
if (the sun shines && (you have the time ¦¦ it is Sunday))
    let's go for a walk;
else
    let's stay home;
```

can be difficult to understand and maintain, programmers sometimes prefer to replace them by a number of simpler ones. Fortunately, there is a purely mechanical, if somewhat verbose, technique for doing so. Create the truth table for the if statement and then implement each line of the truth table by a separate if statement involving only && (AND) and ! (NOT). Applying the technique here yields:

```
if ( the sun shines &&  you have time &&  it is Sunday) walk;
if ( the sun shines &&  you have time && !it is Sunday) walk;
if ( the sun shines && !you have time &&  it is Sunday) walk;
if ( the sun shines && !you have time && !it is Sunday) stay home;
if (!the sun shines &&  you have time &&  it is Sunday) stay home;
if (!the sun shines &&  you have time && !it is Sunday) stay home;
if (!the sun shines && !you have time &&  it is Sunday) stay home;
if (!the sun shines && !you have time && !it is Sunday) stay home;
```

In this particular example, the verbosity can be reduced without reintroducing complexity by noticing that the last four `if` statements are equivalent to:

```
if (!the sun shines) stay home;
```

Of course, it is also possible to go in the other direction, that is, combine several `if` statements into a single more complex one. But remember that no matter how one chooses to represent complex alternatives, truth tables are an essential tool for verifying the accuracy of the result. One should use them whenever one has the slightest doubt about the meaning of an `if` statement.

PRECEDENCE OF OPERATORS

Table 6-3 shows how the logical operators fit into Java's precedence scheme.

TABLE 6-3
Precedence of logical operators

OPERATION	SYMBOL	PRECEDENCE (HIGHEST TO LOWEST)	ASSOCIATION
Grouping	( )	1	Not applicable
Method selection	(.)		Right to left
Unary minus	–	2	Not applicable
Unary plus	+		
Increment	++		
Decrement	– –		
Logical NOT	!		
Multiplication	*	3	Left to right
Division	/		
Remainder	%		
Addition	+	4	Left to right
Subtraction	–		
Less than	<	5	Not applicable
Less than or equal	<=		
Greater than	>		
Greater than or equal	>=		
Equal	==	6	Not applicable
Not equal	!=		
Logical AND	&&	7	Left to right
Logical OR	¦¦	8	Left to right
Assignment	=	9	Right to left

Control Statements

At this point, we have developed considerable facility in working with `if` and `while` statements. Although these two control statements are adequate for all of our programming needs, Java provides several additional control statements that are often convenient to use.

Do-while Statement

The `do-while` statement is a slight variant of the `while` statement. Its syntax is:

```
do {block of statements} while (some condition);
```

Figure 6-1 illustrates the behavior of this looping statement. Notice that the block of statements is executed before the condition is tested, in contrast to the `while` statement, which tests the condition before entering the loop. Consequently, the `do-while` statement always executes the block of statements at least once.

FIGURE 6-1
Flowchart of a
do-while statement

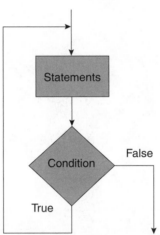

The next example shows a `do-while` loop that sums the numbers between 1 and 10:

```
int counter = 1;
int sum = 0;
do{
    sum = sum + counter;
    counter++;
}while (counter <= 10);
```

for Statement

The `for` statement provides yet another looping construct. The syntax of the statement is:

```
for (statement1; condition; statement2) statement;
```

or

```
for (statement1; condition; statement2) {block of statements};
```

To demonstrate how the `for` loop works, we rewrite it using an equivalent `while` loop:

```
statement1;
while (condition){
   block of statements;
   statement2;
}
```

Here is a `for` loop that adds the numbers between 1 and 100:

```
sum = 0;
for (i = 1; i <= 100; i++)
   sum = sum + i;
```

And here is another that does the same thing counting backward from 100 to 1:

```
sum = 0;
for (i = 100; i >= 1; i--)
   sum = sum + i;
```

Some care must be taken when writing `for` loops. A loop that adds together the numbers 1.00, 1.01, 1.02 . . . , 1.99 might be written as follows:

```
double sum, x;
sum = 0.0;
for (x = 1; x != 2; x = x + 0.01)
   sum = sum + x;
```

Because of the limited precision of floating-point numbers, there is no guarantee that x will ever exactly equal 2, with the consequence that the loop could be infinite. A minor modification corrects the problem:

```
double sum, x;
sum = 0.0;
for (x = 1; x < 2; x = x + 0.01)       // < instead of !=
   sum = sum + x;
```

Java programmers often declare the loop control variable inside of the `for` statement. The next example does this; note that the variable `i` is now visible only within the body of the loop (the code within the { } symbols).

```
sum = 0;
for (int i = 100; i >= 1; i--) {
   sum = sum + i;
}
```

`switch` **Statement**

The `switch` statement behaves very much like a group of nested `if` statements, and although it is not as general as nested `if` statements, it is considerably less cumbersome to use. Here is the syntax:

```
switch (expression){
   case literal 1:
      group of statements;
      break;
   case literal 2:
```

```
      group of statements;
      break;
   ...
   case literal n:
      group of statements;
      break;
   default:                    // This part
      group of statements;     // is
      break;                   // optional.
}
```

The switch statement begins by comparing the expression to the literals. If there is a matching literal, the corresponding group of statements is executed. Otherwise, the statements following the keyword default are executed (if this optional group is present). If the keyword break is missing, execution continues into the next group. The expression must yield a value of type byte, long, int, or char (to be discussed shortly), and the literals must be of the same type as the expression. Figure 6-2 illustrates the logic of the switch statement.

FIGURE 6-2
Flowchart of the switch statement

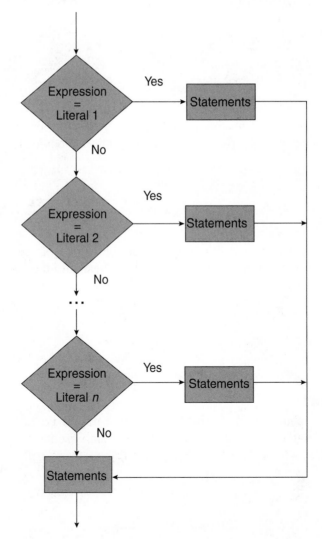

Here is an example:

```
// Generate a random number between 1 and 100.
lotteryNumber = <generate a random number between 1 and 100>
                //we will see how later in this lesson
switch (lotteryNumber){
   case 100:
      messageBox("Congratulations, you have won first prize");
      break;
   case 99:
      messageBox("Congratulations, you have won second prize");
      break;
   case 98:
      messageBox("Congratulations, you have won third prize");
      break;
   default:
      messageBox("Sorry, you didn't win a prize");
      break;
}
```

break Statement

Sometimes we want to break out of a loop prematurely. The `break` statement provides a simple mechanism for doing so. It works equally well with `for`, `while`, and `do-while` loops. For instance, suppose we want to determine if an integer is *prime:*

```
int number, isPrime, divisor;

number = ...;      // Assume number >= 3
isPrime = 1;       // This means we start with the assumption that the
                   // number is prime

for (divisor = 2; divisor < number; divisor++){
   if (number % divisor == 0){
      isPrime = 0;      // We have now discovered that the number is not
      break;            // prime, so we break out of the loop prematurely.
   }
}
if (isPrime == 1)
   messageBox("The number is prime");
else
   messageBox("The number is NOT prime");
```

The `break` statement can always be avoided, as demonstrated in the situation that follows:

```
...
divisor = 2;
while (divisor < number && isPrime == 1){
   if (number % divisor == 0){
      isPrime = 0;
   }
   divisor++;
}
```

The `break` statement, in the form just presented, breaks out of the immediately enclosing loop. The `labeled break`, on the other hand, can be used to break out of nested loops. A label is a user-defined symbol, and it is placed immediately before the loop from which we want to break. For instance:

```
thisIsALabelWithAStrangeName:
while (...){
  ...
  for (...){
    ...
    if (...) break thisIsALabelWithAStrangeName;
    ...
  }
  ...
}
```

The Math Class

Many computations involve the use of standard mathematical functions such as sine, cosine, square root, and logarithm. For the convenience of Java programmers, these and many other mathematical functions have been collected in something called the `Math` class. Here are several snippets of code that illustrate the use of these functions, or methods as they are called in Java.

Given the area of a circle, compute its radius (used in Case Study 1 in Lesson 4):

```
radius = Math.sqrt (area / Math.PI);
```

where `Math.PI` is not a method but a constant that provides a highly accurate approximation to the value of π.

Given a person's height, compute the length of his shadow when the sun is at a known angle above the horizon:

```
radians = Math.PI * angle / 180;
length = height / Math.tan (radians);
```

How much is $100 compounded annually for 8 years at 5% interest? This can be answered by computing $100 * 1.05^8$:

```
amount = 100 * Math.pow (1.05, 8);
```

Generate a random integer between the integers a and b inclusive, where a < b. The method `Math.random()` returns a floating-point number that is greater than or equal to 0 and less than 1.0. Thus, the code to produce a random integer between the integers a and b, inclusive, is

```
number = (int)(a + Math.random() * (b - a + 1));
```

Table 6-4 summarizes some of the methods and constants in class `Math` as described in Java's online documentation. To access complete documentation on Java's features, including the `Math` class, use your Web browser (see Appendix A).

TABLE 6-4
Methods and constants in the Math class

CONSTANT/METHOD	EXPLANATION
abs(aNumber) returns aNumber	Returns the absolute value of a number.
exp(aDouble) returns aDouble	Returns the exponential number e (i.e., 2.718 . . .) raised to the power of a double value.
log(aDouble) returns aDouble	Returns the natural logarithm (base e) of a double value.
max(aDouble, aDouble) returns aDouble	Returns the greater of two values.
max(aFloat, aFloat) returns aFloat	
max(anInt, anInt) returns anInt	
max(aLong, aLong) returns aLong	
min(aDouble, aDouble) returns aDouble	Returns the smaller of two values.
etc.	
pow(aDouble, aDouble) returns aDouble	Returns the value of the first parameter raised to the power of the second parameter.
random()	Returns a random number greater than or equal to 0.0 and less than 1.0.
round(aDouble) returns aLong	Returns the nearest long integer to the parameter.
sin(aDouble) returns aDouble	Returns the trigonometric sine of an angle expressed in radians.
cos(aDouble) returns aDouble	Ditto for cos and tan.
tan(aDouble) returns aDouble	
sqrt(aDouble) returns aDouble	Returns the square root of a double value.
E	The double value that is closer than any other to e, the base of the natural logarithms.
PI	The double value that is closer than any other to π, the ratio of the circumference of a circle to its diameter.

Data Types

Until this point in the text, our programs have been limited to the data types int, double, and String. However, most programming languages support many more. In this section we introduce some data types that represent Boolean, character, and other numeric values.

Booleans

The values true and false are called Boolean in honor of George Boole, a nineteenth-century British mathematician and one of the originators of mathematical logic. In Java, a `boolean` variable is one that can assume just two values: `true` or `false`. For instance, here is a simple but ridiculous example:

```
boolean b1, b2, b3;
int i = 3, j = 4, k = 5;

b1 = i < j;      // The result of this comparison is either true or false
                 // and can be assigned to the Boolean variable b1
b2 = j < k;
b3 = b1 && bs;

if (b3)
   messageBox("i is less than j and j is less than k");
else
   messageBox("i, j, and k are not in order");
```

Not all examples need be so silly. A `boolean` variable works nicely when determining if a number is prime:

```
int number, divisor;
boolean isPrime;

number = ...;    // Assume number >= 3
isPrime = true;  // This means we start with the assumption that the
                 // number is prime

for (divisor = 2; divisor < number; divisor++){
   if (number % divisor == 0){
      isPrime = false;  // We have now discovered that the number is not
      break;            // prime, so we break out of the loop prematurely.
   }
}
if (isPrime)
   messageBox ("The number is prime");
else
   messageBox ("The number is NOT prime");
```

Characters

Programs frequently need to manipulate characters. Word processors are an obvious example. When we think of characters, the English letters of the alphabet immediately spring to mind. To these we must add the ten digits needed to represent numbers and various punctuation marks. Not so obvious are the nonprintable characters needed to represent carriage returns, linefeeds, tabs, backspaces, command key sequences, and other items that are more familiar to computer programmers than to the general public. The total number of all of these special characters is not large, so the entire set of characters is easily represented by an 8-bit code that provides 256 possibilities.

Of course, computer users must agree about which code, or pattern of 0s and 1s, represents which character. Until recently, the most widely used coding scheme in the English-speaking world was the ASCII standard, some examples of which were presented in Lesson 3. The need to represent more of the world's alphabets led to adoption of the 16-bit Unicode scheme used in Java and provides 65,536 patterns. For the sake of convenience, the first 256 Unicode characters match the ASCII character set. A table listing the ASCII character set can be found in Appendix D.

Here is a snippet of code in which we declare some character variables and assign them values using character literals:

```
char c1, c2, c3, c4;
c1 = 'a';
c2 = 'b';
c3 = ' ';
c4 = '8';
c5 = ';';
```

In this book, we have little need to know which ASCII values represent which characters. However, it is important to understand that the letters *a* to *z* are represented by consecutive integer values (that is, when viewed as binary numbers), as are the letters *A* to *Z* and the digits 0 to 9. Therefore, it is not surprising that arithmetic operations can be performed on character variables:

```
char chr;

chr = 'a';              // chr equals 'a'
chr = chr + 2;          // and now 'c'
chr++;                  // and finally 'd'

chr = chr + 'A' - 'a';  // convert from lower to uppercase
messageBox(chr);        // 'D' displayed
```

However, not all arithmetic operations make sense. Adding a large number, say 1000, to a yields a Unicode value that does not correspond to a familiar character, and if displayed on a computer set up for an English alphabet yields ?. Similarly, multiplying a by 6 would not make much sense either.

Because int is more inclusive than char, character values can be assigned to integer variables, but going in the other direction causes a syntax error:

```
char chr;
int i;

chr = 'A';
i = chr;
messageBox(chr);        // 'A' displayed
messageBox(i);          // 65 displayed
chr = i + 1;            // Syntax error: cannot assign int to char.
```

Character variables and literals can be compared to each other. For instance, to see if a character variable contains a lowercase letter, one could write code like this:

```
char chr;
chr = <any character>;
if (chr >= 'a' && chr <= 'z')
    messageBox("lowercase");
else messageBox("not lowercase");
```

A simpler alternative is to use one of the `Character` class methods to test a character for a given property. The `Character` class provides methods for manipulating characters in much the same manner as the `Math` class provides methods for manipulating numbers. For example, the following code segment uses the `Character` methods `isUpperCase`, `isLowerCase`, and `isDigit` to test for one of these properties:

```
char chr;
chr = <any character>;
if (Character.isLowerCase(chr))
    messageBox("lowercase");
else if (Character.isUpperCase(chr))
    messageBox("uppercase");
else if (Character.isDigit(chr, 10))
    messageBox("digit");
else
    messageBox("unkown");
```

For a list of the many `Character` class methods, consult the Java documentation listed in Appendix A.

Some of the nonprintable characters are used so frequently that they are designated by a backslash followed by a code letter:

```
chr = '\b';    // backspace
chr = '\t';    // tab
chr = '\n';    // linefeed
chr = '\r';    // carriage return
```

Characters that already have special significance in Java's syntax also are designated by means of a backslash:

```
chr = '\"';    // double quote
chr = '\'';    // single quote
chr = '\\';    // backslash
```

Finally, it is always possible to use a Unicode value to designate a character literal. Unicode values are of the form \uxxxx, where x = 0..9 or A. .F:

```
chr = '\u0043';
messageBox(chr);  // 'C' displayed
```

Full understanding of this example requires knowledge of hexadecimal numbers. See Appendix E for details.

Other Numeric Data Types

In addition to `int` and `double`, Java supports several other numeric types. A complete list is shown in Table 6-5.

TABLE 6-5
Numeric data types

TYPE	STORAGE REQUIREMENTS	RANGE
byte	1 byte	–128 to 127
short	2 bytes	–32,768 to 32,767
int	4 bytes	–2,147,483,648 to 2,147,483,647
long	8 bytes	–9,223,372,036,854,775,808L to 9,223,372,036,854,775,807L
float	4 bytes	–3.40282347E+38F to 3.40282347E+38F
double	8 bytes	–1.79769313486231570E+308 to 1.79769313486231570E+308

When memory is at a premium, the types short and float are used instead of the types int and double, respectively. We continue to use int and double for numbers in this text.

The Cast Operator and Mixed-Mode Arithmetic

Now that we have more data types, we must revisit the topics of mixed-mode arithmetic expressions and mixed-mode assignment statements first introduced in Lesson 3. There we learned that in mixed-mode arithmetic, less inclusive types, such as int, are automatically converted to more inclusive types, such as double. In mixed-mode assignment statements, the type of the variable on the left must be at least as inclusive as the type of the expression on the right. To see how these rules apply to the data types introduced in this lesson, we list them from the least inclusive to the most inclusive:

```
byte short char int long float double
```

However, there is a way to override mixed-mode restrictions. The programmer can use the *cast operator* to convert a more inclusive type to a less inclusive type before the assignment. The form of the cast operation is:

```
(<less inclusive type name>) <more inclusive value>
```

In the following example, we begin with a double, convert to an int, and finally convert to a char:

```
double d;
int i;
char c;

d = 65.57;
i = (int) d;        // i contains 65, due to truncation.
c = (char) i;       // c contains 'A'.
messageBox(c);      // Displays 'A'.
```

The precedence (2) and association (right to left) of the cast operator are the same as those of unary plus and minus.

Here are some more examples of automatic type conversions during the evaluation of arithmetic expressions:

```
byte * long          becomes     long * long
float * int          becomes     float * float
float * double       becomes     double * double
```

Sometimes, however, the programmer wants to override this automatic conversion, for instance, to treat `float * int` as `int * int`. This can be achieved by using the cast operation, as illustrated next:

```
byte * (byte)long        becomes     byte * byte
(int)float * int         becomes     int * int
float * (float)double    becomes     float * float
```

IMPORTANT:

Use of the cast operation can destroy information. For instance, the fractional part of `double` and `float` is thrown away when cast to `byte`, `short`, `int`, `long`—thus, `(int)3.789` becomes 3. If the number being cast is outside the range of the target type, garbage results—thus, `(int) 8.88e + 009` becomes 290065408.

Now suppose we had declared the variable `incomeTax` as an `int` in the `IncomeTaxCalculator` program of Lesson 3. Then the computation of the income tax would be

```
incomeTax = (int) Math.round(taxableIncome * taxRate);
```

Explanation:

- `taxRate` is double and `taxableIncome` is int.

- `taxableIncome` is temporarily converted to `double` before the multiplication is performed.

- `Math.round` rounds its parameter to the nearest long integer and returns this.

- The result is cast to an `int` and assigned to the integer variable `incomeTax`.

Constants

In the `IncomeTaxCalculator` program of Lesson 3, the numbers 10000, 2000, and 0.20 are the standard deduction, the dependent deduction, and the tax rate, respectively. However, anyone reading the program could hardly guess these meanings from looking at the numbers. A better way to express these values is to give them names, such as STANDARD_DEDUCTION, DEPENDENT_DEDUCTION, and TAX_RATE. Thus, in the statement

```
taxableIncome = grossIncome - 10000 - numberOfDependents * 2000;
```

the meaning of the numbers `10000` and `2000` is not immediately obvious, whereas in the statement

```
taxableIncome = grossIncome - STANDARD_DEDUCTION -
                numberOfDependents * DEPENDENT_DEDUCTION;
```

the meaning of the names `STANDARD_DEDUCTION` and `DEPENDENT_DEDUCTION` is obvious.

These names should be given an initial value when declared and never changed thereafter. They are what one might call symbolic constants. The keyword `final` placed at the beginning of their declarations guarantees that their values cannot be changed later. Attempting to do so constitutes a syntax error.

```
final int STANDARD_DEDUCTION = 10000;
final int DEPENDENT_DEDUCTION = 2000;
final double TAX_RATE = 0.20;
```

Aside from being more readable, programs with symbolic constants are easier to modify than those that use just literals. Imagine a large program that uses the constant `0.08` throughout to denote the sales tax rate. If the rate changes to `0.09`, a programmer might be tempted to replace all instances of `0.08` by `0.09`. But this could be catastrophic if `0.08` is used for other purposes in the program. To avoid a possible calamity, the programmer is forced to read the whole program carefully before making any substitutions. However, if a symbolic constant is used for the tax rate, the programmer can fearlessly change

```
final double SALES_TAX_RATE = 0.08;
```

to

```
final double SALES_TAX_RATE = 0.09;
```

C A S E   S T U D Y   1 :   Metric Conversion

As an illustration of some of the ideas discussed above, we now write a metric conversion program.

Request

Write a program that converts a given number of meters into the equivalent number of yards, feet, and inches.

Analysis

There are approximately 2.540005 centimeters per inch. User input is some number of meters expressed in floating point. Compute the equivalent number of yards, feet, and inches using these requirements:

- Yards and feet are expressed as integers.

- Inches are expressed as a floating-point number, rounded to six digits of precision.

Output is yards, feet, and inches.

Figure 6-3 shows the proposed interface.

FIGURE 6-3

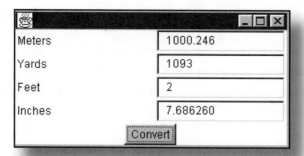

Design and Implementation

Here is the code for some variable declarations and the `buttonClicked` method. The rest of the program is left as an exercise.

```
final double CENTIMETERS_PER_INCH = 2.540005;
double meters, inchesLeft;
int yards, feet;

public void buttonClicked (Button buttonObj){
   meters = metersField.getNumber();

   inchesLeft = meters * 100 / CENTIMETERS_PER_INCH;
   yards = (int)inchesLeft / 36;
   inchesLeft = inchesLeft % 36;
   feet = (int)inchesLeft / 12;
   inchesLeft = inchesLeft % 12;

   yardsField.setNumber (yards);
   feetField.setNumber (feet);
   inchesField.setNumber (inchesLeft);
   inchesField.setPrecision (6);
```

C A S E   S T U D Y   2 : Dice Rolling

Bill loves to play board games that require the use of a pair of dice and challenges strangers wherever he goes. While he never leaves home without a board and a computer, he frequently forgets the dice.

Request

Write a program that simulates the roll of a pair of dice.

Analysis, Design, and Implementation

Figure 6-4 shows a suggested interface. Every time the **Roll** button is clicked, two random numbers between 1 and 6 are generated and displayed. Just to give the user some ensurance that the dice are unbiased, the running average of each die is also displayed.

FIGURE 6-4

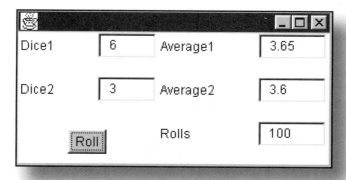

Here is the critical code. The rest is left as an exercise.

```
int numberOfRolls = 0;
int dice1, dice2;
double dice1Total = 0;
double dice2Total = 0;

public void buttonClicked (Button buttonObj){
    numberOfRolls = numberOfRolls + 1;
    dice1 = (int)(1 + Math.random() * 6);
    dice2 = (int)(1 + Math.random() * 6);
    dice1Total = dice1Total + dice1;
    dice2Total = dice2Total + dice2;

    dice1Field.setNumber (dice1);
    dice2Field.setNumber (dice2);
    average1Field.setNumber (dice1Total / numberOfRolls);
    average2Field.setNumber (dice2Total / numberOfRolls);
    rollsField.setNumber (numberOfRolls);
}
```

Strings Revisited

We have been working with strings since Lesson 2. However, further manipulation of strings requires sending messages to string objects. These messages are handled by the methods of class String.

String Methods

Methods have been written for examining individual characters in a string, for comparing the alphabetical order of two strings, for searching strings for particular characters or substrings, for extracting substrings, and for creating a copy of a string in which all characters are translated to uppercase or lowercase.

Many of the methods refer to specific locations within a string. For instance, in the three-character string 'abc' the character 'a' is considered to be at location 0 and not, as one might reasonably expect, at location 1. The characters 'b' and 'c' are in locations 1 and 2, respectively. This rather strange way of counting is a symptom of Java's historic ties to C++, and thus to C, and finally to assembly language, where counting from 0 is generally more convenient than counting from 1.

Table 6-6 contains a list of frequently used `String` methods. To access complete documentation on Java's features, including the `String` class, use your Web browser (see Appendix A).

TABLE 6-6
String methods

METHOD	DESCRIPTION
`charAt (anIndex)` `returns char`	Ex: `chr = myStr.charAt(4);` Returns the character at the position `anIndex`. Remember the first character is at position 0. An exception is thrown (i.e., an error is generated) if `anIndex` is out of range (i.e., does not indicate a valid position within `myStr`).
`compareTo (aString)` `returns int`	Ex: `i = myStr.compareTo("abc");` Compares two strings lexicographically. Returns 0 if `myStr` equals `aString`; a value less than 0 if `myStr` string is alphabetically less than `aString`; and a value greater than 0 if `myStr` string is lexicographically greater than `aString`.
`equals (aString)` `returns boolean`	Ex: `bool = myStr.equals("abc");` Returns `true` if `myStr` equals `aString`, else returns `false`. Because of implementation peculiarities in Java, **never test for equality like this:** `myStr == aString`

`equalsIgnoreCase`
`(aString)`
    `returns boolean`
	Similar to equals but ignores case during the comparison.

`indexOf (aCharacter)`	Ex: `i = myStr.indexOf('z')` Returns the index within `myStr` of the first occurrence of `aCharacter` or −1 if `aCharacter` is absent.

`indexOf (aCharacter,`
        `beginIndex)`
    `returns int`
	Ex: `i = myStr.indexOf('z', 6);`
	Similar to the preceding method except the search starts at position `beginIndex` rather than at the beginning of `myStr`. An exception is thrown if `beginIndex` is out of range.

`indexOf (aSubstring)` `returns int`	Ex: `i = myStr.indexOf("abc")` Returns the index within `myStr` of the first occurrence of `aSubstring` or −1 if `aSubstring` is absent.

`indexOf (aSubstring,`
        `beginIndex)`
    `returns int`
	Ex: `i = indexOf("abc", 6)`
	Similar to the preceding method except the search starts at position `beginIndex` rather than at the beginning of `myStr`. An exception is thrown if `beginIndex` is out of range.

`length()` `returns int`	Ex: `i = myStr.length();` Returns the length of `myStr`.

`replace (oldChar,`
        `newChar)`
    `returns String`
	Ex: `str = myStr.replace('z', 'Z');`
	Returns a new string resulting from replacing all occurrences of `oldChar` in `myStr` with `newChar`. **`myStr` is not changed.**

TABLE 6-6
(continued)

substring (beginIndex) returns String	Ex: str = myStr.substring(6); Returns a new string that is a substring of myStr. The substring begins at location beginIndex and extends to the end of myStr. An exception is thrown if beginIndex is out of range.

substring (beginIndex,
        endIndex)
    returns String
	Ex: str = myStr.substring(4, 8);
	Similar to the preceding method except the substring extends to location endIndex-1 rather than to the end of myStr.

toLowerCase() returns String	Ex: str = myStr.toLowerCase(); str is the same as myStr except that all letters have been converted to lowercase. **myStr is not changed**.
toUpperCase() returns String	Ex: str = myStr.toUpperCase(); str is the same as myStr except that all letters have been converted to uppercase. **myStr is not changed**.
trim() returns String	Ex: str = myStr.trim(); str is the same as myStr except that leading and trailing spaces, if any, are absent. **myStr is not changed**.

Conversion Between Strings and Primitive Data Types

We have seen that Java automatically converts primitive data types to their string representation prior to concatenation. It is also possible to do these conversions outside the context of concatenation. Here are some representative examples in which the String class method valueOf is used to perform the conversions:

```
String s1 = String.valueOf (true);    // Boolean to string
String s2 = String.valueOf ('A');     // Character to string
String s3 = String.valueOf (3);       // Integer to string
String s4 = String.valueOf (3.14);    // Double to string
```

Conversion in the other direction is also supported but is more awkward. Here are some examples:

```
byte   b = Byte.valueOf ("12").byteValue();          // String to byte
double d = Double.valueOf ("3.14e4").doubleValue();  // String to double
float  f = Float.valueOf ("3.14e4").floatValue();    // String to float
int    i = Integer.valueOf ("12").intValue();        // String to int
long   l = Long.valueOf ("12").longValue();          // String to long
short  s = Short.valueOf ("12").shortValue();        // String to short
```

Short Examples of String Manipulations

We now present several short examples of string manipulations:

```
// Count the number of uppercase letters in a string.

String str;
```

```
int count, i;
char chr;

str = " + A x ...G;H";
count  = 0;
for (i = 0; i < str.length(); i++){
    chr = str.charAt(i);
    if (Character.isUpperCase(chr)) count++;
}
messageBox ("str contains " + count + " uppercase letters.");
```

```
// Create a string that consists of all the digits
// in another string.

String digitStr, mainStr;
int i;
char chr;

mainStr = "a12bc3d";
digitStr = "";                          // An empty string

for (i = 0; i < mainStr.length(); i++){
    chr = mainStr.charAt(i);
    if (Character.isDigit (chr))
        digitStr = digitStr + chr;
}
messageBox (digitStr);
```

```
// Extract the substring starting with the first '*' and
// ending with the second '*'.

String str, substr;
int first, second;

str = "ab*cdef*xyz*";
first = str.indexOf ('*');
if (first == -1)
    messageBox ("not present");
else{
    second = str.indexOf ('*', first+1);
    if (second == -1)
        messageBox ("not present");
    else{
        substr = str.substring (first, second+1);
        messageBox (substr);
    }
}
```

```
// Determine the lexicographical order of two strings.

String str1 = "Charles", str2 = "Chuck";
int outcome;

outcome = str1.compareTo (str2);
```

```
if (outcome == 0)
    messageBox ("str1 equals str2");
else if (outcome < 0)
    messageBox ("str1 comes before str2");
else
    messageBox ("str1 comes after str2");
```

CASE STUDY 3: Palindromes

Request

Write a program that determines whether or not an input string is a palindrome.

Analysis

A palindrome is a string that reads the same forward and backward. We accept an input string from a text field. We ignore the case of the letters in the string. All characters (including white space) are examined. We display "Yes, you entered a palindrome" or "No, you did not enter a palindrome" in a message box. Figure 6-5 shows the proposed interface. Figure 6-6 shows the resulting message box.

FIGURE 6-5

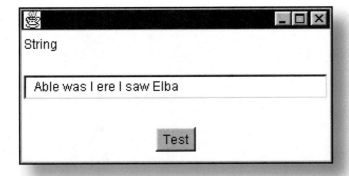

FIGURE 6-6

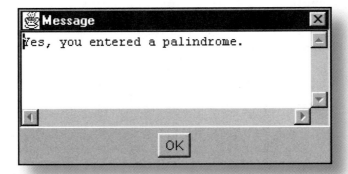

Design

Here is the pseudocode for the `buttonClicked` method:

```
Get aString from text field
Convert aString to uppercase
If isPalindrome (aString)
   output yes
else
   output no
```

The `isPalindrome` method consists of a loop in which we start comparing characters at the opposite ends of the string. If the characters are not the same, we return false. Otherwise, we continue the comparisons after moving both positions toward the middle of the string. If the loop reaches the middle of the string, all the characters have matched, so we return true. Here is the pseudocode:

```
Set forward to first position in string
Set backward to last position in string
While forward < backward
   If string.charAt (forward) != string.charAt (backward)
      Return false
   Increment forward
   Decrement backward
Return true
```

Implementation

```
import java.awt.*;
import BreezyGUI.*;

public class Palindrome extends GBFrame{

   Label stringLabel = addLabel ("String",1,1,2,1);
   TextField stringField = addTextField ("",2,1,2,1);
   Button testButton = addButton ("Test",3,1,2,1);

   public void buttonClicked(Button buttonObj){
      String aString = stringField.getText();
      aString = aString.toUpperCase();
      if (isPalindrome (aString))
         messageBox("Yes, you entered a palindrome.");
      else
         messageBox("No, you did not enter a palindrome.");
   }

   private boolean isPalindrome (String s){
      int lastPosition = s.length() - 1;
      int forward = 0;
      int backward = lastPosition;

      while (forward < backward){
         if (s.charAt (forward) != s.charAt (backward))
```

```
                return false;
            forward++;
            backward--;
        }
        return true;
    }

    public static void main (String[] args){
        Frame frm = new Palindrome();
        frm.setSize (300, 150);
        frm.setVisible (true);
    }
}
```

C S   C A P S U L E :   Data Encryption

Data encryption involves the translation of data into a code that cannot be read by unauthorized users. *Cryptography* is the formal study of methods of data encryption, and *cryptanalysis* is the branch of cryptography that deals with "breaking" codes. Although the practice of data encryption is thousands of years old, its use with computers is almost as old as the computer itself. One of the first uses of a computer was to break the German code during World War II, and Alan Turing, one of the first computer scientists, was a leading engineer in this project.

Although the algorithms for encryption and decryption have become very sophisticated, the processes are straightforward. The inputs to an encryption algorithm are a code (a string of bits) and the source data. The output is the encrypted data. Decryption reverses this process.

Needless to say, the primary use of data encryption during the Cold War (from 1946 to 1992) was military, and the U.S. government closely regulated any new data encryption algorithms. With the advent of networks and their use for commerce, e-mail, and so forth, the use of data encryption has spread, mainly to protect the privacy, security, and reliability of these transactions. For an overview of the technology and policy issues concerning data encryption, see the entire issue of *Communications of the ACM,* Volume 35, No. 7 (July 1992).

Design, Testing, and Debugging Hints

- Use care in constructing the appropriate compound Boolean expressions for a given problem. For example, the expression 80 <= average && average < 90 cannot be rewritten 80 <= average < 90. Much as we would like to have the shorter version, it would produce a syntax error.

- When designing and testing a complex Boolean expression, use a truth table to determine the possible values of the subexpressions. Be sure that the expression covers all of the possibilities.

- A for loop's logic is similar to that of a while loop and should be designed and tested accordingly.

- Remember to include a `break` statement for each case of a `switch` statement and a `default` statement where relevant.

- When concatenating strings and numbers, the position of the operands makes a difference. For example, the expression `5 + 6 + ""` produces the string 11, whereas the expression `"" + 5 + 6` produces the string 56.

- Use constants for data wherever possible. The use of constants enhances program security and maintainability.

- The individual characters in a string are located at positions 0 through the length of the string minus 1. An attempt to access a character at a position outside of this range will result in a run-time error.

Summary

In this lesson, you learned:

- Java includes many more operators than the ones you have used so far, including increment and decrement operators and logical operators such as AND, OR, and NOT.

- Java's `do-while`, `for`, and `switch` control statements can streamline programming but require careful attention. The `break` statement is a useful way to break out of a loop prematurely.

- Additional data types give you considerable control over output. The `boolean` data type has only two values: true or false. The `char` data type allows you to manipulate character data. You can use the cast operator to convert a more inclusive data type to a less inclusive one.

- Using constants clarifies program statements and makes it easy to change values in a program.

- The `Math` class contains many mathematical functions that can simplify programming.

- The `String` class contains a number of methods that let you work with string characters in many ways.

LESSON 6 REVIEW QUESTIONS

WRITTEN QUESTIONS

Write your answers to the following questions.

1. Assume that the variables x and y contain the values 15 and 3, respectively. Indicate if the Boolean expressions below are true, false, or syntactically incorrect.
   a. `x < y || x < y * 6`
   b. `x < y && x < y * 6`
   c. `! x < y`
   d. `! x % y == 0`
   e. `x && y`

2. Write `switch` statements for the problems below.
   a. If the value of the variable x is 2, set it to its square. If it is 3, set it to its cube. If it is 4 or 5, multiply it by 3 and set it to this result. Otherwise, set it to 0.
   b. If the value of the variable ch is A or a, display the string "Outstanding." If the value is B or b, display "Good." If the value is C or c, display "Average." Otherwise, display "Don't know."

3. Write a method that displays a table of integers, their squares, and their square roots, using the integers from parameter x up to parameter y. The third parameter of the method should be a `TextArea`. The method should use a `for` loop.

4. Assume that the variables `char1`, `int1`, and `double1` are of type `char`, `int`, and `double`, respectively. Indicate which of the statements below are syntactically correct and which are not. Explain any errors.
   a. `int1 = double1;`
   b. `double1 = int1;`
   c. `int1 = char1;`
   d. `int1 = (double) double1;`
   e. `int1 = int1 + char1;`
   f. `int1 = int1 + (int1) char1;`

5. Write a method that expects three `int` parameters and returns the smallest of the three values. The method should use logical operators and a multiway `if` statement.

6. Write a method that expects three `int` parameters and returns the smallest of the three values. The method should use the method `Math.min`.

7. What is a `final` variable? When is its use appropriate? Give an example of a standard Java `final` variable.

LESSON 6 PROJECTS

For these projects, we will not specify the data validation requirements or the headers of the user-defined methods. However, you should strive to maintain the standards set in earlier lessons, including the use of preconditions and postconditions for user-defined methods.

1. Complete the first two case studies in this lesson and test them.

2. Modify the program of Case Study 2 (rolling dice) so that it takes as an additional input the number of sides on a die (there need not be six sides). When the user clicks the **Roll** button, the program should use the number of sides to calculate the value of each die. Whenever the user changes the number of sides, reset the totals and the number of rolls.

3. Write a tester program that displays the characters that have the ASCII values 0 through 127. Display 12 characters per line. By the way, not all characters are printable. The newline character will cause a break to a new line. One of the characters will ring the bell, and another will cause a backspace. Notice that the digits precede the capital letters. See Appendix D for more details.

4. In the game of PNZ, one player thinks of a number consisting of three distinct digits. The other player repeatedly guesses the number and receives the following evaluation of the guess from the opponent:

- PPP means that each digit is in the correct position—the player has guessed the number.

- Each P means that a digit is in the correct position, without saying which position that is.

- Each N means that a digit occurs in the number, but it's not in the correct position.

- A single Z means no digits are in the number.

Assuming that the number is 123, here are some sample guesses and evaluations:

GUESS	EVALUATION
134	PN
213	PNN
143	PP
300	N
555	Z
123	PPP

So as not to provide too many clues, the evaluator always displays the Ps before the Ns in the output.

Write a program that plays this game with the user. The interface should have three window objects: a text field for entering a three-digit string, a button to register the guess, and a text area to display the results. The results should be displayed in a table similar to the one just shown. Your program should have the following methods:

- `void startNewGame()` starts a new game when the user selects the button.

- `char randomDigit()` returns a randomly generated digit between 0 and 9.

- `String randomString()` returns the string representation of a number that has three unique, randomly generated digits.

- `String evaluateGuess(String target, String guess)` takes the target string and the guess string as parameters and applies the rules of PNZ to generate and return a result string.

- `void displayResults(String guess, String result)` takes the guess string and the result string as parameters and updates the text area by adding a new line to its text.

The user interacts with two buttons. The program should handle invalid guesses (strings not having three distinct digits) by displaying the error in a message box.

5. Most verbs form a participle by adding *ing* to the present singular. For example, the participle of *go* is *going* and of *eat* is *eating*. In cases of verbs ending in *e*, the *e* is dropped, as in *date/dating*. Write a program that takes the present singular form of a verb as input and displays the participle form as output.

CRITICAL THINKING ACTIVITY

A number guessing game begins with one player saying, "I'm thinking of a number between *x* and *y*," where *x* is the smaller number and *y* is the larger number. The other player responds with a guess. The first player then replies, "It's larger," "It's smaller," or "You've got it!" This process goes on until the second player guesses the number. Write a program that plays this game. Basic requirements:

■ At startup, the program waits for the user to click a button to start the game. The user can also click this button at any time to start a new game.

■ There is a second button that the user clicks to register a guess.

■ When the user correctly guesses the number, the program should display a count of the number of guesses and end the game.

■ Guessing when no game is in progress results in an error message.

USER-DEFINED CLASSES

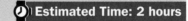
Overview of Classes and Objects

In Lesson 1, we first introduced the terms *object* and class. An object is a run-time entity that contains data and responds to messages. A class is a software package or template that describes the characteristics of similar objects. These characteristics are of two kinds: variable declarations that define an object's data requirements and methods that define its behavior in response to messages. We call these characteristics *instance variables* and *instance methods,* respectively. The combining of data and behavior into a single software package is called *encapsulation.* An object is said to be an *instance* of its class, and the process of creating a new object is called *instantiation.*

When a Java program is executing, a computer's memory must hold

■ Templates for all classes used (in their compiled form, of course).

■ Variables that refer to objects.

■ Objects.

Memory for methods is allocated within class templates. Memory for data is allocated within objects. Although class templates must be in memory at all times, individual objects can come and go. An object first appears and occupies memory when instantiated, and it disappears automatically when no longer needed. Java keeps track of whether objects are referenced. Because unreferenced objects cannot be used, Java assumes that it is OK to delete them from memory. Java does this during a process called *garbage collection.*

In contrast, C++ programmers have the onerous responsibility for deleting objects explicitly. Forgetting to delete unneeded objects wastes scarce memory resources, and accidentally deleting an object too soon or more than once may cause programs to crash. In large programs, these mistakes are easy to make and difficult to detect. Fortunately, Java programmers do not have to worry about this problem.

Three Characteristics of an Object

An object has three characteristics worth emphasizing. First, an object has *behavior* as defined by the methods of its class. Second, an object has *state,* which is another way of saying that at any particular moment its instance variables have particular values. Typically, the state changes over time in response to messages sent to the object. Third, an object has its own unique *identity,* which distinguishes it from all other objects in the computer's memory, even those that might momentarily have the same state. An object's identity is handled behind the scenes by the JVM and should not be confused with the variables that might refer to the object. Of these, there can be none, one, or several. When there are none, the garbage collector will soon purge the object from memory. We will see an example in which two variables refer to the same object later.

Clients and Servers

When messages are sent, two objects are involved—the sender and the receiver, also called the *client* and *server.* A client's interactions with a server are limited to sending messages, so a client does not need to know anything about the internal workings of a server. The server's data requirements and the implementation of its methods are hidden from the client, an approach called *information hiding.* From the client's perspective, the server is a *black box.* Information hiding allows a class's users to focus on the services it provides, while only the class's implementer needs to understand its internal workings. Another term used to refer to a server is *abstract data type* (ADT). An ADT is abstract in that a client knows only the interface of the data type—the set of messages that objects of that type understand.

A Student Class

The first class we develop is called Student. We begin by considering the class from the perspective of a user. Later we will show how to implement it. A user needs to know that a student object keeps track of a real student's name and three test scores and responds to the messages listed in Table 7-1.

Using Student Objects

Some snippets of code illustrate how to create and manipulate student objects. First, we declare several variables, including two variables of type Student.

```
Student s1, s2;        // Declare the variables
String str;
int i;
```

TABLE 7-1
Messages in the Student class

MESSAGE	RESPONSE
setName(aString) returns void	Ex: stud.setName ("Bill"); Sets the name of stud to aString.
getName() returns String	Ex: str = stud.getName(); Returns the name of stud.

setScore(whichTest,
      testScore)
  returns void
	Ex:: stud.setScore (3, 95);
	Sets the score on whichTest to testScore. If whichTest is not
	1, 2, or 3, then uses 3 as whichTest.

getScore(whichTest) returns int	Ex: score = stud.getScore (3); Returns the score on whichTest. If whichTest is not 1, 2, or 3, then uses 3 as whichTest.
getAverage() returns int	Ex: average = stud.getAverage(); Returns the average of the test scores.
getHighScore() returns int	Ex: highScore = stud.getHighScore(); Returns the highest test score.
toString() returns String	Ex: str = stud.toString(); Returns a string that describes the student.

As usual, we do not use variables until we have assigned them initial values. We assign a new student object to s1 using the operator new:

```
s1 = new Student();     // Instantiate a student and associate it with the
                        // variable s1
```

It is important to emphasize that the variable s1 is a reference to a student object and is *not* a student object itself.

A student object keeps track of the name and test scores of an actual student. Thus, for a brand-new student object, what are the values of these data attributes? That is determined by the programmer who implemented the Student class, but we can easily find out by sending messages to the student object via its associated variable s1:

```
str = s1.getName();      // str equals ""
i = s1.getHighScore();   // i equals 0
```

Apparently, the name was initialized to an empty string and the test scores to 0. Now we set the object's data attributes using what are called *mutator* methods:

```
s1.setName ("Bill");     // Set the student's name to "Bill"
s1.setScore (1,84);      // Set the score on test 1 to 84
s1.setScore (2,86);      //                on test 2 to 86
s1.setScore (3,88);      //                on test 3 to 88
```

To see if the previous step worked correctly, we use *accessor* methods to ask the object for the values of its data attributes:

```
str = s1.getName();       // str equals "Bill"
i = s1.getScore (1);      // i equals 84
i = s1.getHighScore();    // i equals 88
i = s1.getAverage();      // i equals 86
```

The object's string representation can be obtained by sending the object the `toString` message:

```
str = s1.toString();
  // str  now equals
  // "Name:    Bill\nTest 1:  84\nTest2:  86\nTest3:  88\nAverage: 86"
```

If displayed in a text area, the string would be broken into several lines as determined by the placement of the newline characters (\n). In addition to the above explicit use of the `toString` method, in some situations the method is called automatically. For instance, `toString` is used when a student object is concatenated with a string or sent to a message box (Figure 7-1):

```
str = "The best student is: \n" + s1;
messageBox (s1);
```

FIGURE 7-1
The output in the Message box

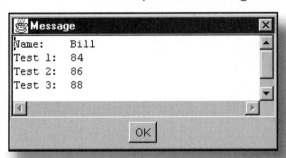

Hence, if you anticipate using an object in either context, provide the class with a `toString` method. But, if you forget to do so, Java provides a very simple version of the method through the mechanism of inheritance (discussed in Lesson 9). This simplified version does little more than return the name of the class to which the object belongs.

We close this demonstration by associating an object with the variable s2. Rather than instantiating a new object, we assign s1 to s2:

```
s2 = s1;                  // s1 and s2 now refer to the same object
```

The variables s2 and s1 now refer to the *same* student object. This might come as surprise, because one might reasonably expect the assignment statement to create a second student object equal to the first, but that is not how Java works. To demonstrate that s1 and s2 now refer to the same student object, we change the student's name using s2 and retrieve the student's name using s1:

```
s2.setName ("Ann");       // Set the name
str = s1.getName();       // str equals "Ann". Therefore, s1 and s2 refer
                          // to the same object.
```

Table 7-2 clarifies the manner in which variables are affected by assignment.

TABLE 7-2
Assigning variables

CODE	DIAGRAM	COMMENTS
`int i, j;`	i `?` j `???`	`i` and `j` are memory locations that have not yet been initialized, but which will hold integers.
`i = 3;` `j = i;`	i `3` j `3`	`i` holds the integer 3. `j` holds the integer 3.
`Student s, t;`	s `???` t `???`	`s` and `t` are memory locations that have not yet been initialized, but which will hold references to student objects.
`s = new Student();` `t = s;`	s t Student Object	`s` holds a reference to a student object. `t` holds a reference to the same student object.

At any time, it is possible to break the connection between a variable and the object it references. Simply assign the value `null` to the variable:

```
Student s1;
s1 = new Student();     // s1 references the newly instantiated student
...                     // Do stuff with the student
s1 = null;              // s1 no longer references anything
```

Structure of a Class Template

A class template consists of four parts:

1. The class's name and some modifying phrases.

2. A description of the instance variables.

3. One or more methods that indicate how to initialize a new object (called *constructor* methods).

4. One or more methods that specify how an object responds to messages.

Here is a typical class template:

```
public class <name of class> extends <some other class>{

    // Declaration of instance variables
    private <type> <name>;
    ...
```

```
    // Code for the constructor methods
    public <name of class>() {
        // Initialize the instance variables
        ...
    }
    ...

    // Code for the other methods
    public <return type> <name of method> (<parameter list){
        ...
    }
    ...
}
```

Some of the phrases used in the template need to be explained:

■ `public class`. Class definitions usually begin with the keyword `public`, indicating that the class is accessible to all clients desiring access. There are some alternatives to `public` that we overlook for now.

■ `<name of class>`. Class names are user-defined symbols, and, as such, they must adhere to the rules for naming variables and methods. It is common to start class names with a capital letter and variable and method names with a lowercase letter. The names of variables that are declared to be `final`, and therefore act as constants, are often completely capitalized.

■ `extends <some of other class>`. Java organizes its classes in a *hierarchy* (see Lesson 1). At the *root,* or *base,* of this hierarchy is a class called `Object`. In the hierarchy, if a class A is immediately above another class B, we can say that

  ● A is the s*uperclass* or *parent* of B.

  ● B is a *subclass* or *child* of A. See Figure 7-2.

FIGURE 7-2
Class hierarchy

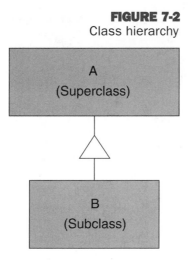

Whenever a new class is created, it must be incorporated into the hierarchy by extending an existing class. The new class's exact placement in the hierarchy is important because a new class inherits the characteristics of its superclass through a process called *inheritance.* The new class then adds to and modifies these inherited characteristics. In other words, the new class *extends* the superclass. For now, whenever we define a new class, we will extend the base class `Object`, which has no characteristics of concern to us at the moment. (Later in the book, we get away from the restriction of extending only the root class `Object`.) Finally, if the clause `extends <some other class>` is omitted from the new class's definition, then, by default, the new class is assumed to be a subclass of `Object`.

- `private <type> <name>`. Instance variables are nearly always declared to be private. This prevents the class's clients from referring to the instance variables directly. Making instance variables private is an important aspect of information hiding.

- `public <return type> <name of method>`. Methods are usually declared to be public, which allows the class's clients to refer to them.

`private` and `public` are called *visibility modifiers*. If both `private` and `public` are omitted, the consequences vary with the circumstances. Without explaining why, suffice it to say that omitting the visibility modifier is often equivalent to using `public`. In earlier lessons, we never bothered to use a visibility modifier when declaring variables. From this point on, we continue this practice for window objects, but use `private` for other variables wherever possible.

To illustrate the difference between `private` and `public`, suppose the class `Student` has a private instance variable `name` and a public method `setName`. Then

```
Student s;
s = new Student();
s.name = "Bill";      // Rejected by compiler because name is private
s.setName ("Bill")    // Accepted by compiler because setName is public
```

Notice that the constructor does not have a return type. All other methods must have a return type.

Implementation of the Student Class

```
public class Student extends Object{

    // Instance variables
    // Each student object will have a name and three test scores
    private String name;
    private int test1;
    private int test2;
    private int test3;

    // Constructor method

    // Initialize a new student's name to the empty string and his test
    // scores to zero.
    public Student(){
        name = "";
        test1 = 0;
        test2 = 0;
        test3 = 0;
    }

    // Other methods

    // Set a student's name.
    public void setName (String nm){
```

```
        name = nm;
    }

    // Get a student's name
    public String getName (){
        return name;
    }

    // Set the score on the indicated test.
    public void setScore (int i, int score){
        if       (i == 1) test1 = score;
        else if (i == 2)  test2 = score;
        else              test3 = score;
    }

    // Get the score on the indicated test.
    public int getScore (int i){
        if       (i == 1) return test1;
        else if (i == 2)  return test2;
        else              return test3;
    }

    // Compute and return a student's average.
    public int getAverage(){
        int average;
        average = (int) Math.round((test1 + test2 + test3) / 3.0);
        return average;
    }

    // Compute and return a student's highest score.
    public int getHighScore(){
        int highScore;
        highScore = test1;
        if (test2 > highScore) highScore = test2;
        if (test3 > highScore) highScore = test3;
        return highScore;
    }

    // Return a string representation of a student's name, test scores
    // and average.
    public String toString(){
        String str;
        str = "Name:     " + name  + "\n" +     // "\n" denotes a newline
              "Test 1:   " + test1 + "\n" +
              "Test 2:   " + test2 + "\n" +
              "Test 3:   " + test3 + "\n" +
              "Average:  " + getAverage();
        return str;
    }
}
```

The meaning of the above code is fairly obvious. All the methods, except the constructor method, have a return type, although the return type may be void, indicating that the method, in fact, returns nothing.

When an object receives a message, the object activates the corresponding method. The method then manipulates the object's data by means of the instance variables. Notice that a method can also declare its own local variables. Whereas local variables retain their values only during the period in which the method is executing, an object's instance variables hold their values for the lifetime of the object.

163

Once the Student class has been compiled, an application can declare and manipulate student objects. Actually, there is a restriction. The code for the application and the Student class must reside in the same directory, unless some extra steps are taken (see Appendix G).

Editing, Compiling, and Testing the Student Class

The Student class must be saved in a file called Student.java and is compiled in the same way you compile any other program. The compiler then lists syntax errors in the usual manner. The Student class is also compiled automatically anytime you compile an application that uses the Student class, so even if you forget to recompile it, the latest version will be used.

We can test the Student class by using the Tester program first introduced in Lesson 3. Here is a small sample of test code. The result obtained when it is run is shown in Figure 7-3.

```
import BreezyGUI.*;

public class Tester{
    public static void main (String[] args){
        Student s1, s2;
        String str;
        int i;

        s1 = new Student();        // Instantiate a student object
        s1.setName ("Bill");       // Set the student's name to "Bill"
        s1.setScore (1,84);        // Set the score on test 1 to 84
        s1.setScore (2,86);        //                  on test 2 to 86
        s1.setScore (3,88);        //                  on test 3 to 88
        System.out.println("\nHere is student s1\n" + s1);

        s2 = s1;                   // s1 and s2 now refer to the same object
        s2.setName ("Ann");        // Set the name through s2
        System.out.println ("\nName of s1 is now: " + s1.getName());
        GBFrame.pause();
    }
}
```

FIGURE 7-3

Results of the Tester program

```
C:\javafiles>javac Tester.java

C:\javafiles>java Tester

Here is student s1
Name:     Bill
Test 1:   84
Test 2:   86
Test 3:   88
Average:  86

Name of s1 is now: Ann

Hit Enter to continue: _
```

We now introduce a run-time error into the `Student` class and run the `Tester` program again. Here is a listing of the modified and erroneous lines of code. Figure 7-4 shows the error messages generated when `Tester` is run.

```java
public int getAverage(){
    int average = 0;
    average = (int) Math.round ((test1 + test2 + test3) / average);
    return average;
}
```

FIGURE 7-4
Java throws an arithmetic exception

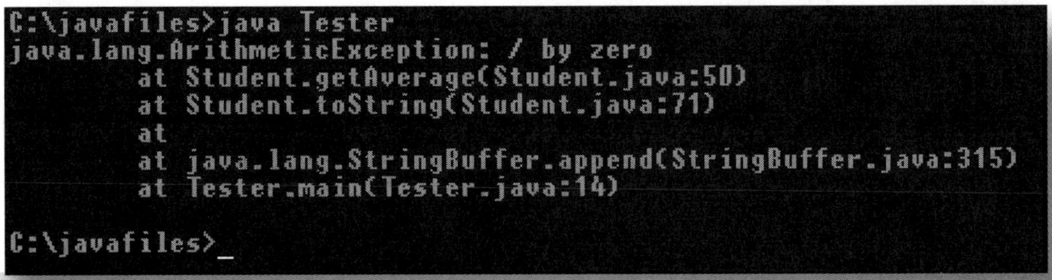

```
C:\javafiles>java Tester
java.lang.ArithmeticException: / by zero
        at Student.getAverage(Student.java:50)
        at Student.toString(Student.java:71)
        at
        at java.lang.StringBuffer.append(StringBuffer.java:315)
        at Tester.main(Tester.java:14)

C:\javafiles>_
```

The messages indicate that an attempt was made to divide by 0 in the `Student` class's `getAverage` method (line 50), which had been called from the `Student` class's `toString` method (71), which had been called by some methods we did not write, which had been called from the `Tester` class's `main` method (line 14). Here are the actual lines of code mentioned:

```
Student getAverage line 50 :
                average = (int)(test1 + test2 + test3 + 0.5) / average;
Student toString line 71   :
                "Average: " + getAverage();
Tester main line 14        :
                System.out.println ("\nHere is student s1\n" + s1);
```

BreezyGUI: Menus and the Title

W e are just about ready to present a case study that uses the `Student` class, but before doing so, we must introduce some new window objects.

Menus

Menus provide a convenient mechanism for entering commands into a program. A menu system consists of a menu bar, a number of menus, and, for each menu, several selections. It is also possible to have submenus, but we ignore these for now. It is easy to add a menu system to an application. Simply declare a menu item object for each menu selection. For instance, the following code adds two menus to an application's interface:

```java
MenuItem highTest1MI   = addMenuItem ("HighStudent", "Test1");
MenuItem highTest2MI   = addMenuItem ("HighStudent", "Test2");
MenuItem highTest3MI   = addMenuItem ("HighStudent", "Test3");
MenuItem highOverallMI = addMenuItem ("HighStudent", "Overall");
```

```
MenuItem highAverageMI = addMenuItem ("HighStudent", "Average");

MenuItem displayStudent1MI = addMenuItem ("Display", "Student1");
MenuItem displayStudent2MI = addMenuItem ("Display", "Student2");
```

The first menu is called **HighStudent** and has five items, while the second, called **Display**, has two. When the user selects a menu item, a method called `menuItemSelected` is activated. Here is a typical snippet of code from this method:

```
public void menuItemSelected (MenuItem menuItemObj){
   if (menuItemObj == highTest1MI)
      ... do something appropriate ...
   else if (menuItemObj == highTest2MI){
      ... do something else ...

   etc.
}
```

The setTitle Method

Most applications include a title at the top of the window. To display a title in our applications, we need to add a constructor to the interface class and include the line:

```
SetTitle (<"the title">);
```

We are now ready to begin the case study.

C A S E   S T U D Y : Student Test Scores

Request

Write a program that allows one to compare two students' test scores. Each student takes three tests.

Analysis

Figure 7-5 shows the proposed interface.

FIGURE 7-5

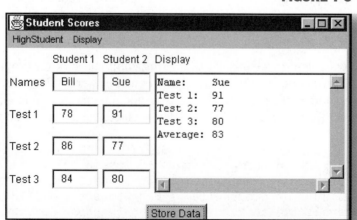

To use the interface,

1. Enter the names and test scores of two students and click the **Store Data** button. Anytime the data is updated, it is necessary to click the **Store Data** button again.

2. Select an option from either of the two menus. The menu options are explained in Table 7-3.

TABLE 7-3
Menu options

HIGHSTUDENT MENU

MENU OPTION	EXPLANATION
Test1	Display the name of the student who scored higher on test 1, unless the scores are equal. For instance, see Figure 7-6:

FIGURE 7-6

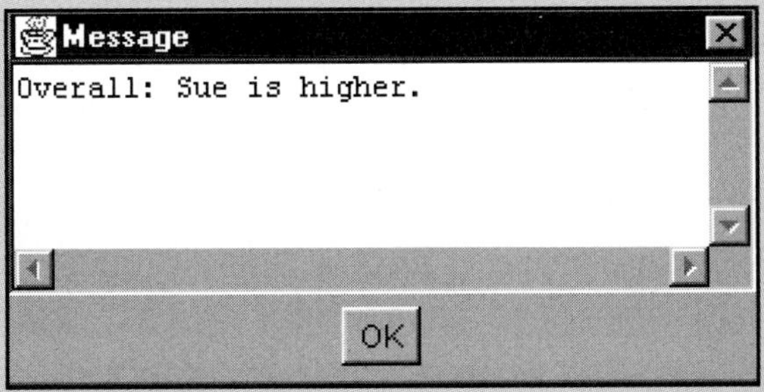

Test2	Display the name of the student who scored higher on test 2, unless the scores are equal.
Test3	Display the name of the student who scored higher on test 3, unless the scores are equal.
Overall	Display the name of the student who had the higher test score overall, unless they both have the same highest score.
Average	Display the name of the student who had the higher average, unless they both have the same average. For instance, see Figure 7-7:

FIGURE 7-7

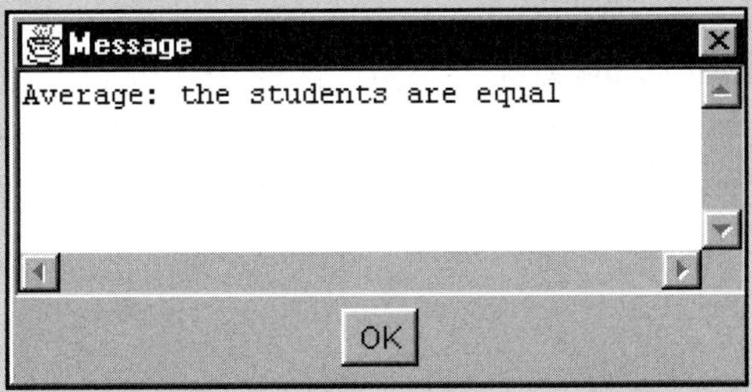

DISPLAY MENU

MENU OPTION	EXPLANATION
Student1	Display the name, test scores, and average of student 1.
Student2	Display the name, test scores, and average of student 2.

Classes

During analysis, we determine which classes will be needed to support the application, and we decide each class's overall responsibilities. The nature of the current problem suggests the use of two classes:

1. `Student`. Not surprisingly, the `Student` class has capabilities that exactly fit the needs of this program.

2. `StudentInterface`. This class will support the user interface and declare and manipulate two student objects.

Design

During analysis, we decided to base the implementation on two classes: `Student` and `StudentInterface`. Now, during design, we specify the characteristics of these classes in detail. This involves determining the data requirements of each class and the methods that will be needed by the users of the classes. This process is usually straightforward. To illustrate, let us pretend for the moment that we have not written the `Student` class.

Designing the Student Class

We know from the work completed during analysis that a student object must keep track of a name and three test scores. The high score and the average can be calculated when needed. Thus, the data requirements are clear. The `Student` class must declare four instance variables:

```
private String name;
private int test1;
private int test2;
private int test3;
```

To determine the `Student` class's methods, we look at the class from the perspective of the clients who will be sending messages to student objects. In this application, the interface is the only client. Here are the clues for the methods:

■ The interface needs to instantiate two student objects. This indicates the need for a constructor method, which we always include anyway.

■ When the user clicks the **Store** button, the interface needs to tell each student object its name and three test scores. This can be handled by two mutator methods: `setName(theName)` and `setScore(whichTest, testScore)`.

■ When the user makes selections from the **HighStudent** menu, the interface needs to ask the student object for the scores on specific tests, or the highest score, or the average. This suggests three accessor methods: `getScore(whichTest)`, `getHighScore()`, and `getAverage()`.

■ When the user makes a selection from the **Display** menu, the interface needs a string representation of a student object, which can be provided by the method `toString()`.

We summarize our findings in a *class summary* box:

```
Class:
    Student extends Object
Private Instance Variables:
    String name
    int test1
    int test2
    int test3
Public Methods:
    constructors
    void setName (theName)
    String getName()
    void setScore
       (whichTest, testScore)
    int getScore (whichTest)
    int getAverage()
    int getHighScore()
    String toString()
```

Normally, we would complete a class's design by writing pseudocode for methods whose implementation is not obvious, but we skip this step here.

Designing the `StudentInterface` Class

The design of an interface class is largely predetermined. There is little point in listing all the window objects required to support the interface. The person writing the code can easily determine these. However, it is necessary to note that two student objects will be needed. Let us call these `student1` and `student2`.

There must, of course, be a constructor and methods to handle button clicks and menu selections. These methods in turn can call helper methods, as illustrated in Lesson 5. Here is pseudocode for the methods:

```
public StudentInterface(){
    // This is the constructor
    instantiate the student objects
    set window's title to "Student Scores"
}

public void buttonClicked (buttonObj){
    get the data from the screen and use it to set data values for student1
    and student2
}

public void menuItemSelected (menuItemObj){
  if (menu item is "Test1")
    compareAndReport ("Test 1", score1 student1, score1 student2)
  else if (menu item is "Test2")
```

```
         compareAndReport ("Test 2", score2 student1, score2 student2)
      else if (menu item is "Test 3")
         compareAndReport ("Test 3", score3 student1, score3 student2)
      else if (menu item is "Overall")
         compareAndReport ("Overall", high score student1, high score student2)
      else if (menu item is "Average")
         compareAndReport ("Average", average student1, average student2)
      else if (menu item is "Display student 1")
        display string for student1 in text area
      else if (menu item is "Display student 2")
        display string for student2 in text area
   }

   private void compareAndReport (String description, int num1, int num2){
      if num1 == num2
        display description + "the students are equal"
      else if num1 > num2
        display description + name student1 + "is higher"
      else
        display description + name student2 + "is higher"
   }
```

Here is the class summary box for the StudentInterface class:

```
Class:
    StudentInterface extends GBFrame
Private Instance Variables:
    window objects as needed
    Student student1
    Student student2
Public Methods:
    constructor
    void buttonClicked (buttonObj)
    void menuItemSelected (menuItemObj)
    static void main (args)
Private Methods:
    void compareAndReport (description, num1, num2)
```

Implementation

The code for the Student class has already been presented. Code for the StudentInterface class follows:

```
import java.awt.*;
import BreezyGUI.*;


public class StudentInterface extends GBFrame{
```

```
Label student1Label = addLabel ("Student 1",1,2,1,1);
... etc.

private Student student1;
private Student student2;

// Constructor
public StudentInterface(){
    student1 = new Student();
    student2 = new Student();
    setTitle ("Student Scores");
}

// Other methods
public void buttonClicked (Button buttonObj){
    student1.setName (stud1NameField.getText());
    student1.setScore (1, stud1Test1Field.getNumber());
    student1.setScore (2, stud1Test2Field.getNumber());
    student1.setScore (3, stud1Test3Field.getNumber());

    student2.setName (stud2NameField.getText());
    student2.setScore (1, stud2Test1Field.getNumber());
    student2.setScore (2, stud2Test2Field.getNumber());
    student2.setScore (3, stud2Test3Field.getNumber());
}

public void menuItemSelected (MenuItem menuItemObj){

    if      (menuItemObj == highTest1MI)
        compareAndReport ("Test 1", student1.getScore(1),
                                    student2.getScore(1));
    else if (menuItemObj == highTest2MI)
        compareAndReport ("Test 2", student1.getScore(2),
                                    student2.getScore(2));
    else if (menuItemObj == highTest3MI)
        compareAndReport ("Test 3", student1.getScore(3),
                                    student2.getScore(3));
    else if (menuItemObj == highOverallMI)
        compareAndReport ("Overall", student1.getHighScore(),
                                    student2.getHighScore());
    else if (menuItemObj == highAverageMI)
        compareAndReport ("Average", student1.getAverage(),
                                    student2.getAverage());
    else if (menuItemObj == displayStudent1MI)
        displayField.setText(student1.toString());
    else if (menuItemObj == displayStudent2MI)
        displayField.setText("" + student2);
}

private void compareAndReport (String description,
                                    int num1, int num2)
{
    String str = description + ": ";
```

171

```
        if (num1 == num2)
            str = str + "the students are equal";
        else if (num1 > num2)
            str = str + student1.getName() + " is higher.";
        else
            str = str + student2.getName() + " is higher.";
        messageBox (str);
    }

    public static void main (String[] args){
        Frame frm = new StudentInterface();
        frm.setSize (400, 250);
        frm.setVisible (true);
    }
}
```

Having introduced user-defined classes and worked our way through an example, we need to consider a few more details concerning their use.

The Static Modifier

The static modifier can be used in the declarations of variables and methods. It indicates that the variable or method applies to the class as a whole rather than to individual objects. Such variables and methods are called *class variables* and *class methods,* respectively. An example will help to clarify this somewhat vague description.

Counting the Number of Students Instantiated

Consider the Student class. Let us suppose we want to count all the student objects instantiated during the execution of an application. To do so, we introduce a variable called studentCount. This variable will be incremented every time a student object is instantiated, and the natural place to do so is inside the class's constructor. Clearly, this variable is independent of any particular student object and therefore cannot be an instance variable. Instead, it must be associated with the class as a whole and thus be a class variable. In addition, we need two methods to manipulate the studentCount variable: one to initialize the variable to 0 at the beginning of the application and the other to return the variable's value on demand. These methods will be called setStudentCount and getStudentCount, respectively. Because these methods do not manipulate any particular student object, sending a message to a student object cannot activate them. Instead, they are activated when a message is sent to the class as a whole. Hence, they need to be class methods.

Modifying the Student Class

Here are the modifications needed for the Student class. Notice that the class variables and methods have been added at the end of the class's template. There is no rule that says they must be placed in that particular location, but it is as good as any other and is the one we always use.

```
public class Student extends Object{

    private String name;
    ... rest of the instance variables go here ...

    public Student(){
```

```
            studentCount++;        // Increment the count when a student is
                                   // instantiated
            name = "";
            test1 = 0;
            test2 = 0;
            test3 = 0;
        }

        public void setName (String nm){
            name = nm;
        }

        ... rest of the methods without change go here ...


        //---------------- static variables and methods ----------------

        static private int studentCount;

        static public void setStudentCount(int count){
            studentCount = count;
        }

        static public int getStudentCount(){
            return studentCount;
        }
    }
```

Here is some code that illustrates the new capabilities of the Student class:

```
Student.setStudentCount (0);                // Initialize count to 0
s1 = new Student();                         // Instantiate a student object

s2 = new Student();                         // Instantiate a student object

s1 = new Student();                         // Instantiate a student object
messageBox (Student.getStudentCount());     // Displays 3
```

Notice that class messages are sent to a class and not to an object. Also, notice that we do not attempt to manipulate the studentCount variable directly, because in accordance with the good programming practice of information hiding, we declared the variable to be private.

Class Constants

By using the modifier final in conjunction with static, one can create a *class constant*. To illustrate the use of class constants, we modify the Student class again by adding two constants: MIN_SCORE and MAX_SCORE. Now, when a student's score is set, it will be held within the limits defined by these two constants. Such an approach is not ideal but perhaps is better than allowing a score to take on a negative value or a ridiculously large value. Here, then, are the modifications needed for the Student class:

```
public class Student extends Object{

    private String name;
    ... rest of the instance variables go here ...

    ... no changes in the methods up to this point ...
```

173

```
    public void setScore (int i, int score){
        // Limit the score to the interval [MIN_SCORE, MAX_SCORE]
        score = Math.max (MIN_SCORE, score);
        score = Math.min (MAX_SCORE, score);

        if      (i == 1) test1 = score;
        else if (i == 2) test2 = score;
        else             test3 = score;
    }

    ... no changes in the methods here ...

//--------------- static variables and methods ----------------

    static final private int MIN_SCORE = 0;
    static final private int MAX_SCORE = 100;

    ... no changes in the rest of the static stuff ...
}
```

And here is a snippet of code that illustrates the Student class's new features:

```
s = new Student();
s.setScore(1, -20);     // Too small, will be set to MIN_SCORE
s.setScore(2, 150);     // Too large, will be set to MAX_SCORE
s.setScore(3, 55);      // Value is acceptable
messageBox (s);         // Displays scores of 0, 100, and 55
```

Rules for Using the Static Modifier

There are two simple rules to remember when using the static modifier:

1. Class methods can reference static variables but never instance variables.

2. Instance methods, on the other hand, can reference all variables.

The Math Class Revisited

By now you may have guessed that all the methods and variables in the Math class are static. Math.PI refers to a static constant, whereas Math.max(MIN_SCORE, score) activates a static method.

The Static Method Main

All the many interface classes presented so far have included the static method main. Now we can understand more about how main works. Consider the following example:

```
import java.awt.*;
import BreezyGUI.*;

public class MyApp extends GBFrame{

    ... declare window objects ...
    ... declare instance variables ...

    public MyApp(){              // Constructor
        ...
    }
```

```
        public void buttonClicked (Button buttonObj){
            ...
        }

        public void menuItemSelected (MenuItem menuItemObj){
            ...
        }

        public static void main (String[] args){
            Frame frm = new MyApp();
            frm.setSize (200,300);
            frm.setVisible (true);
        }
    }
```

When the user runs this program by typing

```
java MyApp
```

the following sequence of events occurs:

1. The Java interpreter sends the message `main` to the class `MyApp`.

2. The method `main` instantiates an object called `frm` of type `MyApp`, at which point the `MyApp` constructor is activated.

3. The method `main` sends the object `frm` two messages, `setSize` and `setVisible`.

4. The object `frm` responds by setting its window size and displaying the interface.

5. Thereafter, the object `frm` becomes inactive until the user clicks a button or selects a menu option, at which point the Java interpreter sends the `frm` object either the message `buttonClicked` or `menuItemSelected`.

Notice that the methods `main`, `buttonClicked`, and `menuItemSelected` must be `public`, and the method `main` must also be `static`.

Restriction on the Use of the messageBox Method

We have finally introduced enough terminology to state a restriction on the use of the `messageBox` method more fully than we did in Lesson 3. The method can be used only in subclasses of `GBFrame`, and then only in methods that are not static. We must postpone the explanation until we have said more about inheritance.

Constructors

The purpose of a constructor is to initialize the instance variables of a newly instantiated object. It is activated when the keyword `new` is used and in no other way. It can never be used with an existing object to reset the object's instance variables.

A class template can include more than one constructor provided each has a unique parameter list. However, all the constructors must have the same name, that is, the name of the class. This is another example of overloaded methods, first encountered in Lesson 5. The constructors we have seen so far have had empty parameter lists and are called *default constructors*.

If a class template contains no constructors, the Java virtual machine provides a minimal default constructor behind the scenes. This constructor initializes numeric variables to 0 and object variables to null, a special value that indicates the object variable currently references no object. However, if a class template contains even one constructor, the Java virtual machine will no longer provide a default constructor automatically.

To illustrate these ideas, we add several constructors to the Student class. The code lists the original default constructor and two additional ones:

```
public Student(){
    studentCount++;      // Increment the count when a student is
                         // instantiated
    name = "";
    test1 = 0;
    test2 = 0;
    test3 = 0;
}

public Student(String nm, int t1, int t2, int t3){
    studentCount++;      // Increment the count when a student is
                         // instantiated
    name = nm;
    test1 = t1;
    test2 = t2;
    test3 = t3;
}

public Student(Student s){
    studentCount++;      // Increment the count when a student is
                         // instantiated
    name = s.name;
    test1 = s.test1;
    test2 = s.test2;
    test3 = s.test3;
}
```

A class is easier to use when it has a variety of constructors. Here is some code that shows how to use the different Student constructors. In a program, one would use whichever constructor best suited one's purpose:

```
Student s1, s2, s3;
s1 = new Student();                  // First student object has
                                     // name "" and scores 0,0,0

s2 = new Student ("Bill",70,80,90);  // Second student object has
                                     // name "Bill" and scores 70,80,90

s3 = new Student (s2);               // Third student object also has
                                     // name "Bill" and scores 70,80,90

s3.setName ("Ann");                  // Third student object now has
s3.setScore (1,75);                  // name "Ann" and scores 75,80,90
```

There are now three completely separate student objects. For a moment, two of them had the same state, that is, the same values for their instance variables.

Primitive Types, Reference Types, and the null Value

We mentioned earlier that two or more variables can refer to the same object. We now explore how this is possible, in terms of Java's way of classifying data types. Java classifies all data into two fundamental kinds of types:

1. *Primitive types*—int, double, boolean, char, and the shorter and longer versions of these.

2. *Reference types*—any classes, such as String, Student, TextArea, GBFrame, and so forth.

Variables of these two kinds of types differ in the way in which they are represented in memory. A variable of a primitive type can be viewed as a little box that contains a value of that primitive type. A variable of a reference type can be viewed as a little box that contains a pointer to an object of that type. Thus, the state of memory after the following code

```
int number = 45;
String word = "Hi";
```

is executed could be depicted as shown in Figure 7-8.

FIGURE 7-8
Primitive and reference
types display different data

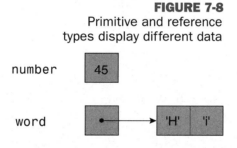

What happens when no initial values are specified for these variables? An instance variable of a primitive type such as int contains a standard default value such as 0. An instance variable of a reference type, such as String or Employee, contains the special pointer value null. Thus, the code segment

```
int number;
String word;
```

would produce the memory shown in Figure 7-9.

FIGURE 7-9
No initial values produce
these results in memory

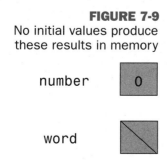

177

The programmer can assign the `null` value to a variable of any reference type. If the variable previously pointed to an object, and no other variable currently points to that object, the computer would reclaim the object's memory during the next garbage collection. This situation is shown in the following code segment and Figure 7-10.

```
Student student = new Student("Mary", 70, 80, 90);
student = null;
```

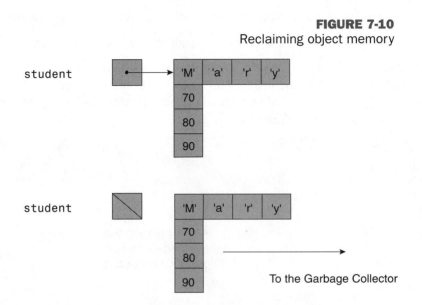

FIGURE 7-10
Reclaiming object memory

A variable of any reference type can be compared to the `null` value, as follows:

```
if (student = null)
    // Don't try to run a method with that student!
else
    // Process the student

while (student != null)
    // Process the student
    // Obtain the next student from whatever source
```

When a program attempts to run a method with an object that is `null`, Java throws a *null pointer exception,* as in the following example:

```
String str = null;
System.out.println (str.length());  // Oops! str is null, so Java throws a
                                     // null pointer exception.
```

Copying Objects

We are now in a position to remedy the potential problems caused by attempting to copy objects with simple assignment statements. The following code creates two references to one student object, when the intent is to copy the contents of one student object to another:

```
Student s1, s2;

s1 = new Student("Mary", 70, 80, 90);
s2 = s1;                                // s1 and s1 refer to the same object
```

When the intent is to copy an object, we must provide a method for doing so. Assuming that a Student method copy exists, we now rewrite the above code so it creates a copy of a student object:

```
Student s1, s2;

s1 = new Student("Mary", 70, 80, 90);
s2 = s1.copy();                         // s1 and s1 refer to distinct objects
```

The implementation of this method does the following:

1. Creates a new instance of Student with the values of the instance variables of the source student.

2. Returns the new student object.

Here is the code:

```
public Student copy(){
    Student s = new Student(name, test1, test2, test3);
    return s;
}
```

 IMPORTANT:

In cases in which instance variables are themselves objects that recognize copy methods, it is a good idea to run the copy methods on them before passing them to the constructor. This process is called *deep copying* and can help to minimize program errors.

Comparing Objects for Equality

We are now in a position to understand why we said, in Lesson 6, that you should always use the method equals instead of the operator == when comparing two strings for equality. Consider the following code segment, which extracts a string from a text field, uses both methods to compare this string to a string literal, and outputs the results:

```
String str = textField.getText();       // Extract string from field.

System.out.println (str == "Java");      // Displays false no matter what
                                         // string was entered.
System.out.println (str.equals ("Java")); // Displays true if the string
                                         // entered was "Java" and false
                                         // otherwise.
```

Explanation:

1. The objects referenced by the variable `str` and the literal `"Java"` are two different string objects in memory, even though the characters they contain are the same. The first string object was created in the text field during user input. The second string object was created internally within the program.

2. The operator `==` compares the references to the objects, not the contents of the objects. Thus, if the two references do not point to the same object in memory, `==` returns `false`. Because the two strings in our example are not the same object in memory, `==` returns `false`.

3. The method `equals` returns `true`, even when two strings are not the same object in memory, if their characters happen to be the same. If at least one pair of characters fails to match, the method `equals` returns `false`.

4. A corollary of these facts is that the operator `!=` can return `true` for two strings, even though the method `equals` also returns `true`.

As you have seen, the operator `==` can also be used with other objects, such as buttons and menu items. In these cases, too, the operator tests for object identity—a reference to the same object in memory. With window objects, the use of `==` is appropriate, because most of the time we want to compare references. In case of other objects, however, such as the student objects discussed in this lesson, the use of `==` should be avoided. To test two student objects for equality, it would be better to implement a method `equals` in the `Student` class. This method would compare the internal components of two students for equality, or would focus perhaps on a single, privileged component, such as the student's name. This component is sometimes called the *key field*.

C S   C A P S U L E : Reliability of Software Systems

The next time you step onto an airliner or lie down beneath an X-ray machine, you might ask yourself about the quality of the software that helps to run them. There are several measures of software quality, and we have mentioned some already in this book, such as readability, maintainability, correctness, and robustness. But perhaps the most important measure is *reliability*. Reliability should not be confused with correctness. Software is correct if its design and implementation are consistent with its specifications. That means that the software actually does what it is supposed to do, as described in what we have called analysis. However, software can be correct in this sense yet still be unreliable.

Recall that during analysis, we construct a model of what the user wants the software to do, and from this model we build a model of what the software will do. Our design and implementation may reflect this second model correctly, but the software may still be unreliable. It is unreliable if we have built the wrong models during analysis—that is, we have misunderstood the user's request (have the wrong model of the user) or we have built a model of the software that does not do what we correctly have understood the user to require.

For example, several decades ago, the Navy contracted with a software firm to build a software system to detect the movements of missiles. The software worked just fine in detecting missiles but was thrown off by the presence of the moon in certain cases.

There have been many reports of software unreliability in commercial software installations as well. One of the more tragic cases is that of the X-ray machine Therac-25, which killed several patients a few years ago.

A classic discussion of software reliability in military applications can be found in Alan Borning, "Computer System Reliability and Nuclear War," *Communications of the ACM,* Volume 30, No. 2 (February 1987): 112–131. Almost every textbook on computer ethics has case studies on computer reliability in commercial applications. A good place to start is Sara Baase, *A Gift of Fire* (Upper Saddle River, NJ: Prentice Hall, 1997), Chapter 4.

Design, Testing, and Debugging Hints

- When developing a user-defined class, write a short tester program that does the following:
  - Creates objects of that class, using each of the different constructor methods.
  - Runs the accessor methods and displays the values of the objects' instance variables.
  - Runs the mutator methods and then displays the values of the variables once again.
  - Tests any class variables and class methods in a similar manner.

- In general, it is useful for testing and debugging to write a `toString` method for each new user-defined class. The `toString` method returns a formatted string that contains the values of an object's instance variables.

- Be sure that each new object of a user-defined class has all of its instance variables initialized when the object is instantiated. Defining one or more constructor methods can do this.

- When clients will need to copy objects, provide a `copy` method. Beware that simple assignment of variables causes multiple references to the same object.

- When clients will need to compare two objects for equality, implement the `equals` method. Remember that `==` and `equals` mean different things.

Summary

In this lesson, you learned:

- An object is an instance of its class, and the process of creating new objects is called instantiation. All objects have three characteristics: behavior, state, and identity. Objects can be either clients or servers.

- A new class template consists of four parts: the class name and modifying phrases; a description of the instance variables; constructor methods; and methods that specify how objects respond to messages. Classes are organized in a hierarchy, with superclasses and subclasses. A new class inherits the characteristics of its superclass.

- Menus and titles are window objects that provide additional information about a program interface and a means of entering commands into a program.

- The `static` modifier indicates that a variable or method belongs to the class as a whole rather than to individual objects.

- Java classifies all data into two types: primitive and reference.

- The `copy` method provides a safe way of copying data from one object to another.

WRITTEN QUESTIONS

Write your answers to the following questions.

1. Explain the difference between a class and an instance of a class.

2. Explain the difference between the visibility modifiers `public` and `private`.

3. What are accessor and mutator methods?

4. Develop a design for a new class called `BaseballPlayer`. The attributes of this class are

   name (a `String`)
   team (a `String`)
   home runs (an `int`)
   batting average (a `double`)

   Express your design in terms of a class summary box. The class should have a constructor and methods for accessing and modifying all of the attributes.

5. Explain the difference between a class variable and an instance variable. What are the appropriate uses of each kind of variable?

6. Describe how to set up a menu of options for modifying a baseball player's attributes as specified in Question 4.

7. Implement the method for handling the menu events specified in Question 6. This method should assume that other methods have been implemented to obtain data from the user and update the baseball player's attributes.

LESSON 7 PROJECTS

1. Add the extra constructors and the `copy` method to the `Student` class of this lesson's Case Study, and test these methods thoroughly with a `Tester` program.

2. A student object should validate its own data. The client runs this method, called `validateData()`, with a student object, as follows:

```
String result = student.validateData();
if (result == null)
    <use the student>
else
    messageBox(result);
```

If the student's data are valid, the method returns the value `null`. Otherwise, the method returns a string representing an error message that describes the error in the data. The client can then examine this result and take the appropriate action.

A student's name is invalid if it is an empty string. A student's test score is invalid if it lies outside of the range from `MIN_SCORE` to `MAX_SCORE`, as discussed in this lesson. Thus, sample error messages might be

```
"SORRY: name required"
```

and

```
"SORRY, must have 50 <= test score <= 100"
```

Implement and test this method.

3. Redo the dice-playing program of Lesson 6 so that it uses dice objects. That is, design and implement a `Dice` class. Each instance of this class should have as attributes its current side, the total number of times it has been rolled, and the average of all of the sides it has displayed. There should be accessor methods for all of these attributes, as well as a `toString` method. Two other methods, `roll` and `reset`, are the mutator methods. Be sure to test the `Dice` class in a simple tester program before incorporating it into the GUI-based application.

4. The game of blackjack is played with cards numbered 2 through 10, and the ace, king, queen, and jack. The last three cards each count 10, while the ace can count 1 or 11, depending on the total count in the player's hand. The object of the game for each player is to hit (be dealt cards that total) up to 21 without going over. A player who goes over 21 busts (loses). The player who has the count closest to 21 wins. Players may stay, or pass on further hits, when they get close to 21 and do not wish to risk a bust. When a player draws an ace, it counts as either 1 or 11, depending on which of these two values brings the count closest to 21 without going over. A hand containing an ace that currently counts as 11 is soft, because this ace's value may be changed to a 1 after a subsequent hit. Thus, a hand may contain all four aces, but at most one of these can count as 11.

The dealer has several restrictions. If the dealer's count is less than or equal to 16, the dealer must hit. If the dealer's count is greater than 16, the dealer must stay. Otherwise, the dealer plays the same as any other player.

Design and implement three classes, `Card`, `Dealer`, and `Player`, that allow the user to play blackjack with the computer.

Each instance of the `Card` class should have one attribute, a point. A card's point is initialized with a random number between 1 and 11 when the card is instantiated. The `Card` class provides an accessor method for the point.

A `Player` object maintains a total count of the cards in a hand, and a Boolean flag indicating whether the hand is soft (an ace counting as 11 rather than 1). These values are initially 0 and false, respectively. The `Player` class provides an accessor method for the total count and a mutator method that adds a card's point to the total count.

A `Dealer` object maintains the same attributes as a player. However, the dealer is also responsible for generating cards and returning them to all players, including the dealer. An accessor method should be defined that does this.

Begin by defining each class and testing it with a short tester program. For example, you could create a dealer and ask it to hit until its count equals 16 or exceeds 16.

Then, provide an interface that allows the user to select two buttons, **Hit** or **Stay.** When the user selects **Hit,** a `Dealer` object generates a card and passes it to a `Player` object. A display area should show the player's card points and the total count after each hit.

Finally, make the `Dealer` object a player also. If one of the two players busts, declare the other the winner. If one of the two players stays, let the other continue according to the rules until there is a winner.

5. The blackjack game program of Project 4 has a shortcoming. There are four aces, four twos, four threes, and so on, but there are 16 tens (all the face cards). The `Card` class uses a random-number generator to instantiate a card whose point is between 1 and 10, making it equally likely that an ace will be dealt as a face card. Suggest a method for increasing the probability of dealing a face card and implement it in the program.

CRITICAL THINKING ACTIVITY

The blackjack game of Project 4 has one other shortcoming. Using our current methods, there is a chance, although a remote one, that more than four of the cards dealt will be aces, or twos, or some other small nonface card. Suggest a method for solving this problem, and implement it in the program. (You will see an easy way to solve this problem with arrays in Lesson 8.)

UNIT 2 REVIEW QUESTIONS

TRUE/FALSE

On a separate piece of paper, type True if the statement is true or False if it is not.

T   F   1. Each method can declare its own private variables, called local variables.

T   F   2. The lifetime of a variable is the region on the program within which it can be used.

T   F   3. Recursion is when a method calls itself.

T   F   4. The logical operator OR is indicated by !.

T   F   5. A `boolean` variable is used to manipulate characters and strings.

T   F   6. The keyword `final` placed at the beginning of a declaration means that values cannot be changed later.

T   F   7. A mutator method is used to ask an object for the values of its data attributes.

T   F   8. A new class inherits the characteristics of its superclass.

T   F   9. Variables can apply to a class as a whole, rather than to an individual object.

T   F   10. The purpose of a constructor is to change the data type of an object.

FILL IN THE BLANKS

On a separate piece of paper, type the information necessary to complete the following statements.

1. A method that has a single clearly defined reponsibility is said to have _____.

2. Two methods in a program that have the same name but not the same number and types of parameters are said to be _____.

3. If a variable is declared outside all methods, it is said to be _____.

4. Simplified methods that contain only enough code to indicate that they are called appropriately are called _____.

5. The _____ statement provides a simple way to get out of a loop before all the statements in the loop process.

6. The _____ data type can be used for numbers in the range of –128 to 127.

7. The easiest way to increase numbers by 1 in a program is to use the _____ operator.

8. The process of creating a new object is called _____.

9. The process of deleting unreferenced objects from memory is called _____.

10. A variable that applies to a class as a whole is called a(n) _____.

WRITTEN QUESTIONS

On a separate piece of paper, type the answers to the following questions or problems.

1. Explain the difference between a global variable and a local variable, and give an example of each.

2. Assume that x, y, and z are `boolean` variables. Draw truth tables for the expressions below.
   a. `x && y || z`
   b. `!(x || y || z)`
   c. `x && (y || z)`

3. Write a method that returns a randomly generated lowercase letter. The method expects no parameters and returns a value of type `char`.

4. What is data encapsulation? Why is it important?

5. Describe what a class constructor does.

UNIT 2 APPLICATIONS

1. Write a program that takes as inputs the lengths of three sides of a triangle and displays in a message box whether the triangle is scalene, isosceles, and equilateral. Useful facts:

   ■ In a triangle, the longest side must be less than the sum of the other two sides.

   ■ A scalene triangle has all sides unequal.

   ■ An isosceles triangle has two sides equal.

   ■ An equilateral triangle has all sides equal.

2. In the game of craps, a player provides an initial bankroll and bets from this amount on each roll of the dice. On each roll, the sum of the faces is taken. The outcomes are as follows:

   ■ If 7 or 11 is rolled, the player wins.

   ■ If 2, 3, or 12 is rolled, the player loses.

- Otherwise, the number rolled becomes the player's point. The player rolls the dice repeatedly until the player wins by making point (getting the same number as on the first roll) or loses by crapping out (getting a 7).

Design and implement a craps machine that allows the user to play craps. This machine should be defined as a new class. The interface accepts an amount of money representing an initial bankroll. Before each roll of the dice, the user must make a bet. The interface should control the user's options by enabling and disabling the appropriate command buttons. At the end of the game, program should display the amount of the user's current bankroll (after adding the gains and deducting the losses).

3. A perfect number is a positive integer such that the sum of the divisors equals the number. Thus, $28 = 1 + 2 + 4 + 7 + 14$ is a perfect number. If the sum of the divisors is less than the number, it is deficient. If the sum exceeds the number, it is abundant. Write a program that takes a positive integer as input and displays a message box that indicates whether the number entered is perfect, deficient, or abundant. Your program should define the following two methods:

```
boolean isDivisor (int number, int divisor)
int divisorSum (int number)
```

The method `isDivisor` returns `true` if the `divisor` parameter is a divisor of the `number` parameter, and `false` otherwise. The `divisorSum` method uses `isDivisor` to accumulate and return the sum of the proper divisors of the `number` parameter. Be sure to design and test the program incrementally, that is, verify that `isDivisor` works correctly before using it in `divisorSum`.

4. A standard experiment is to drop a ball to see how high it bounces. Once the "bounciness" of the ball is determined, the ratio gives a bounciness index. For example, if a ball dropped from a height of 10 feet bounces 6 feet high, the index is 0.6 and the total distance traveled by the ball is 16 feet after one bounce. If the ball continues bouncing, the distance after two bounces would be $10 + 6 + 3.6 = 25.6$ feet. Note that the distance traveled for each bounce is the distance to the floor plus 0.6 of that distance as the ball comes back up.

Write a program that takes as inputs the initial height of the ball (in feet), the index of the ball's bounciness, and the number of times the ball is allowed to continue bouncing. The program should output the total distance traveled by the ball. At some point in the process, the distance traveled by the ball after a bounce might become negligible, for example, less than 0.00001 inches. If that stage is reached, terminate the process and output the total distance.

CRITICAL THINKING ACTIVITY

A number is prime if it has no divisors (other than 1) that are less than or equal to its square root. The number 1 is not prime. Design and implement a method, `isPrime`, that returns `true` if its parameter is a prime number and `false` otherwise. You should use the `isDivisor` method developed in Application 3 in the implementation of `isPrime`. Then use these methods in a program that takes as input a number N, and displays as output a list of the first N prime numbers.

ARRAYS, INHERITANCE, AND GRAPHICS

UNIT 3

Unit 3 Estimated Time: 11 hours

ARRAYS, SEARCHING, AND SORTING

Upon completion of this lesson, you should be able to:

■ Write programs using arrays to handle collections of similar items.

■ Add window objects such as check boxes, radio buttons, and lists to programs.

■ Construct programs using the model/view pattern.

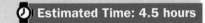 **Estimated Time: 4.5 hours**

Arrays

There are situations in which programs need to manipulate many similar items, a task that would be extremely awkward using the Java language features encountered so far. The Student class from Lesson 7 gives a glimpse of the problem. Currently, a student has three test scores, but imagine how tedious and lengthy the code would become if a student had 20 test scores, instead. The declarations for the instance variables would look like this:

```
private String name;
private int test1,  test2,  test3,  test4,  test5;
private int test6,  test7,  test8,  test9,  test10;
private int test11, test12, test13, test14, test15;
private int test16, test17, test18, test19, test20;
```

and the computation of the average like this:

```
// Compute and return a student's average
public int getAverage(){
    long average;
    average = Math.round((test1 + test2  + test3  + test4  + test5 +
                          test6  + test7  + test8  + test9  + test10 +
                          test11 + test12 + test13 + test14 + test15 +
                          test16 + test17 + test18 + test19 + test20) / 20);
    return (int) average;
}
```

The other methods in the program would also require similar changes.

Fortunately, there is an easier way of handling the situation. Most programming languages, including Java, provide a data structure called an *array*. In Java, an array is an ordered collection of similar *items* or *elements*—for instance, a collection of integers, or doubles, or characters, or objects of the same type.

An array, as a whole, has a single name, and the items in an array are referred to in terms of their *position* within the array. Figure 8-1 clarifies these ideas.

FIGURE 8-1
Arrays are collections of similar items

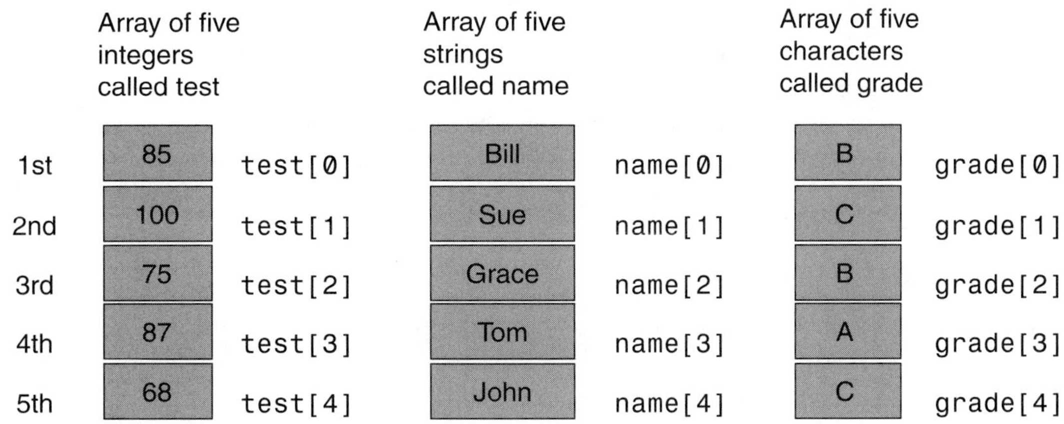

	Array of five integers called test		Array of five strings called name		Array of five characters called grade	
1st	85	test[0]	Bill	name[0]	B	grade[0]
2nd	100	test[1]	Sue	name[1]	C	grade[1]
3rd	75	test[2]	Grace	name[2]	B	grade[2]
4th	87	test[3]	Tom	name[3]	A	grade[3]
5th	68	test[4]	John	name[4]	C	grade[4]

In the diagram, each array contains five elements or has a *size* of five. The first element in the array test is referred to as test[0], the second as test[1], and so on. Here we encounter again Java's convention of numbering from 0 rather than from 1, a convention that is guaranteed to cause you grief whenever you accidentally revert to your lifelong habit of counting from 1. Thus, the elements in an array of size 100 are numbered from 0 to 99. An item's position within an array is indicated by a number (0 refers to the first item in the array, 1 refers to the second item, and so on). This number is called its *index* or *subscript*.

Simple Manipulations

The following snippets of code illustrate some basic array manipulations. First we declare and instantiate an array of 500 integer values. By default, all the values are initialized to 0. More will be said later about declaring arrays.

```
int[] abc = new int[500];
```

Now we declare some other variables:

```
int i = 3;
int temp;
double avFirstFive;
```

The basic syntax for referring to an array element has the form

```
<array name>[<index>]
```

where <index> must be between 0 and the array's size less 1. (Remember that 0 refers to the first item in the array, 1 refers to the second item, and so on, so the last subscript is the array's size less 1.) The subscript operator ([ ]) has the same precedence as the method selector (.).

Assign values to the first five elements:

```
abc[0] = 78;                   //1st element 78
abc[1] = 66;                   //2nd element 66
abc[2] = (abc[0] + abc[1]) / 2; //3rd element average of first two
abc[i] = 82;                   //4th element 82
abc[i + 1] = 94;               //5th element 94
```

Assign a value to the 500th element:

```
abc[499] = 76;                 //500th element 76
```

The Java interpreter checks subscripts before use to make sure that they are within bounds, and throws an exception if they are not. This is similar to the interpreter's behavior when a program attempts to divide by 0. In the present situation, subscripts must be between 0 and 499.

```
abc[-1] = 74;                  //NO! NO! NO! Out of bounds
abc[500] = 88;                 //NO! NO! NO! Out of bounds
```

Compute the average of the first five elements:

```
avFirstFive = (abc[0]+abc[1]+abc[2]+abc[3]+abc[4])/5;
```

Interchange the fourth and fifth elements of the array. Initially i is 3, abc[i] is 82, and abc[i + 1] is 94.

```
temp = abc[i];         //temp now equals 82
abc[i] = abc[i+1];     //abc[i] now equals 94
abc[i + 1] = temp;     //abc[i + 1] now equals 82
```

You do not have to remember an array's size. The array itself makes this information available by means of a public instance variable called length:

```
System.out.println ("The size of abc is: " + abc.length);
```

Looping Through Arrays

There are many situations in which one needs to loop through all the elements of an array. Here are several of the most common. Assume in these examples that abc is an array of 500 integers.

SUM THE ELEMENTS

Here is code that adds the numbers in an array. Each time through the loop we add a different array element to the sum. On the first iteration we add abc[0] and on the last abc[499].

```
int sum;
sum = 0;
for (i = 0; i < 500; i++)
    sum = sum + abc[i];
```

COUNT THE OCCURRENCES

One can determine how many times a number x occurs in an array by comparing x to each element and incrementing count every time there is a match:

```
int x;
int count;
```

```
x = ...;                        //Assign the search number to x
count = 0;
for (i = 0; i < 500; i++){
    if (abc[i] == x) count++;
}
```

DETERMINE PRESENCE OR ABSENCE

To determine if a number is present in an array, one could count the occurrences, but alternatively one could save time by breaking out of the loop as soon as the first match is found. Here is code based on this idea. The Boolean variable found indicates the outcome of the search:

```
int x;
boolean found;
x = ...;
found = false;              // Initially assume x is not present
for (i = 0; i < 500; i++){
    if (abc[i] == x){
        found = true;
        break;                  // No point in continuing once x is found
                                // so break out of the loop
    }
}
if (found) messageBox ("Found");
else       messageBox ("Not Found");
```

DETERMINE FIRST LOCATION

As a variation on the preceding example, we find the first location of x in an array. The variable loc initially equals -1, meaning that we have not found x yet. We then iterate through the array, comparing each element to x. As soon as we find a match, we set loc to the location and break out of the loop. If x is not found, loc remains equal to -1.

```
int x;
int loc;
x = ...;
loc = -1;
for (i = 0; i < 500; i++){
    if (abc[i] == x){
        loc = i;
        break;
    }
}
if (loc == -1) messageBox ("Not Found");
else            messageBox ("Found at index " + loc);
```

LOCATE THE LARGEST NUMBER

To locate the largest number in an array, we begin by saying that the first element is the largest so far. On the first iteration through the loop, we compare the largest so far to the second element. If the second element is larger, we say it is the largest so far. On the second iteration we compare the largest so far to the third element and so on. Sooner or later we encounter the largest element and remember its location.

```
int loc = 0;                        // Largest so far is at index 0
for (i = 1; i < 500; i++){
```

```
    if (abc[i] > abc[loc])
        loc = i;                    // Largest so far is at index i
}
```

To illustrate the above, consider the list shown in Figure 8-2, whose largest element is 97.

FIGURE 8-2

87	abc[0]
75	abc[1]
89	abc[2]
84	abc[3]
...	...
97	abc[120]
...	...
64	abc[499]

Initially, the largest so far is at location 0 (loc = 0).

During 1st iteration compare   abc[loc] and abc[1].

During 2nd iteration compare   abc[loc] and abc[2].
                                      Largest so far is at location 2 (loc = 2).

During 3rd iteration compare   abc[loc] and abc[3].
...

During 120th iteration compare   abc[loc] and abc[120].
                                      Largest so far is at location 120 (loc = 120)

...

MOVE THE SMALLEST TO THE FIRST POSITION

It is easy to move the smallest number in an array to the first position. Compare the first number to each of the remaining ones. Anytime a smaller number is found, interchange it with the first number and continue the comparisons. The smallest number will end up in the first position, and the rest of the numbers will be shuffled around a little:

```
int j;
int temp;
for (j = 1; j < 500; j++){
    if (abc[j] < abc[0]){
        temp = abc[j];
        abc[j] = abc[0];
        abc[0] = temp;
    }
}
```

Here is an illustration based on an array of five elements. Table 8-1 shows the initial order of the numbers in the array and their order after each iteration through the loop. After the last iteration, the smallest number is at the top and the remaining numbers are somewhat shuffled.

TABLE 8-1
Order of numbers after all iterations

	INITIAL	J = 1	J = 2	J = 3	J = 4
abc[0]	24	15	15	10	10
abc[1]	15	24	24	24	24
abc[2]	20	20	20	20	20
abc[3]	10	10	10	15	15
abc[4]	16	16	16	16	16

MOVE THE SECOND SMALLEST NUMBER TO SECOND POSITION

After we have moved the smallest number to the top, we can move the second smallest to the second position in a similar manner. This time we compare abc[1] to each of the numbers below it and interchange whenever we encounter a smaller number:

```
int j;
int temp;
for (j = 2; j < 500; j++){
    if (abc[j] < abc[1]){
        temp = abc[j];
        abc[j] = abc[1];
        abc[1] = temp;
    }
}
```

SORT IN ASCENDING ORDER

The idea behind the two previous snippets of code can be extended to yield an algorithm for sorting the numbers in an array from smallest to largest. It is called an *exchange sort*:

```
int i, j;
int temp;
for (i = 0; i < (500-1); i++){
    for (j = i + 1; j < 500; j++){
        if (abc[j] < abc[i]){
            temp = abc[j];
            abc[j] = abc[i];
            abc[i] = temp;
        }
    }
}
```

The outer loop is executed 499 times. Table 8-2 shows what happens on each pass through the outer loop and the corresponding range of activity for the inner loop.

TABLE 8-2
Sorting in ascending order

OUTER LOOP VALUE OF i	INNER LOOP RANGE OF VALUES FOR j	INNER LOOP ELEMENTS COMPARED	RESULT ACHIEVED BY INNER LOOP
0	1...499	abc[0] to abc[1...499]	abc[0] smallest
1	2...499	abc[1] to abc[2...499]	abc[1] next smallest
2	3...499	abc[3] to abc[3...499]	abc[2] next smallest
...	...	...	
498	499...499	abc[498] to abc[499]	abc[498] next smallest

SORT IN DESCENDING ORDER

A trivial modification of the above code yields an algorithm that sorts the numbers from largest to smallest. Simply replace

```
if (abc[j] < abc[i]){
```

with

```
if (abc[j] > abc[i]){
```

INSERT AN ELEMENT

Sometimes only an array's initial slots are in use. For instance, an array might be capable of holding 500 integers, but only the first 154 positions might be occupied. Additional values can then be added to the array, either between values already present or after the last one. When inserting between existing values, care must be taken. All the values at and below the insertion point must first be moved down one position.

To illustrate, suppose that:

- An array abc can hold up to 500 numbers.

- The variable indexLastElement indicates the position of the last element currently in use.

Suppose further that:

- The array is not full (indexLastElement < 499).

- The variable newValue contains the value to insert.

- The variable insertionPoint indicates the insertion point, and insertionPoint <= indexLastElement + 1.

The code to perform the insertion is quite simple. Notice that the variable i decreases on successive iterations. The last element is first moved. The next to last element is then moved into the newly vacated slot and so forth. Finally, the new value is assigned to the array at the insertion point.

```
for (i = indexLastElement; i >= insertionPoint; i--)
    abc[i + 1] = abc[i];
```

```
abc[insertionPoint] = newValue;
indexLastElement++;
```

Figure 8-3 is an illustration of the process showing an array before and after the insertion of the number 6. The active or used portion of the array is shaded.

FIGURE 8-3

An array before and after an insertion

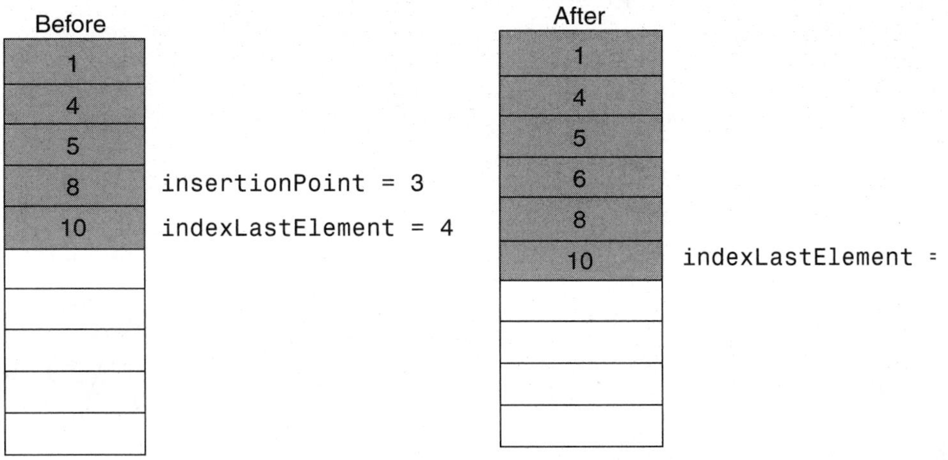

Before

| 1 |
| 4 |
| 5 |
| 8 |
| 10 |
| |
| |
| |
| |

insertionPoint = 3

indexLastElement = 4

After

| 1 |
| 4 |
| 5 |
| 6 |
| 8 |
| 10 |
| |
| |
| |

indexLastElement =

DELETE AN ELEMENT

Deleting elements from partially full arrays is also a common task. Assume the situation is the same as described in the previous section, except that now we want to delete the element at position deletionPoint. We assume that 0 <= deletionPoint <= indexLastElement. Starting at the deletion point, the code overwrites each array element with the element below it.

```
for (i = deletionPoint; i < indexLastElement; i++)
    abc[i] = abc[i + 1];
indexLastElement--;
```

Figure 8-4 shows an array before and after the deletion of the number 5.

FIGURE 8-4

An array before and after a deletion

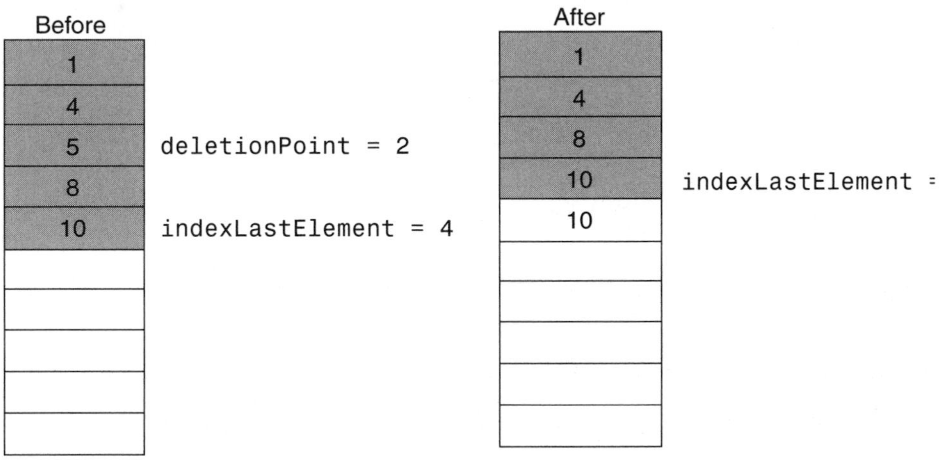

Before

| 1 |
| 4 |
| 5 |
| 8 |
| 10 |
| |
| |
| |
| |

deletionPoint = 2

indexLastElement = 4

After

| 1 |
| 4 |
| 8 |
| 10 |
| 10 |
| |
| |
| |
| |

indexLastElement =

197

Notice that the array now contains two copies of the number 10. This does not cause a problem because the second instance is in the unused portion of the array.

Declaring Arrays

Earlier we declared an array of 500 integers as follows:

```
int[] abc = new int[500];
```

In doing so, we combined two separate statements:

```
int[] abc;                  // Declare abc to be a variable that can
                            // reference an array of integers.
abc = new int[500];         // Instantiate an array of 500 integers for abc to
                            // reference.
```

Arrays are in fact objects and must be instantiated before being used. Several array variables can be declared in a single statement like this:

```
int[] abc, xyz;
abc = new int[500];
xyz = new int[10];
```

or like this:

```
int[] abc = new int[500], xyz = new int[10];
```

Because arrays are objects, two variables can refer to the same array:

```
int[] abc, xyz;
abc = new int[10];                   // Instantiate an array of 10 integers.
xyz = abc;                           // xzy and abc refer to the same array.
xyz[3] = 100;                        // Changing xyz changes abc as well.
System.out.println ("" + abc[3]);    // 100 is displayed.
```

If we want abc and xyz to refer to two separate arrays that happen to contain the same values, we could copy all of the elements from one array to the other, as follows:

```
int[] abc, xyz;             // Declare two array variables.
int i;
abc = new int[10];          // Instantiate an array of size 10.
for (i = 0; i < 10; i++)    // Initialize the array
    abc[i] = i*i;           //    a[0]=0 and a[1]=1 and a[2]=4, etc.
xyz = new int[10];          // Instantiate another array of size 10.
for (i = 0; i < 10; i++)    // Initialize the second array.
    xyz[i] = abc[i];
```

Also, because arrays are objects, Java's garbage collector sweeps them away when they are no longer referenced:

```
int[] abc, xyz;
abc = new int[10];          // Instantiate an array of 10 integers.
```

```
xyz = new int[5];        // Instantiate an array of 5 integers.
xyz = abc;               // The array of 5 integers is no longer referenced
                         // so the garbage collector will sweep it away.
```

Arrays can be declared, instantiated, and initialized all in one step. The list of numbers between the braces is called an *initializer list*.

```
int[] abc = {1,2,3,4,5} // abc now references an array of five integers.
```

As mentioned at the outset, arrays can be formed from any collection of similar items. Here then are arrays of doubles, characters, Booleans, strings, and students:

```
double[]    ddd = new double[10];
char[]      ccc = new char[10];
boolean[]   bbb = new boolean[10];
String[]    ggg = new String[10];
Student[]   sss = new Student[10];
String      str;

ddd[5] = 3.14;
ccc[5] = 'Z';
bbb[5] = true;
ggg[5] = "The cat sat on the mat.";
sss[5] = new Student();

sss[5].setName ("Bill");
str = sss[5].getName() + ggg[5].substring(7);
    // str now equals "Bill sat on the mat."
```

There is one more way to declare array variables, but its use can be confusing. Here it is:

```
int aaa[];               // aaa is an array variable
```

That does not look confusing, but what about this:

```
int aaa[], bbb, ccc[];   // aaa and ccc are array variables.
                         // bbb is not. This fact might go unnoticed.
```

which is equivalent to:

```
int[] aaa, ccc;          // aaa and ccc are array variables
int bbb;                 // bbb is not. This fact is obvious.
```

 **IMPORTANT:**

Once an array is instantiated, its size cannot be changed, so make sure the array is large enough from the outset.

199

Parallel Arrays

In some situations it is convenient to declare what are called *parallel arrays*. Suppose you want to keep a list of people's names and ages. This can be achieved by using two arrays in which the corresponding elements are related, for instance:

```
String[] name = {"Bill", "Sue", "Shawn", "Mary", "Ann"};
int[]    age  = {20    , 21   , 19     , 24    , 20};
```

Thus, Bill's age is 20 and Mary's is 24.

Here is a snippet of code that finds the age of a particular person:

```
String searchName;
int correspondingAge;
int i;

searchName = ...;                        // Set this to the desired name
for (i = 0; i < name.length; i++){       // name.length is the array's size
    if (searchName.equals (name[i]){
        correspondingAge = age[i];
        break;
    }
}
```

If for some reason the array of names must be sorted, the correspondence with the ages can be preserved. To achieve this, every time we switch two names, we switch the corresponding ages as well. Here is the relevant code. Figure 8-5 shows the output it produces.

```
String[] name = {"Bill", "Sue", "Shawn", "Mary", "Ann"};
int[]    age  = {20    , 21   , 19     , 24    , 20};

int i, j;
int tempAge;
String tempName;

for (i = 0; i < name.length-1; i++){
    for (j = i + 1; j < name.length; j++){
        if (name[j].compareTo(name[i]) < 0){
            tempName = name[j];
            name[j] = name[i];
            name[i] = tempName;
            tempAge = age[j];
            age [j] = age [i];
            age [i] = tempAge;
        }
    }
}

for (i = 0; i < name.length; i++){
    System.out.println (name[i] + ":" + age[i]);
}
```

FIGURE 8-5
Output from the array

```
Ann:20
Bill:20
Mary:24
Shawn:19
Sue:21
```

There are many more uses for parallel arrays. These examples only hint at the possibilities.

Two-Dimensional Arrays

The arrays we have been studying so far can represent only simple lists of items and are called one-dimensional. For many applications, *multidimensional arrays* are more useful. A table of numbers, for instance, is best implemented as a *two-dimensional array*. Figure 8-6 illustrates a two-dimensional array that has four rows and five columns.

FIGURE 8-6
An array of 20 numbers arranged in
four rows and five columns called a **table**

	column 0	column 1	column 2	column 3	column 4
row 0	0	1	2	3	4
row 1	10	11	12	13	14
row 2	20	21	22	23	24
row 3	30	31	32	33	34

To indicate an element in the array, we specify its row and column position, remembering that indices start at 0:

```
x = table[2][3]  // Set x to 23, the value in (row 2, column 3)
```

Sum the Elements

Manipulating a two-dimensional array is straightforward. For instance, here is code that sums all the numbers in table. The outer loop iterates four times and moves down the rows. Each time through the outer loop, the inner loop iterates five times and moves across a different row.

```
int i, j;
int sum = 0;
for (i = 0; i < 4; i++){      // There are four rows: i = 0,1,2,3
   for (j = 0; j < 5; j++){ // There are five columns: j = 0,1,2,3,4
      sum += table[i][j];
   }
}
```

The above segment of code can be rewritten without using the numbers 4 and 5. The value `table.length` equals the number of rows, and `table[i].length` the number of columns in row `i`.

```
int i, j;
int sum = 0;
for (i = 0; i < table.length; i++){
   for (j = 0; j < table[i].length; j++){
      sum += table[i][j];
   }
}
```

Sum the Rows

Rather than accumulate all the numbers into a single sum, we now compute the sum of each row separately and place the results in a one-dimensional array called `rowSum`. This array has four elements, one for each row of the table. The elements in `rowSum` are initialized to 0.

```
int i, j;
int[] rowSum = {0,0,0,0};
for (i = 0; i < table.length; i++){
   for (j = 0; j < table[i].length; j++){
      rowSum[i] += table[i][j];
   }
}
```

Locate the Largest Number

The next piece of code finds the location of the largest number in the array. The technique is similar to the one we used to find the largest number in a one-dimensional array. We begin by assuming that the largest number is at location (0,0). We then traverse the complete table, comparing each value to the one at location (0,0). Whenever we encounter a larger value, we remember its location and use it in future comparisons.

```
int i, j;
int rowLoc = 0, colLoc = 0;
for (i = 0; i < table.length; i++){
   for (j = 0; j < table[i].length; j++){
      if (table[i][j] > table[rowLoc][colLoc]){
         rowLoc = i;
         colLoc = j;
      }
   }
}
```

Declare and Instantiate

Declaring and instantiating a two-dimensional array extends the same processes as for a one-dimensional array:

```
int[][] table;            // The variable table can reference a
                          // two-dimensional array of integers.
table = new int[4][5];    // Instantiate table as an array of size 4,
                          // each of whose elements will reference an array
                          // of 5 integers.
```

Figure 8-7 is another diagram of `table` that illustrates the perspective revealed in the previous piece of code. The variable `table` references an array of four elements. Each of these elements in turn

FIGURE 8-7

table references an array of four elements

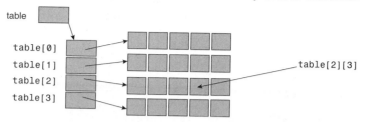

references an array of five integers. Although the diagram is complex, specifying an element in the resulting two-dimensional array is the same as before, for instance, table[2][3].

Initializer lists can be used with two-dimensional arrays. This requires a list of lists. The number of inner lists determines the number of rows, and the size of each inner list determines the size of the corresponding row. The rows do not have to be the same size, but they are in this example:

```
int[][] table = {{0,1,2,3,4},       // row 0
                 {10,11,12,13,14},   // row 1
                 {20,21,22,23,24},   // row 2
                 {30,31,32,33,34}};  // row 3
```

Variable Length Rows

Occasionally the rows of a two-dimensional array are not the same size, although they usually are. Consider the following improbable declaration:

```
int[][] table;
table = new int[4][];       // table has 4 rows
table[0] = new int[6];      // row 0 has 6   elements
table[1] = new int[10];     // row 1 has 10  elements
table[2] = new int[100];    // row 2 has 100 elements
table[3] = new int[1];      // row 3 has 1   element
```

Finally, remember that all the elements of a two-dimensional array must be of the same type, be they integers, doubles, strings, or whatever.

Arrays and Methods

An array can be passed as a parameter to a method. The method then manipulates the array in whatever manner is appropriate. Because the method manipulates the original array itself and not a copy, changes made to the array are still in effect after the method has completed its execution. Consequently, passing an array to a method can be dangerous, for how can one be sure that the method does exactly what is intended, and neither more nor less? A method can also instantiate a new array and return it using the return statement. Here are some illustrations based on examples presented earlier.

Sum the Elements

Here is a method that computes the sum of the numbers in an integer array. When the method is written, there is no need to know the array's size. The method works equally well with integer arrays of all sizes. However, the method cannot be used with arrays of other types, for instance, doubles. Notice that the method makes no changes to the array and therefore is "safe."

```
int sum (int[] a){
   int i, result = 0;
   for (i = 0; i < a.length; i++)
      result = result + a[i];
   return result;
}
```

Use of the method is straightforward:

```
int[] array1 = {10, 24, 16, 78, -55, 89, 65};
int[] array2 = {4334, 22928, 33291};
...
if (sum(array1) > sum(array2)) ...
```

Search for a Value

The code to search an array for a value is used so frequently in programs that it is worth placing in a method. Here is a method to search an array of integers. The method returns the location of the first array element equal to the search value and –1 if the value is absent:

```
int search (int[] a, int searchValue){
   int location;
   location = -1;
   for (i = 0; i < a.length; i++){
      if (a[i] == searchValue){
         location = i;
         break;
      }
   }
   return location;
}
```

Sort in Ascending Order

The code to sort an array can easily be packaged in a method:

```
void sort (int[] a){
   int i, j;
   int temp;
   for (i = 0; i < a.length-1; i++){
      for (j = i + 1; j < a.length; j++){
         if (a[j] < a[i]){
            temp = a[j];
            a[j] = a[i];
            a[i] = temp;
         }
      }
   }
}
```

This method must be used with caution because it changes the array passed to it.

Sum the Rows

Here is a method that instantiates a new array and returns it. The method computes the sum of each row in a two-dimensional array and returns a one-dimensional array of row sums. The method works even if the rows are not all the same size. We also rely on the fact that Java provides a default value of 0 at each position in the array.

```
int[] sumRows (int[][] a){
    int i, j;
    int[] rowSum = new int[a.length];
    for (i = 0; i < a.length; i++){
        for (j = 0; j < a[i].length; j++){
            rowSum[i] = rowSum[i] + a[i][j];
        }
    }
    return rowSum;
}
```

Here is code that uses the method. Notice that we do not have to instantiate the array oneD, because that task is done in the method sumRows.

```
int[][] twoD = {{1,2,3,4}, {5,6}, {7,8,9}};
int[] oneD;

oneD = sumRows (twoD);      // oneD now equals {10, 11, 24}
```

Copy an Array

Earlier we saw that copying an array must be done with care. Assigning one array variable to another does not do the job. It merely yields two variables referencing the same array. Here is a method that attempts to solve this problem. The first parameter represents the original array and the second, the copy. The original is instantiated before the method is called, and the copy is instantiated in the method.

```
void copyOne (int[] original, int[] copy){
    int i;
    copy = new int[original.length];
    for (i = 0; i < original.length; i++){
        copy[i] = original[i];
    }
}
```

We now run this method in the following code segment:

```
int[] orig = {1,2,3,4,5};
int[] cp;
...
copyOne (orig, cp);
```

When copyOne terminates, we expect the variable cp to refer to an array of five integers. However, that does not happen. Even though the method created a copy of the original array and assigned it to the array parameter, the original variable cp was not changed. The only way to change the cp array is to change the contents of the cells within it. Howver, the cp array had no cells of its own to begin with.

In a correct solution, the method returns the copy, as shown next:

```
int[] copyTwo (int[] original){
    int i;
```

```
      int[] copy = new int[original.length];
      for (i = 0; i < original.length; i++){
         copy[i] = original[i];
      }
      return copy;
   }
```

Here is some code that illustrates the use of `copyTwo`:

```
int[] orig = {1,2,3,4,5};
int[] cp;
...
cp = copyTwo (orig);
```

Other Objects and Methods

Objects of all types, not just arrays, can be passed to and returned from methods. The lessons you have just learned when using arrays in this manner apply equally to all objects.

BreezyGUI: Checkboxes, Radio Buttons, Scrolling Lists, and Choice Lists

To our growing list of window objects we now add checkboxes, radio button groups, scrolling lists, and popup choice lists. Before diving into the details, we present a simple demo program. An initial illustration for the demo program is shown in Figure 8-8 and contains:

- A *checkbox* labeled **Driver** that is currently checked.

- A *radio button* group containing buttons labeled **Married, Single,** and **Divorced** with the option **Single** selected.

- A *scrolling list box.* The list contains the words *Swimming, Reading, Golf, Fishing, Dusting, Cooking,* and *Movies.* Only some of these are visible, and the word *Golf* has been selected

- A *popup choice list.* The list contains the words *Swimming, Reading, Golf, Fishing, Dusting, Cooking,* and *Movies,* but because the word *Golf* has been selected, it is the only word visible.

- A *text area.* This area displays a message when the user selects an item in the scrolling list.

FIGURE 8-8
The demo program produces this window

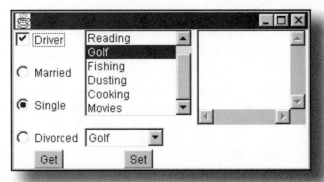

The user and the program can manipulate the settings of the various window objects. The program made the settings shown in Figure 8-8 at startup. When the user clicks the **Get** button, the program reads the current settings and displays them in a Message box such as the one shown in Figure 8-9.

FIGURE 8-9
The message resulting from the program window

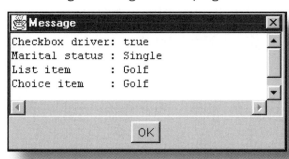

When the user clicks the **Set** button, the program modifies the contents of the scrolling and popup lists and makes several selections, as shown in Figure 8-10.

FIGURE 8-10
The **Set** button produces this window

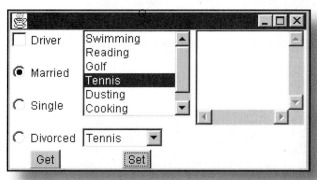

Whenever the user selects, with a single-click, an item in a scrolling list, the program can respond to this selection. Figure 8-11 shows a message displayed in the text area.

FIGURE 8-11
Message displayed in the text area

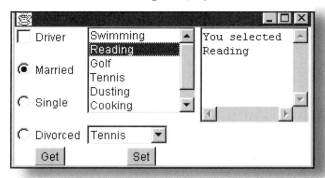

Any time the user double-clicks an item in a scrolling list, the program is informed of both a single click (see previous example) and a double-click. Our demo program displays a message box indicating the item double-clicked and updates the text area with the results of a single-click (Figure 8-12).

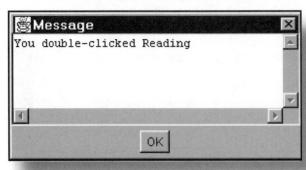

FIGURE 8-12
Message resulting from a double-click

Now that we have seen a simple demonstration, let us look at some of the details.

Checkboxes

Checkboxes are declared in a now familiar manner, for instance,

```
Checkbox cbDriver = addCheckbox ("Driver", 1,1,1,1);
```

Table 8-3 contains four frequently used `Checkbox` methods.

TABLE 8-3
Frequently used `Checkbox` methods

NAME OF METHOD	WHAT THE METHOD DOES
`setState (aBoolean)`	If aBoolean is true, draw a check mark; else clear check mark.
`getState()` `returns aBoolean`	Return true if checked; else return false.
`setLabel(aString)`	Set the label to a string.
`getLabel()` `returns aString`	Return the current label.

Radio Buttons

When checkboxes are placed in a group, they behave like radio buttons, meaning that selecting one automatically deselects the others. To use radio buttons, one must declare a `CheckboxGroup`, several checkboxes, and then add each checkbox to the group. Later, when the program needs to know which checkbox has been selected, it sends the `getSelectedCheckbox()` message to the checkbox group object. Here are relevant lines of code from the demo program:

```
CheckboxGroup cbgMaritalStatus = new CheckboxGroup();   // Radio button
Checkbox cbMarried  = addCheckbox ("Married", 2,1,1,1); // group
Checkbox cbSingle   = addCheckbox ("Single", 3,1,1,1);  //
```

```
Checkbox cbDivorced = addCheckbox ("Divorced", 4,1,1,1); //

// Place the married, single, and divorced checkboxes in a
// radio button group, and select the "Single" option
cbMarried.setCheckboxGroup (cbgMaritalStatus);
cbSingle.setCheckboxGroup (cbgMaritalStatus);
cbDivorced.setCheckboxGroup (cbgMaritalStatus);
cbSingle.setState (true);

... cbgMaritalStatus.getSelectedCheckbox().getLabel()
```

Table 8-4 contains a summary of the methods just discussed.

TABLE 8-4

TYPE OF OBJECT	NAME OF METHOD	WHAT THE METHOD DOES
Checkbox	setCheckboxGroup (aCheckboxGroup)	Adds the checkbox to aCheckboxGroup.
CheckboxGroup	getSelectedCheckbox() returns aCheckbox	Returns the selected checkbox.

Scrolling Lists

The strings in a scrolling list can be manipulated by the user and by the program. When the user clicks on a string, it is automatically highlighted. Later the program can query the list to determine which string the user selected. When the user double-clicks on a string, it is highlighted, and the program is notified immediately. The program is also able to select and, thus, highlight, a string. Finally, the program can add strings to and remove strings from the list. Here are some fragments of code that show how the demo program declares and manipulates a scrolling list.

```
List ltHobbies  = addList       (1,2,1,3);          // Scrolling list

// Load up the list object
ltHobbies.add ("Swimming", 999);   // 999 is larger than list size
ltHobbies.add ("Reading", 999);    // therefore string added to
ltHobbies.add ("Golf", 999);       // end of list
ltHobbies.add ("Fishing", 999);
ltHobbies.add ("Dusting", 999);
ltHobbies.add ("Cooking", 999);
ltHobbies.add ("Movies", 999);
ltHobbies.select (2);              // select the 3rd string

// Determine which string has been selected and retrieve it
i = ltHobbies.getSelectedIndex();
selection = ltHobbies.getItem(i);

ltHobbies.remove (3);              // Remove 4th item, "Fishing"
ltHobbies.add ("Tennis", 3);      // Add "Tennis" in 4th position
ltHobbies.select (3);             // Select 4th item
```

Table 8-5 summarizes the commonly used Java `List` methods. Note that positions within a list are zero based.

TABLE 8-5
Commonly used `List` methods

NAME OF METHOD	WHAT THE METHOD DOES
add(aString,anInteger) returns void	To the list, adds a string at the indicated position. If anInteger is –1 or is larger than the list's size, adds the string to the list's end.
getItem(anInteger) returns aString	Returns the string at the indicated position. An exception is thrown if anInteger is out of bounds.
getItemCount() returns anInteger	Returns the list's length.
getItems() returns arrayOfString	Returns an array containing all the strings in the list.
getSelectedIndex() returns anInteger	Returns the index of the selected item and –1 if no item is selected.
remove(anInteger) returns void	Removes the indicated item. An exception is thrown if anInteger is out of bounds.
remove(aString) returns void	Removes the first instance of aString. An exception is thrown if aString is absent.
removeAll() returns void	Removes all the items from the list.
replaceItem (aString, anInteger)	Replaces the item at the indicated position with aString.
select(anInteger) returns void	Selects the item at the indicated position. An exception is thrown if anInteger is out of bounds.

The method `addList` is provided for your convenience by **BreezyGUI**. This package also provides two methods for responding to events that occur in scrolling lists, as listed in Table 8-6.

TABLE 8-6
Methods used in scrolling lists

NAME OF THE METHOD	WHAT THE METHOD DOES
void listItemSelected(List listObj)	The framework invokes this method when the user selects a list item with a single-click or a double-click. The application may or may not implement this method to take the appropriate action. The parameter is the list in which the item was selected. The programmer can use the List methods getSelectedIndex() and getItem(int) to determine the selected item.

TABLE 8-6

(continued)

Lesson ⑧ Arrays, Searching, and Sorting

NAME OF THE METHOD	WHAT THE METHOD DOES
void listDoubleClicked(List listObj, String itemClicked)	The framework invokes this method when a list item is double-clicked. The application should implement this method to take the appropriate action. The parameters are the list and the list item where the event occurred. **Note:** This method is invoked *after* the method listItemSelected.

Applications are free to ignore single-clicks in a scrolling list and omit the implementation of listItemSelected. However, if the application is to ignore double-clicks, the programmer must implement a listDoubleClicked method that does nothing. Otherwise, a Message box displays a reminder to implement this method.

Popup Choice Lists

A popup choice list and a scrolling list look very different, but in other respects they have much in common. Their main difference, from the perspective of this demonstration, is that double-clicking on a popup list has no effect. Table 8-7 is a summary of some useful Choice methods:

TABLE 8-7

Choice methods

NAME OF METHOD	WHAT THE METHOD DOES
insert (aString,anInteger) returns void	In the list, inserts a string at the indicated position. If anInteger is larger than the list's size, adds the string to the list's end. An exception is thrown if anInteger is negative.
getItem(anInteger) returns aString	Returns the string at the indicated position. An exception is thrown if anInteger is out of bounds.
getItemCount() returns anInteger	Returns the list's length.
getSelectedIndex() returns anInteger	Returns the index of the selected item and −1 if no item is selected.
remove(anInteger) returns void	Removes the indicated item. An exception is thrown if anInteger is out of bounds.
remove(aString) returns void	Removes the first instance of aString. An exception is thrown if aString is absent.
removeAll() returns void	Removes all the items from the list.
select(anInteger) returns void	Selects the item at the indicated position. An exception is thrown if anInteger is out of bounds.

Code for the Demo

Here is the complete code for the demonstration program.

```java
import java.awt.*;
import BreezyGUI.*;

public class Test extends GBFrame{

    // Declare the window objects. The variables have been given prefixes
    // that indicate their type. Doing this is not necessary, but hopefully
    // it makes the program more readable.
    //
    // Prefix          Type of Object
    //   cb              Checkbox
    //   ch              Choice
    //   lt              List
    //   bt              Button

    Checkbox cbDriver    = addCheckbox ("Driver", 1,1,1,1);    // Checkbox

    CheckboxGroup cbgMaritalStatus = new CheckboxGroup();      // Radio button
    Checkbox cbMarried   = addCheckbox ("Married", 2,1,1,1);   // group
    Checkbox cbSingle    = addCheckbox ("Single", 3,1,1,1);    //
    Checkbox cbDivorced  = addCheckbox ("Divorced", 4,1,1,1);  //

    Choice   chHobbies   = addChoice   (4,2,1,1);              // Popup choice list

    List     ltHobbies   = addList     (1,2,1,3);              // Scrolling list
    TextArea ltHobbyOut  = addTextArea ("", 1,3,1,3);          // Output of selected
                                                              // list item.

    Button   btGet       = addButton   ("Get", 5,1,1,1);  // Command buttons
    Button   btSet       = addButton   ("Set", 5,2,1,1);

    // Constructor
    public Test(){
        // Load up the list object
        ltHobbies.add ("Swimming", 999);   // 999 larger than list size
        ltHobbies.add ("Reading", 999);    // therefore string added to
        ltHobbies.add ("Golf", 999);       // end of list
        ltHobbies.add ("Fishing", 999);
        ltHobbies.add ("Dusting", 999);
        ltHobbies.add ("Cooking", 999);
        ltHobbies.add ("Movies", 999);
        ltHobbies.select (2);              // select the 3rd string

        // Load up the choice object
        chHobbies.insert ("Swimming", 999);  // 999 larger than list size
        chHobbies.insert ("Reading", 999);   // therefore inserts at end
        chHobbies.insert ("Golf", 999);      // of list
        chHobbies.insert ("Fishing", 999);
        chHobbies.insert ("Dusting", 999);
        chHobbies.insert ("Cooking", 999);
        chHobbies.insert ("Movies", 999);
```

```
        chHobbies.select (2);                    // select the 3rd string

    // Mark the driver checkbox
    cbDriver.setState (true);

    // Place the married, single, and divorced checkboxes in a
    // radio button group, and select the "Single" option
    cbMarried.setCheckboxGroup (cbgMaritalStatus);
    cbSingle.setCheckboxGroup (cbgMaritalStatus);
    cbDivorced.setCheckboxGroup (cbgMaritalStatus);
    cbSingle.setState (true);
}

public void buttonClicked (Button buttonObj){
    String str;
    int i;
    if (buttonObj == btGet){

        // Read the data from the screen and display it in a message box.

        // Examine the driver checkbox
        str  = "Checkbox driver: " + cbDriver.getState() + "\n";

        // Examine the radio button group
        str = str +
            "Marital status : " +
            cbgMaritalStatus.getSelectedCheckbox().getLabel() + "\n";

        // Examine the scrolling list
        i = ltHobbies.getSelectedIndex();
        str = str + "List item      : " + ltHobbies.getItem(i) + "\n";

        // Examine the popup choice list
        i = chHobbies.getSelectedIndex();
        str = str + "Choice item    : " + chHobbies.getItem(i) + "\n";

        // Display the data in a message box
        messageBox (str);

    }
    else{

        // Modify some of the data on the screen.
        cbDriver.setState (false);        // Uncheck driver
        cbMarried.setState (true);        // Choose radio button "Married"

        ltHobbies.remove (3);             // Remove 4th item, "Fishing"
        ltHobbies.add ("Tennis", 3);      // Add "Tennis" in 4th position
        ltHobbies.select (3);             // Select 4th item

        chHobbies.remove (3);             // Remove 4th item, "Fishing"
        chHobbies.insert ("Tennis", 3);   // Add "Tennis" in 4th position
        chHobbies.select (3);             // Select 4th item
    }
}
```

213

```
public void listDoubleClicked (List listObj, String itemClicked){
    // Handle double-clicks on a list item.
    messageBox ("You double-clicked " + itemClicked);
}

public void listItemSelected (List listObj){
    // Handle selection (single click) of a list item.
    int index = listObj.getSelectedIndex();
    String item = listObj.getItem(index);
    ltHobbyOut.setText("You selected \n" + item);
}

public static void main (String[] args){
    Frame frm = new Test();
    frm.setSize (325, 175);
    frm.setVisible(true);
}
}
```

C A S E   S T U D Y   1 : Polynomial Evaluator

A polynomial is an expression that can consist of constants, variables, and exponents. For example, the expressions

- $3x^2 + 2x - 1$

- $5x^3$

- 6

are polynomials. To evaluate a polynomial, we substitute a value for the variable and perform the specified arithmetic. Thus, when $x = 2$, our example polynomials evaluate to 15, 40, and 6, respectively.

A polynomial's constants are called coefficients. Coefficients can be nonnegative integers or real numbers. In this case study, we restrict them to nonnegative integers. Exponents are always nonnegative integers. There can be more than one variable in a polynomial, but in this case study, we allow just one variable, called x. The arithmetic operators in a polynomial are just addition and subtraction. Our example polynomials are actually written in shorthand form. They are equivalent to the complete forms shown below:

SHORTHAND FORM	**COMPLETE FORM**
$3x^2 + 2x - 1$	$3x^2 + 2x^1 - 1x^0$
$5x^3$	$5x^3 + 0x^2 + 0x^1 + 0x^0$
6	$6x^0$

Recall that $x^1 = x$ and $x^0 = 1$. Normally, when we write polynomials, we use the shorthand form. However, when a computer represents a polynomial, it is convenient to translate it to its complete form.

In this case study, we develop a program to evaluate a given polynomial for its value at x. In the Projects at the end of this lesson, we ask you to develop a calculator that manipulates polynomials as a pocket calculator manipulates numbers.

Request

Develop a program to evaluate polynomials.

Analysis

A polynomial has the form:

$$a_n x^n + a_{n-1} x^{n-1} + \ldots + a_1 x + a_0$$

Figure 8-13 shows a suggested interface for the evaluator. To input a polynomial, the user enters the coefficients at the desired positions. The coefficients are displayed in the list labeled **Coef. List** and the polynomial is displayed in the text area labeled **Polynomial.**

FIGURE 8-13

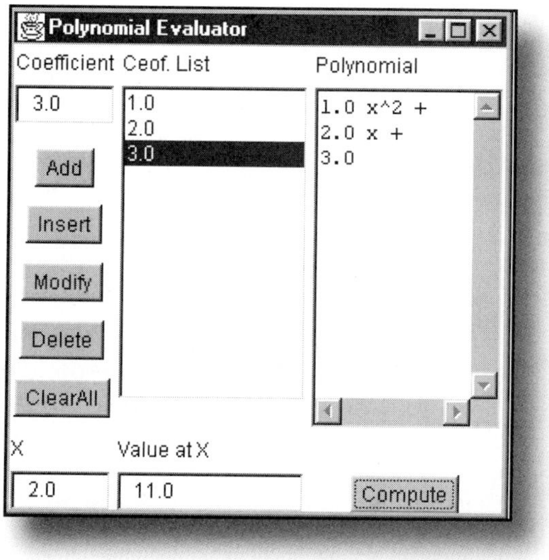

To manipulate the list, the user enters a value in the field labeled **Coefficient** and then clicks one of the buttons below it. The actions of each button are given in Table 8-8.

TABLE 8-8
Functions of buttons in the interface

BUTTON	FUNCTION
Add	Adds the number in the **Coefficient** field to the end of the list.
Insert	Inserts the number in the **Coefficient** field immediately before the selected item.
Modify	Replaces the selected item by the number in the **Coefficient** field.
Delete	Deletes the selected item from the list.
Clear All	Erases all items in the list.

Double-clicking on an item in the list copies it to the **Coefficient** field.

To evaluate the polynomial at *x*, the user enters a number in the field labeled **X** and then clicks the **Compute** button.

Classes

Two classes are needed for this application, an interface class and a polynomial class, called `PolynomialEvaluator` and `Polynomial`, respectively. Because the interface includes so many window objects, we can expect the interface class to be fairly large. However, it is, as usual, straightforward, and we will not discuss it further. The `Polynomial` class is responsible for keeping track of a polynomial's coefficients and implementing any manipulations we intend to perform on polynomials.

Design

The `Polynomial` class will use an array called `coef` to keep track of a polynomial's coefficients. The array's first element holds the polynomial's constant term, and the array's size is one larger than the degree of the polynomial. For instance, the coefficients of the polynomial

$$6x^4 + 3x + 1$$

would be stored as follows:

```
coef[0] = 1      constant term
coef[1] = 3      coefficient of x
coef[2] = 0      coefficient of x²
coef[3] = 0      coefficient of x³
coef[4] = 4      coefficient of x⁴
```

It is always a good idea to provide a class with a rich repertoire of constructors. For the `Polynomial` class, these might include the constructors listed in Table 8-9.

TABLE 8-9
Constructors for the `Polynomial` class

CONSTRUCTOR	WHAT IT DOES
`Polynomial()`	The default constructor initializes a polynomial object with a single coefficient set equal to 0. This is the "zero" polynomial.
`Polynomial(double ccc)`	Initializes a polynomial with a single coefficient set equal to ccc. This is a constant polynomial.
`Polynomial(double[] ddd)`	Initializes a polynomial object by setting its coefficients to the values in the array ddd.
`Polynomial(String[] sss)`	Initializes a polynomial object by setting its coefficients to the values in the array sss. This requires converting the entries in sss from strings to doubles. Also, in the array sss, the coefficients are in reverse order, with the constant term last. This is in keeping with the organization of the interface's **Coef. List** field.

Naturally, the `Polynomial` class should include a `toString` method. To support the needs of this application, a polynomial's string representation has `"\n"` inserted after every term, with the result that each term appears on a separate line when displayed in a text area.

The remaining method, `valueAt`, is listed below:

METHOD	WHAT IT DOES
`valueAt(aDouble)` `returns aDouble`	Returns the value of this polynomial at the parameter.

Implementation

Here is the implementation of the Polynomial class:

```
public class Polynomial extends Object{

    private double[] coef;

        // Suppose that the degree of the polynomial is n, then
        //   coef[0] is the constant term
        //   coef[n] is the highest term
        //   if n > 0, coef[n] must be different from zero
        // In other words the polynomial looks like:
        //   coef[n]*x^n + coef[n - 1]*x^(n - 1) + ... + coef[1]*x + coef[0]


    // -------------- constructors ------------------------------------

    // Construct the zero polynomial

    public Polynomial(){
       coef = new double[1];
       coef[0] = 0;
    }


    // Construct a polynomial from an array of strings. Each string in
    // the array represents a coefficient of the polynomial. The first
    // element contains the coefficient of the highest powered term.

    public Polynomial (String[] inArray){

       // inArray[0] is highest powered term, thus we must reverse the
       // order of inArray when transferring its values to coef

       int i,m = inArray.length;
       int n;

       // The array inArray may be empty. If so, create the zero polynomial
       if (m == 0){
          coef = new double[1];
          coef[0] = 0;
```

217

```
            return;
        }

        // Some of the leading terms of inArray may be zero. After skipping
        // over these, the effective degree of inArray becomes less and is
        // denoted by n.

        for (i = 0; i < m; i++)
            if (Double.valueOf (inArray[i]).doubleValue() != 0) break;
        n = Math.max (m - i, 1);

        // Instantiate a new array of degree n and load it up. Strings in
        // inArray must be converted to doubles.

        coef = new double[n];
        for (i = 0; i < n; i++)
            coef[i] = Double.valueOf (inArray[m - 1 - i]).doubleValue();
    }

// -------------- toString -----------------------------------------
// Create a string representation with line breaks after each term

public String toString(){
    String c;
    String str = "";
    int i, n = coef.length;

    for (i = n - 1; i >= 2; i--){
        if (coef[i] != 0){
            c = String.valueOf (coef[i]);
            str = str + c + " x^" + i + " +\n";
        }
    }

    if (n >= 2){
        if (coef[1] != 0){
            c = String.valueOf (coef[1]);
            str = str + c + " x +\n";
        }
    }
    str += String.valueOf (coef[0]);
    return str;
}

// ------------- valueAt ------------------------------------------
// Return the value of this polynomial at x

public double valueAt (double x){
    int i, n = coef.length;
    double value = coef[n - 1];
    for  (i = n - 2; i >= 0; i--)
        value = value * x + coef[i];
```

```
            return value;
        }

}


import java.awt.*;
import BreezyGUI.*;

public class PolynomialEvaluator extends GBFrame{

    // Window objects-------------------------------------

    // Labels across the top
    Label lbCoefficient = addLabel ("Coefficient" , 1,1,1,1);
    Label lbCoefList    = addLabel ("Coef. List"  , 1,2,1,1);
    Label lbPolynomial  = addLabel ("Polynomial"  , 1,3,1,1);

    // Data entry areas for the coefficients
    DoubleField dfCoefficient = addDoubleField (0  ,2,1,1,1);
    List        ltCoefList    = addList         (   2,2,1,6);

    // Display area for polynomials
    TextArea    taPolynomial    = addTextArea    ("", 2,3,1,6);

    // Labels and data entry areas for x and value
    Label       lbX      = addLabel          ("X"        , 8,1,1,1);
    DoubleField dfX       = addDoubleField (0           , 9,1,1,1);
    Label       lbValue  = addLabel        ("Value at X" , 8,2,1,1);
    DoubleField dfValue = addDoubleField (0             , 9,2,1,1);

    // Command button for polynomial evaluation
    Button btCompute  = addButton ("Compute" ,9,3,1,1);

    // Command buttons for building coefficient list
    Button btAdd      = addButton ("Add"     , 3,1,1,1);
    Button btInsert   = addButton ("Insert"  , 4,1,1,1);
    Button btModify   = addButton ("Modify"  , 5,1,1,1);
    Button btDelete   = addButton ("Delete"  , 6,1,1,1);
    Button btClearAll = addButton ("ClearAll" , 7,1,1,1);

    // Other instance variables-------------------------

    private Polynomial polynomial;

    // Constructor
    public PolynomialEvaluator(){
        setTitle ("Polynomial Evaluator");

        // Initialize and display polynomial
        polynomial = new Polynomial();
        taPolynomial.setText (polynomial.toString());
    }
```

```
// buttonClicked method----------------------------------

public void buttonClicked (Button buttonObj){
    double value;
    String coef                         // Coefficient entered by user
        = String.valueOf (dfCoefficient.getNumber());
    int index                           // Index of selected coefficient
        = ltCoefList.getSelectedIndex();       //   -1 if no selection

    if (buttonObj == btCompute){
        value = polynomial.valueAt (dfX.getNumber());
        dfValue.setNumber (value);


    }
    else{
        if (buttonObj == btAdd){                    // Add coefficient
            ltCoefList.add (coef, -1);
            ltCoefList.select (ltCoefList.getItemCount() - 1);


        }
        else if (buttonObj == btInsert){        // Insert coefficient
            ltCoefList.add (coef, index);
            if (index == -1) index = ltCoefList.getItemCount() - 1;
            ltCoefList.select (index);


        }
        else if (buttonObj == btModify){        // Modify coefficient
            if (index == -1) return;
            ltCoefList.replaceItem (coef, index);
            ltCoefList.select (index);


        }
        else if (buttonObj == btDelete){        // Delete coefficient
            if (index == -1) return;
            ltCoefList.remove (index);


        }
        else if (buttonObj == btClearAll){      // Clear all coefficients
            ltCoefList.removeAll();
        }
        resetPolynomial();
    }

}

// listDoubleClicked method-----------------------------

public void listDoubleClicked (List listObj, String itemClicked){
    // Transfer selected item from "Coefficient" list
    // to "Coefficient" field
    int index = ltCoefList.getSelectedIndex();
    String coef = ltCoefList.getItem(index);
```

```
        dfCoefficient.setText (coef);
    }

    // Private methods--------------------------------------

    private void resetPolynomial(){
        String[] coefArray;                     // Array containing strings in
                                                // list of coefficients

        coefArray = ltCoefList.getItems();
        polynomial = new Polynomial (coefArray);
        taPolynomial.setText (polynomial.toString());
    }

    // main method-----------------------------------------

    public static void main (String[] args){
        Frame frm = new PolynomialEvaluator();
        frm.setSize (300, 300);
        frm.show();
    }
}
```

CASE STUDY 2 : Student Test Scores Again

In the Case Study of Lesson 7, we developed a program to tally the grades of an individual student. The next case study builds on that program in two ways:

1. We extend the program so that it allows the user to maintain a list of students.

2. We modify the Student class so that the three grades are stored in an array rather than in three separate instance variables.

    Both changes illustrate the use of arrays to maintain lists of data.

Request

Modify the student test scores program of Lesson 7 so that it allows the user to maintain a list of students.

Analysis

As before, the interface displays the data for an individual student and allows the user to modify these data. However, the interface now provides a window on the current student in a list of students. The window's buttons allow the user to navigate through this list by moving to the beginning, to the end, to the next student, or to the previous student. Buttons also allow the user to add a student to the end of the list, insert a student before the current student, modify the current student, or delete the current student. The interface displays the index of the current student and the current length of the list in text fields. Finally, the user can sort the list of students by selecting a menu option.

221

Figure 8-14 shows the proposed interface.

FIGURE 8-14

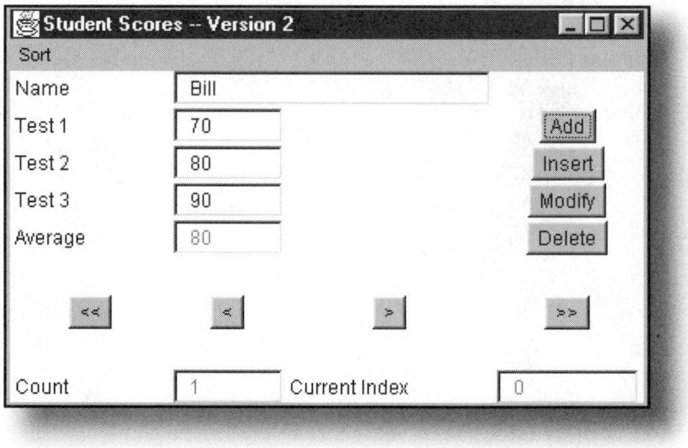

Table 8-10 describes the functions provided by the buttons.

TABLE 8-10
Functions of the buttons in the interface

BUTTON LABEL	EFFECT
Add	Creates a new student object with the data displayed and inserts it at the end of the list. The new student becomes the current student.
Insert	Creates a new student object with the data displayed and inserts it before the current student. The new student becomes the current student.
Modify	Replaces the current student's data with the data displayed.
Delete	Removes the current student from the list. If the list becomes empty or the deleted student was the last student, the data fields are cleared. Otherwise, the next student becomes the current student.
<<	Moves to the first student in the list and displays its data.
<	Moves to the previous student in the list and displays its data.
>	Moves to the next student in the list and displays its data.
>>	Moves to the last student in the list and displays its data.

Design of the StudentTestScores Class

The interface class StudentTestScores now contains three private instance variables for the data:

- An array of Student objects.

- The selected index (an int).

- The current number of students (an int).

This will allow us to use some simple loops to transfer scores between the student and the interface.

The `buttonClicked` method now selects from several methods. These methods either move through the list or update its contents in some way. We provide implementations of several of these methods and leave the others as exercises.

We now use a method to validate the student's data before entering a new student or modifying an existing student.

Design of the Student Class

There are two primary changes to the `Student` class of Lesson 7:

1. The three test scores are stored in an array. This allows much more flexibility than does the use of a separate instance variable for each score.

2. The `Student` class provides a `validateData` method that allows clients to validate a student's data.

Implementation

```java
import java.awt.*;
import BreezyGUI.*;

public class StudentTestScores extends GBFrame{

    // Window objects ------------------------------------------

    Button addButton    = addButton ("Add"   ,2,4,1,1);
    Button insertButton = addButton ("Insert",3,4,1,1);
    Button modifyButton = addButton ("Modify",4,4,1,1);
    Button deleteButton = addButton ("Delete",5,4,1,1);

    Label  blankLine1     = addLabel  (""  , 6,1,1,1);
    Button firstButton    = addButton ("<<", 7,1,1,1);
    Button previousButton = addButton ("<",  7,2,1,1);
    Button nextButton     = addButton (">",  7,3,1,1);
    Button lastButton     = addButton (">>", 7,4,1,1);

    Label nameLabel    = addLabel ("Name"    ,1,1,1,1);
    Label test1Label   = addLabel ("Test 1"  ,2,1,1,1);
    Label test2Label   = addLabel ("Test 2"  ,3,1,1,1);
    Label test3Label   = addLabel ("Test 3"  ,4,1,1,1);
    Label averageLabel = addLabel ("Average" ,5,1,1,1);

    TextField    nameField    = addTextField    ("",1,2,2,1);
    IntegerField test1Field = addIntegerField (0 ,2,2,1,1);
    IntegerField test2Field = addIntegerField (0 ,3,2,1,1);
    IntegerField test3Field = addIntegerField (0 ,4,2,1,1);
    IntegerField averageField = addIntegerField (0 ,5,2,1,1);

    Label        blankLine2
            = addLabel          (""               ,8,1,1,1);
```

```
Label          countLabel
          = addLabel         ("Count"          ,9,1,1,1);

IntegerField countField
          = addIntegerField (0                 ,9,2,1,1);

Label          indexLabel
          = addLabel         ("Current Index" ,9,3,1,1);

IntegerField indexField
          = addIntegerField (-1                ,9,4,1,1);

MenuItem sortByNameMI    = addMenuItem ("Sort","By Name");
MenuItem sortByAverageMI = addMenuItem ("Sort","By Average");

// Other instance variables -------------------------------

private Student[] students = new Student[10];
private int indexSelectedStudent;
private int studentCount;

// Constructor --------------------------------------------

public StudentTestScores(){
   setTitle ("Student Scores -- Version 2");

   indexSelectedStudent = -1;
   studentCount = 0;

   averageField.setEditable (false);
   countField.setEditable (false);
   indexField.setEditable (false);

   displayCurrentStudent();
}


// buttonClicked method -----------------------------------

public void buttonClicked (Button buttonObj){
   if      (buttonObj == addButton)      addStudent();

   // insert, modify, and delete are left as an exercise

   else if (buttonObj == firstButton)    displayFirstStudent();
   else if (buttonObj == previousButton) displayPreviousStudent();
   else if (buttonObj == nextButton)     displayNextStudent();
   else if (buttonObj == lastButton)     displayLastStudent();
}

// menuSelected method-------------------------------------

public void menuItemSelected (MenuItem menuItemObj){
```

```java
        if (menuItemObj == sortByNameMI){
            if (studentCount == 0) return;
            sortStudentsByName ();
            indexSelectedStudent = 0;
            displayCurrentStudent ();
        }

        // Sorting by average left as an exercise
    }

    // Private methods -------------------------------------------

    private void addStudent (){
        if (studentCount == students.length){
            messageBox ("SORRY: student array is full");
            return;
        }

        Student stud = getDataOnScreen ();
        String str = stud.validateData ();
        if (str != null){
            messageBox (str);
            return;
        }

        students[studentCount] = stud;
        indexSelectedStudent = studentCount;
        studentCount++;

        displayCurrentStudent ();
    }

    private Student getDataOnScreen (){
        String nm = nameField.getText ().trim ();

        int[] tests = new int[Student.NUM_TESTS];
        tests[0] = test1Field.getNumber ();
        tests[1] = test2Field.getNumber ();
        tests[2] = test3Field.getNumber ();

        Student stud = new Student (nm, tests);
        return stud;
    }

    private void displayFirstStudent (){
        if (studentCount == 0)
            indexSelectedStudent = -1;
        else
            indexSelectedStudent = 0;
        displayCurrentStudent ();
    }

    private void displayPreviousStudent (){
```

```java
        // Exercise
    }

    private void displayNextStudent(){
        if (studentCount == 0)
            indexSelectedStudent = -1;
        else
            indexSelectedStudent
                = Math.min (studentCount - 1, indexSelectedStudent + 1);
        displayCurrentStudent();
    }

    private void displayLastStudent(){
        // Exericse
    }

    private void displayCurrentStudent(){
        if (indexSelectedStudent == -1){
            nameField.setText ("");
            test1Field.setNumber (0);
            test2Field.setNumber (0);
            test3Field.setNumber (0);
            averageField.setNumber (0);
        }else{
            Student stud = students[indexSelectedStudent];
            nameField.setText (stud.getName());
            test1Field.setNumber (stud.getScore(1));
            test2Field.setNumber (stud.getScore(2));
            test3Field.setNumber (stud.getScore(3));
            averageField.setNumber (stud.getAverage());
        }
        countField.setNumber (studentCount);
        indexField.setNumber (indexSelectedStudent);
    }

    private void sortStudentsByName(){
        for (int i = 0; i < studentCount - 1; i++){
            String namei = students[i].getName();
            for (int j = i + 1; j < studentCount; j++){
                String namej = students[j].getName();
                if (namei.compareTo (namej) > 0){
                    Student temp = students[i];
                    students[i] = students[j];
                    students[j] = temp;
                }
            }
        }
    }

    public static void main (String[] args){
        Frame frm = new StudentTestScores();
        frm.setSize (400, 250);
```

```
            frm.setVisible(true);
    }
}
```

```java
public class Student extends Object{

    public final static int NUM_TESTS = 3;
    private final static int MIN_SCORE = 0;
    private final static int MAX_SCORE = 100;

    private String name;
    private int[] tests = new int[NUM_TESTS];

    public Student(){
        name = "";
        for (int i = 0; i < NUM_TESTS; i++)
            tests[i] = 0;
    }

    public Student(String nm, int[] t){
        name = nm;
        for (int i = 0; i < NUM_TESTS; i++)
            tests[i] = t[i];
    }

    public Student(Student s){
        name = s.name;
        for (int i = 0; i < NUM_TESTS; i++)
            tests[i] = s.tests[i];
    }

    public void setName (String nm){
        name = nm;
    }

    public String getName (){
        return name;
    }

    public void setScore (int i, int score){
        // where 1 <= i <= NUM_TESTS

        tests[i - 1] = score;
    }

    public int getScore (int i){
        // where 1 <= i <= NUM_TESTS

        return tests[i - 1];
    }
```

```
        public int getAverage(){
            int sum = 0;
            for (int i = 0; i < NUM_TESTS; i++)
                sum += tests[i];
            return sum / NUM_TESTS;
        }

        public int getHighScore(){
            int highScore;
            highScore = tests[0];
            for (int i = 1; i < NUM_TESTS; i++){
                highScore = Math.max (highScore, tests[i]);
            }
            return highScore;
        }

        public String toString(){
            String str;
            str = "Name:     " + name  + "\n";
            for (int i = 0; i < NUM_TESTS; i++){
                str += "tests " + i + ":   " + tests[i] + "\n";
            }
            str += "Average: " + getAverage();
            return str;
        }

        public String validateData(){
            if (name.equals ("")) return "SORRY: name required";
            for (int i = 0; i < NUM_TESTS; i++){
                if (tests[i] < MIN_SCORE ¦¦ tests[i] > MAX_SCORE){
                    String str = "SORRY: must have "+ MIN_SCORE
                                + " <= test score <= " + MAX_SCORE;
                    return str;
                }
            }
            return null;
        }
    }
```

The Model/View Pattern

The successful development of large applications depends on the principle of divide and conquer. A large, complex task is best accomplished by dividing it into simpler, cooperating subtasks. However, we did not take full advantage of this precept in the preceding case study. We mixed code for controlling the interface with code for managing the application's underlying data. The StudentTestScores class manages a complex interface and at the same time performs basic manipulations on the array of students— adding, inserting, deleting, and sorting students in the array. Now we modify the case study by dividing the StudentTestScores class in two. The first class, StudentTestScoresView, will manage the interface, and the second class, StudentTestScoresModel, will support all manipulations of the student array.

The breakdown of programs into a model and a view is used widely by computer professionals, and we recommend it highly. It simplifies the task of writing complex applications and increases their maintainability as well. It is common for users to request changes to an application's interface, so it is advantageous to make these changes without getting entangled in the intricacies of the model. Similarly, changes can be made to the model without worrying about the interface. The separation of model and view is also beneficial when an application requires several windows. A separate class supports each window, or view, and all views communicate with a common model.

In general, when we separate an application into a model and view, the responsibilities of the view are:

1. Instantiate and arrange the window objects.

2. Instantiate and initialize the model.

3. Handle user-generated events such as button clicks and menu selections by sending messages to the model.

4. Accurately represent the model to the user.

The responsibilities of the model are:

1. Define and manage the application's data (this usually requires coordinating the activities of several programmer-defined classes).

2. Respond to messages from the view.

The division of labor between the model and the view has proven itself useful in many different situations and is called a *pattern*. There are many other patterns in the realm of object-oriented programming. Each describes how a common programming situation can be handled by a collection of classes with predefined roles communicating in a predefined manner. In Lesson 13 we will see how the model/view pattern can be extended to the famous model/view/controller pattern, also called the MVC pattern.

Throughout the rest of the book, we invite you to modify the case studies so that they use the model/view pattern. On large projects, two programmers can work independently on the view and the model, provided they specify ahead of time the public methods included in the model.

We now illustrate how a segment of code taken from the `StudentTestScores` class can be split between the classes `StudentTestScoresView` and `StudentTestScoresModel`. This will give you a feeling for how the separation is made between the model and view. The code deals with the task of adding a new student to the array of students. First, here is the code as it appears in the `StudentTestScores` class:

```
public void buttonClicked (Button buttonObj){
   if (buttonObj == addButton) addStudent();
   ...
}


void addStudent(){
   // See if the array is full
   if (studentCount == students.length){
      messageBox ("SORRY: student array is full");
      return;
   }

   // Get the data from the screen and make sure it is valid
   Student stud = getDataOnScreen();
   String str = stud.validateData();
   if (str != null){
      messageBox (str);
```

```
        return;
    }

    // Place the new student in the array
    students[studentCount] = stud;
    indexSelectedStudent = studentCount;
    studentCount++;

    // Display the student just added
    displayCurrentStudent();
}
```

In this segment, the code is split fairly equally between managing the interface (getting data from the screen and displaying error messages) and manipulating the array (including worrying about whether the array is full and updating the student count and the index of the selected student).

The corresponding code in the `StudentTestScoresView` class follows. The code deals primarily with the interface and calls a method in the model to manipulate the data.

```
public void buttonClicked (Button buttonObj){
    if (buttonObj == addButton){

        // Get the data from the screen
        Student stud = getDataOnScreen();

        // Ask the model to add the student to the array.
        // If model encounters any problems, it returns an error message
        // else it returns null.
        String str = model.addStudent (stud);
        if (str != null)
            messageBox (str);
        else
            displayCurrentStudent();
    }
    ...
}
```

Here is the code in the model. It is completely independent of the view. The code checks the length of the array and makes sure the data are valid before adding the student to the array. The model keeps track of the student count and the index of the selected student.

```
public String addStudent (Student stud){
    if (studentCount == students.length)
        return "SORRY: student array is full";

    String str = stud.validateData();
    if (str != null)
        return str;

    students[studentCount] = stud;
    indexSelectedStudent = studentCount;
    studentCount++;

    return null;
}
```

Here are complete listings for the StudentTestScoresView and StudentTestScoresModel classes:

```java
import java.awt.*;
import BreezyGUI.*;

public class StudentTestScoresView extends GBFrame{

    // Window objects --------------------------------------

    Button addButton    = addButton ("Add"   ,2,4,1,1);
    Button insertButton = addButton ("Insert",3,4,1,1);
    Button modifyButton = addButton ("Modify",4,4,1,1);
    Button deleteButton = addButton ("Delete",5,4,1,1);

    Label  blankLine1     = addLabel  (""  , 6,1,1,1);
    Button firstButton    = addButton ("<<", 7,1,1,1);
    Button previousButton = addButton ("<",  7,2,1,1);
    Button nextButton     = addButton (">",  7,3,1,1);
    Button lastButton     = addButton (">>", 7,4,1,1);

    Label nameLabel    = addLabel ("Name"    ,1,1,1,1);
    Label test1Label   = addLabel ("Test 1"  ,2,1,1,1);
    Label test2Label   = addLabel ("Test 2"  ,3,1,1,1);
    Label test3Label   = addLabel ("Test 3"  ,4,1,1,1);
    Label averageLabel = addLabel ("Average" ,5,1,1,1);

    TextField    nameField    = addTextField    ("",1,2,2,1);
    IntegerField test1Field   = addIntegerField (0 ,2,2,1,1);
    IntegerField test2Field   = addIntegerField (0 ,3,2,1,1);
    IntegerField test3Field   = addIntegerField (0 ,4,2,1,1);
    IntegerField averageField = addIntegerField (0 ,5,2,1,1);


    Label        blankLine2
            = addLabel        (""                ,8,1,1,1);

    Label        countLabel
            = addLabel        ("Count"           ,9,1,1,1);

    IntegerField countField
            = addIntegerField (0                 ,9,2,1,1);

    Label        indexLabel
            = addLabel        ("Current Index"   ,9,3,1,1);

    IntegerField indexField
            = addIntegerField (-1                ,9,4,1,1);

    MenuItem sortByNameMI    = addMenuItem ("Sort","By Name");
    MenuItem sortByAverageMI = addMenuItem ("Sort","By Average");
```

```java
// Other instance variables ----------------------------------

StudentTestScoresModel model;

// Constructor ------------------------------------------------

public StudentTestScoresView(){
   setTitle ("Student Scores -- Version 3");

   model = new StudentTestScoresModel();

   averageField.setEditable (false);
   countField.setEditable (false);
   indexField.setEditable (false);

   displayCurrentStudent();
}


// buttonClicked method ---------------------------------------

public void buttonClicked (Button buttonObj){
   if (buttonObj == addButton){
      Student stud = getDataOnScreen();
      String str = model.addStudent (stud);
      if (str != null)
         messageBox (str);
      else
         displayCurrentStudent();
   }

   // insert, modify, and delete are left as an exercise

   else if (buttonObj == firstButton){
      model.moveToFirstStudent();
      displayCurrentStudent();
   }
   else if (buttonObj == previousButton); // left as an exercise

   else if (buttonObj == nextButton){
      model.moveToNextStudent();
      displayCurrentStudent();
   }
   else if (buttonObj == lastButton);      // left as an exercise
}

// menuSelected method ----------------------------------------

public void menuItemSelected (MenuItem menuItemObj){

   if (menuItemObj == sortByNameMI){
      model.sortStudentsByName();
```

```
               model.moveToFirstStudent();
               displayCurrentStudent();
         }


         // Sorting by average left as an exercise
      }


      // Private methods ------------------------------------------

      Student getDataOnScreen(){
         String nm = nameField.getText().trim();

         int[] tests = new int[Student.NUM_TESTS];
         tests[0] = test1Field.getNumber();
         tests[1] = test2Field.getNumber();
         tests[2] = test3Field.getNumber();

         Student stud = new Student (nm, tests);
         return stud;
      }


      void displayCurrentStudent(){
         Student stud = model.getCurrentStudent();
         if (stud == null){
            nameField.setText ("");
            test1Field.setNumber (0);
            test2Field.setNumber (0);
            test3Field.setNumber (0);
            averageField.setNumber (0);
         }
         else{
            nameField.setText (stud.getName());
            test1Field.setNumber (stud.getScore(1));
            test2Field.setNumber (stud.getScore(2));
            test3Field.setNumber (stud.getScore(3));
            averageField.setNumber (stud.getAverage());
         }
         countField.setNumber (model.getStudentCount());
         indexField.setNumber (model.getIndexSelectedStudent());
      }

      public static void main (String[] args){
         Frame frm = new StudentTestScoresView();
         frm.setSize (400, 250);
         frm.setVisible(true);
      }
   }
```

```
public class StudentTestScoresModel extends Object{

   // Instance variables ------------------------------------
```

```java
Student[] students = new Student[10];
int        indexSelectedStudent;
int        studentCount;

// Constructor -----------------------------------------------

public StudentTestScoresModel(){
    indexSelectedStudent = -1;
    studentCount = 0;
}

public String addStudent (Student stud){
    if (studentCount == students.length)
        return "SORRY: student array is full";

    String str = stud.validateData();
    if (str != null)
        return str;

    students[studentCount] = stud;
    indexSelectedStudent = studentCount;
    studentCount++;

    return null;
}

public Student getCurrentStudent(){
    if (indexSelectedStudent == -1)
        return null;
    else
        return students[indexSelectedStudent];
}

public int getIndexSelectedStudent(){
    return indexSelectedStudent;
}

public int getStudentCount(){
    return studentCount;
}

void moveToFirstStudent(){
    if (studentCount == 0)
        indexSelectedStudent = -1;
    else
        indexSelectedStudent = 0;
}

void moveToPreviousStudent(){
    // Exercise
}
```

```
        void moveToNextStudent(){
            if (studentCount == 0)
                indexSelectedStudent = -1;
            else
                indexSelectedStudent
                    = Math.min (studentCount - 1, indexSelectedStudent + 1);
        }

        void moveToLastStudent(){
            // Exercise
        }

        void sortStudentsByName(){
            for (int i = 0; i < studentCount - 1; i++){
                String namei = students[i].getName();
                for (int j = i + 1; j < studentCount; j++){
                    String namej = students[j].getName();
                    if (namei.compareTo (namej) > 0){
                        Student temp = students[i];
                        students[i] = students[j];
                        students[j] = temp;
                    }
                }
            }
        }
}
```

Design, Testing, and Debugging Hints

■ Three things should be done to set up an array:

1. Declare an array variable.

2. Instantiate an array object and assign it to the array variable.

3. Initialize the cells in the array with data, as appropriate.

■ When creating a new array object, try to come up with an accurate estimate of the number of cells for the data. If you underestimate, some data will be lost. If you overestimate, some memory will be wasted.

■ To avoid range errors, remember that the index of an array cell ranges from 0 (the first position) to the length of the array minus one.

■ To access the last cell in an array, use the expression <array>.length - 1.

■ As a rule of thumb, it is best to avoid aliasing, that is, having more than one array variable refer to the same array object. When you want to copy the contents of one array to another, do not use the assignment A = B. Write a copy method, instead, and use the assignment A = arrayCopy(B).

■ Aliasing is appropriate when an array is passed as a parameter to a method. In this case, the formal array parameter automatically serves as an alias for the actual array parameter.

Summary

In this lesson, you learned:

- Arrays are ordered collections of similar items or elements. Arrays are useful when a program needs to manipulate many similar items, such as scores for a number of tests. An array can be passed to a method as a parameter

- Parallel arrays are useful for organizing information with corresponding elements.

- Two-dimensional arrays store values in a row-and-column arrangement similar to a table.

- Checkboxes, radio buttons, and lists are window objects that allow the user to control window data.

- Breaking programs into a model and a view simplifies writing and helps with program maintenance. Dividing a program into a model and a view is called a pattern.

LESSON 8 REVIEW QUESTIONS

WRITTEN QUESTIONS

Write your answers to the following questions.

1. Assume the following declarations are made and indicate which items below are valid subscripted variables.

```
int a[] = new int[10];
char b[] = new char[6];
int x = 7, y = 2;
double z = 0.0;
```

   a. a[0]
   b. b[0]
   c. c[1.0]
   d. b['a']
   e. b[a]
   f. a[x + y]
   g. a[x % y]
   h. a[10]
   i. c[-1]
   j. a[a[4]]

2. Assume that the array a defined in Question 1 contains the following values. Indicate if the following are valid subscripts of a and, if so, state the value of the subscript. If invalid, explain why.

```
1  4  6  8  9  3  7  10  2  9
```

   a. a[2]
   b. a[5]
   c. a[a[2]]

    d. `a[4 + 7]`

    e. `a[a[5] + a[2]]`

    f. `a[Math.sqrt(2)]`

3. List the errors in the array declarations below.

    a. `int intArray[] = new double[10];`

    b. `int intArray[] = new int[1.5];`

    c. `double doubleArray = new double[-10]`

    d. `int intMatrix[] [] = new int[10];`

4. Write a method `selectRandom` that expects an array of integers as a parameter. The method should return the value of an array element at a randomly selected position.

5. Write code to declare and instantiate a two-dimensional array of integers with five rows and four columns.

6. Write code to initialize the array of Question 5 with randomly generated integers between 1 and 20.

LESSON 8 PROJECTS

1. Write a program that takes ten integers as input. The program places the even integers into an array called `evenList`, the odd integers into an array called `oddList`, and the negative integers into an array called `negativeList`. The program displays the contents of the three arrays after all the integers have been entered.

2. Write a program that takes as input an unknown number of integer test scores. Assume that there are at most 50 scores, and provide an **Enter** button to accept each score. When the user selects the **Results** button, the program displays the scores sorted from low to high, the scores sorted from high to low, the highest score, the lowest score, and the average score. Write separate methods that take an array of integers as a parameter and compute each of these results.

3. The mode of a list of numbers is the number listed most often. Write a program that takes ten numbers as input and displays the mode of these numbers. Your program should use parallel arrays and a method that takes an array of numbers as a parameter and returns the maximum value in the array.

4. The median of a list of numbers is the value in the middle of the list if the list is arranged in order. Add the capability of displaying the median of the list of numbers to the program of Project 3 .

5. Modify the program of Project 4 so that it displays not only the median and mode of the list of numbers but also a table of the numbers and their associated frequencies.

6. Design, implement, and test a class that represents a deck of cards. First, modify the `Card` class of Project 4 of Lesson 7 so that it maintains the suit of a card (spade, club, heart, or diamond). The constructor of this class should randomly generate not only the number but also the suit of a new card. Then equip the `Deck` class with the methods shown in Table 8-11.

TABLE 8-11
Methods for the Deck class

METHOD	WHAT IT DOES
Deck()	Creates a new deck of 52 cards.
boolean empty()	Returns true if the deck has no cards left and false otherwise.
int size()	Returns the number of cards left in the deck.
Card [] deal(int number)	Precondition: The deck is not empty. Deals a hand (array) of cards from the top of the deck, reducing the size of the deck by the specified number.
Card deal()	Precondition: The deck is not empty. Deals the next card from the top of the deck, reducing the size of the deck by one.

Write a short tester program that creates two decks of cards. The program should deal one card at a time, and display all 52 cards from the first deck. It should also deal four hands of 13 cards each and display them from the second deck.

7. Use the Deck class developed in Project 7 to solve the problems mentioned in the blackjack program of Lesson 7.

8. In this and the next three problems, you will build on the polynomial evaluator of Case Study 1 to develop a polynomial calculator. When completed, the calculator should allow the user to input two polynomials, then select an arithmetic operation and compute the result. The user can also evaluate a polynomial for its value at x (as before), and find where the polynomial's graph crosses the x-axis. Figure 8-15 shows a possible interface.

FIGURE 8-15

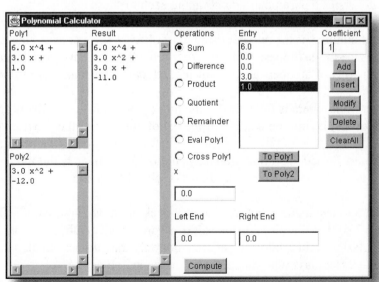

The first step is to update the interface class, `PolynomialEvaluator`, to display the entry of only two polynomials. Note from the sample interface that the entry of a single polynomial takes place as before. However, the user selects the button **To Poly1** or **To Poly2** to determine which polynomial will be updated. Thus, all you need to add at this point are these two buttons and the extra text area for the second polynomial. Test your changes before doing the next project.

9. Modify the `Polynomial` class (see Project 8) by adding methods to perform arithmetic and to test two polynomials for equality. As examples of the computations that the calculator should perform, consider the two polynomials:

P1: $6x^4 + 3x + 1$

P2: $3x^2 - 12$

Table 8-12 shows the results of some computations.

TABLE 8-12

COMPUTATION	RESULT
P1 + P2	$6x^4 + 3x^2 + 3x - 11$
P1 − P2	$6x^4 - 3x^2 + 3x + 13$
P1 * P2	$18x^6 - 72x^4 + 9x^3 + 3x^2 - 36x - 12$
P1 / P2	
Quotient	$2x^2 + 8$
Remainder	$3x + 97$
P1 evaluated at 3	496
In the interval (−.5,0) P1 crosses the x-axis at approximately	−0.371378

Table 8-13 lists the specifications of the methods.

To compute the crossing point, the calculator expects that

■ The left end, a, is less than the right end, b.

■ The polynomial's graph at the left and right ends is on opposite sides of the x-axis.

Test these methods with a short tester program that creates two polynomials, runs all the methods on them, and displays the results in the terminal window.

10. Return to the polynomial calculator's interface (see Project 8) and add the radio buttons that will allow the user to select an arithmetic operation. Then add the text fields for the endpoints, a and b, that will allow the user to determine where the graph of P1 crosses the x-axis. Run the program to verify that the interface is correctly displayed.

TABLE 8-13

METHOD	WHAT IT DOES
equals(aPolynomial) returns aBoolean	Returns true if this and the parameter polynomial are equal.
plus(aPolynomial) returns aPolynomial	Returns the sum of this and the parameter polynomial.
minus(aPolynomial) returns aPolynomial	Returns the difference of this and the parameter polynomial.
times(aPolynomial) returns aPolynomial	Returns the product of this and the parameter polynomial.
quotient(aPolynomial) returns aPolynomial	Returns the quotient obtained when this polynomial is divided by the parameter polynomial.
remainder(aPolynomial) returns aPolynomial	Returns the remainder obtained when this polynomial is divided by the parameter polynomial.

getCrossingPoint
  (double a, double b)
  returns double
	Approximates and returns the point in the interval [*a*,*b*] where this polynomial's graph crosses the *x*-axis. The following constraints must be met:
	
	■ *a* < *b*
	■ The polynomial's graph is on opposite sides of the *x*-axis at *a* and *b*

11. Complete the program for the polynomial calculator (Projects 8 to 10). When the user selects the **Compute** button, examine which radio button is currently on and perform the appropriate operation. Be sure that the results displayed are consistent with those you obtained in Project 10.

12. Complete the student test scores application of Case Study 2 and test it thoroughly.

13. Add menu options to the student test scores application of Case Study 2 that find the highest average grade and the highest overall grade among the students.

14. A magic square is a two-dimensional array of positive integers such that the sum of each row, column, and diagonal is the same constant. For example, Figure 8-16 shows a magic square whose constant is 34. Write a program that takes 16 integers as inputs. The program should determine whether the square is a magic square and display the result in a Message box.

FIGURE 8-16

16	3	2	13
5	10	11	8
9	6	7	12
4	15	14	1

15. Pascal's triangle can be used to recognize coefficients of a quantity raised to a power. The rules for forming this triangle of integers are such that each row must start and end with a 1, and each entry in a row is the sum of the two values diagonally above the new entry. Thus, four rows of Pascal's triangle are

This triangle can be used as a convenient way to get the coefficients of a quantity of two terms raised to a power (binomial coefficients). For example,

$(a + b)^3 = \times a^3 + 3a^2b + 1 \times b^3$

where the coefficients 1, 3, 3, and 1 come from the fourth row of Pascal's triangle.

Write a program that takes the number of rows as input and displays Pascal's triangle for those rows.

16. In the game of Penny Pitch, a two-dimensional board of numbers is laid out as follows:

1 1 1 1 1

1 2 2 2 1

1 2 3 2 1

1 2 2 2 1

1 1 1 1 1

A player tosses several pennies on the board, aiming for the number with the highest value. At the end of the game, the total of the tosses is returned. Develop a program that plays this game. The program should perform the following steps each time the user selects the **Toss** button:

■ Generate two random numbers for the row and column of the toss.

■ Add the number at this position to a running total.

■ Display the board, replacing the numbers with Ps where the pennies land.

Hint: You should use a two-dimensional array of Square objects for this problem. Each square contains a number like those shown above and a Boolean flag that indicates whether a penny has landed on that square.

CRITICAL THINKING ACTIVITY

You have been using a method for searching for data in arrays like the one described in this lesson, but your friend tells you that it's a poor way to search. She says that you're examining every element in the array to discover that the target element is not there. A better way, she says, is to assume that the elements in the array are in alphabetical order. Then examine the element at the middle position in the array first. If that element matches the target element, you're done. Otherwise, if that element is less than the target element, continue the same kind of search in just the portion of the array to the left of the element just examined. Otherwise, continue the same kind of search in just the portion of the array to the right of the element just examined.

Write an algorithm for this search process (a recursive algorithm will be greatly appreciated), and explain why it is better than the search algorithm discussed in this lesson.

INHERITANCE, ABSTRACT CLASSES, AND POLYMORPHISM

OBJECTIVES

Upon completion of this lesson, you should be able to:

■ Organize a set of classes using inheritance.

■ Distinguish abstract and concrete classes.

■ Write polymorphic methods.

■ Pass objects appropriately as parameters to methods.

Estimated Time: 3.5 hours

Introduction

This lesson explores ideas first introduced in Lesson 1: inheritance, abstract classes, and polymorphism.

Inheritance

Java organizes classes in a hierarchy. Classes inherit the instance variables and methods of the classes above them in the hierarchy. A class can extend its inherited characteristics by adding instance variables and methods and by overriding inherited methods. Thus, inheritance provides a mechanism for reusing code and can greatly reduce the effort required to implement a new class.

Abstract Classes

Some classes in a hierarchy must never be instantiated. They are called abstract classes. Their sole purpose is to define features and behavior common to their subclasses. The class `Object`, which is at the base or root of Java's class hierarchy, is an example of an abstract class.

Polymorphism

Methods in different classes, but with a similar function, are usually given the same name. This is called *polymorphism*. Polymorphism makes classes easier to use, because programmers need to memorize fewer method names. In a well-designed class hierarchy, polymorphism is used as much as possible. A good example of a polymorphic message is `toString`. Every object, no matter which class it belongs to, understands the `toString` message and responds by returning a string that describes the object.

We begin by examining some of these ideas in the context of a simple inheritance structure.

Implementing a Simple Shape Hierarchy

Suppose we need to perform some basic manipulations on circles and rectangles. These manipulations include positioning, moving, and stretching these basic geometric shapes. In addition, we want to determine a shape's area, and we want to be able to flip the dimensions of rectangles, that is, interchange a rectangle's width and height. For good measure, we require each shape to respond to the toString message by returning a description of the shape's attributes.

We proceed by defining classes for circles and rectangles. These classes will be called Circle and Rect, respectively. We do not use the more obvious name Rectangle because Java already includes a class with that name. To minimize the coding involved, we first implement a class Shape and from it derive subclasses Circle and Rect. Because we do not intend to instantiate a generic shape object, we designate the Shape class as abstract. (Figure 9-1).

FIGURE 9-1
The Shape class hierarchy

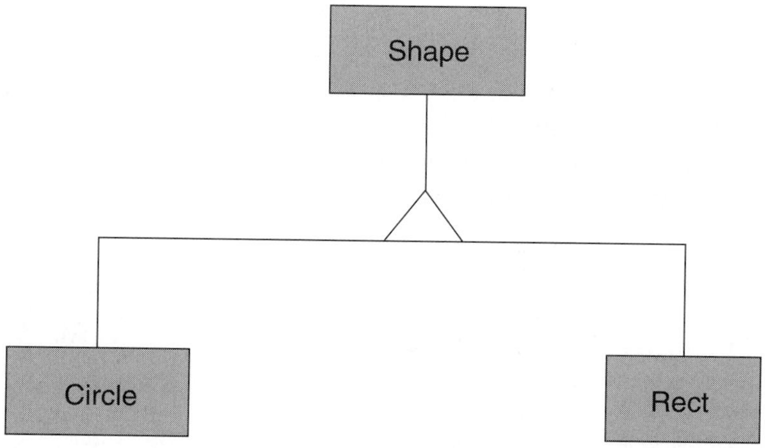

Because we do intend to instantiate circles and rectangles, the classes Circle and Rect are known as *concrete classes*.

The implementation begins like this:

```
abstract public class Shape extends Object{
    ...
}

public class Circle extends Shape{
    ...
}

public class Rect extends Shape{
    ...
}
```

Notice the use of the word abstract at the beginning of the Shape class definition.

Implementing the Shape Class

Now, what characteristics are shared by the classes `Circle` and `Rect`? These can be extracted and defined in the Shape class:

- **Position.** All shapes have an *x, y* position in an underlying coordinate system. This position can be stored in instance variables xPos and yPos. The Shape class's constructors will initialize the variables, and accessor methods will make their values available to clients.

- **Movement.** All shapes are movable. Moving a shape is accomplished by changing its *x, y* coordinates. A method moveTo can perform the task.

- **Area Computation.** All shapes must be able to calculate their areas. However, this is done differently for circles and rectangles. Consequently, we cannot write code in the Shape class to perform the needed calculations, but we can designate in the Shape class that all subclasses must implement an area method. To do this, we declare area as an abstract method in the Shape class. As a result, the Java compiler will complain if a subclass of Shape forgets to implement an area method.

- **Stretching.** All shapes must be stretchable. This is achieved by changing a circle's radius or by changing a rectangle's width and height. The code cannot be written in the Shape class, so we declare an abstract method called stretchBy.

- **toString.** All shapes must respond to the toString message. The response should include a shape's position. Other details will differ for circles and rectangles. Therefore, the Shape class implements a toString method that indicates just the position. The subclasses will need to extend this method to include the other information.

That exhausts the list of attributes shared by circles and rectangles. Here is the complete listing for the Shape class.

```
abstract public class Shape extends Object{

    private double xPos;
    private double yPos;

    public Shape (){
        xPos = 0;
        yPos = 0;
    }

    public Shape (double x, double y){
        xPos = x;
        yPos = y;
    }

    abstract public double area();

    abstract public void stretchBy (double factor);

    public final double getXPos(){
        return xPos;
    }

    public final double getYPos(){
        return yPos;
    }
```

```
    public void moveTo (double xLoc, double yLoc){
       xPos = xLoc;
       yPos = yLoc;
    }

    public String toString(){
       String str = "(X,Y) Position: (" + xPos + "," + yPos + ")\n";
       return str;
    }

}
```

Notice there are two new features in the listing:

1. *Abstract methods.* The methods area and stretchBy begin with the word abstract, end with a semicolon, and include no code. The purpose of an abstract method is to notify subclasses that they must implement the method or they will not compile successfully.

2. *Final methods.* In earlier lessons, you saw how programs define constants. A constant is specified as a final variable. This means that once it is defined, its value cannot be changed. A similar syntax is used to define methods that cannot be redefined in subclasses. For example, the access methods for the instance variables of the Shape class are defined as final:

```
public final double getXPos(){
    return xPos;
}

public final double getYPos(){
    return yPos;
}
```

The use of final in this code implies that subclasses of Shape cannot redefine these methods. Classes can also be declared as final. This implies that such classes cannot have subclasses.

Implementing the Circle Class

To implement the Circle class, we extend the Shape class. Only those features of a circle not shared with a rectangle need to be considered. Thus, the Circle class must

- Declare a variable to keep track of a circle's radius.

- Implement the abstract methods area and stretchBy.

- Extend Shape's constructors and toString method.

Here is the listing:

```
public class Circle extends Shape{

    private double radius;

    public Circle(){
       super();
```

```
        radius = 0;
    }

    public Circle (double xLoc, double yLoc, double rds){
        super (xLoc, yLoc);
        radius = rds;
    }

    public double getRadius(){
        returns radius;
    }

    public double area(){
        return Math.PI * radius * radius;
    }

    public void stretchBy (double factor){
        radius = radius * factor;
    }

    public String toString(){
        String str = "CIRCLE\n"
                    + super.toString()
                    + "Radius: " + radius + "\n"
                    + "Area: " + area();
        return str;
    }

}
```

The word super in the above listing activates code in the superclass. The details of how this is done are different in constructors than in other methods.

Constructors and super

When an object is instantiated, a constructor is activated to initialize the object's variables. The constructor is, of course, located in the object's class. If variables are also declared in the superclass, these too need to be initialized. This initialization is achieved most easily by activating the constructor in the superclass. To activate the default constructor in the superclass, use the method super:

```
super();
```

To activate a different constructor in the superclass, use the method super with the parameter list of the desired constructor, for instance:

```
super (xLoc, yLoc);
```

Other Methods and super

The Circle class also uses the word super in a completely different manner. Any method can include code that looks like this:

```
super.<method name> (<parameter list>);
```

Such code activates the named method in the superclass. In comparison, the code

```
<method name> (<parameter list>);
```

activates the named method in the current class. We saw an example in the `Circle` class's `toString` method:

```
public String toString(){
    String str = "CIRCLE\n"
               + super.toString()              // <<<< super used here
               + "Radius: " + radius + "\n"
               + "Area: " + area();
    return str;
}
```

Implementing the Rect Class

The `Rect` class's implementation is similar to that of the `Circle` class. There is one minor difference. The `Rect` class includes a method, `flipDimensions`, that is not part of either the `Shape` or `Circle` classes. Here is the code:

```
public class Rect extends Shape{

    private double width;
    private double height;

    public Rect(){
        super();
        width = 0;
        height = 0;
    }

    public Rect (double xLoc, double yLoc, double wdth, double hght){
        super (xLoc, yLoc);
        width = wdth;
        height = hght;
    }

    public double area(){
        return width * height;
    }

    public void flipDimensions(){
        double temp = width;
        width = height;
        height = temp;
    }

    public void stretchBy (double factor){
        width = width * factor;
        height = height * factor;
    }
```

```
    public String toString(){
        String str = "RECTANGLE\n"
                   + super.toString()
                   + "Width & Height: " + width + " & " + height +"\n"
                   + "Area: " + area();
        return str;
    }

}
```

Protected Variables and Methods

In Lesson 7, we learned the difference between `public` and `private` visibility. A name can be declared `public` in a class, and thus be visible to the rest of an application. Or a name can be declared `private` in a class and be visible only within that class's implementation. Subclasses cannot see `private` names declared in their parent classes.

To make a method or variable visible to subclasses, but not to the rest of an application, we declare it to be `protected`. As a demonstration, we could modify the `Shape` class as follows:

```
abstract public class Shape extends Object{

    protected double xPos;
    protected double yPos;
    ...
}
```

The variables `xPos` and `yPos` would now be visible to all descendants of `Shape`, including `Circle`, so we could rewrite `Circle`'s constructors as follows:

```
public Circle (){
    xPos = 0;
    yPos = 0;
    radius = 0;
}

public Circle (double xLoc, double yLoc, double rds){
    xPos = xLoc;
    yPos = yLoc;
    radius = rds;
}
```

Obviously, this is not an improvement over our previous manner of coding `Circle`'s constructors. Generally, it is best to limit the visibility of instance variables as much as possible, so `private` instance variables are preferred to `protected` and `public` ones in most situations.

Implementation, Extension, Overriding, and Finality

From the foregoing discussion, we can see that there are four ways in which methods in a subclass can be related to methods in a superclass:

1. *Implementation* of an abstract method. As we have seen, each subclass is forced to implement the abstract methods specified in its superclass. Abstract methods are thus a means of requiring certain behavior in all subclasses.

2. *Extension.* There are two kinds of extension:

   a. The subclass method does not exist in the superclass.

   b. The subclass method invokes the same method in the superclass and then extends the superclass's behavior with its own operations.

3. *Overriding.* In this case, the subclass method does not invoke the superclass method. Instead, the subclass method is intended as a complete replacement of the superclass method.

4. *Finality.* The method in the superclass is complete and cannot be modified by the subclasses. We declare such a method to be `final`.

Using the Shape Classes

Here is a little program that tests the shape classes:

```
import BreezyGUI.*;

public class TestShapes {

    public static void main (String[] args){
        Circle circ;
        circ = new Circle (0, 0, 1);
        circ.moveTo (1, 2);
        circ.stretchBy (2);
        System.out.println ("\n" + circ.toString());

        Rect rect;
        rect = new Rect (0, 0, 1, 2);
        rect.moveTo (1, 2);
        rect.stretchBy (2);
        rect.flipDimensions();
        System.out.println ("\n" + rect.toString());
        GBFrame.pause();
    }
}
```

The program produces the output shown in Figure 9-2.

FIGURE 9-2
Output from the TestShapes program

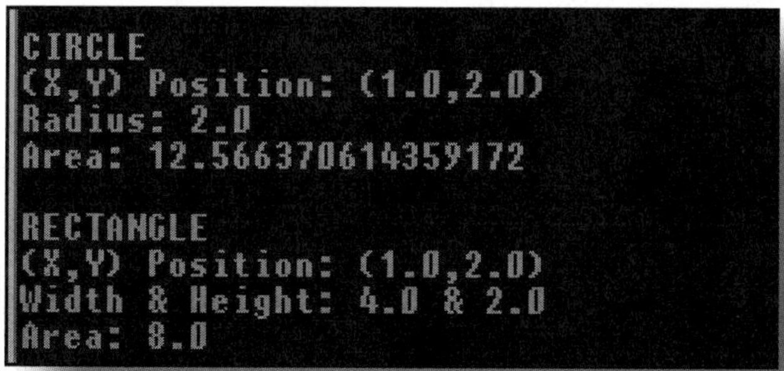

```
CIRCLE
(X,Y) Position: (1.0,2.0)
Radius: 2.0
Area: 12.566370614359172

RECTANGLE
(X,Y) Position: (1.0,2.0)
Width & Height: 4.0 & 2.0
Area: 8.0
```

Finding the Right Method

When a message is sent to an object, Java looks for a matching method. The search starts in the object's class and, if necessary, continues up the class hierarchy. Consequently, in the above program, when the moveTo message is sent to a circle or a rectangle, the moveTo method in the Shape class is activated. There is no moveTo method in either the Circle or Rect classes. On the other hand, when the stretchBy message is sent to a circle, Java finds a corresponding method in the Circle class.

Extending the Shape Hierarchy

We now introduce a new shape, cylinder, which looks like a soft drink can. We will implement the shape by means of a Cylinder class. A cylinder shares several characteristics with the other shapes. It has a position, but in a three-dimensional coordinate system. It has a surface area and can be moved and stretched. In addition, it has a new quality, volume, which we have not seen before. Because its dimensions are determined by the radius of its top and by its height, perhaps we can simplify the Cylinder class's implementation by extending the Circle class as shown in Figure 9-3.

FIGURE 9-3
Extending the Circle class

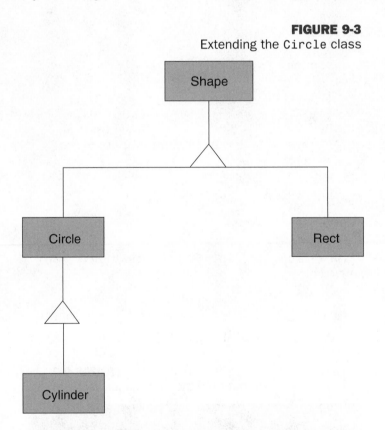

Implementing the Cylinder Class

Here is the code for the Cylinder class:

```
public class Cylinder extends Circle{

    private double zPos;
    private double height;
```

```
    public Cylinder(){
        super();
        zPos = 0;
        height = 0;
    }

    public Cylinder (double xLoc, double yLoc, double zLoc,
                     double rds, double hght){
        super (xLoc, yLoc, rds);
        zPos = zLoc;
        height = hght;
    }

    public double area(){
        return 2 * super.area() + 2 * Math.PI * getRadius() * height;
    }

    public void moveTo (double xLoc, double yLoc, double zLoc){
        super.moveTo (xLoc, yLoc);
        zPos = zLoc;
    }

    public void stretchBy (double factor){
        super.stretchBy (factor);
        height = height * factor;
    }

    public double volume(){
        return super.area() * height;
    }

    public String toString(){
        String str = "CYLINDER\n"
                    + "(X,Y,Z) Position: (" + getXPos() + ","
                                            + getYPos() + ","
                                            + zPos + ")\n"
                    + "Radius & Height: "   + getRadius() + " & "
                                            + height + "\n"
                    + "Area: " + area() + "\n"
                    + "Volume: " + volume();
        return str;
    }

}
```

More About the Use of super

Notice that in the Cylinder class, when we refer to a method in a superclass, sometimes we use the prefix super and sometimes we do not:

```
public double volume(){
    return super.area() * height;                          // in Circle
}
```

251

```
public String toString(){
    String str = "CYLINDER\n"
                + "(X,Y,Z) Position: (" + getXPos() + ","      // in Shape
                                        + getYPos() + ","       / in Shape
                                        + zPos + ")\n"
                + "Radius & Height: "   + getRadius() + " & "   // in Circle
                                        + height + "\n"
                + "Area: " + area() + "\n"                      // in Cylinder
                + "Volume: " + volume();
    return str;
}
```

Remember that Java normally starts its search for a method in the current class, which would be Cylinder in the present example. The effect of the prefix super is to force the search to start in the current class's parent. For instance, because there is an area method in Cylinder and in Circle,

```
... area() ...         // Refers to the method in Cylinder
... super.area() ...   // Refers to the method in Circle
```

But because the getRadius method appears only in the Circle class, super is unnecessary:

```
... getRadius() ...        // Refers to the method in Circle
... super.getRadius()...   // Refers to the method in Circle
```

Testing the Cylinder Class

Here is a program that tests the Cylinder class. The program's output is shown in Figure 9-4.

```
import BreezyGUI.*;

public class TestShapes {

    public static void main (String[] args){
        Cylinder cyl;
        cyl = new Cylinder (0, 0, 0, 1, 2);
        cyl.moveTo (1, 2, 3);
        cyl.stretchBy (2);
        System.out.println ("\n" + cyl.toString());
        GBFrame.pause();
    }
}
```

FIGURE 9-4

Output of the Cylinder class

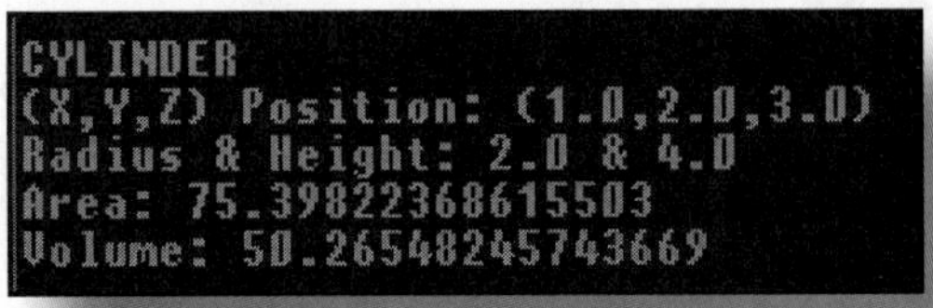

```
CYLINDER
(X,Y,Z) Position: (1.0,2.0,3.0)
Radius & Height: 2.0 & 4.0
Area: 75.39822368615503
Volume: 50.26548245743669
```

Arrays of Shapes

There are many situations in which we might want to work with arrays of shapes. In this section, we learn some simple rules that must be observed.

Declaring an Array of Shapes

Suppose we want to work with an array of circles. We might begin as follows:

```
Circle[] circles;                  // Declare an array variable
circles = new Circle[10];          // Reserve space for 10 circles
circles[0] = new Circle (1,1,2);   // Assign a circle to the 1st element
circles[1] = new Circle (6,3,15);  // Assign a circle to the 2nd element
...
```

For greater flexibility we might instead prefer an array that can hold all the different types of shapes simultaneously, that is, circles, rectangles, and cylinders, as demonstrated next:

```
Shape[] shapes;                        // Declare an array variable
shapes = new Shape[10];                // Reserve space for 10 shapes
shapes[0] = new Circle (1,1,1);        // Assign a circle to the 1st element
shapes[1] = new Rect (2,2,2,2);        // Assign a rectangle to the 2nd
shapes[2] = new Cylinder (3,3,3,3,3);  // Assign a cylinder to the 3rd
shapes[3] = new Rect (4,4,4,4);        // Assign a rectangle to the 4th
...
```

An important rule must be followed when objects of different classes are mixed in an array:
Rule for Mixing Objects of Different Classes in an Array. If we declare an array variable of type ClassX

```
ClassX[] theArray = new ClassX[10];
```

then we can store in the array objects of ClassX or objects of any class below ClassX in the class hierarchy.

```
theArray[0] = new ClassX();
theArray[1] = new ClassY(); // where ClassY is a subclass of ClassX
theArray[2] = new ClassZ(); // where ClassZ is a subclass of ClassY
... etc ...
```

A similar rule applies to nonarray variables:
Rule for Assigning Objects of Different Classes to a Variable. If we declare a variable of type ClassX

```
ClassX theVariable;
```

then we can assign to the variable objects of ClassX or objects of any class below ClassX in the class hierarchy.

```
theVariable = new ClassX();
theVariable = new ClassY(); // where ClassY is a subclass of ClassX
theVariable = new ClassZ(); // where ClassZ is a subclass of ClassY
... etc. ...
```

Sending Messages to Objects in an Array of Shapes

Suppose we have an array of various shapes—circles, rectangles, and cylinders. We can easily find the combined area of all the shapes by sending each an `area` message.

```
Shape[] shapes = new Shapes[10];
shapes[0] = new Circle (...);
shapes[1] = new Cylinder (...);
...
totalArea = 0;
for (int i = 0; i < 10; i++)
   totalArea = totalArea + shapes[i].area();
```

THE `instanceof` OPERATOR

In a similar manner, we might try to find the combined volume of all the shapes. However, now we confront a problem. Some shapes do not have a volume and do not recognize the `volume` message. We can overcome the difficulty by sending the `volume` message to just those shapes that have a volume, that is, to the cylinder objects. Java provides an operator that allows us to determine an object's class. It is called `instanceof`. Here is a first attempt at finding the total volume of all the shapes:

```
Shape[] shapes = new Shapes[10];
shapes[0] = new Circle (...);
shapes[1] = new Cylinder (...);
...
totalVolume = 0;
for (int i = 0; i < 10; i++){
   if (shape[i] instanceof Cylinder)
      totalVolume = totalVolume + shapes[i].volume();   // <<<<<< Problem here
}
```

That looks good, but there is a problem in the indicated line. There is no `volume` method in the Shape class, so the Java compiler will complain. We did not have a similar problem when we were computing the `totalArea` because the Shape class does have an `area` method, even if it is an abstract method. Hence the Java compiler accepts the line of code:

```
totalArea = totalArea + shapes[i].area();
```

When the preceding line of code is executed, the `area` method used depends on the actual shape being processed at that moment—circle, rectangle, or cylinder.

CASTING TO THE RESCUE

We overcome our problem by using the cast operator. We replace the line of code

```
totalVolume = totalVolume + shapes[i].volume();          // <<<<<< Problem here
```

with the line

```
totalVolume = totalVolume + (Cylinder)shapes[i].volume(); // <<<<<< Problem gone
```

However, the cast operator must be used with caution, and two rules must be observed.

1. Before casting an object, be sure that the object is of the target type. Thus, before casting a generic shape to a cylinder, we must be certain that the shape is in fact a cylinder. There will be a run-time error if it is not.

2. Never cast up, only cast down. Thus, it is acceptable to cast a Shape to a Cylinder, but not vice versa. Class Cylinder is below class Shape in the hierarchy.

A SHORT EXAMPLE

A short example recaps the points we have been making:

```
import BreezyGUI.*;

public class TestShapes {

    public static void main (String[] args){
        Shape[] shapes = new Shape[3];
        shapes[0] = new Circle (0,0,1);        // Radius 1
        shapes[1] = new Rect (0,0,1,1);        // Width 1, height 1
        shapes[2] = new Cylinder (0,0,0,1,1); // Radius 1, height 1

        double totalArea = 0;
        double totalVolume = 0;
        for (int i = 0; i < shapes.length; i++){
            totalArea = totalArea + shapes[i].area();
            if (shapes[i] instanceof Cylinder)
                totalVolume = totalVolume + ((Cylinder)shapes[i]).volume();
        }
        System.out.println ("\nTotal area: " + totalArea);
        System.out.println ("Total volume: " + totalVolume);
        GBFrame.pause();
    }
}
```

The output is shown in Figure 9-5.

FIGURE 9-5
Output of the example

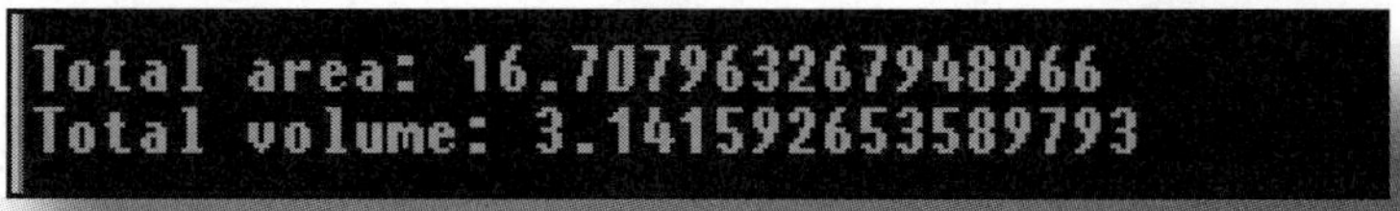

```
Total area: 16.707963267948966
Total volume: 3.141592653589793
```

Shapes as Parameters and Return Values

Objects can be passed to and returned from methods. Actually, objects themselves are not passed, but references to objects are. We do not usually bother to make the distinction. Objects are passed to methods as parameters and passed back in return statements.

It is obvious that an object must exist before it is passed to a method. Less obvious is the fact that the changes the method makes to the object are permanent. The changes are still in effect after the method stops executing. An object returned by a method is usually created in the method, and the object continues to exist after the method stops executing.

If a parameter specifies that an incoming object belongs to ClassX, then an object of any subclass can be substituted. Similarly, if a method's return type is ClassX, then objects of ClassX or any subclass can be returned.

We now illustrate these ideas with some examples.

Rectangle In, Circle Out

For our first example, we write a method that takes a rectangle as an input parameter and returns a circle. The circle has the same area and position as the rectangle. The method makes no changes to the rectangle, and it has to instantiate the circle:

```
static private Circle makeCircleFromRectangle (Rect rectangle){
    double area = rectangle.area();
    double radius = Math.sqrt (area / Math.PI);
    Circle circle = new Circle (rectangle.getXPos(),
                                rectangle.getYPos(),
                                radius);
    return circle;
}
```

Here is a short program that shows the method in action:

```
import BreezyGUI.*;

public class TestShapes {

    public static void main (String[] args){
        Circle circ;
        Rect rect;

        rect = new Rect (1,1,4,6);
        circ = makeCircleFromRectangle (rect);

        System.out.println ("\nRectangle Area: " + rect.area() +
                            "\nCircle Area:    " + circ.area());
        GBFrame.pause();
    }

    static private Circle makeCircleFromRectangle (Rect rectangle){
        ... code as shown above ...
    }
}
```

The output is shown in Figure 9-6.

FIGURE 9-6

Output of the circle from rectangle program

```
Rectangle Area: 24.0
Circle Area:    24.000000000000004
```

Any Shape In, Circle Out

We now modify the previous method so that it accepts any shape as an input parameter—circles, rectangles, or cylinders. The fact that all shapes understand the area method makes the task easy:

```
static private Circle makeCircleFromAnyShape (Shape shape){
    double area = shape.area();
```

```
        double radius = Math.sqrt (area / Math.PI);
        Circle circle = new Circle (shape.getXPos(),
                                    shape.getYPos(),
                                    radius);

        return circle;
    }
```

Any Shape In, Any Shape Out

It is also possible for a method to return any shape rather than a prespecified one. The next method has two input parameters. The first parameter is a shape, and the second indicates the type of shape to return:

```
static private Shape makeOneShapeFromAnother (Shape inShape, String type){
    Shape outShape;                                  // declare outShape
    double area, radius, width, height;
    double x = inShape.getXPos();
    double y = inShape.getYPos();

    area = inShape.area();
    if (type.equals ("circle")){
        radius = Math.sqrt (area / Math.PI);
        outShape = new Circle (x, y, radius);        // assign a circle
    }
    else if (type.equals ("rectangle")){
        width = height = Math.sqrt (area);
        outShape = new Rect (x, y, width, height);   // assign a rectangle
    }
    else{
        radius = Math.sqrt (area / (Math.PI * 3));
        height = radius / 2;
        outShape = new Cylinder (x, y, 0,
                                 radius, height);     // assign a cylinder
    }
    return outShape;
}
```

In the above code, notice that outShape is declared to be of type Shape, an abstract class. However, when it comes time to assign a value to outShape, one of the concrete shapes is used—Circle, Rect, or Cylinder. This is consistent with the rule stated earlier in the lesson. If we declare a variable of type ClassX, then we can assign to the variable objects of ClassX or objects of any class below ClassX in the class hierarchy.

Here is a test of the above method:

```
public class TestShapes {

    public static void main (String[] args){
        Rect rect;
        Shape shape1, shape2, shape3;

        rect = new Rect (1,1,4,6);
        shape1 = makeOneShapeFromAnother (rect, "circle");
        shape2 = makeOneShapeFromAnother (rect, "rectangle");
        shape3 = makeOneShapeFromAnother (rect, "cylinder");

        System.out.println ("\nRectangle Area: " + rect.area() +
```

```
                          "\nCircle Area:     " + shape1.area() +
                          "\nRectangle Area: " + shape2.area() +
                          "\nCylinder Area:  " + shape3.area());
    }

    static private Shape makeOneShapeFromAnother (Shape inShape,
                                                  String    type){
    ... code as shown above ...
    }
}
```

The output is shown in Figure 9-7.

FIGURE 9-7
Output of the `makeOneShapeFromAnother` code

```
Rectangle Area: 24.0
Circle Area:    24.000000000000004
Rectangle Area: 23.999999999999996
Cylinder Area:  24.000000000000007
```

An Employee Hierarchy

Well, enough about shapes already. Let us talk about employees instead. Suppose a company has three types of employees: code testers, regular programmers, and lead programmers. Code testers get paid by the hour, with overtime for hours over 40. Regular programmers are on salary. (Programmers work such long hours that the company would go broke if it had to pay them overtime.) Lead programmers are also on salary, with a bonus for each programmer they supervise. The task is to design classes that can be used in a payroll system. See the hierarchy shown in Figure 9-8.

FIGURE 9-8
An employee hierarchy

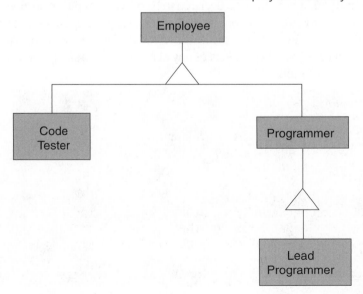

In the hierarchy, the following statements are true:

■ Employee is an abstract class that keeps track of name, number of dependents, deduction per dependent, and tax rate.

■ CodeTester is a concrete class that keeps track of hourly rate and overtime rate.

■ Programmer is a concrete class that keeps track of salary.

■ LeadProgrammer is a concrete class that keeps track of the number of programmers supervised.

All the classes need to provide methods for manipulation of variables and a method to compute pay according to applicable rules.

Figure 9-9 shows a more complete specification of each class. The accessor and mutator methods needed for the class and instance variables are not shown.

FIGURE 9-9
Specifications for each class

abstract **Employee extends Object**
Class Variables double DEDUCTION_PER_DEPENDENT double TAX_RATE
Instance Variables String name int numDependents double payRate int unitsWorked
Instance Methods protected double   computeTax (double grossPay)

CodeTester extends Employee
Class Variables double OVERTIME_FACTOR
Instance Variables none, but here unitsWorked and payRate represent hourly amounts
Instance Methods public double   computeNetPay (double hoursWorked)

Programmer extends Employee
Class Variables none
Instance Variables none, but here unitsWorked and payRate represent weekly amounts
Instance Methods public double computeNetPay ()

LeadProgrammer extends Programmer
Class Variables double BONUS_PER_PROGRAMMER
Instance Variables int numProgrammersSupervised
Instance Methods public double computeNetPay ()

The implementation of these classes is straightforward. Only the rules for computing pay need further explanation. Here are the methods that compute an employee's pay:

IN THE Employee CLASS

```
protected double computeTax (double grossPay){
   double deductions = DEDUCTION_PER_DEPENDENT * numDependents;
   double tax = Math.max (0, (grossPay - deductions)) * TAX_RATE;
   return tax;
}
```

IN THE CodeTester CLASS

```
public double computeNetPay(double unitsWorked){
    double grossPay = 0;
    if (unitsWorked > 40){
        grossPay = (unitsWorked - 40) * payRate * (OVERTIME_FACTOR - 1);
        hoursWorked = 40;
    }
    grossPay += unitsWorked * payRate;
    double netPay = grossPay - computeTax (grossPay * unitsWorked);
    return netPay;
}
```

IN THE Programmer CLASS

```
public double computeNetPay(){
    return payRate - computeTax (payRate);
}
```

IN THE LeadProgrammer CLASS

```
public double computeNetPay(){
    double grossPay = payRate
                    + BONUS_PER_PROGRAMMER * numProgrammersSupervised;
    return grossPay - computeTax (grossPay);
}
```

CASE STUDY : The Painter's Friend

Customer Request

Write a program that allows a painter to estimate the number of gallons of paint needed to paint a house.

Analysis

We assume that a painter knows the following things:

1. The number of square feet that a gallon of paint can cover.

2. The number of coats of paint required.

3. The dimensions of each wall, window, door, and gable.

Thus, the interface should provide a way of entering these data and should display the total number of gallons of paint required.

Figure 9-10 shows the proposed interface.

FIGURE 9-10

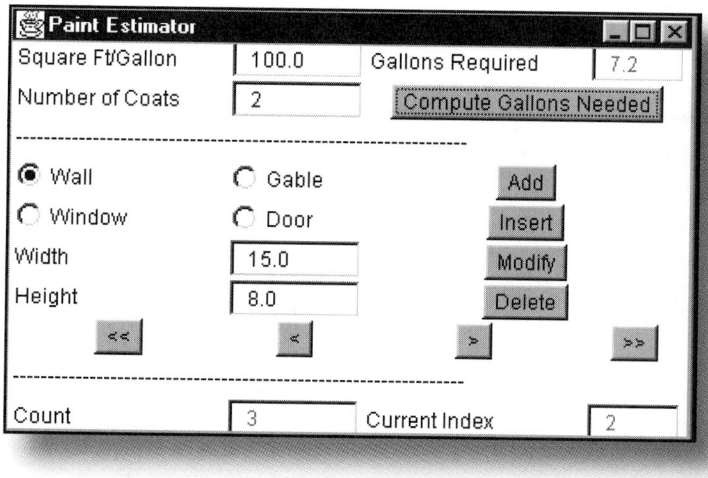

The program maintains a view on a list of different regions: walls, windows, gables, and doors. The user enters a new region by selecting the surface type, entering its width and height, and selecting either **Add** or **Insert.** The user can also modify, delete, or navigate to existing regions in the list by selecting the appropriate buttons.

The user can determine the number of gallons of paint required by entering values for square feet per gallon and number of coats of paint, and selecting **Compute Gallons Needed.**

Classes

1. `PaintEstimatorView`. This class is responsible for setting up the view, handling user inputs, and updating the view with any changes.

2. `PaintEstimatorModel`. This class is responsible for maintaining the data model of the program and computing the total gallons required. The data in the model are the list of regions, the number of square feet per gallon of paint, and the number of coats of paint.

3. `Region`. This class defines the common variables and methods of all regions.

4. `Wall`, `Window`, `Door`, and `Gable`. These classes define the variables and methods of the specific regions.

Design of `Region` and Its Subclasses

The data model for the application requires us to represent different kinds of regions. Each region has a height and width, which are set when the region is constructed. Each region also computes and returns its area. However, only walls and gables contribute to the surface area to be painted. The areas of windows and doors should be negative, so they can be deducted from the total surface area of a house. The fact that some regions share some but not all properties suggests a hierarchy of classes, in which `Region` is abstract and the other classes are concrete. Figure 9-11 shows a class hierarchy.

FIGURE 9-11
Hierarchy of the Region class

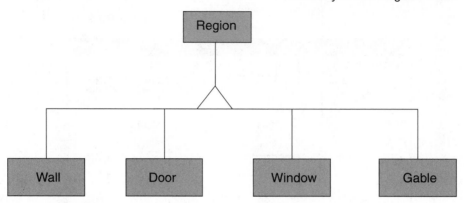

We define `Region` as an abstract class, with the variables and methods specified in the following class summary:

```
Class:
    abstract Region extends Object
Protected Instance Variables:
    double width
    double height
Public Methods:
    constructors
    abstract double area()
    double getWidth()
    double getHeight()
```

The subclasses `Wall`, `Window`, `Door`, and `Gable` have direct access to the protected instance variables variables. Others, such as the data model and interface classes, must run the `getWidth` and `getHeight` methods for access.

The subclasses each implement the `area` method. Here is a summary of one of the subclasses:

```
Class:
    Wall extends Region
Public Methods:
    constructor
    double area()
```

Design of `PaintEstimatorModel`

The design of `PaintEstimatorModel` is similar to the design of the class `StudentTestScores-Model` discussed in Lesson 8. `PaintEstimatorModel` supports the maintenance of a list of objects, with operations that allow insertions, deletions, modifications, and changing the current position in the list. We represent the list of objects as an array. We must also maintain the index of the current object in the array and a count of the number of regions stored. Two additional variables represent the square feet per gallon and the number of coats. The model must provide mutator methods for these variables, as well as a method that computes the number of gallons needed. Here is the class summary:

```
Class:
    PaintEstimatorModel extends Object
Protected Instance Variables:
    Region[] regions
    int indexSelectedRegion
    int regionCount
    double squareFeetPerGallon
    int numberOfCoats
Public Methods:
    constructor
    void setNumberOfCoats (int noc)
    void addRegion (Region rgn)
    double getGallonsOfPaintNeeded()
    Region getCurrentRegion()
    int getRegionCount()
    int getIndexSelectedRegion()
    void moveToFirstRegion()
    void moveToPreviousRegion()
    void moveToNextRegion()
    void moveToLastRegion()
    void addRegion(Region rgn)
    void insertRegion(Region rgn)
    void modifyRegion(Region rgn)
    void deleteRegion(Region rgn)
Private Methods:
    int area()
```

The design for the list maintenance methods is the same as that discussed in Lesson 8. The pseudocode for the methods `getGallonsOfPaintNeeded` and `area` follows:

```
getGallonsOfPaintNeeded
    a = area
    if (a <= 0 || squareFeetPerGallon <= 0)
        return 0
    else
        return numberOfCoats * a / squareFeetPerGallon
```

```
area
    totalArea = 0
    for (i = 0; i < regionCount; i++)
        totalArea = totalArea + regions[i].area()
    return totalArea
```

The design of the class `PaintEstimatorView` is similar to the design of the class `StudentTestScoresView` discussed in Lesson 8 and requires no further comment.

Implementation

```
abstract public class Region extends Object{

    protected double width;
    protected double height;

    public Region(){
        width = 0;
        height = 0;
    }

    public Region (double w, double h){
        width = w;
        height = h;
    }

    abstract public double area();

    public double getWidth(){
        return width;
    }

    public double getHeight(){
        return height;
    }

}
```

```
public class Wall extends Region{

    public Wall (double width, double height){
        super (width, height);
    }

    public double area(){
        return width * height;
    }

}
```

```
public class Gable extends Region{

    public Gable (double width, double height){
        super (width, height);
    }

    public double area(){
        return width * height / 2;
    }

}
```

```java
public class Window extends Region{

    public Window (double width, double height){
        super (width, height);
    }

    public double area(){
        return - width * height;
    }

}
```

```java
public class Door extends Region{

    public Door (double width, double height){
        super (width, height);
    }

    public double area(){
        return - width * height;
    }

}
```

```java
import java.awt.*;
import BreezyGUI.*;

public class PaintEstimatorView extends GBFrame{

    // Window objects--------------------------------------------

    Label sqrftLabel     = addLabel ("Square Ft/Gallon" ,1,1,1,1);
    Label numCoatsLabel  = addLabel ("Number of Coats"  ,2,1,1,1);
    Label gllnReqLabel   = addLabel ("Gallons Required" ,1,3,1,1);

    DoubleField sqrftField    = addDoubleField  (0,1,2,1,1);
    IntegerField numCoatsField = addIntegerField (0,2,2,1,1);
    DoubleField gllnReqField   = addDoubleField  (0,1,4,1,1);

    Button computeButton = addButton ("Compute Gallons Needed", 2,3,2,1);

    Label separator1 = addLabel
    ("--------------------------------------------------------------"
    , 3,1,4,1);

    CheckboxGroup cbgRegion = new CheckboxGroup();
    Checkbox       cbWall    = addCheckbox ("Wall"  ,4,1,1,1);
    Checkbox       cbGable   = addCheckbox ("Gable" ,4,2,1,1);
    Checkbox       cbWindow  = addCheckbox ("Window",5,1,1,1);
    Checkbox       cbDoor    = addCheckbox ("Door"  ,5,2,1,1);
```

```
Label widthLabel  = addLabel ("Width"  , 6,1,1,1);
Label heightLabel = addLabel ("Height", 7,1,1,1);

DoubleField widthField  = addDoubleField (0,6,2,1,1);
DoubleField heightField = addDoubleField (0,7,2,1,1);

Button addButton    = addButton ("Add"   ,4,3,2,1);
Button insertButton = addButton ("Insert",5,3,2,1);
Button modifyButton = addButton ("Modify",6,3,2,1);
Button deleteButton = addButton ("Delete",7,3,2,1);

Button firstButton    = addButton ("<<", 8,1,1,1);
Button previousButton = addButton ("<",  8,2,1,1);
Button nextButton     = addButton (">",  8,3,1,1);
Button lastButton     = addButton (">>", 8,4,1,1);

Label separator2 = addLabel
("----------------------------------------------------------------"
, 9,1,4,1);

Label        countLabel
             = addLabel        ("Count"         ,10,1,1,1);

IntegerField countField
             = addIntegerField (0               ,10,2,1,1);

Label        indexLabel
             = addLabel        ("Current Index" ,10,3,1,1);

IntegerField indexField
             = addIntegerField (-1              ,10,4,1,1);

// Other instance variables---------------------------------

PaintEstimatorModel model;

// Constructor----------------------------------------------

public PaintEstimatorView(){
   setTitle ("Paint Estimator");
   model = new PaintEstimatorModel();
   gllnReqField.setEditable (false);

   cbWall.setCheckboxGroup (cbgRegion);
   cbGable.setCheckboxGroup (cbgRegion);
   cbWindow.setCheckboxGroup (cbgRegion);
   cbDoor.setCheckboxGroup (cbgRegion);
   cbWall.setState (true);

   countField.setEditable (false);
   indexField.setEditable (false);
   displayCurrentRegion();
}

// buttonClicked method-------------------------------------

public void buttonClicked (Button buttonObj){
```

```
            if (buttonObj == computeButton)
                computePaintNeeded();

            else if (buttonObj == addButton){
                Region rgn = getDataOnScreen();
                if (rgn != null){
                    model.addRegion (rgn);
                    displayCurrentRegion();
                }
            }

            // insert, modify, and delete are left as an exercise

            else if (buttonObj == firstButton){
                model.moveToFirstRegion();
                displayCurrentRegion();
            }
            else if (buttonObj == previousButton); // left as an exercise

            else if (buttonObj == nextButton){
                model.moveToNextRegion();
                displayCurrentRegion();
            }
            else if (buttonObj == lastButton);      // left as an exercise
    }

    // Private methods------------------------------------------------

    private void computePaintNeeded(){
        double sqrftPerGal = sqrftField.getNumber();
        int numCoats = numCoatsField.getNumber();

        if (sqrftPerGal <= 0 || numCoats <= 0)
            messageBox ("SORRY: sqr ft/gl and num coats \n" +
                        "must be > 0");
        else{
            model.setSquareFeetPerGallon (sqrftPerGal);
            model.setNumberOfCoats (numCoats);
            gllnReqField.setNumber (model.getGallonsOfPaintNeeded());
        }
    }

    private Region getDataOnScreen(){
        double width = widthField.getNumber();
        double height = heightField.getNumber();
        if (width <= 0 || height <= 0){
            messageBox ("SORRY: width and height \n" +
                        "must be positive");
            return null;
        }

        String str = cbgRegion.getSelectedCheckbox().getLabel();

        Region reg;
        if (str.equals ("Wall"))
            reg = new Wall (width, height);
        else if (str.equals ("Gable"))
```

```java
            reg = new Gable (width, height);
        else if (str.equals ("Window"))
            reg = new Window (width, height);
        else
            reg = new Door (width, height);
        return reg;
    }

    void displayCurrentRegion(){
        Region rgn = model.getCurrentRegion();
        if (rgn == null){
            widthField.setNumber (0);
            heightField.setNumber (0);
        }
        else{
            if (rgn instanceof Wall)
                cbWall.setState (true);
            else if (rgn instanceof Gable)
                cbGable.setState (true);
            else if (rgn instanceof Window)
                cbWindow.setState (true);
            else
                cbDoor.setState (true);
            widthField.setNumber (rgn.getWidth());
            heightField.setNumber (rgn.getHeight());
        }
        countField.setNumber (model.getRegionCount());
        indexField.setNumber (model.getIndexSelectedRegion());
    }

    public static void main (String[] args){
        Frame frm = new PaintEstimatorView();
        frm.setSize (400, 250);
        frm.setVisible(true);
    }
}


public class PaintEstimatorModel extends Object{

    Region[] regions;
    int indexSelectedRegion;
    int regionCount;

    double squareFeetPerGallon;
    int numberOfCoats;


    public PaintEstimatorModel(){
        regions = new Region[5];
        regionCount = 0;
        indexSelectedRegion = -1;
    }

    public void setSquareFeetPerGallon (double sfpg){
        squareFeetPerGallon = sfpg;
    }
```

```
public void setNumberOfCoats (int noc){
    numberOfCoats = noc;
}

public void addRegion (Region rgn){
    if (regionCount == regions.length){
        Region[] temp = new Region[regionCount + 5];
        for (int i = 0; i < regionCount; i++)
            temp[i] = regions[i];
        regions = temp;
    }
    regions[regionCount] = rgn;
    indexSelectedRegion = regionCount;
    regionCount++;
}

public double getGallonsOfPaintNeeded(){
    double a = area();
    if (a <= 0 || squareFeetPerGallon <= 0)
        return 0;
    else
        return numberOfCoats * a / squareFeetPerGallon;
}

private double area(){
    double totalArea = 0;
    for (int i = 0; i < regionCount; i++)
        totalArea = totalArea + regions[i].area();
    return totalArea;
}

public Region getCurrentRegion(){
    if (indexSelectedRegion == -1)
        return null;
    else
        return regions[indexSelectedRegion];
}

public int getRegionCount(){
    return regionCount;
}

public int getIndexSelectedRegion(){
    return indexSelectedRegion;
}

void moveToFirstRegion(){
    if (regionCount == 0)
        indexSelectedRegion = -1;
    else
        indexSelectedRegion = 0;
}

void moveToPreviousRegion(){
    // Exercise
}
```

```
void moveToNextRegion(){
    if (regionCount == 0)
        indexSelectedRegion = -1;
    else
        indexSelectedRegion
            = Math.min (regionCount - 1, indexSelectedRegion + 1);
}

void moveToLastRegion(){
    // Exercise
}

}
```

Object-Oriented Analysis and Design Guidelines

Now that you are familiar with the major concepts of object-oriented programming—encapsulation, inheritance, and polymorphism—let us summarize some guidelines for object-oriented analysis and design.

Objects—A Universal Means of Representation

Objects can represent just about anything. We have seen examples of computational objects, such as buttons, text fields, menus, strings, arrays, and vectors. We have also seen examples of objects that represent "real" things, such as students and employees. The list of these things is in fact inexhaustible: human beings, artifacts, institutions, natural objects, events, abstract concepts, and so on.

Analyzing Objects

Recall that analysis describes what a software system does, whereas design describes how the software system accomplishes these tasks. In general, we should do analysis before we do design. In object-oriented analysis, we describe what the objects in a system are. In object-oriented design, we describe their attributes (instance and class variables) and their behavior (instance and class methods). During analysis, we determine which objects are needed by the system. Each object should have a clearly defined role and responsibility in the system. Thus, an object should be cohesive, even if it will have many methods. That is, an object should have closely related responsibilities, even if it might need many methods to carry out its responsibilities well.

As a rule of thumb, the nouns in the problem description of a system supply hints about the objects required. If the organization of a system reflects some kind of natural or organizational hierarchy, the objects should reflect that in the form of a hierarchy of subclasses. Thus, if a system contains the objects manager, staff, and programmer, it will likely be convenient to organize these classes as subclasses of an abstract employee class.

Designing Objects

In the design of objects, we start with the classes determined by analysis and add instance variables and methods to each class. Once again, there are some rules of thumb for determining class attributes and methods:

- Nouns in a problem description give a hint about attributes.

- Verbs in a problem description give a hint about methods.

Occasionally, a class is simply a convenient way of organizing a collection of related methods. Java's `Math` class is a good example.

We also determine the relationships among classes in the system. Objects (and their classes) are related in one of the following ways:

- Class A uses class B. This is true if a method of class A sends a message to an object of class B, or if a method of class A creates, receives, or returns an object of class B.

- Class A contains class B (sometimes called the "has a" relation). This is true if class A defines an attribute (an instance variable) of class B.

- Class A is a subclass of class B (sometimes called the "is a" relation).

During design, we try to maximize the power of encapsulation, inheritance, and polymorphism.

Maximizing Encapsulation

Here are some guidelines for taking advantage of encapsulation:

- With the exception of some constants, all data should be declared `private`.

- An object should always initialize its own data when it is created.

- A method should be declared `public` only when other objects must use it.

- If a datum does not need an accessor or a mutator, the object should not provide it.

- If a datum should not be changed, or a method should not be overridden by a subclass, it should be declared `final`.

Maximizing Inheritance

The first way to make use of inheritance is to define a class that extends some existing class provided by the language. Even a top-level class must extend the class `Object`. Otherwise, we define an abstract class and its appropriate subclasses.

An abstract class should define the data and methods that the subclasses have in common. Here are some guidelines for taking advantage of inheritance:

- Declare a datum or method `protected` when it should be visible to subclasses but not to the rest of the system.

- Declare a method `abstract` (in an abstract class) when that method must be implemented by all subclasses. Declare a method `final` when that method should be inherited but not overridden by any subclass.

- When overriding a superclass method, use that superclass method (that is, the Java variable `super`) to take care of the superclass's responsibilities, if any.

Maximizing Polymorphism

Use conventional names (`draw` for drawing an image, `toString` for returning a string) for methods wherever possible. Provide abstract classes with abstract methods for situations in which polymorphism might be used.

Summary

In this lesson, you learned:

- Java organizes classes in a hierarchy. Classes inherit variables and methods from their superclasses and can extend their inherited characteristics to other classes. Inheritance can greatly reduce the labor required to create new classes.

- Abstract classes are never instantiated. Abstract classes define features and behavior common to subclasses.

- Polymorphism is when methods in different classes (but with similar functions) are given the same name. Polymorphism helps in the programming process because programmers need to memorize fewer method names.

LESSON 9 REVIEW QUESTIONS

WRITTEN QUESTIONS

Write your answers to the following questions.

1. Name a built-in Java class that inherits features from another class, and name this superclass.

2. What is an abstract class? How does an abstract class differ from a concrete class?

3. What does the Java keyword super refer to? How is it used?

4. Explain how the Java visibility modifier protected works.

5. When would you declare an abstract method?

6. Describe how Java looks for a method when a message is sent to an object.

7. When can objects of one class be assigned to variables of another class, and when is casting necessary?

LESSON 9 PROJECTS

SCANS

1. Design a hierarchy of classes that model the taxonomy of your favorite region of the animal kingdom. Your hierarchy should be at most three classes deep, and use abstract classes on the first two levels.

2. Design a hierarchy of classes that represents the taxonomy of artifacts, such as vehicles.

3. Institutions are rich in hierarchies. Design a hierarchy of classes that represents the organizational tree of your favorite institution.

4. Complete the Case Study program of this lesson by finishing the methods marked as exercises.

5. Redo the blackjack program of Project 7 in Lesson 8 so that the Dealer class is a subclass of the Player class.

CRITICAL THINKING ACTIVITY

Browse Java's class hierarchy on Sun Microsystems' Web site (see Appendix A). Write an essay that describes the design ideas underlying a class hierarchy that you find interesting among Java's classes.

SIMPLE GRAPHICS

LESSON

10

OBJECTIVES

Upon completion of this lesson, you should be able to:

■ Explain the graphics coordinate system.

■ Draw text and graphics at specific locations.

■ Control the color of images.

■ Define a class to control geometric objects.

■ Change text properties to alter color, font, style, and size.

⏱ Estimated Time: 3 hours

The Conceptual Framework for Computer Graphics

The window objects used thus far are in fact nothing more than patterns of bits displayed on a two-dimensional bitmapped screen. Java provides classes and methods for manipulating bit patterns directly. Applications that do this are known as graphics applications.

Coordinate Systems

The basis of any graphics application is a *coordinate system*. Positions in this system are specified in terms of points. Points in a two-dimensional system have *x* and *y* coordinates. For example, the point (10, 30) has an *x* coordinate of 10 and a *y* coordinate of 30.

The *x* and *y* coordinates of a point express its position relative to the system's *origin* at (0,0). Figure 10-1 presents some examples of points in the familiar *Cartesian coordinate system.*

In Java and most other programming languages, the coordinate system is oriented as shown in Figure 10-2. Note that the only quadrant shown is the one that defines the coordinates of the computer's screen, extending from the point (0,0) in the upper left corner. The other three quadrants exist, but the points in them never appear on the screen.

In a windows-based application, the coordinate system is usually relative to a given window. Thus, the origin (0,0) is at the upper left corner of the window (including the title bar and window border). Each point in a coordinate system, extending from the origin to the lower right corner of a window, locates the position of a pixel, or picture element, in the window. The (*x*, *y*) coordinates of a point are represented as integers.

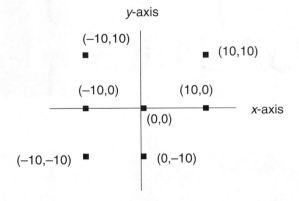

FIGURE 10-1
The Cartesian coordinate system

y-axis

(−10,10)

(10,10)

(−10,0)

(10,0)

(0,0)

x-axis

(−10,−10)

(0,−10)

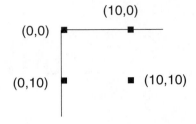

FIGURE 10-2
The Java coordinate system

(10,0)

(0,0)

(0,10)

(10,10)

The Graphics Class

Java provides a Graphics class for drawing in a window. A window maintains an instance of this class, called a *graphics context,* which allows the programmer to access and modify the window's bitmap. The programmer sends messages to this graphics context to perform all graphics operations. Hereafter, we refer to the graphics context with the variable name g. Some commonly used Graphics drawing methods are listed in Table 10-1.

TABLE 10-1
Common Graphics drawing methods

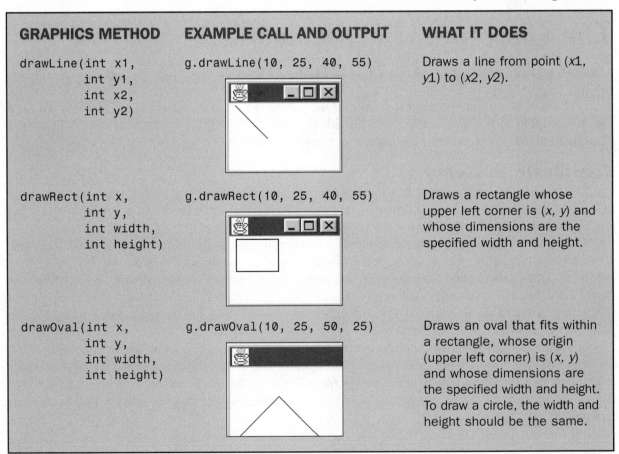

GRAPHICS METHOD	EXAMPLE CALL AND OUTPUT	WHAT IT DOES

drawLine(int x1,
         int y1,
         int x2,
         int y2)
	g.drawLine(10, 25, 40, 55)	Draws a line from point (*x1, y1*) to (*x2, y2*).

drawRect(int x,
         int y,
         int width,
         int height)
	g.drawRect(10, 25, 40, 55)	Draws a rectangle whose upper left corner is (*x, y*) and whose dimensions are the specified width and height.

drawOval(int x,
         int y,
         int width,
         int height)
	g.drawOval(10, 25, 50, 25)	Draws an oval that fits within a rectangle, whose origin (upper left corner) is (*x, y*) and whose dimensions are the specified width and height. To draw a circle, the width and height should be the same.

TABLE 10-1
(continued)

Lesson 10 Simple Graphics

GRAPHICS METHOD	EXAMPLE CALL AND OUTPUT	WHAT IT DOES

drawArc(
    int x,
    int y,
    int width,
    int height,
    int startAngle,
    int arcAngle)
	g.drawArc(10, 25, 50, 50, 0, 90)	Draws an arc that fits within a rectangle whose upper left corner is (x, y) and whose dimensions are the specified width and height. The arc is drawn from startAngle to startAngle + arcAngle. The angles are expressed in degrees. The start angle of 0 indicates the 3 o'clock position. A positive arc indicates a counterclockwise rotation, and a negative arc indicates a clockwise rotation, from 3 o'clock.

drawPolygon(
    int x[],
    int y[],
    int n)
	int x[] = {10, 40, 60, 30, 40};
	int y[] = {25, 25, 50, 60, 40};
	g.drawPolygon(x, y, 5);
		Draws a polygon defined by n line segments, where the first n − 1 segments run from (x[i − 1], y[i − 1]) to (x[i], y[i]), for 1 <= i < n. The last segment starts at the final point and ends at the first point.

drawRoundRect(
    int x,
    int y,
    int width,
    int height,
    int arcWidth,
    int arcHeight)
	g.drawRoundRect(10, 25, 40, 30,
	                20, 20)
		Draws a rounded rectangle.

drawString(
    String str,
    int x,
    int y)
	g.drawString("Java rules!",
	             10, 50)
		Draws a string. The point (x, y) indicates the position of the baseline of the first character.

The methods fillArc, fillRect, and fillOval draw filled shapes. In the examples that follow, we assume that the variable g represents the graphics context of the current window, which is 200 pixels wide and 200 pixels high.

Drawing Triangles

The following code segment draws a triangle with vertices (50,50), (100,100), and (0,100):

```
g.drawLine(50, 50, 100, 100);
g.drawLine(100, 100, 0, 100);
g.drawLine(0, 100, 50, 50);
```

Note that the origin (0,0) is at the upper left corner of the window's border and the vertex (0,100) is also on the window's border, as shown in Figure 10-3.

FIGURE 10-3
Triangle drawn using `Graphics` method

Drawing Circles

The next code segment draws five expanding circles. Figure 10-4 shows the result.

```
int x = 50, y = 50, width = 50, height = 50;
int i;

for (i = 1; i <= 5; i++){
    g.drawOval (x, y, height, width);
    width = (int) (width * 1.25);
    height = (int) (height * 1.25);
}
```

FIGURE 10-4
A drawing of expanding circles

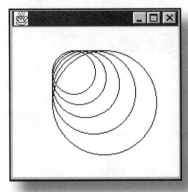

Drawing Text

The following code segment draws the string `"Java is way cool!"` at position (100,100). The resulting window is shown in Figure 10-5.

```
g.drawString ("Java is way cool!", 100, 100);
```

FIGURE 10-5
The string at its specified location

Java is way cool!

Accessing a Graphics Context

Now that we have seen how to use the `Graphics` methods, it is natural to ask how an application accesses a window's `Graphics` context. The easiest way to do this is to invoke the method `getGraphics()`. This method returns the graphics context of the window. Thus, the following code would draw the string displayed in Figure 10-5.

```
Graphics g = getGraphics();
g.drawString ("Java is way cool!", 100, 100);
```

The Method paint

We now know how to make drawings, but two problems remain. First, graphics cannot be done in constructors, so how does one display a drawing when a window first opens? Second, every time a window is resized or uncovered, the window is refreshed and drawings in the window are lost. We call this the *transient image* problem. There is a common solution to both problems. One of `GBFrame`'s superclasses contains a method named `paint`, which is called automatically when a window first opens and every time it is refreshed thereafter. Normally, `paint` does nothing, but we can override it in our applications and load it up with the desired drawing instructions.

The `paint` method has one parameter, which is of type `Graphics`. Here is an example:

```
public void paint (Graphics g){
    g.drawString ("Java is way cool!", 100, 100);
}
```

The string `"Java is way cool!"` is now displayed when the window first opens and every time the window is refreshed.

The Method repaint

Although an application can call the `paint` method to reapply a group of drawing commands, there is generally little point in its doing so. Before reapplying drawing commands, one normally would want to erase the current drawing. The `repaint` method provides the needed capability. This method, which is also implemented in one of `GBFrame`'s superclasses, first erases the current drawing and then calls `paint`. Actually, `repaint` does more. It also tells all the window objects (text fields, labels, buttons, etc.) to redisplay themselves.

Thus, one way for an application to clear a window of graphical images (other than our standard window objects) is to leave `paint` unimplemented and to invoke `repaint`. We take this approach in the first case study. In later case studies, we examine how to use `paint` to refresh our images.

CASE STUDY 1:
Drawing Text at Different Positions

Request

Write a program that allows the user to draw text at different positions in a window.

Analysis

The application allows the user to enter some text and a point. The **Draw** option in the **Command** menu draws the text at the specified point. The **Clear** option in the **Command** menu erases all of the drawings in the window.

Figure 10-6 shows the proposed interface. In this figure, the data were entered as indicated in Table 10-2.

FIGURE 10-6

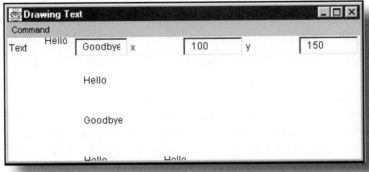

TABLE 10-2
Coordinates for the text shown in Figure 10-6

TEXT	X	Y
Hello	50	50
Hello	100	100
Hello	100	200
Hello	200	200
Goodbye	100	150

Design

When the user selects the **Draw** command, the menuItemSelected method invokes the draw method. This method performs these tasks:

■ Extracts the data from the input fields.

■ Obtains the graphics context of the window.

■ Invokes the drawString method on the graphics context with the input data as parameters.

When the user selects the **Clear** command, the menuItemSelected method invokes the repaint method. Because the paint method is not implemented, the strings just drawn by the application will be erased.

Implementation

```
import java.awt.*;
import BreezyGUI.*;

public class DrawText extends GBFrame{

    MenuItem drawItem = addMenuItem ("Command", "Draw");
    MenuItem clearItem = addMenuItem ("Command", "Clear");
    Label textLabel = addLabel ("Text", 1,1,1,1);
    TextField textField = addTextField ("", 1,2,1,1);
    Label xLabel = addLabel ("x", 1, 3, 1, 1);
    IntegerField xField = addIntegerField (0, 1, 4, 1, 1);
    Label yLabel = addLabel ("y", 1, 5, 1, 1);
    IntegerField yField = addIntegerField (0, 1, 6, 1, 1);

    public DrawText(){
        setTitle ("Drawing Text");
    }

    public void menuItemSelected (MenuItem mi){
        if (mi == drawItem)
            draw();
        else if (mi == clearItem)
            repaint();
    }

    private void draw(){
        String text = textField.getText();
        int x = xField.getNumber();
        int y = yField.getNumber();
        Graphics g = getGraphics();
        g.drawString (text, x, y);
    }

    public static void main (String[] args){
        Frame frm = new DrawText();
        frm.setSize (350, 200);
        frm.setVisible (true);
    }
}
```

This application demonstrates the transient image problem. When the user resizes the window, the text disappears.

Color

A Java programmer can control the color of images by using the Color class. The Color class provides the class constants listed in Table 10-3.

TABLE 10-3
Color class constants

color CONSTANT	COLOR
public static final Color red	Red
public static final Color yellow	Yellow
public static final Color blue	Blue
public static final Color orange	Orange
public static final Color pink	Pink
public static final Color cyan	Cyan
public static final Color magenta	Magenta
public static final Color black	Black
public static final Color white	White
public static final Color gray	Gray
public static final Color lightGray	Light gray
public static final Color darkGray	Dark gray

Thus, the expression Color.red would yield the Color constant for red.

The Graphics class provides the following methods for examining and modifying the color of images:

METHOD	WHAT IT DOES
Color getColor()	Returns the current color of the graphics context.
void setColor(Color c)	Sets the color of the graphics context to c.

Images are drawn in the current color until the color is changed. Changing the color does not affect the color of previously drawn images. The next code segment draws a string in red and a line in blue in the graphics context g:

```
g.setColor (Color.red);
g.drawString ("Colors are great!", 50, 50);
g.setColor (Color.blue);
g.drawLine (50, 50, 150, 50);
```

Java allows the programmer finer control over colors by using RGB (red/green/blue) values. In this scheme, there are 256 shades of red, 256 shades of green, and 256 shades of blue. The programmer "mixes" a new color by selecting an integer from 0 to 255 for each color, and passing these integers to a `Color` constructor as follows:

```
new Color (<int for red>, <int for green>, <int for blue>)
```

The next code segment shows how to create a random color with RGB values:

```
// Create a random color from randomly generated RGB values
int r = (int) (Math.random() * 256);
int g = (int) (Math.random() * 256);
int b = (int) (Math.random() * 256);
Color randomColor = new Color (r, g, b);
```

The value 0 indicates the absence of a color in the mixture, while the value 255 indicates the maximum saturation of that color. Thus, black has RGB (0,0,0), and white has RGB (255, 255, 255). There are $256 * 256 * 256 = 2^{24}$ possible colors in this scheme.

Tracking the Mouse

Interactive input in graphical applications is often accomplished with a pointing device, such as a mouse, trackball, or trackpad. The application tracks and registers mouse events, such as button clicks, movement, and dragging. Our **BreezyGUI** class `GBFrame` specifies methods for handling mouse events. Each method has two parameters:

1. The *x* coordinate of the mouse when the event occurs.

2. The *y* coordinate of the mouse when the event occurs.

The mouse-handling methods are listed in Table 10-4.

TABLE 10-4
Mouse-handling methods

METHOD	WHAT IT DOES
void mouseClicked (int x, int y)	This method is called when a mouse button is clicked.
void mousePressed (int x, int y)	This method is called when a mouse button is pressed.
void mouseReleased (int x, int y)	This method is called when a mouse button is released.
void mouseMoved (int x, int y)	This method is called when the mouse is moved.
void mouseDragged (int x, int y)	This method is called when the mouse button is pressed and the mouse is moved.

To detect and handle mouse input, an application must implement one or more of these methods. A mouse-handling method typically transfers the values of the mouse coordinates to the application's instance variables, and then performs some action and updates the display with the results. For example, the following definition of mousePressed does just that for instance variables mouseX and mouseY:

```
public void mousePressed (int x, int y){
mouseX = x;
mouseY = y;
repaint();
}
```

CASE STUDY 2 : A Simple Sketching Program

Request

Write a program that allows the user to draw a figure by repeatedly pressing the mouse.

FIGURE 10-7

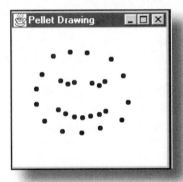

Analysis

The application called Sketchpad1 supports the simplest kind of drawing. When the user presses the mouse button in the window, a pellet-sized dot appears. The user can drop several of these dots to construct a figure.

Figure 10-7 shows the proposed interface.

Design

mousePressed uses the current coordinates of the mouse to draw a 5-by-5 pellet.

Implementation

```
import java.awt.*;
import BreezyGUI.*;

public class Sketchpad1 extends GBFrame{

    public Sketchpad1(){
        setTitle ("Pellet Drawing");
    }

    public void mousePressed (int x, int y){
        Graphics g = getGraphics();
        g.fillOval (x, y, 5, 5);
    }

    public static void main (String[] args){
        Frame frm = new Sketchpad1();
```

```
              frm.setSize (200, 200);
              frm.setVisible (true);
         }
    }
```

Transient and Refreshable Images

Our sketchpad application has the same transient image problem that we saw in Case Study 1 in this lesson. To see the problem, draw a few dots and then resize the window by making it smaller and then larger, or hide a portion of the window beneath another window and then reselect the application window. All the dots have disappeared!

To draw a permanent or *refreshable image,* one that reappears when the window is resized, the application must maintain a record of that image and redraw it when necessary. We now modify Sketchpad1 as follows:

1. When the mousePressed method is invoked, the *x* and *y* coordinates are stored in two parallel arrays.

2. We implement the paint method. It loops through all available points in the arrays and draws all the pellets.

The application handles the details of saving and displaying points in two new methods, savePoint(int x, int y) and displayPoints(Graphics g). Here is the listing of the modified program, called Sketchpad2:

```java
import java.awt.*;
import BreezyGUI.*;

public class Sketchpad2 extends GBFrame{

   private static int MAX_POINTS = 500;
   private int numPoints;
   private int xArray[];
   private int yArray[];

   public Sketchpad2(){
      setTitle ("Pellet Drawing");
      numPoints = 0;
      xArray = new int[MAX_POINTS];
      yArray = new int[MAX_POINTS];
   }

   public void paint (Graphics g){
      displayPoints (g);
   }

   public void mousePressed (int x, int y){
```

```
            if (numPoints < xArray.length){
                Graphics g = getGraphics();
                g.fillOval (x, y, 5, 5);
                savePoint (x, y);
            }
            else
                messageBox ("Sorry: cannot draw another pellet.");
        }

        private void displayPoints (Graphics g){
            int i;
            for (i = 0; i < numPoints; i++){
                g.fillOval (xArray[i], yArray[i], 5, 5);
            }
        }

        private void savePoint (int x, int y){
            xArray[numPoints] = x;
            yArray[numPoints] = y;
            numPoints++;
        }

        public static void main (String[] args){
            Frame frm = new Sketchpad2();
            frm.setSize (200, 200);
            frm.setVisible (true);
        }
    }
```

Although this version of the program behaves correctly, there is still a problem. When the arrays of the coordinates become full, the program can no longer accept mouse clicks, so the user sees a message box. There are several ways to deal with this problem. One way, which we leave as an exercise, is to resize the arrays when they become full, perhaps by adding 50 new cells each time this happens.

The current version of the Sketchpad application can easily be modified to support freehand brush-stroke drawing. We implement the mouseDragged method. This method should do the same thing as the mousePressed method. Then, as long as the user moves the mouse with the button pressed, a series of pellets will be drawn in a stroke. This change is also left as an exercise.

Defining and Using a Geometric Class

Many applications implement classes to represent geometric objects such as points, lines, and circles. In this section, we develop a Circle class.

Specification and Use of Circles

A circle object has a center, a radius, and a color. Instances of class Circle recognize messages to observe and modify these attributes and to draw themselves in a given graphics context. Table 10-5 lists these methods.

TABLE 10-5
Methods of the Circle class

METHOD	WHAT IT DOES
Circle(int x, int y, int r, Color c)	Creates a circle with center point (x, y), radius r, and color c.
int getX()	Returns the x coordinate of the center.
int getY()	Returns the y coordinate of the center.
int getRadius()	Returns the radius.
Color getColor()	Returns the color.
int setX(int x)	Modifies the x coordinate of the center.
int setY(int y)	Modifies the y coordinate of the center.
int setRadius(int r)	Modifies the radius.
Color setColor(Color c)	Modifies the color.
void draw(Graphics g)	Draws the circle in the graphics context. The circle is filled with its color.
void drawOutline(Graphics g)	Draws an outline of the circle in the graphics context.
boolean containsPoint(int x, int y)	Returns true if the point (x, y) lies within the circle.
void move(int xAmount, int yAmount)	Moves the circle by xAmount horizontally and yAmount vertically. Negative amounts move to the left and up.

An application's `paint` method might create and draw a circle with center point (100,100), radius 50, and color red, as in this example:

```
public void paint (Graphics g){
    Circle circle = new Circle (100, 100, 50, Color.red);
    circle.draw (g);
}
```

Implementation of Circle Class

The implementation of the instance variables, the constructor, and the accessors and mutators for the Circle class requires no comment.

The draw method uses drawOval to draw the circle. drawOval expects not the coordinates of the center of the circle, but the coordinates of the upper left corner of the rectangle that bounds the circle.

drawOval also expects not the radius of the circle, but the width and height of the bounding rectangle. Thus, we must translate the circle's attributes to the attributes of the enclosing rectangle:

```
public void draw (Graphics g){
    // Save the current color of the graphics context
    // and set it to the circle's color.
    Color oldColor = g.getColor();
    g.setColor(color);

    // Translate the circle's data to the rectangle's data for drawing.
    g.fillOval(centerX - radius, centerY - radius, radius * 2, radius * 2);

    // Restore the color of the graphics context.
    g.setColor(oldColor);
}
```

The user detects the presence of a point in a circle by running the `containsPoint` method. To determine whether a point (*x, y*) lies within the circumference of a circle, begin with the equation of a circle,

$$(x - xc)^2 + (y - yc)^2 = r^2$$

or

$$(x - xc)^2 + (y - yc)^2 - r^2 = 0$$

and plug in the values of the center point, the radius, and the coordinates. If the left side of this equation is less than or equal to 0, then the point lies within the circle. For example, given a circle of radius 2 and center point (0,0), the point (1,1) produces the result

$$1^2 + 1^2 - 2^2 = -2$$

so this point lies within the circle.

Here is the method that results from this design:

```
public boolean containsPoint (int x, int y){
    int xSquared = (x - centerX) * (x - centerX);
    int ySquared = (y - centerY) * (y - centerY);
    int radiusSquared = radius * radius;
    return xSquared + ySquared - radiusSquared <= 0;
}
```

CASE STUDY 3 : Dragging Circles

Request

Write a program that allows the user to drag circles in a window.

Analysis

The application, called `DragCircles`, draws some randomly generated circles at startup. When the user drags a circle, the circle object is modified and redrawn.

Figure 10-8 shows the proposed interface.

FIGURE 10-8

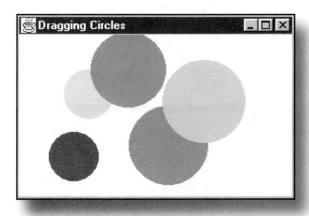

Design

The program maintains an array of circle objects that appear in the window. When the user drags a circle, one of these objects is modified and redrawn. The program also maintains a currently selected circle, the coordinates of the current mouse point, and a Boolean flag, initially false, indicating that a circle has been selected.

mousePressed searches the array of circles to determine whether the user has pressed the mouse button in a circle. If so, these events occur:

- A Boolean flag, circleHasBeenSelected, is set to true.

- A Circle variable, selectedCircle, is set to the circle that was selected.

- The coordinates currentX and currentY are set to the mouse's current coordinates.

    mouseDragged performs the following steps:

- The incremental amount by which the mouse has just moved is determined. This is done by subtracting the old mouse point coordinates from the new ones.

- The move method is called to move the circle by the given amount.

- repaint is invoked, which clears the window and then calls paint to redraw all the circles.

- The new mouse position is saved in the variables currentX and currentY.

Implementation

```
import java.awt.*;
import BreezyGUI.*;

public class DragCircles extends GBFrame{

    private final static int MAX_CIRCLES = 5;
    private final static int MIN_CENTER_X = 50;
    private final static int MAX_CENTER_X = 150;
```

```
private final static int MIN_CENTER_Y = 50;
private final static int MAX_CENTER_Y = 150;
private final static int MIN_RADIUS = 10;
private final static int MAX_RADIUS = 50;

private int mouseX = 0, mouseY = 0;
private boolean circleHasBeenSelected = true;
private int currentX = 0;
private int currentY = 0;
private Circle selectedCircle;
private Circle circles[] = new Circle[MAX_CIRCLES];

public DragCircles(){
    int i;
    for (i = 0; i < MAX_CIRCLES; i++){
        int centerX = randomInt(MIN_CENTER_X, MAX_CENTER_X);
        int centerY = randomInt(MIN_CENTER_Y, MAX_CENTER_Y);
        int radius = randomInt(MIN_RADIUS, MAX_RADIUS);
        Color color = randomColor();
        Circle circle = new Circle(centerX, centerY, radius, color);
        circles[i] = circle;
    }
    setTitle ("Dragging Circles");
}

public void paint (Graphics g){
    int i;
    for (i = 0; i < MAX_CIRCLES; i++)
        circles[i].draw(g);
}

public void mousePressed (int x, int y){
    currentX = x;
    currentY = y;
    circleHasBeenSelected = findCircle();
}

public void mouseReleased (int x, int y){
    circleHasBeenSelected = false;
}

public void mouseDragged (int x, int y){
    if (circleHasBeenSelected){
        selectedCircle.move(x - currentX, y - currentY);
        repaint();
        currentX = x;
        currentY = y;
    }
}

private boolean findCircle(){
    int i;
    for (i = MAX_CIRCLES - 1; i >= 0; i--)
```

```
            if (circles[i].containsPoint(currentX, currentY)){
                selectedCircle = circles[i];
                return true;
            }
        return false;
    }

    private int randomInt (int low, int high){
        return (int) (low + Math.random() * (high - low + 1));
    }

    private Color randomColor(){
        Color color;
        int number = randomInt (1, 5);
        switch (number){
            case 1:
                color = Color.red;
                break;
            case 2:
                color = Color.blue;
                break;
            case 3:
                color = Color.green;
                break;
            case 4:
                color = Color.magenta;
                break;
            case 5:
                color = Color.cyan;
                break;
            default: color = Color.orange;
        }
        return color;
    }

    public static void main (String[] args){
        Frame frm = new DragCircles();
        frm.setSize (300, 200);
        frm.setVisible (true);
    }
}
```

The above program has a problem. As we drag a circle around, the window seems to flicker. The cause lies in the mouseDragged method. Every time we move a circle, the repaint method is called. This method clears the window and then calls paint to redraw the circles. Unless the computer is very fast, the human eye reads the cycles of clear and redraw as a flicker.

Fortunately, there is a way to overcome this problem. Java allows drawing to be done in two different modes. In the default mode, which we have been using exclusively so far, images (lines, text, shapes) overwrite whatever happens to be underneath them. This mode is called *paint*. The second mode is called *XOR*. The result of drawing an image in XOR mode depends on two colors—the current color and the XOR color. Wherever the image overlays the XOR color, it is drawn in the current color, and vice versa. A consequence of this strange convention is that if an image is redrawn on top of itself, it disappears, and the window returns to its original appearance before the image was first drawn. Pixels of a different color (neither the current color nor the XOR color) underneath the image are changed in a manner too difficult to explain here. However, redrawing over these pixels returns them to their original color, too.

In the code that follows, we use the XOR mode to solve the flicker problem. When a circle is selected, we draw an outline of it in XOR mode. Then, as the user drags the mouse, we redraw the outline using XOR (restoring the pixels covered by the outline) and draw another outline in XOR mode at the mouse's new location. Drawing an outline involves so few pixels that the user sees no flicker and believes the outline is smoothly following the mouse around the window. When the user finally releases the mouse, we repaint the window. Here are the modifications to the program:

```
public void mousePressed (int x, int y){
     currentX = x;
     currentY = y;
     circleHasBeenSelected = findCircle();
     if (circleHasBeenSelected)
        selectedCircle.drawOutline(getGraphics());
}

public void mouseReleased (int x, int y){
     circleHasBeenSelected = false;
     repaint();
}

public void mouseDragged (int x, int y){
     if (circleHasBeenSelected){
        Graphics g = getGraphics();
        selectedCircle.drawOutline (g);                    // Old location
        selectedCircle.move (x - currentX, y - currentY);
        selectedCircle.drawOutline (g);                    // New location
        currentX = x;
        currentY = y;
     }
}
```

To complete the modifications, we must add the drawOutline method to the Circle class. Here is the code:

```
public void drawOutline (Graphics g){
   Color oldColor = g.getColor();
   g.setColor (Color.black);
   g.setXORMode (Color.white);
   g.drawOval (centerX - radius, centerY - radius, radius * 2, radius *
             2);
   g.setColor (oldColor);
   g.setPaintMode ();
}
```

Text Properties

As you have seen, text (a string of characters) is drawn like any other image in a bitmapped display. Text can have several properties, as shown in Table 10-6.

TABLE 10-6
Text properties

TEXT PROPERTY	EXAMPLE
Color	Red, green, blue, white, black, etc.
Font style	Plain, **bold**, *italic*
Font size	10 point, 12 point, etc.
Font name	Courier, Times New Roman, etc.

The color and font properties of text are set by adjusting the color and font properties of the window (or window object) in which the text is drawn. We first provide an overview of Java's Font class, and then show some examples of how to control the properties of text.

The Class Font

An object of class Font has three basic properties: a name, a style, and a size. The following code creates one Font object to represent the font **Courier bold 12**, and another Font object to represent the font *Arial bold italic 10:*

```
Font courierBold12 = new Font("Courier", Font.BOLD, 12);
Font arialBoldItalic10 = new Font("Arial", Font.BOLD + Font.ITALIC, 10);
```

The Font constants PLAIN, BOLD, and ITALIC define the font styles. The font size is an integer representing the number of points, where one point equals $1/72$ inch. The values of the font names depend on your particular computer platform. To see what they are, run the code segment

```
String fontNames[] = Toolkit.getDefaultToolkit().getFontList();
int i;
for (i = 0; i < fontNames.length; i++)
    System.out.println (fontNames[i]);
```

This code performs the following tasks:

- Declares the variable fontNames as an array of strings.

- Runs the Toolkit class method getDefaultToolkit, which returns the default toolkit for the particular computer platform.

- Runs the method getFontList on the toolkit. This method returns a list of the available font names.

- Sets the variable fontNames to this list.

- Runs a loop that displays the contents of fontNames in the terminal window.

Table 10-7 lists the important Font methods.

TABLE 10-7
Font methods

FONT METHOD	WHAT IT DOES
`public Font(String name,` `        int style, int size)`	Creates a new Font object with the specified properties; style must be PLAIN, BOLD, ITALIC, or a combination of these using +.
`public String getName()`	Returns the current font name.
`public int getStyle()`	Returns the current font style.
`public int getSize()`	Returns the current font size.

Setting the Color and Font Properties of Text

The programmer sets the color and font properties of text by setting the color and font properties of the GUI object's graphics context. For example, assume that we want to display the text `"Hello world!"`, in green with the font Courier bold 14, in an application window. The following code would do this:

```
Font ourFont = new Font ("Courier", Font.BOLD, 14);
Color ourColor = Color.GREEN;
Graphics g = getGraphics();
g.setColor (ourColor);
g.setFont (ourFont);
g.drawString ("Hello world!", 100, 100);
```

Changing the font and color of a graphics context affects all subsequent graphics operations (`drawString`, in particular) in that context, but does not alter the font or color of existing images.

Design, Testing, and Debugging Hints

■ Computer screen coordinates are not the same as conventional Cartesian coordinates. Computer screen coordinates place the origin (0, 0) in the upper left corner, and get larger as they move to the left and to the bottom of the screen.

■ The `repaint` method always clears the graphics context. Thus, any displayed images will be erased when `repaint` is invoked. This will occur automatically when the window is resized, unless you override the `paint` method to redraw the images.

Summary

In this lesson, you learned:

■ A coordinate system is required for any graphics application. In Java and other programming languages, coordinate start with (0,0) in the upper left corner.

■ Java provides a `Graphics` class for drawing in a window. When a window that contains a graphic is resized, Java refreshes the window objects. The `paint` method can be used to redraw window objects when the screen is updated.

■ Java controls the color of images and text using the `Color` class. Text properties of font, font style, and font size are controlled by the `Font` class.

LESSON 10 REVIEW QUESTIONS

WRITTEN QUESTIONS

Write your answers to the following questions.

1. Assume that g refers to a graphics context for drawing shapes. Write method calls that draw the shapes requested below.
   a. A line with end points (50,70) and (300,200).
   b. An oval with an upper left corner (50,50), a width of 100, and a height of 200.
   c. An arc that spans 90 degrees from 12 o'clock to 3 o'clock, with an upper left corner of (50,50), a width of 100, and a height of 200.
   d. A string, "I'm getting really good at Java Programming," at (100,100).

2. Write a method, `drawCircle`, that expects three parameters—the *x* and *y* coordinates of the center point and the length of the radius—and draws a circle.

3. When is it a good idea to implement the method `paint` in a Java application?

4. Write a code segment that saves the color of graphics context g, changes its color to blue, draws a filled oval, and restores the original color of the graphics context.

5. Implement a method that displays the string "Mouse pressed at" and the coordinates of the mouse when the mouse is pressed.

6. Write a code segment that displays your name in green letters with the font Courier bold italic 14.

LESSON 10 PROJECTS

1. Write a program that allows the user to change the color of the application window and to view its size. The program should provide a menu of colors. When the user selects a color, the program sets the window's graphics context to that color. The program also displays the height and width of the window's graphics context at the center of the window. These values should be updated whenever the user resizes the window.

2. Modify the program of Project 3 in Lesson 7, so that it displays the faces of the dice on each roll. To do this, the `Dice` class should define a `draw` method. This method's parameters are a graphics

context and a pair of coordinates representing the point at the center of the die's rectangular face. Thus, the application is responsible for computing the location of the dice, but the dice are responsible for drawing themselves. After each roll, the application should clear the window and redraw the dice.

3. Modify the program of Project 5 in Lesson 7, so that it displays the user's blackjack hand. To do this, the Card class should define a draw method. This method is similar to the draw method for dice in Project 2. A card can be visualized as a rectangle that displays the card's number in the upper left corner and the lower right corner. In the case of the ace or a face card, use the letters A, K, Q, or J. In addition, you should display the name of the suit (spade, club, heart, or diamond) in the middle of the rectangle. When the suit of the card is spade or club, the information displayed within the rectangle should be black. Otherwise, this information should be red.

4. The twentieth-century Dutch painter Piet Mondrian developed a style of abstract painting that exhibited simple recursive patterns. For example, an "idealized" pattern from one of his paintings might look like Figure 10-9. To generate such a pattern with a computer, an algorithm would begin by drawing a rectangle, and then repeatedly draw two unequal subdivisions, as shown in Figure 10-10.

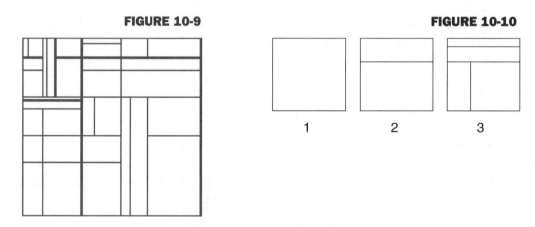

FIGURE 10-9   FIGURE 10-10

As you can see, the algorithm continues this process of subdivision for a number of levels, until an "aesthetically right moment" is reached. In this version, the algorithm appears to divide the current rectangle into portions representing $1/3$ and $2/3$ of its area and appears to randomly alternate the subdivisions along the horizontal and vertical axes. Design, implement, and test a program that uses a recursive method to draw such patterns. The user should be able to draw several pictures with different levels.

5. Modify the program in Project 4 so that it fills the rectangular areas in the picture with randomly generated colors.

6. The programs in Projects 4 and 5 use constant factors of $1/3$ and $2/3$ to subdivide the rectangle on the recursive steps. Modify the program in Project 5 so that the factors randomly alternate among $1/5$ and $4/5$, $1/4$ and $3/4$, and $1/3$ and $2/3$.

7. In the Sketchpad2 program of Case Study 2, saving the points in arrays causes a problem: The size of the arrays is fixed when they are created, so the number of pellets the user can draw is limited. Modify the program so that the arrays can accommodate any number of points. When the

arrays become full, invoke a method that creates two new arrays that are 50 cells larger than the old arrays, copy the data from the old arrays to the new arrays, and reset the instance variables to the new arrays. Test the program thoroughly.

8. Modify the Sketchpad2 program of Case Study 2 so that it supports freehand drawing, as suggested in the text. Also, add a menu that allows the user to select the width of a pellet (1, 3, or 5 pixels).

9. The freehand drawing program of Project 8 works well as long as the user drags the mouse slowly. However, when dragging speeds up, large gaps appear between the pellets. To solve this problem, modify the program so that it draws lines between the points during dragging. Simply pressing the mouse should still draw a pellet. The two arrays should contain the coordinates of these pellets, as well as the coordinates of the end points of each line segment. To distinguish a pellet from a line segment, use the value −1 as a separator in each array. For example, if the user draws a pellet at (100,100) and then two line segments at (100,100), (150,160) and (150,160), (200,45), the two arrays should contain the values

100 −1 100 150 −1 150 200
100 −1 100 160 −1 160 45

You should continue to use the method fillOval to draw pellets, but use drawLine to draw line segments.

CRITICAL THINKING ACTIVITY

Java's RGB color scheme supports 2^{24} colors. Describe the design of a program that would cycle through all these colors and display each one. Write a pseudocode algorithm for the process that generates the colors and displays them.

UNIT 3 REVIEW QUESTIONS

TRUE/FALSE

On a separate piece of paper, type True if the statement is true or False if it is not.

T F **1.** In Java, an array is an ordered collection of methods.

T F **2.** Because arrays are objects, two variables can refer to the same array.

T F **3.** You can select more than one radio button at a time.

T F **4.** One responsibility of the view portion of a program is to instantiate and arrange window objects.

T F **5.** Methods in different classes that have similar functions can have the same name.

T F **6.** Subclasses can see both public and private names declared in their parent classes.

T F **7.** If you need to use the cast operator, remember that you never cast down, only cast up.

T F **8.** The coordinate system in Java and other programming languages is the Cartesian coordinate system.

T F **9.** Java automatically invokes the default `paint` method.

T F **10.** To change the look of text in program output, use the methods in the `Font` class.

FILL IN THE BLANKS

On a separate piece of paper, type the information necessary to complete the following statements.

1. A(n) _____ is an ordered collection of similar items or elements.

2. An item's position within an array is called its _____.

3. Two arrays in which the corresponding elements are related are called _____ arrays.

4. The division of labor between a model and a view is called a(n) _____.

5. Classes that are never instantiated are called _____.

6. Java organizes classes in a(n) _____.

7. The `toString` message, which is understood by every object no matter which class it belongs to, is a good example of _____.

8. Java provides the _____ class for drawing in windows.

9. An image that reappears when a window is resized is called a(n) _____ image.

10. The `Font` method that returns the current font name is _____.

WRITTEN QUESTIONS

On a separate piece of paper, type the answers to the following questions or problems.

1. Write statements for the following items that declare array variables and assign the appropriate array objects to them.
   a. `intNumbers`, an array of 5 integers.
   b. `realNumbers`, an array of 100 real numbers.
   c. `bools`, an array of 10 Booleans.
   d. `words`, an array of 20 strings.

2. Write a `for` loop that initializes an array of ten integers to the first ten positive integers.

3. Repeat Question 2, but use an initializer list.

4. There are several ways in which methods in a subclass can be related to methods in its superclass. Describe at least two of these.

5. Explain what happens when your program calls the method `repaint`.

UNIT 3 APPLICATIONS

1. Write a program that takes ten floating-point numbers as inputs. The program displays the average of the numbers followed by all the numbers that are greater than the average. As part of your design, write a method that takes an array of doubles as a parameter and returns the average of the data in the array.

2. Write a program to keep statistics for a basketball team consisting of 12 players. Statistics for each player should include shots attempted, shots made, and shooting percentage; free throws attempted, free throws made, and free throw percentage; offensive rebounds and defensive rebounds; assists; turnovers; and total points. Place these data in parallel arrays. Appropriate team totals should be listed as part of the output.

3. Modify the program of Application 2 so that it uses a two-dimensional array instead of parallel arrays for the statistics.

4. Sketching programs typically allow users to draw lines, rectangles, and ovals by selecting an item from a menu and clicking the mouse in the desired area of the sketchpad. Write a program that supports this kind of drawing. The program should have a **Shape** menu and a **Color** menu. When the user selects **Shape/Line**, for example, double-clicking in the drawing area will establish the end points of a line. Other lines can then be drawn until the user selects a different shape. This program does not have to refresh the images when the window size is modified.

5. Modify the program of Application 4 so that it can refresh the images. To do this, define the classes `Line`, `Circle`, and `Rectangle`, and maintain arrays of each kind of shape. Each of these classes should have a `draw` method.

CRITICAL THINKING ACTIVITY

A bank provides several kinds of accounts, among them checking accounts and saving accounts. Design a simple banking system data model that represents these accounts. Be sure to make use of abstract classes, inheritance, polymorphism, and encapsulation. The result of your work should be a set of class summary boxes for the data model of the banking system.

FILES, WEB-BASED PROGRAMMING, AND AWT

UNIT 4

 Unit 4 Estimated Time: 10.5 hours

11 FILES

Files are software objects used to model the transfer of data to and from storage media. Files provide machine-independent methods that hide the details of physical storage media.

Secondary Storage

Data stored in variables are temporary, existing only for the lifetime of a method call or the run of an application. Data stored in files can be saved permanently on a secondary storage medium, such as a magnetic disk, an optical disk (CD), or a magnetic tape. When needed, the data can be loaded into program variables from the secondary storage medium.

Figure 11-1 shows the path traveled by data during file input and output.

FIGURE 11-1
The file input/output process

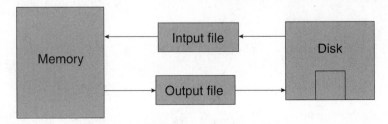

File Classes

At the lowest level, Java views the data in files as a *stream* of bytes. A stream of bytes from which data are read is called a *file input stream*. A stream of bytes to which data are written is called a *file output stream*.

Java provides a set of classes for connecting a program to a file stream and for manipulating data in the stream. These classes are defined in the **java.io** package. Figure 11-2 shows a portion of Java's class hierarchy used in file processing. The concrete classes are shaded. The remaining classes are abstract.

The classes FileInputStream and FileOutputStream are used to connect programs to files. The classes DataInputStream and DataOutputStream are used for input and output of data of specific types, such as int, double, and String. When these data are written to a data output stream, they can be read back in, as ints, doubles, and Strings, from a data input stream. Terminal output uses the object System.out, which is an instance of the PrintStream class.

Several other classes involving files are in a separate branch of Java's class hierarchy, as shown in Figure 11-3. Once again, the concrete classes are shaded.

FIGURE 11-2
Classes used in file processing

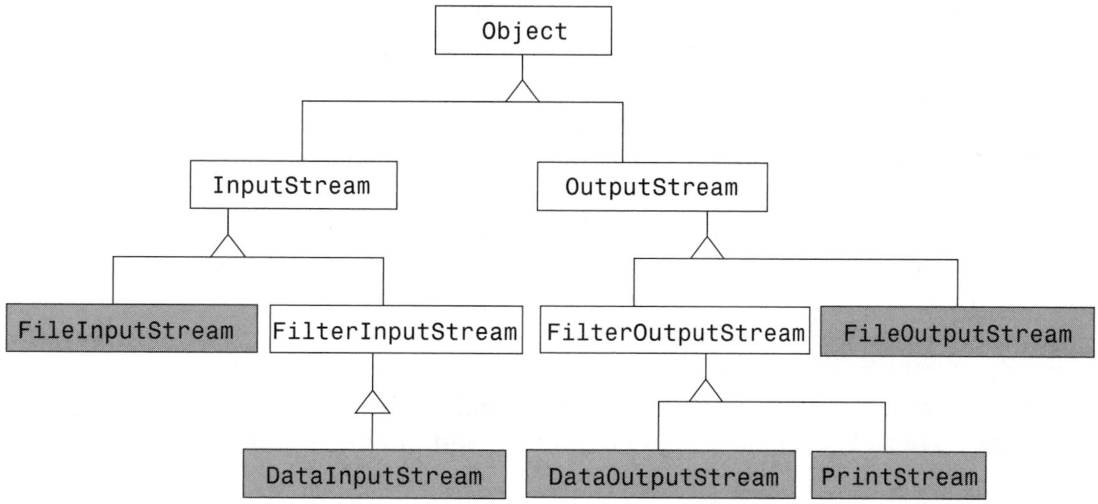

FIGURE 11-3
Other classes relating to files

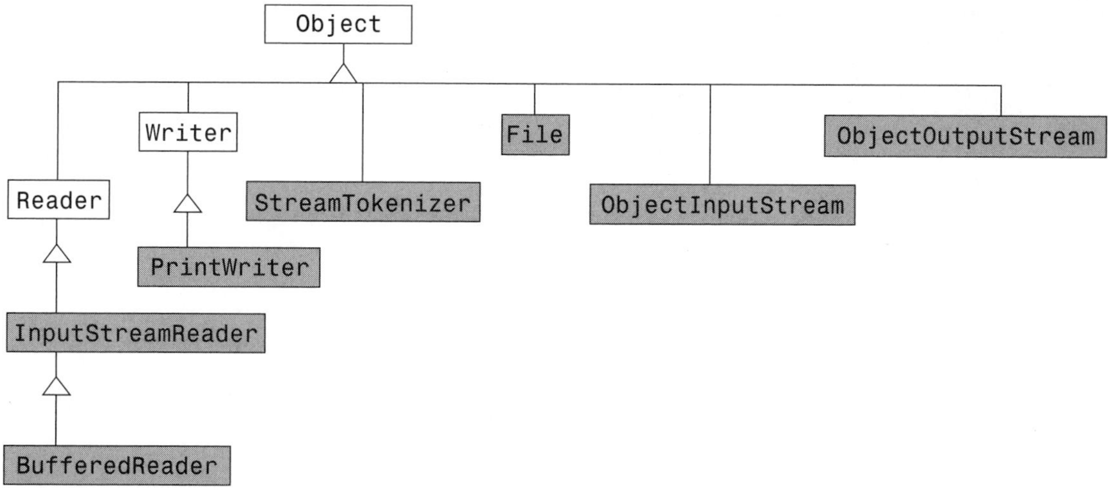

301

The class `InputStreamReader` is used to read character data from a file input stream. The class `BufferedReader` is used to read input one line at a time. The class `StreamTokenizer` is used to read words and numbers from an input stream reader. The class `PrintWriter` takes data of different types (`int`, `double`, `String`, etc.) and writes them as byte-level data to a file output stream. The `File` class is used to establish connections with the file and directory system on a disk. Several of these classes, such as `FileInputStream`, `InputStreamReader`, and `StreamTokenizer`, are typically used in combination to process files.

Although the number of these classes might seem intimidating, they can be used in some rather simple combinations. We focus on some standard methods of establishing connections with files and performing input and output operations.

File Input

A typical file input process is described in the following pseudocode algorithm:

```
Open an input connection to a file
Read the data from the file and process it
Close the input connection to the file
```

We now present a short program that serves as an example of this process. The program's interface allows the user to type a file name in a text field. When the user selects the **Display the Contents** button, the program opens the file for input, calls the method `readAndProcessData`, and closes the file. `readAndProcessData` in the first version of the program is a simple stub. In later versions, this method will read the text from the file, convert it to uppercase, and display the results in a text area.

Run-Time Tip

Make sure the file you want to open is in the same folder with your Java files.
If you have to type a file name, be sure to type the file extension as well.

```java
import java.awt.*;
import java.io.*;
import BreezyGUI.*;

public class ConvertText extends GBFrame{
    Label nameLabel = addLabel ("File Name:", 1, 1, 1, 1);
    TextField nameField = addTextField ("", 1, 2, 1, 1);
    Button displayButton = addButton ("Display the Contents", 2, 1, 1, 1);
    TextArea output = addTextArea ("", 3, 1, 6, 6);

    public ConvertText(){
        nameField.requestFocus();
        output.setEditable (false);
        setTitle ("Open the File");
    }

    public void buttonClicked (Button buttonObj){
        String fileName = nameField.getText();
```

```
        try{
            FileInputStream stream = new FileInputStream (fileName);
            readAndProcessData (stream);
            stream.close();
        }
        catch(IOException e){
            messageBox ("Error in opening input file:\n" + e.toString());
        }
        nameField.requestFocus();
        nameField.selectAll();
    }

    private void readAndProcessData (FileInputStream stream){
        messageBox ("Running readAndProcessData\n" +
                    "File opened successfully");
    }

    public static void main (String[] args){
        Frame frm = new ConvertText();
        frm.setSize (300, 300);
        frm.setVisible(true);
    }
}
```

Opening and Closing a `FileInputStream`

The `buttonClicked` method in our example program performs the following operations:

■ Opens a file input stream on the user's file name.

■ Passes the stream to a method for reading and processing the data.

■ Closes the stream.

```
public void buttonClicked (Button buttonObj){
    String fileName = nameField.getText();
    try{
        FileInputStream stream = new FileInputStream (fileName);
        readAndProcessData (stream);
        stream.close();
    }
    catch(IOException e){
        messageBox ("Error in opening input file:\n" + e.toString());
    }
    nameField.requestFocus();
    nameField.selectAll();
}
```

Note that the code is embedded in Java's `try-catch` statement. The `try-catch` statement provides a way of catching and responding to run-time errors. This statement consists of two parts:

1. A `try` statement. A block of code is included here. If a run-time error occurs in this block, Java throws an exception and control immediately passes to a `catch` statement.

2. One or more `catch` statements. Each `catch` statement is qualified by a particular kind of exception that might be thrown in the `try` statement. In this case, an `IOException`, such as failure

to find the file, might occur. Our example has just one `catch` statement, which expects an instance of `IOException`, here named e, as a parameter. When the `catch` statement is invoked, the code in our example sends the object e the `toString` message to obtain information about the error. Our example then displays this information in a message box.

The code for opening and closing a file stream must be embedded in a `try-catch` statement. Otherwise, the Java compiler objects with a syntax error.

Exception Handling

As you saw in earlier lessons, Java responds to run-time errors by throwing exceptions. The examples in those lessons, such as divide-by-zero exceptions and array subscript exceptions, are thrown automatically. The program remains alive, and Java displays system-defined error messages in a terminal window.

The `try-catch` statement provides a general way of handling exceptions under program control. In what follows, we are concerned only with exceptions related to files. Techniques for handling other kinds of exceptions are presented in Appendix F.

Reading Data from a Text File

After a file input stream has been successfully opened, we can read data from it. We now examine the input of data from *text files*. A text file contains characters. Java provides several ways to read these characters from a file:

1. One character at a time, using the class `InputStreamReader`.

2. One line at a time, using the class `BufferedReader`.

3. One word at a time, using the class `StreamTokenizer`.

To perform the desired kind of input, the Java programmer uses the appropriate class and methods. We now show how this is done by returning to our example program.

READING DATA ONE CHARACTER AT A TIME

The next code segment shows how the method `readAndProcessData` would be completed to read the text from the file one character at a time:

```java
private void readAndProcessData (FileInputStream stream){
    InputStreamReader reader = new InputStreamReader (stream);
    try{
        output.setText("");
        int data = reader.read();
        while (data != -1){
            char ch = (char) data;
            ch = Character.toUpperCase (ch);
            output.append (ch + "");
            data = reader.read();
        }
    }
    catch(IOException e){
        messageBox ("Error in file input:\n" + e.toString());
    }
}
```

The first step is to connect an instance of the class `InputStreamReader` to the `FileInputStream` parameter. This is done by passing the file input stream as a parameter to the input stream reader's constructor. The result is shown in Figure 11-4.

FIGURE 11-4
The file input stream is passed to
the input stream reader's constructor

The next step is to enter a `try-catch` statement to read data from the stream. The form of the input loop is fairly general:

```
Get the first datum from the stream
While the datum does not indicate that the end of stream has been reached
    Process the datum
    Get the next datum from the stream
```

Note three other points:

1. The value –1 indicates that the end of the stream has been reached.

2. The data returned by `read()` are of type `int`. These are the ASCII values of the characters in the file. Thus, you must cast them to characters for further processing.

3. The `catch` statement should handle an `IOException`, which might occur during the input of a datum.

READING DATA ONE LINE AT A TIME

The next code segment shows how the method `readAndProcessData` would be completed to read the text from a file, one line at a time:

```java
private void readAndProcessData (FileInputStream stream){
    InputStreamReader iStrReader = new InputStreamReader (stream);
    BufferedReader reader = new BufferedReader (iStrReader);
    try{
        output.setText("");
        String data = reader.readLine();
        while (data != null){
            data = data.toUpperCase();
            output.append (data + "\n");
            data = reader.readLine();
        }
    }
    catch(IOException e){
        messageBox ("Error in file input:\n" + e.toString());
    }
}
```

To set up the reader, we proceed as before, by first connecting an input stream reader to the file input stream. We then connect an instance of `BufferedReader` to the input stream reader. The result is shown in Figure 11-5.

FIGURE 11-5

BufferedReader has been connected to the input stream reader

Once again, the method uses a try-catch statement. The structure of the input process is the same as before. However, note the following variations:

1. We now call the method readLine to obtain a string representing the next line of text in the stream.

2. When this string has the value null, we have reached the end of the stream.

3. We use the String instance method toUpperCase to convert the entire string to uppercase.

4. The newline character is not part of the string obtained from readLine. Thus, we have to append a newline before output.

The use of a BufferedReader not only allows us to work with whole lines of text, but also can improve the speed at which the data are input. When the programmer uses BufferedReader for input, Java uses an area of memory called a *buffer* to read large chunks of text from the file, rather than single characters.

READING DATA ONE WORD AT A TIME

When sequences of characters are separated by white space characters (blanks, tabs, newlines, punctuation marks, arithmetic operators, and other special characters), these sequences can be processed as words or *tokens*. For example, suppose a file contains the sequence "16 cats sat on 4 mats." It contains the separate tokens

16
cats
sat
on
4
mats

In our example, there are actually two types of tokens: strings (beginning with a letter) and numbers (consisting of digits and perhaps a leading sign and an embedded decimal point).

Java provides a StreamTokenizer class for reading tokens from a file. The next code segment revisits our example program to show how tokens are read from a file stream:

```
private void readAndProcessData (FileInputStream stream){
    InputStreamReader iStrReader = new InputStreamReader (stream);
    BufferedReader bufReader = new BufferedReader (iStrReader);
    StreamTokenizer reader = new StreamTokenizer (bufReader);
    try{
        output.setText("");
        String data = "";
        reader.nextToken();
        while (reader.ttype != StreamTokenizer.TT_EOF){
            if (reader.ttype == StreamTokenizer.TT_WORD){
                data = reader.sval;
                data = data.toUpperCase();
            }
```

```
            else if (reader.ttype == StreamTokenizer.TT_NUMBER)
                data = reader.nval + "";
            output.append (data + "\n");
            reader.nextToken();
        }
    }
    catch (IOException e){
        messageBox ("Error in file input:\n" + e.toString());
    }
}
```

The setup of the stream extends our previous setup only, by connecting an instance of `Stream-Tokenizer` to a buffered reader. The result is shown in Figure 11-6.

FIGURE 11-6
`StreamTokenizer` has been connected to a buffered reader

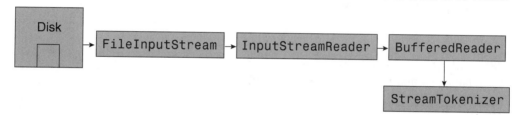

Our example uses an if statement to distinguish words and numbers. To support this, the class `StreamTokenizer` defines the public instance variables listed in Table 11-1.

TABLE 11-1
Variables of the `StreamTokenizer` class

VARIABLE	WHAT IT IS
ttype	An int variable containing the type of the current token. Tokens can be of four types: end of file, end of line, word, and number, represented by the constants TT_EOF, TT_EOL, TT_WORD, and TT_NUMBER, respectively.
sval	A String variable containing the current token if it is a word.
nval	A double variable containing the current token if it is a number.

The `StreamTokenizer` method `nextToken()` reads the next token from the file input stream, and updates the tokenizer's instance variables with information about the type and value of the token. `nextToken` skips white space between words and numbers by default.

IMPORTANT:

Some versions of Java seem to contain a bug in their treatment of the "." character. When placed in or at the end of a word, the period is treated as part of the word rather than as white space. The problem is illustrated in the next case study but can be overcome by using the `StreamTokenizer` method `whiteSpaceChar`. (For more details, see Java's online documentation as discussed in Appendix A.)

Request

Count the number of words in a text file, find the longest word, and determine the length of the longest word.

FIGURE 11-7

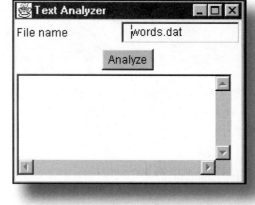

Analysis

The program takes a file name as input from the user. When the user selects the **Analyze** button, the program opens the file, counts the number of words in it, and determines which of these words is the longest. The program then displays the word count, the longest word, and the length of the longest word in a text area.

Figure 11-7 shows the proposed interface.

Example: Assume that the file **words.dat** contains the text

This is a short file. There
are only a few words in it. The
longest word has 7 letters.

The results of an analysis of this file would be displayed as shown in Figure 11-8.

FIGURE 11-8

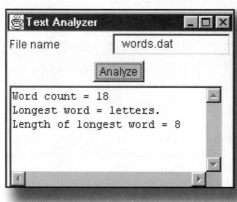

Special considerations include these:

■ If the file name provided by the user is not on disk, the program displays a message box with an error message.

■ A default file name, **words.dat**, appears in the text field initially.

■ Numbers in the file will be ignored.

Design

The following pseudocode describes the operations performed in the `buttonClicked` method:

```
Open a file input stream with the file name provided by the user
Initialize the counter to 0 and the longest word to the empty string
Call the method analyzeFile to read and process the words in the file
Close the file input stream
Call the method printStatistics to display the statistics
```

The `analyzeFile` method reads words and computes statistics, as follows:

```
Open an input stream reader on the file input stream
Open a stream tokenizer on the input stream reader
Read the first token from the stream tokenizer
While there are more tokens in the stream tokenizer
    If the token is a word
        Increment the word count
        If the length of the word is greater than the longest word
            Set the longest word to the word just input
    Read the next token from the stream tokenizer
```

The structure chart shown in Figure 11-9 illustrates the program's design.

FIGURE 11-9

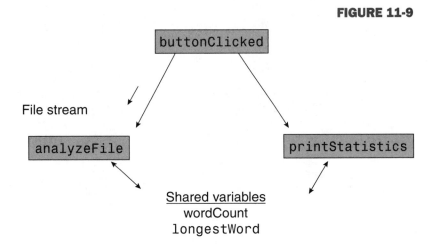

Implementation

```
import java.awt.*;
import BreezyGUI.*;
import java.io.*;

public class TextAnalyzer extends GBFrame{

    Label fileLabel = addLabel ("File name",1,1,1,1);
    TextField fileField = addTextField ("words.dat",1,2,1,1);
    Button doReport = addButton ("Analyze",2,1,2,1);
```

```java
TextArea outputArea = addTextArea ("",3,1,2,3);

private int wordCount;
private String longestWord;

public TextAnalyzer() {
    setTitle ("Text Analyzer");
}

public void buttonClicked (Button buttonObj){

    String fileName = fileField.getText();
    wordCount = 0;
    longestWord = "";

    try{
        FileInputStream fileStream = new FileInputStream (fileName);
        analyzeFile (fileStream);
        fileStream.close();
        printStatistics();
    }
    catch (IOException e){
        messageBox ("File not opened\n" + e.toString());
    }
}

private void analyzeFile (FileInputStream fileStream){

    InputStreamReader reader = new InputStreamReader (fileStream);
    StreamTokenizer tokens = new StreamTokenizer (reader);
    String word = "";

    try{
        tokens.nextToken();
        while (tokens.ttype != StreamTokenizer.TT_EOF){
            if (tokens.ttype == StreamTokenizer.TT_WORD){
                word = tokens.sval;
                wordCount++;
                if (word.length() > longestWord.length())
                    longestWord = word;
            }
            tokens.nextToken();
        }
    }
    catch (IOException e){
        messageBox ("Data not read properly " + e.toString());
    }
}

private void printStatistics(){
```

```
        outputArea.setText ("");
        outputArea.append ("Word count = " + wordCount + "\n");
        outputArea.append ("Longest word = " + longestWord + "\n");
        outputArea.append ("Length of longest word = "
                           + longestWord.length() + "\n");
    }

    public static void main (String[] args){
        Frame frm = new TextAnalyzer();
        frm.setSize (250, 200);
        frm.setVisible (true);
    }
}
```

There is a problem with this program. See Project 1 at the end of this lesson.

File Output

We now turn our attention to file output. The file output process can be described in the following pseudocode algorithm:

```
Open an output connection to a file
Write the data to the file
Close the output connection to the file
```

Opening and Closing a `FileOutputStream`

The code segment below performs these actions:

■ Opens a file output stream on a file named **test.out**.

■ Passes the stream to a method for writing the data.

■ Closes the stream.

```
try{
    FileOutputStream stream = new FileOutputStream ("test.out");
    writeData (stream);
    stream.close();
}
catch(IOException e){
    messageBox ("Error opening output file " + e.toString());
}
```

Writing Data to a `PrintWriter`

We once again examine text file output first. The class `PrintWriter` writes data to a file output stream as bytes. The resulting file can be read with a text editor or an input stream reader. The `Print-Writer` methods `print` and `println` each take a single parameter, which can be an `int`, a `double`, a `String`, or any other type. Each method converts its parameter to a sequence of bytes that is sent to the output stream. `println` also writes a newline character (`\n`) to the *print stream*. Figure 11-10 shows the flow of data from memory to print writer to file output stream to disk.

311

FIGURE 11-10
Data flow from memory to disk

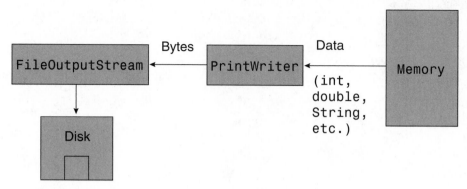

The following code implements the `writeData` method invoked in the previous code segment. This method

- Opens a print writer on the file output stream.

- Writes a header message followed by a newline to the print writer.

- Writes ten random integers between 1 and 10, separated by spaces, to the print writer.

```
void writeData(FileOutputStream fileOutputStream){

    int i;
    PrintWriter printWriter = new PrintWriter (fileOutputStream, true);
    printWriter.println ("Here are 10 random integers: ");

    for (i = 1; i <= 10; i++)
        printWriter.print ((int) (1 + Math.random() * 10) + " ");
}
```

The preferred constructor for a print writer takes a Boolean parameter that indicates whether the application desires the output stream to be flushed. Flushing sends any data left in the output buffer to the disk. A print writer throws no exceptions, so a `try-catch` statement is not necessary.

CASE STUDY 2 : Employees and Payroll

Request

Write a program that reads two files as inputs. Each line in the first file contains employee data. Each line in the second file contains hours worked data for the corresponding employee in the first file. The output of the program is a third file that contains a report of the payroll for all of the employees.

Analysis

Figure 11-11 describes the flow of data for the program.

FIGURE 11-11

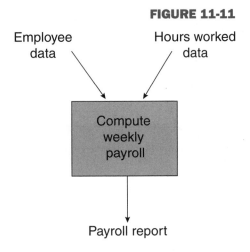

Format of the Input Files

Here is the format of data on each line of the **employee** file:

```
<last name> <first name> <number of dependents> <wage amount>
```

Spaces separate the items on a line.

Here is the format of data on each line of the **hours** file:

```
<regular hours> <overtime hours>
```

Format of the Output File

The output file will consist of six columns, headed as follows:

```
Employee Name    Regular Pay   Overtime Pay   Gross Pay    Tax    Net Pay
```

The format of the columns appears in Table 11-2.

TABLE 11-2
Format for the column output

COLUMN	JUSTIFICATION	SPACING
Employee name	Left	15
Regular pay	Right	15
Overtime pay	Right	15
Gross pay	Right	12
Tax	Right	8
Net pay	Right	10

Each line after the first one will contain the data for the employee and the payroll. For example, given the employee file

```
Lambert Ken 7 5.50
Osborne Martin 3 6.75
```

and the hours worked file

```
40 4
40 6
```

the report file would be

```
Employee Name    Regular Pay    Overtime Pay    Gross Pay      Tax    Net Pay
  Ken, Lambert        220.00           33.00       253.00    37.95     215.05
  Martin, Osborne     270.00           60.75       330.75    49.61     281.14
```

We use an `Employee` class to represent each employee. An `Employee` object is responsible for reading its name and hours worked, computing its pay, and writing the results to the report file. Figure 11-12 shows the proposed interface.

FIGURE 11-12

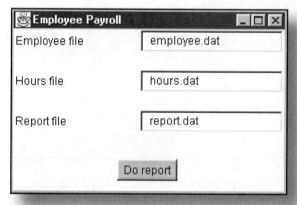

The overtime wage is 1.5 times the regular wage. The tax rate is 15% of the gross pay. The net pay is the gross pay minus the tax.

Design

We use a stream tokenizer for input and a print writer for output. The design of the `Employee Payroll` class focuses on the methods `buttonClicked` and `processFiles`. We first present the pseudocode for these methods. The pseudocode for `buttonClicked` is

```
Open a file input stream on the employee file
Open a file input stream on the hours worked file
Open a file output stream on the report file
Call the method processFiles with the streams as parameters
Close the files
```

Here is the pseudocode for processFiles:

```
Open a stream tokenizer on the employee file stream
Open a stream tokenizer on the hours worked file stream
Open a print writer on the report file stream
Write the header to the report print writer
Read the next token from the employee stream tokenizer
While there are more tokens in the employee stream
    Create an Employee object
    Send message employee.readEmployee(employee stream tokenizer)
    Send message employee.readHoursWorked(hours worked stream tokenizer)
    Send message employee.computeAndPrintPay(report print writer)
Read the next token from the employee stream tokenizer
```

As each line of the employee file is input, we create a new Employee object. This object then extracts its data from the employee file. The employee object is then told to read its payroll data from the hours worked file, process it, and output its result to the report file. The process continues until the last lines of the files are read and processed. The **report** file then appears in the same folder with the other Java files for this project.

The design of the Employee class is outlined in the following class summary box:

```
Class:
    Employee extends Object
Private Class Constant:
    static final double TAX_RATE = 0.15
Private Instance Variables:
    String firstName
    String lastName
    int dependents
    double wage
    int regularHours
    int overtimeHours
Public Methods:
    Constructor
    String toString()
    void readEmployee(StreamTokenizer stream)
    void readHoursWorked(StreamTokenizer stream)
    void computeAndPrintPay(PrintWriter stream)
    static void printHeader(PrintWriter stream)
```

Here is pseudocode for the Employee method readEmployee:

```
Read last name
Read first name
Read wage
Read number of dependents
```

Here is pseudocode for the Employee method readHoursWorked:

```
Read regular hours
Read overtime hours
```

Here is pseudocode for the `Employee` method `computeAndPrintPay`:

```
Calculate my regular pay, overtime pay, gross pay, tax, and net pay
Write these data, in appropriate format, to the print writer
```

Note that we include a class method for printing the header in the `Employee` class. This is appropriate, because this class knows about the number of the data fields and their individual widths.

Implementation

Here is the `EmployeePayroll` class:

```java
import java.awt.*;
import java.io.*;
import BreezyGUI.*;

public class EmployeePayroll extends GBFrame{

    Label employeeLabel = addLabel ("Employee file",1,1,1,1);
    TextField employeeField = addTextField ("employee.dat",1,2,1,1);
    Label hoursLabel = addLabel ("Hours file",2,1,1,1);
    TextField hoursField = addTextField ("hours.dat",2,2,1,1);
    Label reportLabel = addLabel ("Report file",3,1,1,1);
    TextField reportField = addTextField ("report.dat",3,2,1,1);
    Button doReport = addButton ("Do report", 4,1,2,1);

    public EmployeePayroll(){
        setTitle ("Employee Payroll");
    }

    public void buttonClicked (Button buttonObj){

        String employeeFileName = employeeField.getText();
        String hoursFileName = hoursField.getText();
        String reportFileName = reportField.getText();

        try{
            FileInputStream employeeFile =
                new FileInputStream (employeeFileName);
            FileInputStream hoursFile =
                new FileInputStream (hoursFileName);
            FileOutputStream reportFile =
                new FileOutputStream (reportFileName);
            processFiles (employeeFile, hoursFile, reportFile);
            employeeFile.close();
            hoursFile.close();
            reportFile.close();
        }
        catch (IOException e){
            messageBox ("File not opened\n" + e.toString());
        }
    }

    private void processFiles (FileInputStream employeeFile,
```

```
                    FileInputStream hoursFile, FileOutputStream reportFile){

        InputStreamReader employeeReader =
            new InputStreamReader (employeeFile);
        StreamTokenizer employeeStream =
            new StreamTokenizer (employeeReader);
        InputStreamReader hoursReader = new InputStreamReader
        (hoursFile);
        StreamTokenizer hoursStream = new StreamTokenizer (hoursReader);
        PrintWriter reportStream = new PrintWriter (reportFile, true);

        Employee.printHeader(reportStream);

        try{
            employeeStream.nextToken();
            while (employeeStream.ttype != StreamTokenizer.TT_EOF){
                Employee employee = new Employee();
                employee.readEmployee (employeeStream);
                employee.readHoursWorked (hoursStream);
                employee.computeAndPrintPay (reportStream);
                employeeStream.nextToken();
            }
        }
        catch (IOException e){
            messageBox ("Data not read properly " + e.toString());
        }
    }

    public static void main (String[] args){
        Frame frm = new EmployeePayroll();
        frm.setSize (300, 200);
        frm.setVisible (true);
    }
}
```

The next listing shows the Employee class:

```
import java.io.*;
import BreezyGUI.*;

public class Employee extends Object{

    private static final double TAX_RATE = 0.15;
    private String firstName, lastName;
    private double wage;
    private int dependents, regularHours, overtimeHours;

    public Employee(){
        firstName = "NO NAME";
        lastName = "NO NAME";
        wage = 0.00;
        dependents = 0;
        regularHours = 0;
        overtimeHours = 0;
    }
```

```java
    public String toString(){
        return lastName + " "
            + firstName + " "
            + wage + " "
            + dependents + " "
            + regularHours + " "
            + overtimeHours;
    }

    public void readEmployee (StreamTokenizer stream){
        try{
            firstName = stream.sval;
            stream.nextToken();
            lastName = stream.sval;
            stream.nextToken();
            dependents = (int) stream.nval;
            stream.nextToken();
            wage = stream.nval;
        }
        catch (IOException e){
            System.out.println ("Data not read properly " + e.toString());
        }
    }

    public void readHoursWorked (StreamTokenizer stream){
        try{
            stream.nextToken();
            regularHours = (int) stream.nval;
            stream.nextToken();
            overtimeHours = (int) stream.nval;
        }
        catch(IOException e){
            System.out.println ("Data not read properly " + e.toString());
        }
    }

    public void computeAndPrintPay (PrintWriter stream){
        double regPay = wage * regularHours;
        double overPay = wage * 1.5 * overtimeHours;
        double grossPay = regPay + overPay;
        double tax = grossPay * TAX_RATE;
        double netPay = grossPay - tax;
        stream.println(
            Format.justify ('l', lastName + ", " + firstName, 15)
            + Format.justify ('r', regPay, 15, 2)
            + Format.justify ('r', overPay, 15, 2)
            + Format.justify ('r', grossPay, 12, 2)
            + Format.justify ('r', tax, 8, 2)
            + Format.justify ('r', netPay, 10, 2));
    }

    public static void printHeader(PrintWriter stream){
        stream.println (Format.justify('l', "Employee Name", 15)
```

```
                    + Format.justify ('r', "Regular Pay", 15)
                    + Format.justify ('r', "Overtime Pay", 15)
                    + Format.justify ('r', "Gross Pay", 12)
                    + Format.justify ('r', "Tax", 8)
                    + Format.justify ('r', "Net Pay", 10));
      }
}
```

Data Input and Output Streams

It is often convenient to save data of different types, such as int, double, and String, to files in such a way that these data can be read back in as integers, doubles, and strings. It would be difficult to perform these operations with the file classes that we have examined thus far. For example, during input a stream tokenizer can distinguish numbers and words, but not doubles and integers.

Java provides the classes DataInputStream and DataOutputStream for the input and output of several different data types. Table 11-3 shows some of the commonly used input and output operations for data streams.

TABLE 11-3
Common input and output operations for data streams

METHOD	WHAT IT DOES
char readChar()	Reads a character from the data input stream.
double readDouble()	Reads a double from the data input stream.
int readInt()	Reads an int from the data input stream.
String readUTF()	Reads a string from the data input stream.
void writeChar(char ch)	Writes a character to the data output stream.
void writeDouble(double d)	Writes a double to the data output stream.
void writeInt(int i)	Writes an int to the data output stream.
void writeUTF(String s)	Writes a string to the data output stream.

The DataOutputStream methods save additional bytes with each datum to enable the DataInputStream methods to pick out the datum in the input stream. Thus, several data values, such as a double and two strings, can be written consecutively to a data output stream without separating spaces or newlines. For this reason, files created with a data output stream cannot be easily viewed with a text editor or processed by a stream tokenizer. Also, the program must know the order and kind of data exactly during input.

The next example program performs these actions:

■ Generates a user-specified number of random integers (the number is entered as a parameter).

■ Writes these integers to a *data output stream.*

■ Reads them back in from a *data input stream.*

■ Outputs the integers to the terminal window.

```java
import java.io.*;
import BreezyGUI.*;

public class TestDataStreams{

    public static void main (String[] args){

        // Obtain the number of ints from the program's parameter.

        int number = Integer.valueOf (args[0]).intValue();

        // Generate the random ints and output them to a data stream.

        try{
            FileOutputStream foStream = new FileOutputStream ("ints.dat");
            DataOutputStream doStream = new DataOutputStream (foStream);
            int i;
            for (i = 0; i < number; i++)
                doStream.writeInt ((int) (1 + Math.random() * number));
            doStream.close();
        }
        catch (IOException e){
            System.err.println ("Error during output: " + e.toString());
        }

        // Input the ints from a data stream and display on the terminal.

        try{
            FileInputStream fiStream = new FileInputStream ("ints.dat");
            DataInputStream diStream = new DataInputStream (fiStream);
            while (true){
                int i = diStream.readInt();
                System.out.println (i);
            }
        }
        catch (EOFException e){
            System.out.println("\nAll done.");
        }
        catch (IOException e){
            System.err.println("Error in input" + e.toString());
        }
        GBFrame.pause();
    }
}
```

A data input stream is processed within an *exception-driven loop.* Using the expression while (true), the loop continues until an EOFException occurs. This exception is not viewed as an error, but rather as a good reason to exit the loop. The catch statement in this example prints a reassuring message.

Now that we have seen two different ways to handle file input and output, it is natural to ask when to use each one. Here are two rules of thumb:

1. It is appropriate to use a stream tokenizer for input and a print writer for output when the file must be viewed or created with a text editor, or when the order and types of data are unknown.

2. It is appropriate to use a data input stream for input and a data output stream for output when the file need not be viewed or created with a text editor, and when the order and types of data are known.

Serialization and Object Streams

As we saw in Lesson 9, when the data for an application consist of many classes, it is useful to organize these classes in a data model. A data model is *persistent* if it survives between runs of an application. Obviously, the data in a model must be saved to a file and loaded from a file if they are to be considered persistent. When a data model is complex, code for transferring it to and from files can create a real maintenance headache. Java provides a feature called *serialization* that can considerably ease the burden of making a data model persistent. To use this feature, the programmer does these two things:

1. Makes each class in the data model serializable.

2. Uses the classes `ObjectInputStream` and `ObjectOutputStream` to load and save the data model.

For example, consider the student test scores program of Lesson 8. The data model consists of two classes, `Student` and `StudentTestScoresModel`. To serialize these two classes, the programmer must import the package **java.io** and add the qualifier `implements Serializable` to each class definition. The changes are shown below:

```
import java.io.*;

public class StudentTestScoresModel extends Object implements Serializable{
```

```
import java.io.*;

public class Student extends Object implements Serializable{
```

These are the only changes necessary to the data model. The programmer does not have to implement any methods for reading or writing the components of these classes to files.

The next step is to use the appropriate object streams in the interface class to load and save the data model. The following code segment shows how to save a `StudentTestScoresModel` object named `model` to a file:

```
import java.io.*;

public class StudentTestScoresView{

   ...

   private StudentTestScoresModel model;

   ...

   private void saveModel(){
```

```
        try{
            FileOutputStream foStream = new FileOutputStream ("model.dat");
            ObjectOutputStream ooStream = new ObjectOutputStream (foStream);
            ooStream.writeObject (model);
            foStream.flush();
            foStream.close();
        }
        catch (IOException e){
            messageBox ("Error during output: " + e.toString());
        }
    }
    …
}
```

The method `writeObject` outputs the entire data model to the object output stream. Likewise, the method `readObject` can input the entire data model from an object input stream, as shown in the next code segment:

```
import java.io.*;

public class StudentTestScoresView{

    …

    private StudentTestScoresModel model;

    …

    private void loadModel(){
        try{
            FileInputStream fiStream = new FileInputStream ("model.dat");
            ObjectInputStream oiStream = new ObjectInputStream (fiStream);
            model = (StudentTestScoresModel) oiStream.readObject();
            fiStream.close();
        }
        catch (Exception e){
            messageBox ("Error during input: " + e.toString());
        }
    }
}
```

There are two important points to note about this code:

1. The method `readObject` returns an `Object`, which must be cast to a `StudentTestScoresModel` before it can be stored in the variable.

2. The method `readObject` can throw several different kinds of exceptions. To catch any of these, the `catch` statement's parameter is the class `Exception`.

In general, the methods `readObject` and `writeObject` can be used with any objects—strings, arrays, or user-defined objects. When reading an object, the programmer must be aware of its type and its position in the input stream, and store it in the appropriate type of variable. As you can see, object streams and serialization are very powerful tools for managing object-oriented data models, so the time you spend learning to use them will be well worth your while.

Terminal Input and Output

Old-fashioned computers that use operating systems such as DOS support an impoverished style of user interaction known as terminal I/O. In these systems, the terminal screen pretends to be a file output stream, while the keyboard pretends to be a file input stream.

We have been using the stream System.out to display messages in a terminal window. The stream System.err can be used to display messages to an error message window (which, by default, is the same as the terminal window). The stream System.in can be used for input from the keyboard. (**Note:** Java may not support terminal input on a Macintosh.) The two output streams are ready to use (with the methods print and println) immediately. However, some setup is required to use the terminal input stream. The following steps are typical:

1. Open an InputStreamReader on the object System.in.

2. Open a BufferedReader on the resulting input stream reader.

3. Use the method readLine() to read a line of text (a String) from the buffered reader.

The next program uses the three terminal streams in a brief interaction with the user:

```java
import java.io.*;
import BreezyGUI.*;

public class TestTerminal{

    public static void main (String[] args){
        String name;
        int age;
        try{
            InputStreamReader reader = new InputStreamReader (System.in);
            BufferedReader buffer = new BufferedReader (reader);
            System.out.print ("Enter your name: ");
            name = buffer.readLine();
            System.out.print ("Enter your age: ");
            age = Integer.valueOf (buffer.readLine()).intValue();
            if (age < 1)
                System.err.println ("Error: you're too young for this!");
            else
                System.out.println ("Name = " + name + "\nAge = " + age);
        }
        catch (IOException e){
            System.err.println ("Error in terminal input" + e.toString());
        }
        GBFrame.pause();
    }
}
```

Figure 11-13 shows a sample session with this program.

Output of a program that uses terminal input

```
C:\Books\Java\Chapter13>java TestTerminal
Enter your name: James Javahack
Enter your age: 0
Error: you're too young for this!

Hit Enter to continue: _
```

File Dialogs

Thus far in this lesson, file names have come either directly from program code or interactively from a text field. This approach forces the program or the user to get the file name right. Problems can arise if the file does not exist or if the user cannot remember its name.

Windows-based applications provide file dialogs that allow the user to browse directories. The user can point and click to select a file name, or type in a file name, or back out by canceling the dialog. Figure 11-14 shows a typical file dialog for finding input files on a Windows platform.

FIGURE 11-14
A file dialog for Windows 95

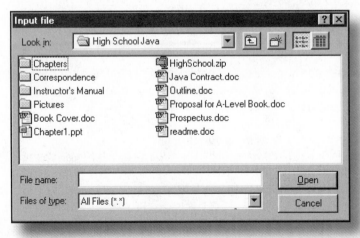

The programmer can use Java's `FileDialog` class to give users easy access to file names. The most important `FileDialog` methods are listed in Table 11-4.

TABLE 11-4

FileDialog methods

Lesson (11) Files

CONSTANT/METHOD	WHAT IT DOES
`FileDialog(Frame parent,` `        String title, int type)`	Creates a file dialog with the specified parent frame, title, and type (either LOAD for input files, or SAVE for output files).
`String getFile()`	Returns the file name if the user has selected a file, or the value null if the user has canceled.
`String getDirectory()`	Returns the directory pathname if the user has selected a file, or the value null if the user has canceled.
`void setSize(int width, int height)`	Sets the width and height of the dialog.
`void setVisible(boolean flag)`	Shows or hides the dialog.

The following code segment presents the user with a dialog for an input file. The code displays the file name and directory pathname if the user has not canceled the dialog. Otherwise, the code displays a message that the user has canceled the dialog. The parent frame passed to the file dialog is the variable `this`, which refers to the application itself:

```
FileDialog fileDialog = new FileDialog (this, "Input file",
                                    FileDialog.LOAD);
fileDialog.setSize(450, 300);
fileDialog.setVisible (true);
String fileName = fileDialog.getFile();
String dirName = fileDialog.getDirectory();
if (fileName != null && dirName != null){
   messageBox ("File name: " + fileName\n" + "Directory: " + dirName);
}
else
   messageBox ("The user has canceled the file dialog.");
```

Once we have the file name and the directory name, we can connect the appropriate file stream to the file. Because the selected file may be located in a directory different from the application, we need both names. The procedure for using these names follows:

1. Create an instance of the class `File` with the file name and the directory name as parameters.

2. Open the appropriate file stream on this `File` object.

The form for creating a `File` object from a file name and a directory name is

```
new File (<dirName>, <fileName>)
```

Here is a modification of the previous code segment that opens a file input stream and processes the data, if the user selects a file name in the dialog:

```
try{
    FileDialog fileDialog = new FileDialog (this, "Input file",
                                            FileDialog.LOAD);
    fileDialog.setSize (450, 300);
    fileDialog.setVisible (true);
    String fileName = fileDialog.getFile();
    String dirName = fileDialog.getDirectory();
    if (fileName != null && dirName != null){
        File file = new File(dirName, fileName);
        FileInputStream stream = new FileInputStream (file);
        processData (stream);
        stream.close();
    }
}
catch (IOException e){
    messageBox ("Error opening input file " + e.toString());
}
```

Note that we have embedded the code segment in a try-catch statement, because Java might throw an IOException when creating a file stream.

CS CAPSULE:
Programming Language Translation

Each time you compile and run a program, a large number of software tools come into play. Two programs in particular, a compiler and a run-time interpreter, play the most significant roles.

The compiler's primary task is to translate the expressions in a source program to a form that can be evaluated by the run-time interpreter. A compiler for a full-blown programming language must analyze many different kinds of expressions (loops, conditionals, assignments, function calls, declarations, etc.) and report specific syntax errors to the programmer.

In addition to a large variety of expressions, a compiler must deal with a complex vocabulary and be capable of generating target expressions that will execute efficiently at run time. A compiler delegates the task of recognizing words in the source program to a module called the scanner and delegates the task of generating efficient object code to a module called the code generator. The work of syntax analysis and error-checking falls to a module called the parser. Most parsers make use of a table of syntax rules and a push down stack to handle backtracking during the processing of expressions.

Most of the real work in compiler design now focuses on the so-called "back end" or code generator. Aside from the task of producing the most efficient code (code that is not only fast but is also small), designers face the challenge of generating code for multiple hardware platforms. As you know, a Java compiler generates platform-independent code called byte code. Each major hardware platform is then responsible for providing an interpreter that understands byte code.

When the executable program is in the machine language of the computer, the computer executes the program's instructions directly. When the executable program is in an intermediate language, such as byte code, an interpreter must decode the program's instructions and invoke the appropriate machine operations. Most interpreters access a program's data in an area of memory called a run-time stack. This stack is also used to store intermediate values of expressions and data belonging to function calls that are currently being evaluated.

Two other software tools that enable compiled programs to be executed are a linker and a loader. The linker combines the code from different modules, such as libraries, into a single executable program. This work usually includes verifying that the functions called in one module have unique definitions in the system. After successful linkage, the loader prepares the run-time system for execution by formatting memory into segments for the program's instructions and for the run-time stack.

Recent advances in programming language translation have led to advances in hardware design. For example, the design of a reduced instruction set chip (RISC) for microprocessors was made possible by new methods of compiler optimization. Thus, programming language translation is an important area of computer science and will become a focus of study as you proceed through upper-level computer science courses.

Design, Testing, and Debugging Hints

■ Attempts to open file streams must be embedded within `try-catch` statements. These statements will catch and respond to errors in I/O operations.

■ When reading data from an input stream, the first datum must be read before testing for the end of the stream. Thus, the form of such a process is

```
Get the next datum from the stream
While not at the end of the stream
    Process the datum
    Get the next datum from the stream
```

Summary

In this lesson, you learned:

■ Files can be used to store data permanently. The **java.io** package contains classes used in file processing. Java views data in files as a stream of bytes.

■ A stream of bytes from which data are read is called an input stream. A stream of bytes to which data are written is an output stream.

■ The `try-catch` statement provides a way of catching and responding to run-time errors. If an error occurs in the block of code included in the `try` statement, Java throws an exception. A `catch` statement then gives specific information about that particular exception.

■ Serialization can be used to make a data model persistent.

■ The `System.in` stream can be used for input from the keyboard.

■ File dialogs can be created using the `FileDialog` class to give users easy access to file names.

WRITTEN QUESTIONS

Write your answers to the following questions.

1. Write a Java code segment that performs the requested task.
   a. Open a file input stream on a file named **Inputfile.**
   b. Open an input stream reader on the file of Question 1a.
   c. Open a buffer reader on the file of Question 1a.
   d. Open a stream tokenizer on the file of Question 1a.
   e. Open a file output stream on a file named **Outputfile.**
   f. Open a print writer on the file of Question 1e.

2. Write a Java code segment that outputs the integers from 1 to 10 to the print writer of Question 1e. Each integer should be followed by newline.

3. What is the purpose of a `try-catch` statement in Java? Why is it used with file operations?

4. Write a Java code segment that inputs characters from the input stream reader of Question 1b and outputs them to a `TextArea` named `output`.

5. Write a Java code segment that inputs lines of text from the buffer reader of Question 1c and outputs them to a `TextArea` named `output`.

6. Write a Java code segment that inputs words from the stream tokenizer of Question 1d and outputs them to a `TextArea` named `output`.

LESSON 11 PROJECTS

SCANS

1. The text analyzer of Case Study 1 has a problem. In the example file, the word *letters* has seven characters and is the longest word, but the program records the word *letters.* as the longest word with eight characters. Consult the online Java documentation on `StreamTokenizer` to diagnose this problem and fix it.

2. Write a program that reads names from a text file. The names are separated by newline characters and are in sorted order. There are some duplicate names. The program should write the names to a different text file, without the duplicate names. Allow the user to specify the file names in text fields.

3. A text file contains a list of salespersons and their total annual sales amounts. Each line of the file contains the person's last name, followed by a blank space, followed by a floating-point number. Write a program that reads the data from such a file and sorts them according to name (ascending order) and then according to sales amount (descending order) and outputs the results of the sorts to two different text files. Allow the user to specify the file names in text fields.

4. Add a checkbox labeled **Save to Disk** to the TidBit Computer Store program of Application 5 in Unit Review 1. When the user checks this box, the program saves the loan schedule to a text file named **loan.dat.**

5. Add a **File** menu to the circle drawing program of Lesson 10. The menu should have the options **New, Open,** and **Save.** When the user selects **New,** the drawing area is cleared, and a new group of randomly generated circles is drawn. When the user selects **Open,** the program clears the drawing area, reads circles from a file, and displays these. When the user selects **Save,** the program writes the currently displayed circles to a file. Use the classes `DataInputStream` and `DataOutputStream` in this program.

CRITICAL THINKING ACTIVITY

Describe how you could use serialization to simplify the program of Project 5.

INTRODUCTION TO HTML AND APPLETS

OBJECTIVES

Upon completion of this lesson, you should be able to:

■ Explain the importance of hypertext language.

■ Format text, lists, and tables using markup tags.

■ Link documents using hyperlinks.

■ Insert multimedia objects using markup tags.

■ Write Java applets.

⏱ **Estimated Time: 3 hours**

Hypertext, Hypermedia, and the World Wide Web

In 1945, Vannevar Bush, a scientist at MIT, published a prophetic essay, "As We May Think," in the *Atlantic Monthly*. According to Bush, even though computers were already wonderful for number crunching, they would soon be used for data storage, data manipulation, and logical reasoning. These predictions came to pass in the 1950s and 1960s, with the advent of database management and AI.

Bush also raised and attempted to answer the following question: How can we improve the way in which we consult our information sources during research? At that time, researchers used indexing schemes such as card catalogs, but this method restricted the user to a blind search. By contrast, the human mind uses association to search its own memory bank. For example, when I hear the word "wife," I instantly think of a particular person, namely, my wife. My mind does not go through a complex search process to retrieve the associated information. Somehow, it just gets it.

Bush proposed to use computer technology to link chunks of information associatively. Now imagine that the entries in a keyed table also contain embedded links to other entries in other tables. Bush called his imaginary machine a *memex*. Each individual would have a desktop memex, as a virtual extension of his or her memory. The memex would receive chunks of information from a photocopy machine, a keyboard, or a stylus. The information would be stored on microfilm. The user would establish links between chunks of information by means of a few simple keystrokes.

The computer would maintain these *associative links* and traces of the user's explorations of them. The user could come back to that trail, or give it to another user to link into a more general trail. Research would involve following the trails blazed by the masters, not just the examination of their end products.

Hypertext and Hypermedia

By the late 1960s, the technology for realizing Bush's dream was available. In 1967, Theodor Holm Nelson coined the term *hypertext* to refer to Bush's machine. Hypertext is a structure consisting of nodes and the links between them. Each node is a document or chunk of text. Normally, links to other nodes are displayed to the user as embedded, highlighted terms within a given chunk of text. The user moves to a node by using an arrow key or a mouse to select an associated term.

Early hypertext systems were Douglas Englebart's NLS/Augment (1968) and Cognetics Corporation's Hyperties (mid-1980s).

In 1987, Apple Computer released Hypercard, one of the first hypermedia platforms. *Hypermedia* is similar to hypertext, but in addition to text links, hypermedia links can include images, sounds, and applications. For example, a link might appear as an icon or image rather than highlighted text. The targeted chunk of information might be a full-screen image, a movie, a musical recording, or a computer application, such as a database program.

Networks and the World Wide Web

All the early hypertext systems ran on separate, stand-alone machines, which maintained data storage for the individual user. With the development of the Internet, people began to think of sharing hypertext across a network of communicating machines. Chunks of information, or pages as they are now called, could be stored on many different physical machines around the world. Each page would be linked in a gigantic hypermedia system, the World Wide Web. The Web is now a reality, taken for granted by millions of users.

The Web consists of two kinds of machines:

- Servers, on which pages of information reside.

- Clients, which run browsers to access information on the servers.

In some cases, the client and server reside on the same machine.

When the user opens a browser, he is presented with an initial page of information. Embedded in this page are links to other nodes. When the user selects a link, the browser sends a message to the node's machine, requesting a transfer of its information. If the request is successful, the information at the node is downloaded to the user's browser.

Because there are different types of computers, a networked hypermedia system requires a uniform means of representing information using a machine-independent *hypertext markup language* (HTML). Such a system also requires a way to designate node addresses using machine-independent *uniform resource locators* (URLs). Information must be transmitted from site to site using machine-independent network transmission protocols. Finally, it must be possible to display information with browsers from different vendors, subject to the restriction that all the browsers behave in a similar manner.

Hypertext Markup Language

HTML was developed as a machine-independent way of representing information in a networked-based hypermedia system. Early word processing systems, such as WordStar, bracketed text with codes that specified print formats. For example, the code ^I (control I) indicated italics and ^B bold. To illustrate, the text

```
Bush, Vannevar, ^BAs We May Think^B, ^IAtlantic Monthly^I, July, 1945.
```

would have been printed as

```
Bush, Vannevar, As We May Think, Atlantic Monthly, July, 1945.
```

HTML uses a similar scheme. Codes called *markup tags* can indicate the format of textual elements or links to other nodes. Browsers interpret these codes as commands and display the text in the desired format. Figure 12-1 shows the relationship between authors and users of HTML documents.

FIGURE 12-1
Relationship between authors and users of HTML documents

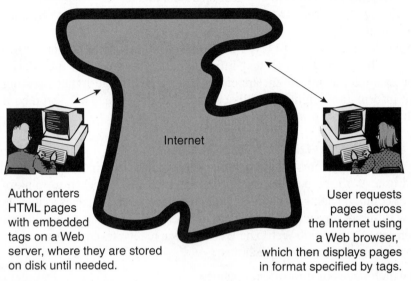

Author enters HTML pages with embedded tags on a Web server, where they are stored on disk until needed.

User requests pages across the Internet using a Web browser, which then displays pages in format specified by tags.

A Short Example

As a first example of using HTML, we will show how to create the Web page shown in Figure 12-2. The page includes markup tags for a title, a heading, and two paragraphs of text.

FIGURE 12-2
A sample Web page

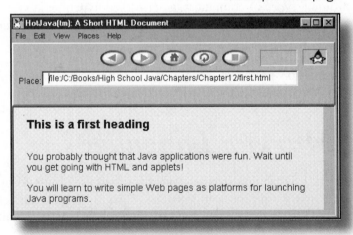

The author of the page wrote an HTML document that looks like this:

```
<html>
<head>
<TITLE>A Short HTML Document</TITLE>
</head>
```

```
<body>
<H1>This is a first heading</H1>
<P>You probably thought that Java applications were fun. Wait until
you get going with HTML and applets!</P>
<P>You will learn to write simple Web pages as platforms
for launching Java programs.</P>
</body>
</html>
```

When a browser displays the document, the title appears at the top of the browser's window.

There is a blank line between the heading and the first paragraph and between the two paragraphs. The browser uses word wrap to fit the text within the window's boundaries. A typical HTML document consists of multiple HTML pages.

The document must be stored in a file having the extension **.html**. Pages can be any size, from a few to many hundreds of lines. We now turn to a discussion of the tags that define the HTML protocol.

Tip

Use the .htm extension if you are running Windows 3.1.

Markup Tags

A markup tag in HTML begins with a left angle bracket (<) and ends with a right angle bracket (>), for example, <title>. Tags are not case sensitive. For instance, the tags <title>, <TITLE>, and< TiTlE> are equivalent, even though they are not equally readable. Tags usually occur in pairs, for example, <title> and </title>. The start tag tells the browser where to begin the format, and the end tag, which includes a slash (/), tells the browser where to end the format.

Tags can include attributes. For example, the tag <P ALIGN=CENTER> tells the browser to align the next paragraph in the center of the window. In this example, ALIGN is the attribute's name and CENTER is the attribute's value. Some commonly used markup tags are listed in Table 12-1.

TABLE 12-1
Common markup tags

MARKUP TAG	WHAT IT DOES
HTML	Designates an HTML document.
HEAD	Designates the head of the document.
BODY	Designates the contents of the document.
TITLE	Designates the title that appears in the browser's window.
P	Designates a paragraph of text.
H1, H2, etc.	Designates a heading. There are six levels of headings.
PRE	Designates text to be formatted literally.
BR	Indicates a line break.
UL	Designates a bulleted list.
OL	Designates a numbered list.
LI	Indicates an item within a list.

Minimal Document Structure

Every HTML document should have the following minimal structure:

```
<HTML>
<HEAD>
<TITLE> the title goes here </TITLE>
</HEAD>
<BODY>
the text for the document goes here
</BODY>
</HTML>
```

Note the following points:

1. The HTML tag informs the browser that it is dealing with an HTML document.

2. The HEAD tag identifies the first part of the document.

3. The TITLE tag identifies the document's title. The title is displayed at the top of the browser's window and is used during searches for the document. The title is also displayed in bookmark lists (a list of the user's favorite links). We recommend short, descriptive titles.

4. The BODY tags enclose the information provided by the HTML document.

5. The browser ignores extra white space, such as blank lines and tab characters.

Commenting an HTML Document

Authors often add comments to an HTML document. The browser does not interpret comments or show them to the reader. The form of a comment is

```
<!-- text of comment -->
```

In the following example, we have modified the first example by inserting blank lines and comments to make it more readable. However, a browser will display this page exactly as before.

```
<html>
<!-- Authors: Kenneth A. Lambert and Martin Osborne
     Last update: November 30, 1997                  -->

<head>
<TITLE>A Short HTML Document</TITLE>
</head>

<body>
<H1>This is a first heading</H1>

<P>You probably thought that Java applications were fun. Wait until
you get going with HTML and applets!</P>

<P>You will learn to write simple Web pages as platforms
for launching Java programs.</P>

</body>
</html>
```

Simple Text Elements

W̲e now describe some simple text elements.

Headings

HTML provides six levels of document headings, numbered H1 through H6. The form of a heading is

```
<Hnumber>Text of heading</Hnumber>
```

Headings are displayed in a font size and style different from normal text. The browser inserts a blank line after each heading.

Paragraphs

The browser uses word wrap to fit a paragraph within the borders of the browser's window. Most browsers insert a blank line after the end of each paragraph. However, they ignore blank lines within a paragraph. The end tag </P> may be omitted. The browser then ends the paragraph at the beginning of the next paragraph or heading tag.

The browser recognizes the following alignment attributes:

- LEFT (the default)

- RIGHT

- CENTER

The next example uses headings of several sizes and paragraphs with different alignments. Figure 12-3 shows a Web page that results from the marked-up text.

```
<H1>The first level heading</H1>
<P ALIGN=RIGHT>The first paragraph.</P>
<H2>The second level heading</H2>
<P ALIGN=CENTER>The second paragraph.</P>
<H3>The third level heading</H3>
<P>The third paragraph.</P>
```

FIGURE 12-3
You can use several alignments
and sizes in an HTML document

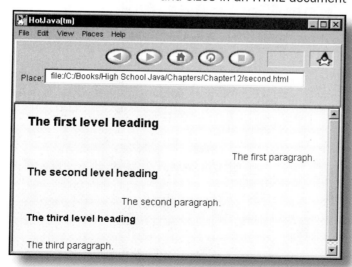

Forced Line Breaks

Occasionally, you might want to display several lines of text each on a separate line, without word wrap. The line break tag <BR> is used for this purpose. For example, the following HTML segment would display the author's address:

```
Department of Computer Science<BR>
Washington and Lee University<BR>
Lexington, VA 24450<BR>
```

Because a line break tag tells the browser where to break a line, no end tag is required.

Preformatted Text

Suppose you want the browser to display text "as is," with line breaks, extra spaces, and tabs. The <PRE> tag accomplishes this. For example, the following HTML segment displays some Java program code with the indicated indention and line breaks:

```
<PRE>
    public static void main (String[] args){
        Frame frm = new FahrenheitToCentigrade();
        frm.setSize (200, 150);
        frm.setVisible (true);
    }
</PRE>
```

In general, you should not use other markup tags within a chunk of preformatted text.

Character-Level Formatting

HTML provides some control over the format of characters. Table 12-2 lists some of the commonly used tags and their effects.

TABLE 12-2
Common formatting tags

MARKUP TAG	WHAT IT DOES	EXAMPLE HTML	DISPLAYED TEXT
EM	Emphasis, usually italics.	<EM>Italics</EM>, for emphasis.	*Italics*, for emphasis.
STRONG	Strong emphasis, usually bold.	<STRONG>Bold</STRONG>, for more emphasis.	**Bold,** for more emphasis.
CITE	Used for titles of books, etc., usually italics.	Plato's <CITE>Republic</CITE>	Plato's *Republic*
B	Bold text.	<B>Bold</B> text.	**Bold** text.
I	Italic text.	<I>Italic</I> text.	*Italic* text.
TT	Typewriter text, a fixed-width font.	<TT>Typewriter</TT> text.	Typewriter text.

Escape Sequences

HTML treats the characters <, >, and & as special characters. For example, the characters < and > are treated as the delimiters of an HTML tag. If you want the browser to display these characters rather than interpret them, you must use the escape sequences listed in Table 12-3.

TABLE 12-3
HTML escape sequences

CHARACTER	ESCAPE SEQUENCE	EXAMPLE HTML	DISPLAYED TEXT
<	&lt;	The character < begins an HTML markup tag.	The character < begins an HTML markup tag.
>	&gt;	The character > ends an HTML markup tag.	The character > ends an HTML markup tag.
&	&amp;	& is an ampersand.	The character & is an ampersand.

Lists

HTML supports the display of three kinds of lists:

- Unnumbered (bulleted) lists—tag UL.

- Numbered (ordered) lists—tag OL.

- Definition (association) lists—tag DL.

For bulleted and numbered lists, you perform the following steps:

1. Start with the desired list tag (UL or OL).

2. For each item, enter the LI (list item) tag followed by the text of the item. No closing tags are needed for the items.

3. End with the desired list tag.

An Unnumbered List Example

The next HTML segment displays a bulleted list of courses that one of the authors taught last year. Figure 12-4 shows the resulting Web page.

```
<UL>
<LI>Fundamentals of Data Structures
<LI>Programming Language Design
<LI>Operating Systems
<LI>Artificial Intelligence
</UL>
```

FIGURE 12-4

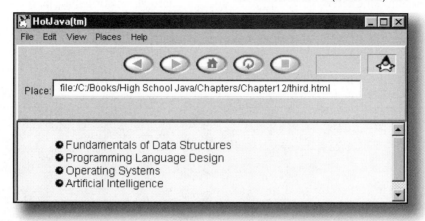

A Definition List Example

A *definition list* displays terms and their associated definitions. Several tags are used with these lists:

■ The tag <DL> begins the definition list and ends it.

■ The tag <DT> precedes each term in a definition list.

■ The tag <DD> precedes each definition in a definition list.

The following example uses a definition list to add course numbers to the course list. The resulting Web page is shown in Figure 12-5.

```
<DL>

<DT>CSCI111
<DD>Fundamentals of Data Structures

<DT>CSCI312
<DD>Programming Language Design

<DT>CSCI330
<DD>Operating Systems

<DT>CSCI315
<DD>Artificial Intelligence

</DL>
```

FIGURE 12-5
A definition list

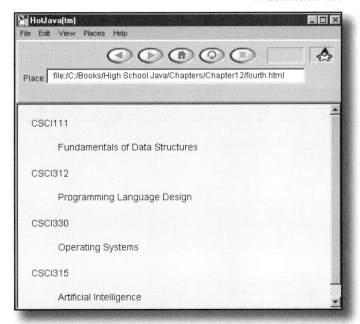

A Nested List Example

Lists can be nested within other lists to any depth, but any more than three levels deep can be hard to read. The following HTML segment nests a numbered list in an unnumbered one. The resulting Web page is shown in Figure 12-6.

```
<UL>
<LI>Fundamentals of Data Structures

<!--The nested, numbered list begins here. -->
<OL>
<LI>Analysis of algorithms
<LI>Collections
<LI>Linked lists
<LI>Stacks
<LI>Queues
<LI>Recursion
<LI>Binary search trees
</OL>
<!--The nested list ends here. -->

<LI>Programming Language Design
<LI>Operating Systems
<LI>Artificial Intelligence
</UL>
```

FIGURE 12-6
A numbered list nested in an unnumbered list

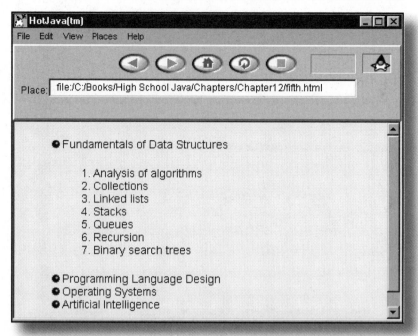

Linking to Other Documents

Links, sometimes also called *hyperlinks* or hypertext references, allow readers to move to other pages on the Web. The markup tag for a link is <A>, which stands for anchor. Placing a link in an HTML document involves the following steps:

1. Identify the target document that will be at the other end of the link. This identifier should be a pathname or an URL.

2. Determine the text that labels the link in the browser.

3. Place this information within an anchor, using the following format:

```
<A HREF=target document identifier>text of link</A>
```

For example, the next HTML anchor sets up a link to the file **courses.html** and labels the link "courses last year":

```
<A HREF="courses.html">courses last year</A>
```

Links or anchors can appear within any HTML element. They are often embedded as items in a list or as terms in a paragraph. For example, the following segment displays a link to the file **courses.html** in a sentence that mentions the author's courses:

```
<P>
My <A HREF="courses.html">courses last year</A> were Fundamentals of Data
Structures, Programming Language Design, Operating Systems, and Artificial
Intelligence.
</P>
```

When the user browses this page, the link is highlighted in color and underlined as shown in Figure 12-7. When the user clicks on the link, the browser retrieves and displays the target document, if the document has been placed at the appropriate location.

FIGURE 12-7
A hyperlink is in a different color and is underlined

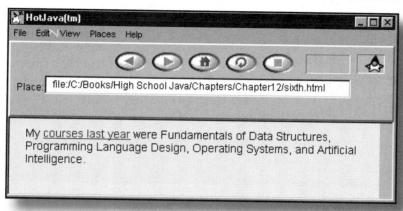

Pathnames

Note the pathname in the Place field in the header portion of the previous figure. The pathname specifies the path to or location of the file **sixth.html** on the author's computer. This file contains the page currently being displayed. The pathname is said to be *absolute* because it specifies the exact or absolute position of the file in the computer's directory structure.

In HTML anchors, we can use absolute or *relative* pathnames to specify the location of a target document. A relative pathname specifies a document's position relative to that of the currently displayed document. Table 12-4 lists some examples that show the relative pathname to **MyPage.html.**

Tip

A directory is the same as a folder on Windows and Macintosh systems. A subdirectory is the same as a folder stored within a folder.

TABLE 12-4
Relative pathname

POSITION OF MyPage.html RELATIVE TO CURRENT PAGE	RELATIVE PATHNAME
In the same directory	MyPage.html
Below, in a subdirectory called Sub1	/Sub1/MyPage.html
In the directory immediately above	../MyPage.html
In the directory two levels above	../../MyPage.html
In a directory Twin1, which is up one and then down one from the current directory	../Twin1/MyPage.html

In general, relative pathnames are easier to use than absolute pathnames, because

- They are shorter, and require less figuring out and typing.

- They need not be changed when a group of documents is moved, even to another computer, provided the documents retain their relative positions.

URLs

When a target document resides on another server in the network, a pathname is no longer enough to locate the document. Instead, we use a Uniform Resource Locator (URL)—usually pronounced "earl"—to locate the document on another machine. An URL to another Web site (called a host) has the following format:

```
http://server name/document pathname
```

For instance, the URL for Ken Lambert's home page is:

```
http://www.wlu.edu/~lambertk
```

Please feel free to visit.

Multimedia

HTML supports the presentation of a range of nontextual information such as images, sound, and movies.

Inline Images

Inline images are graphical images that are displayed when the user opens a page. The form of the markup tag for an inline image is

```
<IMG SRC=ImageLocation>
```

where ImageLocation is an URL or pathname. Images can be encoded in the GIF or JPEG format and are stored in files whose extensions are .gif, .jpg, or .jpeg.

Several parameters can be used with the markup tag of an inline image:

- **Size attributes.** These specify the height and width of the image in pixels. Example:

```
<IMG SRC="mypicture.gif" HEIGHT=100 WIDTH=100>
```

- **Alignment attribute.** This specifies the position of text relative to the image. By default, text that follows an image starts at the image's lower right corner. The text moves to the top right or to the center right of the image when TOP or CENTER is specified. For example:

```
<IMG SRC="mypicture.gif" ALIGN=CENTER>
```

To detach an image from surrounding text, place the image in a separate paragraph. For instance:

```
<p ALIGN=CENTER>
<IMG SRC="mypicture.gif">
</p>
```

External Images

Inline images increase a document's size and slow its transfer across the net. For that reason documents sometimes provide links to *external images*, which are not displayed until the user clicks on a link. The following HTML segment shows two ways of linking to an external image. The first link is a string of text. The second link is a smaller version of the image (sometimes called a thumbnail):

```
<A HREF="mypicture.gif">Sample picture</A>

<A HREF="mypicture.gif"><IMG SRC="mythumbnail.gif"</A>
```

This kind of strategy is also used with other media, such as sound recordings and movies.

Colors and Backgrounds

Browsers normally display black text on a gray background with links highlighted in color. However, an HTML author can easily change the colors of these elements. Background, text, and link colors are controlled by the BGCOLOR, TEXT, and LINK attributes of the BODY tag. For example, the following tag sets the background to black, text to white, and links to red:

```
<BODY BGCOLOR="#000000" TEXT="#FFFFFF" LINK="#FF0000">
```

A string of three two-digit hexadecimal numbers specifies a color by indicating the RGB components of the color. The first two digits represent the red component, the second the green, and the third the blue. Thus, a total of 2^{24} colors is possible. The string "#000000" indicates black, a total absence of any color, while "#FFFFFF" represents white, a total saturation of all colors. Bright red is "#FF0000" and bright green "#00FF00."

Another way to customize a background is to display an image on it. The following tag shows how to use an image as a background:

```
<BODY BACKGROUND="mybackground.jpg">
```

If the image is small, the browser fills the window with the image by a process called tiling, which repeatedly displays the image across and down the screen, creating a wallpaper-like effect.

Other Media

Table 12-5 shows file name extensions for some typical media used in HTML documents.

TABLE 12-5
File name extensions for media used in HTML documents

FILE NAME EXTENSION	TYPE OF MEDIUM
.au	AU sound file
.wav	WAV sound file
.mov	QuickTime movie
.mpeg or .mpg	MPEG movie

Tables

HTML allows authors to organize information in tables. Figure 12-8 shows a table on a Web page. As learned in earlier lessons, tables provide a highly structured way of accessing information. This is true of tables in user interfaces as well.

FIGURE 12-8
A table on a Web page

FIGURE 12-8
A table on a Web page

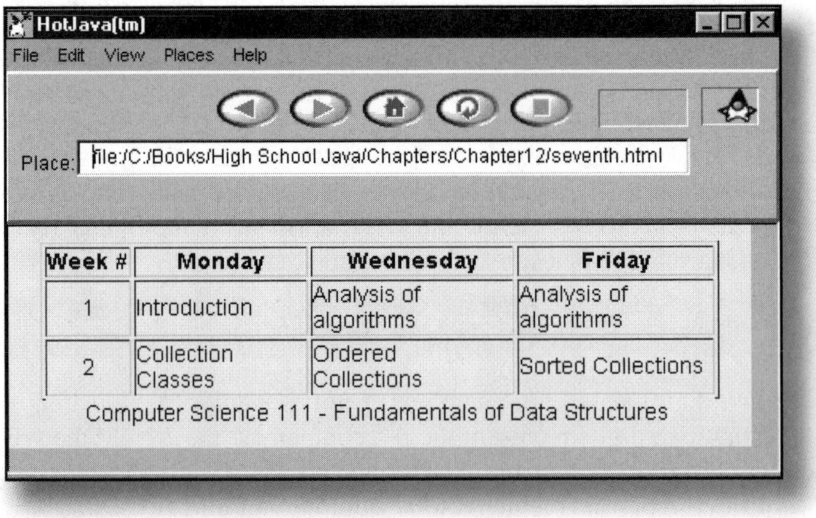

Tables usually contain the following elements:

- A caption or title, normally appearing at the top of the table.
- A first row containing column headers. Each header describes the kind of data contained in the column beneath it.
- Several rows of data. The cells in a row can contain any HTML elements (text, images, links, etc.).

Table 12-6 lists the HTML markup tags used with tables.

TABLE 12-6
HTML markup tags for tables

TABLE MARKUP TAG	WHAT IT DOES
<TABLE>	Defines a table.
<CAPTION>	Defines the title of the table. The default position of the title is at the top of the table, but ALIGN=BOTTOM can also be used.
<TR>	Defines a row within a table.
<TH>	Defines a table header cell.
<TD>	Defines a table data cell.

The table tags accept the attributes listed in Table 12-7.

TABLE 12-7
Attributes used with table markup tags

ATTRIBUTE	TAG	WHAT IT DOES
BORDER	<TABLE>	Displays a border.
ALIGN (LEFT, CENTER, RIGHT)	All except <CAPTION>	Aligns elements horizontally in cells.
VALIGN (TOP, MIDDLE, BOTTOM)	All except <CAPTION>	Aligns elements vertically in cells.
ROWSPAN=n	<TD>	Sets the number of rows that a cell spans.
COLSPAN=n	<TD>	Sets the number of columns that a cell spans.
NOWRAP	All except <CAPTION>	Turns off word wrap within a cell.

Cell attributes override row attributes, and row attributes override table attributes.

Typical Table Format

The format of a typical table follows. The blank lines between rows increase readability but do not affect the manner in which the table is displayed.

```
<TABLE>
<CAPTION> title of the table </CAPTION>

<TR>
<TH> header of first column </TH>
.
.
<TH> header of last column </TH>
</TR>

<TR>
<TD> contents of first data cell </TD>
.
.
<TD> contents of last data cell </TD>
</TR>
.
.
<TR>
<TR>
<TD> contents of first data cell </TD>
.
.
<TD> contents of last data cell </TD>
</TR>
</TABLE>
```

A Simple Example

The table shown at the beginning of this section was created using the following HTML:

```
<TABLE BORDER>

<CAPTION ALIGN=CENTER>
Computer Science 111 - Fundamentals of Data Structures
</CAPTION>

<TR>
<TH>Week #</TH>
<TH>Monday</TH>
<TH>Wednesday</TH>
<TH>Friday</TH>
</TR>

<TR>
<TD ALIGN=CENTER>1</TD> <TD>Introduction</TD>
<TD>Analysis of algorithms</TD> <TD>Analysis of algorithms</TD>
</TR>

<TR>
<TD ALIGN=CENTER>2</TD> <TD>Collection Classes</TD>
<TD>Ordered Collections</TD> <TD>Sorted Collections</TD>
</TR>

</TABLE>
```

Applets

As mentioned in Lesson 2, an applet is a Java application that runs in a Web page. Two components are needed to run an applet:

1. An HTML document that contains an applet markup tag.

2. A byte code file for the applet, that is, a compiled Java applet in a **.class** file.

   An applet markup tag has the following form:

```
<APPLET CODE=byte code file name WIDTH=width HEIGHT=height></APPLET>
```

The width and height are the width and height, respectively, of the applet's screen area in pixels. The HTML document can also contain other markup tags, to display a title in the window, to provide instructions for using the applet, and so forth.

The next case study shows how to create a Web page that runs an applet, and how to create the applet from an existing Java application.

C A S E   S T U D Y   1 :
Fahrenheit to Centigrade as an Applet

User Request

Write a Web page that runs the Fahrenheit to centigrade converter program of Lesson 2.

Analysis

The interface for the converter program itself will not change from the one presented in Lesson 2. However, the Web page in which the interface appears will also display some instructions on the use of the converter and a statement about applets and the Web.

Figure 12-9 shows the proposed interface.

FIGURE 12-9

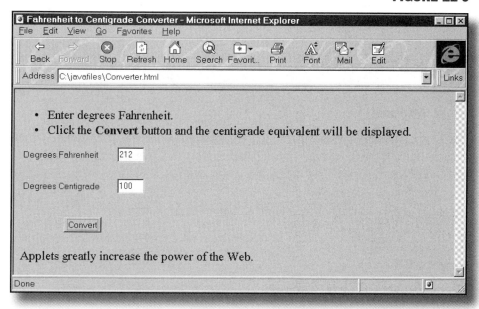

Writing the HTML Document

The first step is to write the HTML document that contains the markup tag for the applet. For this case study, the HTML document should contain the following elements:

■ A tag for the title of the page.

■ A tag for a list of instructions on the use of the applet.

■ A tag for the applet.

■ A tag for the statement about applets and the Web.

Here is the HTML code:

```
<html>
<head>
<TITLE>Fahrenheit to Centigrade Converter</TITLE>
</head>

<body>

<UL>
<LI>Enter degrees Fahrenheit.
<LI>Click the <STRONG>Convert</STRONG> button and the
centigrade equivalent will be displayed.
</UL>

<APPLET CODE="FahrenheitToCentigrade.class" WIDTH=200 HEIGHT=150>
</APPLET>

<P>
Applets greatly increase the power of the Web.

<body>
<html>
```

Implementing the Applet

We have already implemented the converter program as a Java application in Lesson 2. Instead of rewriting the code from scratch, we now show how to convert the Java application to an equivalent applet. Throughout this text, we have used the class GBFrame to provide the framework for GUI-based applications. We now use a similar class, GBApplet, to write a GUI-based applet. In general, to convert a Java application to an applet, we must do four things:

1. Replace the name GBFrame with the name GBApplet at the beginning of the class definition.

2. Delete the method main.

3. Eliminate any use of the setTitle method.

4. Replace the constructor, if any, by the method init:

```
public void init(){
    ...
}
```

The converter application of Lesson 2 does not use the setTitle method and does not define a constructor method. Thus, there are just two changes: delete method main and replace GBFrame with GBApplet. The following listing shows these changes:

```
import java.awt.*;
import BreezyGUI.*;

public class FahrenheitToCentigrade extends GBApplet{

    Label degreesFahrenheitLabel = addLabel ("Degrees Fahrenheit",1,1,1,1);
```

```
    IntegerField degreesFahrenheitField = addIntegerField (0,1,2,1,1);
    Label degreesCentigradeLabel = addLabel ("Degrees Centigrade",2,1,1,1);
    IntegerField degreesCentigradeField = addIntegerField (0,2,2,1,1);
    Button convertButton = addButton ("Convert",3,1,2,1);

    int fahrenheit;
    int centigrade;

    public void buttonClicked (Button buttonObj){
        fahrenheit = degreesFahrenheitField.getNumber();
        centigrade = (fahrenheit - 32) * 5 / 9;
        degreesCentigradeField.setNumber (centigrade);
    }
}
```

Compiling and Running an Applet

After the code for an applet has been edited, the code is compiled in the same way as that of an application. The programmer can then run an applet in two ways:

1.   Run JDK's **appletviewer** tool with the applet's HTML file.

2.   Open the applet's HTML file in a Web browser.

Assuming that the applet's HTML file is named **fahrtocent.html,** Figure 12-10 shows how to compile and run the applet of Case Study 1 with JDK's **javac** and **appletviewer** tools.

Figure 12-11 shows the applet running in the **appletviewer** window.

FIGURE 12-10

Run the applet using the commands shown in this screen

```
C:\javafiles>javac FahrenheitToCentigrade.java

C:\javafiles>appletviewer fahrtocent.html_
```

FIGURE 12-11

The applet is now running in the viewer

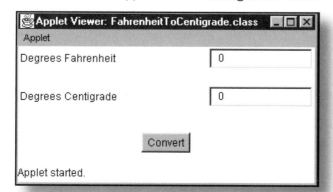

Note that information in the **appletviewer** window is limited to the output of the applet itself. The other output of the HTML file (title, instructions, etc.) is missing. Thus, the **appletviewer** is best used for testing just the code of the applet itself. To test the information in the HTML file as well as the applet, you must open the HTML file with a Web browser.

Differences Between Applets and Applications

One way to look at the differences between applets and applications is to examine why we must take the conversion steps listed earlier. Here are the changes and the reasons why they must be made:

1. **Replace the name GBFrame with the name GBApplet at the beginning of the class definition.** This change is necessary because GBApplet inherits the general behavior of applets, whereas GBFrame inherits the general behavior of applications. We explore these two kinds of general behavior in more detail in Lesson 13.

2. **Delete the method main.** This change is necessary because Java calls the method main at the startup of applications only. Java starts applets differently, as described below.

3. **Eliminate any use of the setTitle method.** Applets run in a Web browser's window rather than in an application window. The title of the Web browser's window is set with a markup tag in an HTML document.

4. **Replace the constructor, if any, by the method init.** Instead of calling a constructor when an applet is created, Java calls the applet's init method. Thus, all the code that normally would go in a constructor, such as initializing instance variables or setting the properties of window objects, should go in the method init.

There are several other major differences between applets and applications:

■ Applets do not have menu bars or pull-down menus. Thus, GBApplet does not support the methods addmenuItem and menuItemSelected. Buttons and popup menus (see Lesson 13) often provide an acceptable substitute.

■ To ensure security on the user's machine, applets cannot access files. Imagine how dangerous it would be to download applets across the Web if the applets could trash the files on your computer.

■ Applets and the HTML documents that use them should be placed in the same directory. This rule can be violated, but doing so is beyond the scope of this book. Java programs, whether they are stand-alone applications or applets, frequently use classes in addition to those in the standard Java libraries. These classes, which might include the **BreezyGUI** package, should be in the same directory as the applet.

■ The programs in this text use Java 1.1, so only Web browsers that support Java 1.1 can run the applets in this chapter. One such browser is available from Sun Microsystems at www.sun.com.

CASE STUDY 2 : A Game of Tic-Tac-Toe

User Request

Write an applet that plays games of tic-tac-toe with the user.

Analysis

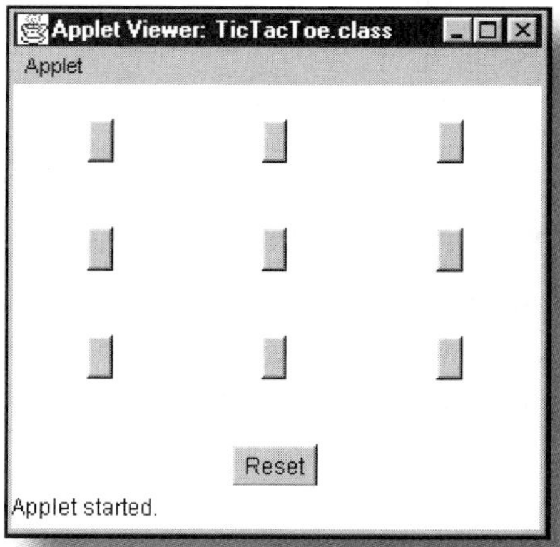

For those of you not acquainted with tic-tac-toe, two players take turns marking a 3-by-3 grid of empty squares until one player has three marks in a row, column, or diagonal. That player wins. One player typically uses an "X" for a mark, and the other player uses an "O."

FIGURE 12-12

Thus, the interface for the applet will consist of a 3-by-3 grid of buttons on which the user and the computer will make their marks. In addition, the interface provides a **Reset** button, which the user can select at any time to play a new game. The proposed interface is shown in Figure 12-12.

Note that the interface is displayed in the **appletviewer,** which gives no hint about other information provided by the HTML document. We assume for now that there is none, except for a title, and leave the development of such information as an exercise.

At program startup, the computer randomly assigns the user and the computer the marks X and O. The user plays the game by clicking empty buttons to try to get three marks in a row. Each time the user clicks a button, the computer responds by making its own selection. When one of the players gets three marks in a row, the program announces the winner in a Message box and disables the buttons in the grid. The user can then select **Reset** to clear the buttons for a new game.

Design

The program requires instance variables to refer to the ten buttons and to the user's mark and the computer's mark. To facilitate the processing of the nine buttons in the grid, we place these in a two-dimensional array at program startup. Thus, we actually need only four instance variables.

The program is then structured in terms of several methods, which are listed in Table 12-8.

TABLE 12-8
Methods used in the tic-tac-toe program

NAME OF METHOD	WHAT IT DOES
void init()	Sets up the interface and initializes the instance variables.
void buttonClicked (Button buttonObj)	Responds to a player's move by marking a button, testing for a win, or resetting the grid of buttons.
void clearAndEnableButtons()	Resets the grid of buttons by setting their labels to " " and enabling them.
void disableButtons()	Disables all the buttons in the grid when a player wins.
void clickForComputer()	Picks a button as the computer's selection and marks it.
boolean playerWins (String playerMark)	Tests the grid of buttons to determine whether a given player has won.

In several of the pseudocode algorithms that follow, we use the expression "For each button in the grid." Because the grid is actually a two-dimensional array of buttons, this expression expands to a nested loop in the Java code.

Here is pseudocode for init.

```
Instantiate the grid (a two-dimensional array of buttons)
For each button in the grid
    Add the button with label "" to position (row + 1, column + 1) in the
    interface
Set up the reset button
Assign the user and the computer the marks "X" and "O" at random
```

Here is pseudocode for buttonClicked.

```
If the button is the reset button
    Call clearAndEnableButtons
Else if the button has not been marked
    Set the button's label to the user's mark
    If the user wins
        Display the message "You win!"
        Call disableButtons
    Else
        Call clickForComputer
        If the computer wins
            Display the message "I win!"
            Call disableButtons
```

Here is pseudocode for clearAndEnableButtons.

```
For each button in the grid
    Set the button's label to ""
    Enable the button
```

Pseudocode for clickForComputer appears below. The algorithm for setting a button with the computer's mark simply selects the first available empty button. Other possible algorithms for this task are left as exercises.

```
For each button in the grid
    If the button's label is ""
        Set the button's label to the computer's mark
        Return from the method
```

The Method playerWins

The method playerWins examines the buttons in the grid to determine whether the given mark appears as the only one in a row, a column, or a diagonal. Thus, the code is implemented as a long chain of Boolean expressions connected by logical operators. The method returns the value of this compound Boolean expression.

Implementation

```java
import java.awt.*;
import BreezyGUI.*;

public class TicTacToe extends GBApplet{

    Button buttons[][];
    Button resetButton;
    private String userMark;
    private String computerMark;

    public void init(){

        // Initialize grid of buttons.
        buttons = new Button[3][3];
        Button button;
        int row, col;
        for (row = 0; row < 3; row++)
            for (col = 0; col < 3; col++){
                button = addButton ("", row + 1, col + 1, 1, 1);
                buttons[row][col] = button;
            }

        // Set up Reset button.
        resetButton = addButton ("Reset", 4, 1, 3, 1);

        // Choose button labels for user and computer.
        if (randomInt(1, 2) == 1){
            userMark = "X";
            computerMark = "O";
        }
        else{
            userMark = "O";
            computerMark = "X";
        }

    }

    public void buttonClicked (Button buttonObj){
        if (buttonObj == resetButton)
            clearAndEnableButtons();
        else if (buttonObj.getLabel().equals("")){
            buttonObj.setLabel (userMark);
            if (playerWins(userMark)){
                messageBox ("You win!");
                disableButtons();
            }
            else{
                clickForComputer();
                if (playerWins(computerMark)){
                    messageBox ("I win!");
                    disableButtons();
                }
            }
        }
    }
```

```java
// Make all the buttons empty and enable them.
private void clearAndEnableButtons(){
    int row, col;
    Button button;
    for (row = 0; row < 3; row++)
        for (col = 0; col < 3; col++){
            button = buttons[row][col];
            button.setLabel ("");
            button.setEnabled (true);
        }
}

// Disable all the buttons.
private void disableButtons(){
    int row, col;
    Button button;
    for (row = 0; row < 3; row++)
        for (col = 0; col < 3; col++){
            button = buttons[row][col];
            button.setEnabled (false);
        }
}

// Selects the first available empty button.
private void clickForComputer(){
    Button button;
    int row, col;
    for (row = 0; row < 3; row++)
        for (col = 0; col < 3; col++){
            button = buttons[row][col];
            if (button.getLabel().equals("")){
                button.setLabel(computerMark);
                return;
            }
        }
}

private boolean playerWins(String playerMark){
    return
        (buttons[0][0].getLabel().equals(playerMark) &&
         buttons[0][1].getLabel().equals(playerMark) &&
         buttons[0][2].getLabel().equals(playerMark)) ||
        (buttons[1][0].getLabel().equals(playerMark) &&
         buttons[1][1].getLabel().equals(playerMark) &&
         buttons[1][2].getLabel().equals(playerMark)) ||
        (buttons[2][0].getLabel().equals(playerMark) &&
         buttons[2][1].getLabel().equals(playerMark) &&
         buttons[2][2].getLabel().equals(playerMark)) ||
        (buttons[0][0].getLabel().equals(playerMark) &&
         buttons[1][0].getLabel().equals(playerMark) &&
         buttons[2][0].getLabel().equals(playerMark)) ||
        (buttons[0][1].getLabel().equals(playerMark) &&
         buttons[1][1].getLabel().equals(playerMark) &&
         buttons[2][1].getLabel().equals(playerMark)) ||
```

```
        (buttons[0][2].getLabel().equals(playerMark) &&
         buttons[1][2].getLabel().equals(playerMark) &&
         buttons[2][2].getLabel().equals(playerMark)) ||
        (buttons[0][0].getLabel().equals(playerMark) &&
         buttons[1][1].getLabel().equals(playerMark) &&
         buttons[2][2].getLabel().equals(playerMark)) ||
        (buttons[2][0].getLabel().equals(playerMark) &&
         buttons[1][1].getLabel().equals(playerMark) &&
         buttons[0][2].getLabel().equals(playerMark));
    }

    int randomInt(int low, int high){
        return low + (int) (Math.random() * (high - low + 1));
    }
}
```

Design, Testing, and Debugging Hints

- The paragraph (<P>) tag ignores blank lines, but inserts one.

- Be sure to test your document whenever you add a new link.

Summary

In this lesson, you learned:

- Hypertext and hypermedia are links that can take you from one Web page to another.

- Hypertext markup language (HTML) was developed to represent information in a hypermedia system. HTML uses markup tags to format text, lists, tables, and multimedia elements.

- Hyperlinks allow you to reference a target document or Web page that appears when you click the link.

- Applets are Java applications that run in Web pages. You can easily modify an existing Java application to create an applet.

LESSON 12 REVIEW QUESTIONS

WRITTEN QUESTIONS

Write your answers to the following questions.

1. Describe the basic idea underlying hypertext.

2. What does HTML stand for?

3. What is the minimal structure of an HTML document?

4. Write an HTML code segment that displays a bulleted list containing the names of your five favorite foods.

5. Modify the code segment of Question 4 so that each name in the list is a link to another HTML document. The destination file names should have the form <name of food>.html.

6. Assume that your class picture is located in the file picture.jpg. Write the code for an HTML document that would display this picture centered above the appropriate caption.

7. Where are the size and the title of an applet set?

LESSON 12 PROJECTS

1. For a fairly complete reference on HTML and Web page design, enter the following URL in your Web browser: http://www.ncsa.uius.edu/General/Internet/WWW/HTMLPrimer.html. If you have not done so already, create a home page on your local Web server. Include a title, a brief paragraph that states who you are, and a picture of your favorite pastime.

2. Add to your home page a list of courses in which you are enrolled this term.

3. Make each item in the list of Project 2 a link to a page that describes that item. Create these pages and test your hypertext thoroughly.

4. Add links to the pages created in Project 3 that return the user to your home page.

5. Write an HTML document to run the applet of Case Study 2. The Web page should display instructions for playing the game.

6. Select an application that uses a menu, such as one of the sketching applications of Lesson 10, and discuss how to convert it to an applet. This will require that you think of a way of displaying commands other than by means of a menu. Test the resulting program on a Web page.

CRITICAL THINKING ACTIVITY

In the tic-tac-toe game of Case Study 2, the computer marks a button after the user does. The algorithm for this task selects the first available empty button. Suggest two other ways of performing this task, and write pseudocode algorithms for them. At least one of your solutions should make the computer play to win.

THE ABSTRACT WINDOWING TOOLKIT

OBJECTIVES

Upon completion of this lesson, you should be able to:

■ Explain the purpose of the AWT.

■ List GUI components of the AWT.

■ Discuss the layouts available for positioning window objects.

■ Define listeners to handle events generated by AWT components.

■ Lay out a dialog using the AWT `Dialog` class.

■ Divide an application into a model, a view, and a controller.

■ Convert programs to applets using the AWT.

Estimated Time: 4 hours

Applications with a GUI are based ultimately on Java's *Abstract Windowing Toolkit (AWT)*. However, for the sake of simplicity, we have until now avoided using the AWT. Instead, we have made all our stand-alone programs subclasses of `GBFrame` and our applets subclasses of `GBApplet`. These are two of the major classes in the **BreezyGUI** package. While using **BreezyGUI** makes it easy to create GUI-based programs, it blocks access to the AWT's full power. Fortunately, we have not noticed the deprivation. But with an eye to your future as Java programmers, we now present the AWT in some detail.

The AWT Philosophy

Traditional programming languages such as Pascal and C++ provide no standard features for programming GUIs, so GUI code must often be rewritten when applications are ported to different machines. Moreover, the GUI features themselves may vary from platform to platform. Java's origi-nators developed the AWT to solve these problems.

The toolkit is abstract in two senses:

1. It provides classes and methods that are platform independent. Write once, run anywhere.

2. It creates user interfaces whose look and feel are platform independent. Run anywhere, look similar.

Applications that use the AWT involve the use of four categories of classes. Table 13-1 contains brief descriptions of each category. Later we will explore the categories in detail and show how they work together to support a GUI.

TABLE 13-1
AWT classes

CATEGORIES	WHAT THEY DO
GUI Component Classes	GUI components include such basic window objects as buttons, text fields, and menu items. Also included in this category are frames, applets, and dialogs, which act as containers for the basic window objects.
Layout Manager Classes	When objects such as buttons are added to a window, their placement is determined by a layout manager. For instance, GBFrame and GBApplet use a grid bag layout. The other layout managers are flow, border, grid, and card.
Event Classes	Event classes define the events that are triggered when users do such things as click buttons, select menu items, and move the mouse.
Listener Classes	Listener classes contain methods that are activated when events occur.

We use these classes to define a GUI as follows:

1. Add window objects to the interface under the control of a layout manager.

2. Decide which events each object should handle by adding listeners for the events to the object.

We can get a feel for all of this by revisiting the Fahrenheit to centigrade conversion program of Lesson 2 and comparing how it is implemented with GBFrame versus directly with the AWT.

Conversion Program Implemented with GBFrame

Here is a version of the program implemented with GBFrame. Figure 13-1 shows the resulting interface.

FIGURE 13-1
Program run with GBFrame

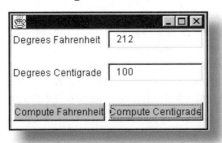

```
import java.awt.*;
import BreezyGUI.*;

public class ConversionWithBreezyGUI extends GBFrame {
```

```
    private Label fahrenheitLabel
                    = addLabel  ("Degrees Fahrenheit",1,1,1,1);
    private IntegerField fahrenheitField
                    = addIntegerField (32           ,1,2,1,1);
    private Label centigradeLabel
                    = addLabel  ("Degrees Centigrade",2,1,1,1);
    private IntegerField centigradeField
                    = addIntegerField (0            ,2,2,1,1);
    private Button fahrenheitButton
                    = addButton ("Compute Fahrenheit",3,1,1,1);
    private Button centigradeButton
                    = addButton ("Compute Centigrade",3,2,1,1);

    public void buttonClicked (Button buttonObj){
       int fahrenheit, centigrade;
       if (buttonObj == fahrenheitButton){
          centigrade = centigradeField.getNumber();
          fahrenheit = centigrade * 9 / 5 + 32;
          fahrenheitField.setNumber (fahrenheit);
       }
       else{
          fahrenheit = fahrenheitField.getNumber();
          centigrade = (fahrenheit - 32) * 5 / 9;
          centigradeField.setNumber (centigrade);
       }
    }

    public static void main (String[] args){
       Frame frm = new ConversionWithBreezyGUI();
       frm.setSize (200, 150);
       frm.setVisible (true);
    }
}
```

From the perspective of this lesson there are several things to notice about the code:

1. The program extends GBFrame.

2. The window objects, or GUI *components*, are instantiated and laid out in the window.

3. The program responds to events that are triggered by the user. In this example, the events of interest are

    -   Clicking on the **Compute Fahrenheit** button.

    -   Clicking on the **Compute Centigrade** button.

    -   Closing the window by clicking the window's close box.

4. There is code to respond to the events. The underlying Java framework activates this listener code when an event occurs. The listener code for the click button event is in the method buttonClicked, while that for handling the window close event is out of sight inside GBFrame.

Conversion Program Implemented with AWT

Now, in contrast, let's look at the program implemented using AWT, without GBFrame. The program is spread out over four files, listed in Table 13-2.

TABLE 13-2
AWT files needed for the program

FILES	WHAT THEY DO
ConversionWithAWT.java	This file contains the program's main class. It defines the GUI and contains code that does the conversion between Fahrenheit and centigrade.
CentigradeButtonListener.java	This file defines the listener for the **Compute Centigrade** button.
FahrenheitButtonListener.java	This file defines the listener for the **Compute Fahrenheit** button.
GenericWindowListener.java	This file defines the listener for closing the window when the close box is clicked.

The Interface

The interface (Figure 13-2) appears essentially the same as it did above when we used GBFrame. The cause of the minor differences will become clear when we discuss layout managers.

FIGURE 13-2
Program run with AWT

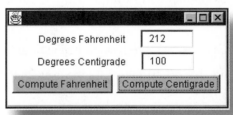

The File ConversionWithAWT.java

The listing is broken by extensive comments that must be read carefully for a proper understanding of how the AWT classes work together to support a GUI.

We begin as usual by importing the awt package:

```
import java.awt.*;
```

But we extend `Frame` rather than `GBFrame`:

```
public class ConversionWithAWT extends Frame {
```

The variables that reference the window objects are declared next:

```
private Label    fahrenheitLabel;
private TextField fahrenheitField;
```

AWT has no integer fields, so in the line above we use a text field instead.

```
private Label    centigradeLabel;
private TextField centigradeField;
private Button    fahrenheitButton;
private Button    centigradeButton;
```

There are a number of tasks that must be performed in the constructor:

```
public ConversionWithAWT(){
```

First, instantiate the window objects:

```
fahrenheitLabel  = new Label ("Degrees Fahrenheit");
fahrenheitField  = new TextField ("212", 6);  // 6 columns wide
centigradeLabel  = new Label ("Degrees Centigrade");
centigradeField  = new TextField ("100", 6);  // 6 columns wide
fahrenheitButton = new Button ("Compute Fahrenheit");
centigradeButton = new Button ("Compute Centigrade");
```

Second, before adding and positioning window objects, we must instantiate and set the layout:

```
FlowLayout layout = new FlowLayout();
setLayout (layout);
```

Third, add the window objects under the influence of the layout, which controls their actual placement. There are several different types of layouts, flow layout being the simplest. A flow layout displays components in the order in which they are added. As many components as possible are displayed on each line. Those that do not fit on a given line wrap around onto the next line.

```
add (fahrenheitLabel);
add (fahrenheitField);
add (centigradeLabel);
add (centigradeField);
add (fahrenheitButton);
add (centigradeButton);
```

Fourth, it is necessary to tell the buttons where their listener code is located. This is done by instantiating *listener* objects and associating them with the buttons. The Java framework sends messages to the listener objects when the buttons are clicked. The listener object for the first button is an instance of the class `FahrenheitButtonListener` and for the second button the class `CentigradeButtonListener`. The need for the parameter `this` will be explained soon.

```
        fahrenheitButton.addActionListener
                              (new FahrenheitButtonListener (this));
        centigradeButton.addActionListener
                              (new CentigradeButtonListener (this));
```

Fifth, a listener is needed to close the window. The listener is activated when the user clicks the window's close box. We call the listener class `GenericWindowListener`. Here we instantiate the listener object and associate it with the window.

```
        addWindowListener (new GenericWindowListener());
    }
```

The conversion from centigrade to Fahrenheit is done in the method below. The `FahrenheitButtonListener` object calls this method. We will see the details soon. Note that the method's code is straightforward:

■ The code retrieves a string from the centigrade field and converts it to a number.

■ The code then converts the number to its Fahrenheit equivalent, converts that back to a string, and displays the string in the Fahrenheit field.

The conversions between strings and numbers are necessary because the AWT does not include the numeric fields that are part of `GBFrame` and `GBApplet`. Instead, we must use the AWT's `TextField`.

```
    public void computeFahrenheit(){
        String str = centigradeField.getText().trim();
        int centigrade = (new Integer (str)).intValue();
        int fahrenheit = centigrade * 9 / 5 + 32;
        fahrenheitField.setText ("" + fahrenheit);
    }
```

The conversion from Fahrenheit to centigrade is handled by the next method. It is similar to the preceding one.

```
    public void computeCentigrade(){
        String str = fahrenheitField.getText().trim();
        int fahrenheit = (new Integer (str)).intValue();
        int centigrade = (fahrenheit – 32) * 5 / 9;
        centigradeField.setText ("" + centigrade);
    }
```

The `main` method is the same as usual:

```
    public static void main (String[] args){
        Frame frm = new ConversionWithAWT();
        frm.setSize (250, 150);
        frm.setVisible (true);
    }
}
```

That ends the code for `ConversionWithAWT.java`. We now examine the code for the listener classes.

The File `FahrenheitButtonListener.java`

When a user clicks on the **Compute Fahrenheit** button, the Java framework sends the `actionPer-formed` message to the `FahrenheitButtonListener` object that we saw instantiated in the code above. Here is an annotated listing of the class.

We begin by importing the package `java.awt.event`:

```
import java.awt.event.*;
```

The class `FahrenheitButtonListener` implements rather than extends the `ActionListener`. The `ActionListener` is an *interface*. Interfaces declare methods and constants, but they are not classes and they cannot be instantiated. The `ActionListener` interface declares just one method, `actionPerformed`, and the `FahrenheitButtonListener` class must provide code to define this method. A button would be nonfunctional if the main GUI class failed to associate it with an `ActionListener` object.

```
public class FahrenheitButtonListener implements ActionListener{
```

Listeners often need to send messages back to the main GUI class. This listener is designed to send a message back to the class `ConversionWithAWT`. To do so, it must declare a variable of type `ConversionWithAWT`.

```
private ConversionWithAWT theGUI;
```

In the constructor below, we assign a value to the variable `theGUI`. The value being assigned corresponds to the word "`this`" in the main GUI class. Here is the line of code, copied from the main GUI class above, that activates the constructor:

```
fahrenheitButton.addActionListener
    (new FahrenheitButtonListener (this));
```

And now here is the constructor itself:

```
public FahrenheitButtonListener (ConversionWithAWT gui){
    theGUI = gui;
}
```

As already mentioned, the Java framework sends the `actionPerformed` message to the `Fahren-heitButtonListener` object when the **Compute Fahrenheit** button is clicked. An event object is passed to the method as a parameter. The event object contains information about the event, such as the identity of the button that triggered the event, which in this case we already know to be the **Compute Fahrenheit** button.

```
public void actionPerformed (ActionEvent e){
```

Listener code is often very simple. In this example all it does is send a message back to the main GUI class, requesting the main GUI class to compute and display the degrees Fahrenheit.

```
        theGUI.computeFahrenheit();
    }
}
```

The File `CentigradeButtonListener.java`

This file is so similar to the listener just discussed that we present the listing without further discussion.

```java
import java.awt.event.*;

public class CentigradeButtonListener implements ActionListener{

    private ConversionWithAWT theGUI;

    public CentigradeButtonListener (ConversionWithAWT gui){
       theGUI = gui;
    }

    public void actionPerformed (ActionEvent e){
       theGUI.computeCentigrade();
    }
}
```

The File `GenericWindowListener.java`

A window listener's principal task is to close the window when the user clicks the window's close box, which in turn triggers the window's closing event. However, there are several other window events that can be handled in a window listener class. These include iconifying and deiconifying the window, and activating and deactivating the window. The listener has a separate method for handling each type of window event. When one of these events occurs, the Java framework sends the appropriate message to the window listener object. As in many applications, this window's closing event is the only one of concern. However, all the methods must be included in the listing, even if some of them have no code. Here is the listing:

```java
import java.awt.event.*;

public class GenericWindowListener implements WindowListener{
    public void windowClosing (WindowEvent e){
       System.exit(0);
    }

    public void windowActivated (WindowEvent e){}
    public void windowClosed (WindowEvent e){}
    public void windowDeactivated (WindowEvent e){}
    public void windowDeiconified (WindowEvent e){}
    public void windowIconified (WindowEvent e){}
    public void windowOpened (WindowEvent e){}
}
```

As you can readily see, the difference between writing GUI applications with and without `GBFrame` is dramatic.

Simplifying the `GenericWindowListener` Class

The `GenericWindowListener` class listed earlier included a number of empty methods. The need to include the empty methods can be avoided if the `GenericWindowListener` extends the `WindowAdapter` class instead of implementing the `WindowListener` interface. The `WindowAdapter` class is part of the package `java.awt.event`. Its code is shown below. As you can see, it implements the `WindowListener` interface and consists of nothing but empty methods.

```
public abstract class WindowAdapter implements WindowListener {
    public void windowOpened(WindowEvent e) {}
    public void windowClosing(WindowEvent e) {}
    public void windowClosed(WindowEvent e) {}
    public void windowIconified(WindowEvent e) {}
    public void windowDeiconified(WindowEvent e) {}
    public void windowActivated(WindowEvent e) {}
    public void windowDeactivated(WindowEvent e) {}
}
```

Here is the `GenericWindowListener` written as an extension of the `WindowAdapter` class. Only one method now needs to be implemented.

```
import java.awt.event.*;

public class GenericWindowListener extends WindowAdapter{

    public void windowClosing (WindowEvent e){
        System.exit(0);
    }
}
```

Altogether there are 11 listener interfaces in the AWT. We have seen two, `ActionListener` and `WindowListener`, and will examine most of the remaining ones later in this lesson. Listeners with more than one method have a corresponding adapter, thus providing programmers with the convenience of extending the adapter rather than implementing the interface.

Adding a Listener to Filter Out Alphabetic Characters

We now modify the program so that it ignores all alphabetic characters entered into the two data entry fields. As the program has been written so far, the user can mix letters and digits when entering degrees Fahrenheit or centigrade, which obviously is undesirable.

To achieve our goal, we implement a listener class that handles keyboard events. Every time the user hits a key, three events are triggered. These occur when a key is first pressed, when the key is released, and when the key is typed (this last event corresponds to the combination of pressing and releasing the key).

The `KeyListener` interface specifies the methods to handle these events. These methods are `keyPressed`, `keyReleased`, and `keyTyped`. Because we only want to implement the method `keyTyped`, our listener class will extend the `KeyAdapter` class rather than implement the `KeyListener` interface. Our new listener class is called `DigitKeyListener`. Here is the code for adding instances of this class to the text fields of the conversion program:

```
        fahrenheitButton.addActionListener
                                (new FahrenheitButtonListener (this));
        centigradeButton.addActionListener
                                (new CentigradeButtonListener (this));

        fahrenheitField.addKeyListener (new DigitKeyListener());
        centigradeField.addKeyListener (new DigitKeyListener());

        addWindowListener (new GenericWindowListener());
```

Here is a listing of the new class, followed by an explanation:

```java
import java.awt.event.*;

public class DigitKeyListener extends KeyAdapter{

    public void keyTyped(KeyEvent e){
        char ch = e.getKeyChar();
        if (! Character.isDigit(ch))
            e.consume();
    }

}
```

When the user types a character in one of the program's text fields, the digit key listener's `keyTyped` method is called and passed an event named e as a parameter. This event object contains the character that the user just typed. If this character is not a digit, the method sends the `consume` message to the event e. The event object responds by

1. Not echoing the character in the field.

2. Not storing the character in the field's data buffer.

One consequence of the way we have implemented the `keyTyped` method is that the backspace character is also consumed. This means that the user cannot delete characters in the text fields of the program. The remedy for this problem is left as an exercise.

Incorporating the Listeners into the Main GUI Class

Listeners do not have to be in separate classes, but can be incorporated into the main GUI class. This is achieved by having the main GUI class implement the desired listeners in addition to extending the `Frame` class. We illustrate the process by incorporating the button and window listeners only. We will, of course, need to implement all the methods in the `ActionListener` and the `WindowListener` interfaces. By the way, a class can extend only one other class, but can implement any number of interfaces. Here is the code with some comments included:

```java
import java.awt.*;
import java.awt.event.*;

public class ConversionWithAWT extends Frame
                               implements ActionListener,
                                          WindowListener{

    private Label     fahrenheitLabel;
    private TextField fahrenheitField;
    private Label     centigradeLabel;
    private TextField centigradeField;
    private Button    fahrenheitButton;
    private Button    centigradeButton;

    public ConversionWithAWT(){
        fahrenheitLabel = new Label ("Degrees Fahrenheit");
        fahrenheitField = new TextField ("212", 6);  // 6 columns wide
        centigradeLabel = new Label ("Degrees Centigrade");
```

```
centigradeField  = new TextField ("100", 6);  // 6 columns wide
fahrenheitButton = new Button ("Compute Fahrenheit");
centigradeButton = new Button ("Compute Centigrade");

FlowLayout layout = new FlowLayout();
setLayout (layout);
add (fahrenheitLabel);
add (fahrenheitField);
add (centigradeLabel);
add (centigradeField);
add (fahrenheitButton);
add (centigradeButton);
```

We still need to associate the buttons and the window with listener objects. But now the only listener object is the application itself, namely, this.

```
fahrenheitButton.addActionListener (this);
centigradeButton.addActionListener (this);
addWindowListener (this);
}
```

A class that implements ActionListener must include the method actionPerformed.

```
public void actionPerformed (ActionEvent e){
   String str;
   int fahrenheit, centigrade;
   Button btn = (Button)e.getSource();

   if (btn == fahrenheitButton){
      str = centigradeField.getText().trim();
      centigrade = (new Integer (str)).intValue();
      fahrenheit = centigrade * 9 / 5 + 32;
      fahrenheitField.setText ("" + fahrenheit);
   }
   else{
      str = fahrenheitField.getText().trim();
      fahrenheit = (new Integer (str)).intValue();
      centigrade = (fahrenheit - 32) * 5 / 9;
      centigradeField.setText ("" + centigrade);
   }
}
```

A class that implements WindowListener must include the seven methods shown below, even if most of them are empty.

```
public void windowClosing (WindowEvent e){
   System.exit(0);
}
public void windowActivated (WindowEvent e){}
public void windowClosed (WindowEvent e){}
public void windowDeactivated (WindowEvent e){}
public void windowDeiconified (WindowEvent e){}
```

3 6 7

```
public void windowIconified (WindowEvent e){}
public void windowOpened (WindowEvent e){}
```

Fortunately, some things never change. Here is the familiar method `main`.

```
public static void main (String[] args){
    Frame frm = new ConversionWithAWT();
    frm.setSize (200, 150);
    frm.setVisible (true);
}
}
```

This completes our overview of the AWT's workings. We now turn to some of the details, beginning with a discussion of GUI components and layouts.

GUI Components

The first category of classes used in developing windows-based applications consists of the GUI components. The visible objects that constitute a window fall into this category. These objects include buttons, text fields, text areas, lists, menu items, and so on. You can find complete documentation for all of the GUI component classes at the Java Web site, as described in Appendix A.

The Component Class Hierarchy

All the GUI components are subclasses of an abstract class called `Component`. This class specifies the most basic attributes and behavior of all GUI objects. For example, every component has attributes that define its size (width and height in pixels), background color, foreground color, text font, and visibility. Commonly used methods for modifying these attributes are listed in Table 13-3.

TABLE 13-3
Common methods from the Component class

COMPONENT METHOD	WHAT IT DOES
void setBackground(Color c)	Sets the background color of the component.
void setEnabled(boolean b)	Enables or disables the component.
void setFont(Font f)	Sets the font of the component.
void setForeground(Color c)	Sets the foreground color of the component.
void setSize(int w, int h)	Sets the width and height of the component.
void setVisible(boolean b)	Displays or hides the component.

The `Component` class also includes methods for adding listener objects to a component, as we saw illustrated in the conversion program above.

Most of the classes of window objects that we have used so far (`Button`, `Checkbox`, `Checkbox-Group`, `Choice`, and `List`) are immediate subclasses of the `Component` class. Others are grouped under intermediate classes. MenuBar and MenuItem are subclasses of MenuComponent. Frame and Applet are subclasses of Container, so called because it can contain other window objects. Figure 13-3 shows most of the Component class hierarchy.

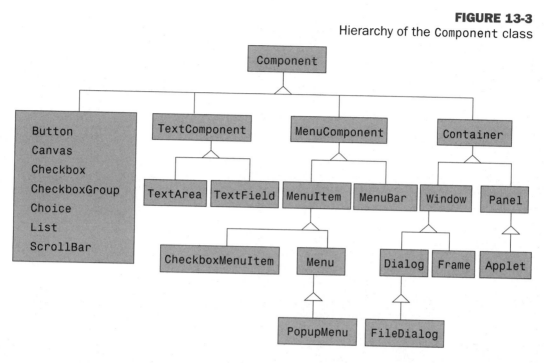

FIGURE 13-3
Hierarchy of the Component class

The classes DoubleField and IntegerField, which we have defined in the **BreezyGUI** package, are subclasses of the TextField class and thus understand all TextField messages. You are already familiar with the capabilities and behavior of many of the component classes, but several deserve further explanation.

Canvases

Canvas is a component not covered earlier. A *canvas* represents a rectangular area within a window. This area can be painted and repainted independently of the rest of the window. A canvas might, for instance, serve as the drawing area in a sketching program.

Scroll Bars

You have seen *scroll bars* along the sides of list and text area components. A case study later in this lesson uses scroll bars and a canvas to create a color meter for your computer.

Menu Components

All of Java's menu classes appear in the MenuComponent hierarchy. In earlier lessons, **BreezyGUI** hid the details of menu setup. For example, the following code segment uses **BreezyGUI** to set up a **File** menu and an **Edit** menu with appropriate options:

```
MenuItem newFileItem  = addMenuItem("File", "New");
MenuItem openFileItem = addMenuItem("File", "Open");
MenuItem saveFileItem = addMenuItem("File", "Save");

MenuItem cutEditItem   = addMenuItem("Edit", "Cut");
MenuItem copyEditItem  = addMenuItem("Edit", "Copy");
MenuItem pasteEditItem = addMenuItem("Edit", "Paste");
```

To perform the equivalent task without **BreezyGUI**, the programmer must do the following things:

1. Create new menu items with the appropriate labels.

2. Create new menus with the appropriate labels.

3. Create a new menu bar.

4. Add the menu items to their respective menus.

5. Add the menus to the menu bar.

6. Add the menu bar to the application window.

These steps are performed in the next code segment:

```
// Create the menu items.
MenuItem newFileItem = new MenuItem ("New");
MenuItem openFileItem = new MenuItem ("Open");
MenuItem saveFileItem = new MenuItem ("Save");
MenuItem cutEditItem = new MenuItem ("Cut");
MenuItem copyEditItem = new MenuItem ("Copy");
MenuItem pasteEditItem = new MenuItem ("Paste");

// Create the menus and the menu bar.
Menu fileMenu = new Menu ("File");
Menu editMenu = new Menu ("Edit");
MenuBar menuBar = new MenuBar();

// Add the menu items to the menus.
fileMenu.add (newFileItem);
fileMenu.add (openFileItem);
fileMenu.add (saveFileItem);
editMenu.add (cutEditItem);
editMenu.add (copyEditItem);
editMenu.add (pasteEditItem);

// Add the menus to the menu bar.
menuBar.add (fileMenu);
menuBar.add (editMenu);

// Add the menu bar to the application window.
setMenuBar (menuBar);
```

The MenuComponent class hierarchy also supports the creation of submenus. To create a submenu, you simply add one menu as an item to another.

The programmer sets up listeners for menu events in the same way as shown earlier for button events, by implementing the interface ActionListener. In this case, an action listener is added to each menu item.

Popup Menus

It is sometimes necessary to provide a popup menu rather than a pull-down menu. For example, we might need a menu in an applet, which does not support pull-down menus. Figure 13-4 shows a simple applet that sets up a popup menu.

When the user clicks in the red area (the portion of the Web page containing the applet's window), the menu pops up. The user can then select a menu option in the same way as with a pull-down menu.

The next segments show the HTML and Java code for this applet. For simplicity, we use the GBApplet class from **BreezyGUI** to define the applet:

FIGURE 13-4
Popup menu in an applet

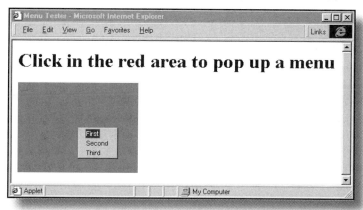

```
<html>
<head>
<TITLE>Menu Tester</TITLE>
</head>

<body>

<H1>Click in the red area to pop up a menu</H1>

<APPLET CODE="MenuApplet.class" WIDTH=200 HEIGHT=150>
</APPLET>

<body>
</html>
```

```
import java.awt.*;
import BreezyGUI.*;

public class MenuApplet extends GBApplet{

    PopupMenu testMenu;
    MenuItem firstItem, secondItem, thirdItem;

    public void init(){
        setBackground (Color.red);
        testMenu = new PopupMenu();
        firstItem = new MenuItem ("First");
        secondItem = new MenuItem ("Second");
        thirdItem = new MenuItem ("Third");
        testMenu.add (firstItem);
        testMenu.add (secondItem);
        testMenu.add (thirdItem);
        add (testMenu);
    }

    public void mouseClicked (int x, int y){
        testMenu.show (this, 100, 75);
    }
}
```

There are two points to note about this code:

1. The method `add`, which is called at the end of the `init` method, simply adds the popup menu to the applet.

2. As you will recall, `GBApplet` triggers the method `mouseClicked` when the mouse is clicked in the applet's window area. Our applet responds by sending the message `show` to the popup menu. The menu in turn responds by displaying itself at the indicated coordinates (100, 75) within the window. The first parameter passed to `show` must be the component relative to which the menu is positioned. In this case, the parameter is `this`, meaning the applet itself.

Container Classes

Container objects are so called because they contain other window objects, including other containers. Table 13-4 describes the uses of several container classes.

TABLE 13-4
Container classes

CONTAINER CLASS	WHAT IT DOES
Frame	Displays components in an application window. All stand-alone GUI applications must extend `Frame` (or `GBFrame` when using **BreezyGUI**).
Applet	Displays components in a Web browser. Applets have neither a menu bar nor a border. All Web-based applications must extend `Applet` (or `GBApplet` when using **BreezyGUI**).
Dialog	Displays components in a dialog window. Dialogs are used as auxiliary windows in stand-alone applications and applets. All dialogs must extend `Dialog` (or `GBDialog` when using **BreezyGUI**).
FileDialog	A subclass of dialog for browsing directory systems (as illustrated in Lesson 11).
Panel	Organizes a set of components as a group. Panels can factor complex interfaces into modular chunks. An applet, frame, or dialog can contain several panels, which in turn can contain buttons, text fields, lists, etc., and other panels.

A container must use a layout manager that determines the arrangement of the components within it. The different types of layouts are discussed next.

Layouts

In many programming environments, the user must specify the location and size of window objects in terms of pixel positions and pixel dimensions. Although this approach provides precise control over a window's appearance, it has a drawback. When a window is resized, its components remain fixed in position and size. Consequently, if the window is too small, some of the components cannot be seen, and if it is too large, the components seem to huddle in the window's top left corner. In contrast, components in a Java window distribute themselves to fill the available space. The exact manner of this distribution depends on the window's layout, as defined by one of Java's layout manager classes. Although you have had no way of knowing it, `GBFrame` and `GBApplet` use the layout manager `GridBagLayout`. Table 13-5 lists the layout manager classes with an illustration and overview of each. A more detailed description of each layout manager follows.

TABLE 13-5
Layout manager classes

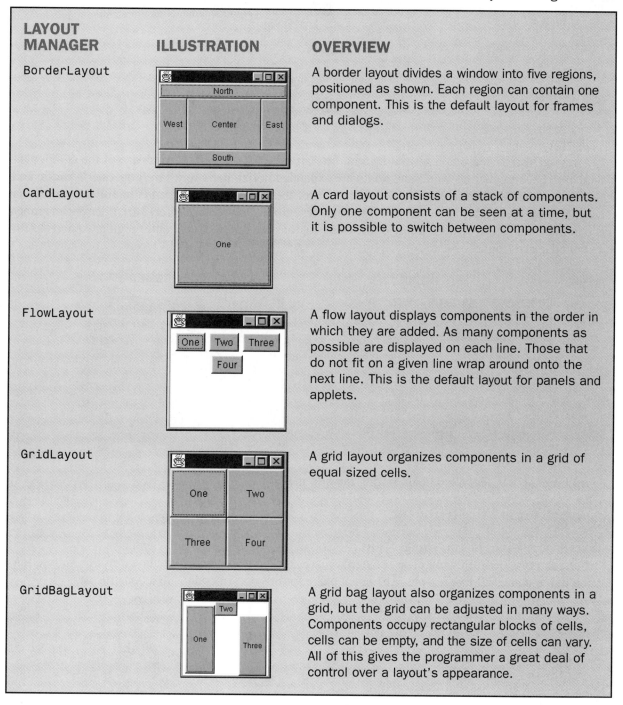

LAYOUT MANAGER	ILLUSTRATION	OVERVIEW
BorderLayout		A border layout divides a window into five regions, positioned as shown. Each region can contain one component. This is the default layout for frames and dialogs.
CardLayout		A card layout consists of a stack of components. Only one component can be seen at a time, but it is possible to switch between components.
FlowLayout		A flow layout displays components in the order in which they are added. As many components as possible are displayed on each line. Those that do not fit on a given line wrap around onto the next line. This is the default layout for panels and applets.
GridLayout		A grid layout organizes components in a grid of equal sized cells.
GridBagLayout		A grid bag layout also organizes components in a grid, but the grid can be adjusted in many ways. Components occupy rectangular blocks of cells, cells can be empty, and the size of cells can vary. All of this gives the programmer a great deal of control over a layout's appearance.

Border Layouts

The default layout for frames and dialogs is BorderLayout. The *border* layout divides a container into five regions, as shown in Figure 13-5.

FIGURE 13-5
The border layout

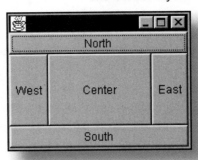

A region's size is based on several factors. First, it depends on the preferred size of the component placed in it. Second, regions North and South are expanded horizontally to fill the container's width, and regions East and West are expanded vertically. Third, the center region expands to fill the remaining space. Not all regions need to be present. If the center region is omitted (Figure 13-6), it leaves an empty space in the container. However, if any of the other regions are omitted, the center region expands to fill the vacated space (Figure 13-7).

FIGURE 13-6

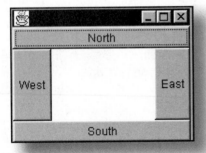

FIGURE 13-7

A component is added to a region using the add method:

```
add (<component>, <region>)
```

where <region> is one of the strings "North," "South," "East," "West," and "Center."

For example, the following code segment creates the first border layout shown in this subsection, the one that includes all five regions. The usual place for this sort of code is in a constructor.

```
// Create and set the layout
BorderLayout layout = new BorderLayout();
setLayout (layout);

// Add components under control of the layout
add (new Button("North"), "North");
add (new Button("East"), "East");
```

```
add (new Button("South"), "South");
add (new Button("West"), "West");
add (new Button("Center"), "Center");
```

In the above, the first two lines of code can be omitted when using a frame or a dialog.

Flow Layouts

The default window layout for panels and applets is `FlowLayout`. A *flow* layout displays components in horizontal lines in the order in which they are added (Figure 13-8). Components that do not fit on a line wrap around onto the next.

FIGURE 13-8
The flow layout

When a user resizes a window, the wrapping points shift, and the appearance of the window changes dramatically. For instance, the two windows in Figures 13-9 and 13-10 were created by the same program.

FIGURE 13-9

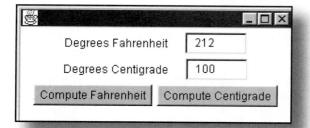

FIGURE 13-10

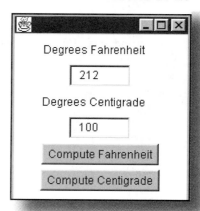

By default, a flow layout centers the components in each row and separates them horizontally and vertically by five pixels. The first flow layout in this subsection can be created as follows:

```
FlowLayout layout = new FlowLayout();
setLayout (layout);

add (new Button("One"));
add (new Button("Two"));
```

```
add (new Button("Three"));
add (new Button("Four"));
```

The first two lines are optional in panels and applets. The programmer has some minor control over a flow layout. The user can align the components to the left, center, or right using the constants

```
FlowLayout.LEFT
FlowLayout.CENTER
FlowLayout.RIGHT
```

For instance, to align the components left, the programmer writes:

```
FlowLayout layout = new FlowLayout (FlowLayout.LEFT);
setLayout (layout);

// Now add the components
```

This code results in the layout shown in Figure 13-11.

FIGURE 13-11
Left-aligned layout

The programmer can control the horizontal and vertical spacing between components. The following example centers window objects with horizontal gaps of 10 pixels and vertical gaps of 15 pixels:

```
FlowLayout layout = new FlowLayout (FlowLayout.CENTER, 10, 15);
setLayout (layout);

// Now add the components
```

The resulting layout is shown in Figure 13-12.

FIGURE 13-12
Centered layout

Grid Layouts

A regular pattern of objects, such as a table of buttons, is easily displayed with a *grid* layout. To use a grid layout,

FIGURE 13-13
A grid layout

1. Create a new instance of class `GridLayout` with the desired number of rows and columns.

2. Set the container's layout to this instance.

3. Add the components to the container.

The components are positioned in the grid from left to right and top to bottom, in the order added, and each cell in the grid is the same size. The following code segment creates the grid layout displayed in Figure 13-13.

```
setLayout (new GridLayout(2, 2));
add (new Button("One"));
add (new Button("Two"));
add (new Button("Three"));
add (new Button("Four"));
```

Grid Bag Layouts

The *grid bag* layout is the most versatile and most complex layout manager. It treats the display area as a grid of cells. The grid starts out with no cells and adds cells as needed to accommodate the components. Components occupy rectangular blocks of cells called display areas. Cells can be empty, and the size of cells can vary. In Figure 13-14, a grid has been superimposed on the window. The button "One" occupies two cells. Each of the other buttons occupies a single cell. The remaining cells are empty. Notice that the cells differ markedly in size and the components fill their display areas in varying degrees.

The classes `GBFrame`, `GBApplet`, and `GBDialog` use a grid bag layout.

FIGURE 13-14
The grid bag layout

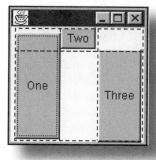

Class `GridBagLayout` must always be used in conjunction with another class—`GridBagCon-straints`. A constraints object specifies the manner in which a component occupies the grid. This is done by assigning values to the constraint object's public instance variables. Here is an illustrative code segment:

```
GridBagLayout layout = new GridBagLayout();
setLayout (layout);
```

```
constraints = new GridBagConstraints();
constraints.gridy = 0;         // row 0
constraints.gridx = 0;         // column 0
constraints.gridheight = 2;
constraints.fill = GridBagConstraints.BOTH;
constraints.insets = new Insets (6,4,3,0);
constraints.weightx = 100;

Button button1 = new Button ("One");
layout.setConstraints (button1, constraints);
add (button1);
```

The public instance variables are described in Table 13-6.

TABLE 13-6

Public instance variables of GridBagLayout

VARIABLES	WHAT THEY DO
anchor	When a component is smaller than its display area, an anchor specifies how to position the component in the area. The valid values are CENTER (the default), NORTH, NORTHEAST, EAST, SOUTHEAST, SOUTH, SOUTHWEST, WEST, and NORTHWEST. These values must be preceded by the name of the class, for instance, GridBagConstraints.NORTH.
fill	When a component's requested size is smaller than its display area, the fill attribute can be used to stretch the component. The valid values are: NONE — Do not stretch the component. This is the default. HORIZONTAL — Stretch the component as much as possible horizontally. VERTICAL — Stretch the component as much as possible vertically. BOTH — Stretch the component as much as possible horizontally and vertically. These values must be preceded by the name of the class, for instance, GridBagConstraints.VERTICAL.
gridx, gridy	Use gridx and gridy to specify the top left cell in a component's display area. Numbering begins at 0. The value GridBagConstraints.RELATIVE (the default value) can be used instead of a number. This value indicates that a component is to be positioned relative to the last component added, to the right for gridx and below for gridy.
gridwidth, gridheight	These variables specify the width and height of a component's display area, as measured in cells. The default value is 1. The values REMAINDER and RELATIVE can be used to specify that the component is the last or next to last, respectively, in a row or column.
ipadx, ipady	These variables are used to increase a component's minimum size by the specified number of pixels on the left and right (ipadx), and on the top and bottom (ipady). The default values are 0.

TABLE 13-6
(continued)

Lesson (13) The Abstract Windowing Toolkit

VARIABLES	WHAT THEY DO
insets	Insets specify how much empty space, as measured in pixels, should be placed between a component and the edges of its display area. The default is 0. Here is an example: `constraints.insets = new Insets (top,left,bottom,right);` where top, left, bottom, and right are nonnegative integers.
weightx, weighty	In a grid bag layout, not all cells need to be the same size. Their sizes can vary depending on values assigned to weightx and weighty. These values do not specify absolute dimensions for a cell, merely a relative size. Thus, all things being equal, a cell with weightx = 100 is twice as wide as one with weightx = 50, while a cell with weightx = 0 is just wide enough to display its component. Of course, all things are seldom equal. The algorithm used for determining a cell's dimensions is not described in Java's online documentation, so the user must acquire an intuitive sense for what happens through experimentation. By the way, if all the weights are 0 (the default), the components huddle together in the center of the container.

Here is code to create the grid bag layout shown in Figure 13-14.

```
// Create and set the layout
   GridBagLayout layout = new GridBagLayout();
   setLayout (layout);

// Create a constraints object
   GridBagConstraints constraints;

// Create three button objects.
   Button button1 = new Button ("One");
   Button button2 = new Button ("Two");
   Button button3 = new Button ("Three");

// Set the constraints object for button1, indicating that
// button1:
//   starts in row 0, column 0
//   has a height of 2 cells
//   fills its display area in both directions
//   is inset within its display area by 6, 4, 3, and 0
//   has a horizontal weighting factor of 100
// with the remaining constraints taking their default values
   constraints = new GridBagConstraints();
   constraints.gridy = 0;          // row 0
   constraints.gridx = 0;          // column 0
   constraints.gridheight = 2;
   constraints.fill = GridBagConstraints.BOTH;
   constraints.insets = new Insets (6,4,3,0);
   constraints.weightx = 100;
```

```
    layout.setConstraints (button1, constraints);
    add (button1);

// Set the constraints object for button2, indicating that
// button2:
//    starts in row 0, column 1
// with the remaining constraints taking their default values
    constraints = new GridBagConstraints();
    constraints.gridy = 0;        // row 0
    constraints.gridx = 1;        // column 1
    layout.setConstraints (button2, constraints);
    add (button2);

// Set the constraints object for button3, indicating that
// button3:
//    starts in row 1, column 2
//    fills its display area in the vertical directions
//    has a horizontal weighting factor of 50
//    has a vertical weighting factor of 100
// with the remaining constraints taking their default values
    constraints = new GridBagConstraints();
    constraints.gridy = 1;        // row 1
    constraints.gridx = 2;        // column 2
    constraints.weightx = 50;
    constraints.weighty = 100;
    constraints.fill = GridBagConstraints.VERTICAL;
    layout.setConstraints (button3, constraints);
    add (button3);
```

Card Layouts

A *card* layout consists of a stack of components. Only one component can be seen at a time, but it is possible to switch between components. When a card layout is created, the top component is visible. Here is the code that created Figure 13-15.

FIGURE 13-15
A card layout

```
CardLayout layout = new CardLayout();
setLayout (layout);
add ("One", new Button("One"));
add ("Two", new Button("Two"));
```

```
add ("Three", new Button("Three"));
add ("Four", new Button("Four"));
```

Several methods are used to move between components. These are first, last, next, previous, and show. Here is some code that demonstrates these methods in action. The word this refers to the container in which the code is running, a frame in this example. At other times, this might be replaced by a variable name that refers to the container associated with the layout.

```
layout.first (this);
layout.next (this);
layout.previous (this);
layout.last (this);
layout.show (this, "Three");
```

Panels

For the sake of simplicity, all of the components in the preceding discussion were buttons. We could have used lists, text areas, canvases, and even panels. A panel is a container that can contain other components, including other panels. Fancy GUIs can be built by combining panels and other components in an imaginative manner. Figure 13-16, for instance, is plenty fancy and more than a bit silly. The code used to generate this window is shown below:

FIGURE 13-16
A fancy panel interface

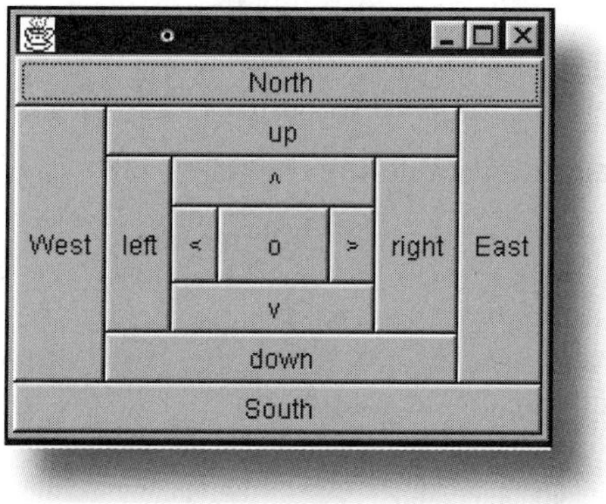

```
BorderLayout layout = new BorderLayout();
setLayout (layout);

add (new Button ("North"), "North");
add (new Button ("East"), "East");
add (new Button ("South"), "South");
add (new Button ("West"), "West");

Panel panel = new Panel();
add (panel, "Center");

BorderLayout layout2 = new BorderLayout();
panel.setLayout (layout2);
panel.add (new Button ("up"), "North");
panel.add (new Button ("down"), "South");
panel.add (new Button ("left"), "West");
panel.add (new Button ("right"), "East");
```

3 8 1

```
Panel panel2 = new Panel();
panel.add (panel2, "Center");

BorderLayout layout3 = new BorderLayout();
panel2.setLayout (layout3);
panel2.add (new Button ("^"), "North");
panel2.add (new Button ("v"), "South");
panel2.add (new Button ("<"), "West");
panel2.add (new Button (">"), "East");
panel2.add (new Button ("o"), "Center");
```

All About Events

When developing a GUI, the programmer is concerned not only with the layout of the window objects, but also with handling the events that they trigger. If we use **BreezyGUI**, then we handle events very easily in methods such as buttonClicked and menuItemSelected. But life becomes complicated when we use Java's AWT directly, as illustrated in the conversion program earlier in the lesson.

Events and Components

From our work with the conversion program, we know that certain events can be associated with certain components. For instance, the action event can be associated with buttons, and keyboard events can be associated with text fields. Table 13-7 lists all the different classes of events, their associated components, and the conditions that trigger the events.

Table 13-7, for example, indicates that the ActionEvent

- Is limited to buttons, lists, menu items, and text fields.

- Can be triggered by clicking a button, double-clicking an item in a list, selecting a menu item, or pressing the Enter key in a text field.

The FocusEvent, on the other hand, is more generally applicable, so it is associated with the class Component and thus with all subclasses of Component.

Events and Listeners

An event is ignored unless the originating component has added a listener to handle the event. In the conversion program we used the addActionListener method to add listeners to buttons and the add-KeyListener method to add listeners to text fields. Table 13-8 lists all the events, their associated listeners, and how to add/remove these listeners. We did not have any reason to remove a component's listener in the conversion program, but the table shows that we could have done so. The table also lists the methods included in each listener interface.

Events and Their Methods

When an event occurs, the event object, e, is passed as a parameter to the appropriate listener method, and the listener method can then send messages to the event object. For instance, consider the following code segment:

```
Button btn = (Button) e.getSource();
```

The getSource message is understood by all events and returns the object in which the event originated—a button in the above example. Table 13-9 lists several different classes of events and the most useful methods in each class.

TABLE 13-7
Event associations

Lesson ⑬ The Abstract Windowing Toolkit

EVENT CLASS	ASSOCIATED COMPONENTS	TRIGGERED WHEN
ActionEvent	Button	The button is clicked.
	List	An item in the list is double-clicked.
	MenuItem	The menu item is selected.
	TextField	The user presses the Enter key in the field.
AdjustmentEvent	Scroll Bar	The scroll tab is moved.
FocusEvent	Component	■ The component gains focus. ■ The component loses focus. Focus can be changed by pressing the Tab key to move from component to component or by clicking the mouse on a component. For text fields and text areas, the field with the focus is the one containing the cursor. It is the field that receives the user's keystrokes.
ItemEvent	Checkbox	The box is checked or unchecked.
	CheckboxMenuItem	■ The checkbox menu item is checked. ■ The checkbox menu item is unchecked.
	Choice	An item is selected from the choice's drop-down list.
	List	An item in the list is single-clicked.
InputEvent	Not applicable	Not applicable.
KeyEvent extends InputEvent	Component	■ A key is pressed. ■ A key is released. ■ A key is typed (i.e., pressed and then released).
MouseEvent extends InputEvent	Component	■ A mouse button is pressed in the component. ■ A mouse button is released in the component (provided it was pressed in the same component). ■ A mouse button is clicked in the component (i.e., pressed and then released). ■ The mouse enters the component. ■ The mouse exits the component. ■ The mouse is dragged in the component (i.e., moved while a button is depressed). ■ The mouse is moved in the component.
TextEvent	TextComponent	The user enters a character in the component.
WindowEvent	Window	■ The window is activated. ■ The window is closed. ■ The window is closing. ■ The window is deactivated. ■ The window is deiconified. ■ The window iconified. ■ The window is opened.

TABLE 13-8
Events and listeners

EVENT CLASS	ASSOCIATED LISTENER INTERFACE	IS THERE AN ADAPTER CLASS?	METHODS TO ADD/ REMOVE LISTENER	LISTENER INTERFACE METHODS
ActionEvent	ActionListener	No	addActionListener () removeActionListener ()	actionPerformed (ActionEvent)
AdjustmentEvent	AdjustmentListener	No	addAdjustment Listener () removeAdjustment Listener ()	adjustmentValueChanged (AdjustmentEvent)
FocusEvent	FocusListener	Yes	addFocusListener () removeFocusListener ()	focusGained (FocusEvent) focusLost (FocusEvent)
ItemEvent	ItemListener	No	addItemListener () removeItemListener ()	itemStateChanged (ItemEvent)
InputEvent	Not applicable	Not applicable	Not applicable	Not applicable
KeyEvent extends InputEvent	KeyListener	Yes	addKeyListener () removeKeyListener ()	keyPressed (KeyEvent) keyReleased (KeyEvent) keyTyped (KeyEvent)

TABLE 13-8
(continued)

EVENT CLASS	ASSOCIATED LISTENER INTERFACE	IS THERE AN ADAPTER CLASS?	METHODS TO ADD/ REMOVE LISTENER	LISTENER INTERFACE METHODS
MouseEvent extends InputEvent	MouseListener	Yes	addMouseListener () removeMouseListener ()	mousePressed (MouseEvent) mouseReleased (MouseEvent) mouseClicked (MouseEvent) mouseEntered (MouseEvent) mouseExited (MouseEvent)
	MouseMotionListener	Yes	addMouse MotionListener () removeMouse MotionListener ()	mouseDragged (MouseEvent) mouseMoved (MouseEvent)
TextEvent	TextListener	No	addTextListener () removeTextListener ()	textValueChanged (TextEvent)
WindowEvent	WindowListener	Yes	addWindowListener () removeWindow Listener ()	windowActivated (WindowEvent) windowClosed (WindowEvent) windowClosing (WindowEvent) windowDeactivated (WindowEvent) windowDeiconified (WindowEvent) windowIconified (WindowEvent) windowOpened (WindowEvent)

TABLE 13-9
Classes of events and their methods

EVENT CLASS	EVENT METHODS	DESCRIPTION
All events	Object getSource ()	Gets the object in which the event originated.
	String toString ()	Returns a string representation of the event.
AdjustmentEvent	int getValue ()	Gets the scroll bar's value.
	int getAdjustmentType ()	Returns the type of adjustment that caused the event. This will be one of the following integer constants: UNIT_INCREMENT, UNIT_DECREMENT, BLOCK_IN-CREMENT, BLOCK_DECREMENT, and TRACK. To reference one of these constants, prefix the class name. For instance, "AdjustmentEvent.TRACK".
FocusEvent	boolean isTemporary ()	Returns true if change in focus is temporary, else false. Permanent changes in focus are of the most interest and are caused by pressing the Tab key or clicking on a component with the mouse.
ItemEvent	int getStateChange ()	Returns the state change type that generated the event. These are ItemEvent.SELECTED and ItemEvent.DESELECTED.
Input	consume ()	Consumes the event. The event, perhaps a keystroke, will not be processed by the component in which the event occurred. For instance, if one wanted to block numeric inputs to a text field, one could consume all numeric keystrokes (0..9) in the field. From the user's perspective, pressing a numeric key would have no effect when this text field has the focus.
Event	boolean isAltDown ()	Returns true if the Alt key is down, else false.
	boolean isMetaDown ()	Returns true if the Meta key is down, else false.
	boolean isControlDown ()	Returns true if the Ctrl key is down, else false.
	boolean is ShiftDown ()	Returns true if the Shift key is down, else false.

TABLE 13-9
(continued)

EVENT CLASS	EVENT METHODS	DESCRIPTION
KeyEvent extends InputEvent	int getKeyCode ()	Returns the integer code for the key that triggered the event.
	char getKeyChar ()	Returns the character code for the key that triggered the event.
	String getKeyText ()	Returns a string representation of the key that triggered the event, i.e., "HOME," or "A," or "h."
	String getKeyModifierText ()	Returns a string describing the modifiers used with the key that triggered the event, i.e., "Alt" or "Alt + Shift."
	boolean isActionKey ()	Returns true if the triggering key is an action key, as defined in Event.java, else false. For instance, on a PC the action keys are Home, Page Up, Page Down, End, the arrow keys, the function keys F1 . . . F12, Print Screen, Scroll Lock, Caps Lock, Num Lock, Pause.
	setKeyCode (int)	Replaces the integer code for the key that triggered the event with the integer code indicated.
	setKeyChar (char)	Replaces the character code for the key that triggered the event with the character code indicated. For instance, many programs replace keystrokes by *s when a password is being entered. This prevents an observer from reading the password as a user types it.
MouseEvent extends InputEvent	int getClickCount ()	Returns the number of mouse clicks associated with the event. Could be 0, 1, or 2.
	Point getPoint ()	Returns the x, y position of the mouse where the event occurs relative to the top left corner of the component in which the event occurs.
	int getX ()	Returns the x position of the mouse where the event occurs relative to the top left corner of the component in which the event occurs.
	int getY ()	Returns the y position of the mouse where the event occurs relative to the top left corner of the component in which the event occurs.
	boolean isPopupTrigger ()	Returns true if this mouse event triggers the popup menu, else false.
Window Event	getWindow ()	Returns the window in which the event occurred.

Dialogs

A *dialog* is a window that pops up during the run of an application. Examples are message boxes and file dialogs. Message boxes merely display information, whereas file dialogs take information from the user and return it to the application. Normally, a dialog is *modal* because the rest of the application is inaccessible as long as the dialog is active. The user quits most dialogs by selecting an **OK** button or a **Cancel** button. The **Cancel** button allows users to back out of changes that are not really desired.

The next program shows how to construct a dialog by extending the class `Dialog`. The application `FirstDialogTester` displays the information for a student of the type defined in Lesson 7 (Figure 13-17). The application also displays a **Modify** button. When the user selects this button, a dialog window pops up, as shown in Figure 13-18.

As shown in Figure 13-17, the window becomes inactive (the title bar is gray) after the **Modify** button is clicked. The dialog shown in Figure 13-18 allows the user to change the student's grades and to return to the application by selecting either **OK** or **Cancel**. If the user selects **Cancel**, the information for the student in the application remains unchanged. If the user selects **OK**, the information in the application is updated with the new information. When the user selects either one of these buttons, the dialog disappears and the application window becomes active again.

FIGURE 13-17
Information is
displayed in a window

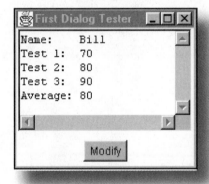

FIGURE 13-18
The dialog window
opens when the **Modify**
button is pressed

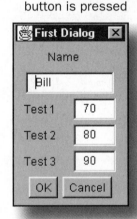

The demo consists of three classes:

1. `Student`—see Lesson 7.

2. `FirstDialog`—the module for the dialog.

3. `FirstDialogTester`—the application that tests the dialog.

The Class `FirstDialogTester`

The class `FirstDialogTester` uses **BreezyGUI** for convenience. Here is the code, followed by a discussion of what it does:

```
import java.awt.*;
import BreezyGUI.*;
```

```
public class FirstDialogTester extends GBFrame{

    TextArea taStudent = addTextArea ("",1,1,2,3);
    Button btModify = addButton ("Modify",4,1,2,1);

    private Student stud;

    public FirstDialogTester(){
        stud = new Student ("Bill", 70, 80, 90);
        taStudent.setText (stud.toString());
        setTitle ("First Dialog Tester");
    }

    public void buttonClicked (Button buttonObj){
        FirstDialog dlg;
        dlg = new FirstDialog (this, stud);
        dlg.show();
        if (dlg.exitType.equals ("OK"))
            taStudent.setText (stud.toString());
    }

    public static void main (String[] args){
        Frame frm = new FirstDialogTester();
        frm.setSize (200, 175);
        frm.setVisible (true);
    }
}
```

When this program starts, it creates a new `Student` object with some information and displays this information in a text area. The program then waits for the user to click the **Modify** button. When the user does this, `buttonClicked`

1. Creates a new instance of `FirstDialog`, passing to it the parameters `this` (the application itself) and the student.

2. Sends the `show` message to the dialog. This will pop up the dialog and pass control to it. At this point, the main interface is blocked until the user closes the dialog.

3. After the dialog is closed, resumes at the statement following `show`, at which point the application determines the manner in which the user closed the dialog and then takes the appropriate action.

Note that the application passes information (references to the student object and to itself) to the dialog when it is created. When the dialog closes, the application examines the dialog's public instance variable `exitType` to determine how the user closed the dialog. The value of this variable will be either "OK," in which case the user closed by selecting the **OK** button, or "Cancel," in which case the user quit by selecting the **Cancel** button.

The Class `FirstDialog`

Here is a listing of the `FirstDialog` class, which uses just the AWT and extends `Dialog`:

```
import java.awt.*;
import java.awt.event.*;

public class FirstDialog extends Dialog implements ActionListener{
```

```java
public String exitType = "Cancel";                        // How I was closed

private Label lbName       = new Label("Name");
private Label lbTest1      = new Label("Test 1");
private Label lbTest2      = new Label("Test 2");
private Label lbTest3      = new Label("Test 3");

private TextField tfName  = new TextField ("", 10);
private TextField ifTest1 = new TextField ("", 3);
private TextField ifTest2 = new TextField ("", 3);
private TextField ifTest3 = new TextField ("", 3);

private Button btnOK       = new Button ("OK");
private Button btnCancel   = new Button ("Cancel");

// The dialog is passed a student object and must refer to it
// at several locations thereafter.

private Student stud;

public FirstDialog (FirstDialogTester fdt, Student s){
   super (fdt, "First Dialog", true);                     // REQUIRED
   stud = s;

   FlowLayout layout = new FlowLayout();     // Default is BorderLayout
   setLayout (layout);

   add (lbName);      add (tfName);
   add (lbTest1);     add (ifTest1);
   add (lbTest2);     add (ifTest2);
   add (lbTest3);     add (ifTest3);
   add (btnOK);       add (btnCancel);
   btnOK.addActionListener (this);
   btnCancel.addActionListener (this);
   setSize (125,200);

   tfName.setText  (stud.getName());
   ifTest1.setText (String.valueOf(stud.getScore(1)));
   ifTest2.setText (String.valueOf(stud.getScore(2)));
   ifTest3.setText (String.valueOf(stud.getScore(3)));
}

public void actionPerformed (ActionEvent evt){
   Button buttonObj = (Button)evt.getSource();
   if (buttonObj == btnOK){
      exitType = "OK";
      stud.setName (tfName.getText());
      stud.setScore (1, new Integer(ifTest1.getText()).intValue());
      stud.setScore (2, new Integer(ifTest2.getText()).intValue());
      stud.setScore (3, new Integer(ifTest3.getText()).intValue());
   }
   dispose();    // This is how we close a dialog.
}
}
```

The programmer uses the AWT to lay out a dialog's window objects and set up their listeners, just as with frames. We used a similar code for an action listener earlier in this lesson. Like the Frame class, which implements application windows, Dialog is a subclass of the Window class. Thus, dialogs are like frames in many other ways. For example, dialogs can have a title, and BorderLayout is the default layout. However, there are some important exceptions:

■ A dialog is modal by default. That is, a dialog prevents the user from accessing the rest of the application before quitting.

■ A dialog must have a *parent*, that is, a frame to which it can refer after it is created. The reference to the parent frame allows a dialog to send messages to the application.

■ A dialog cannot have pull-down menus.

Several constructors allow the programmer to specify a dialog's attributes:

```
public Dialog (Frame parent, String title, boolean modal)
public Dialog (Frame parent, String title)
public Dialog (Frame parent, boolean modal)
public Dialog (Frame parent)
```

To simplify the use of dialogs, **BreezyGUI** contains a **GBDialog** class that has many of the features of GBFrame. Consult the documentation in Appendix H for details.

The Model/View/Controller Pattern

In Lesson 8, we introduced the idea of separating an application into a model and a view. Now we take the idea one step further and show how to divide an application into a model, a view, and a controller, where the controller represents all the application's listener classes. This division of responsibilities is well suited to handling the complexities of large applications, although it will appear a little awkward in the small case study that we present next.

In the MVC pattern, it is the view's responsibility to:

1. Instantiate the window objects, position them in the interface, and attach listeners to them as needed.

2. Instantiate and initialize the model.

3. Accurately represent the model to the user.

The responsibilities of the model are to

1. Define and manage the application's data (this usually requires coordinating the activities of several programmer-defined classes).

2. Respond to messages from the listeners.

3. Inform the view of changes to the model's internal state.

The responsibilities of the controller are to

1. Implement the necessary listeners.

2. Send messages to the model in response to user-generated events.

Here, then, is an illustration of the MVC pattern.

CASE STUDY: A Color Meter Application

Request

Create an application that allows the user to view a color by mixing RGB values.

Analysis

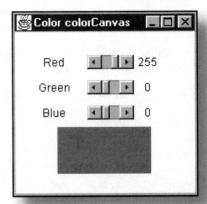

FIGURE 13-19

Figure 13-19 shows the proposed interface.

A color has three components (red, blue, green). The user manipulates each component separately by means of one of the scroll bars. Each scroll bar takes on values in the range 0 . . . 255. The rectangular patch below the scroll bars changes color in response to changes in the scroll bars. In addition, the RGB values are displayed to the right of the scroll bars.

The application uses the four classes listed in Table 13-10.

TABLE 13-10
Classes used in the application

CLASS	ROLE IN THE PROGRAM
ColorMeterView	The view class defines the window's layout, associates listeners with the scroll bars, instantiates the model, and redisplays the color when requested by the model.
ColorMeterModel	The model knows the current color, changes the color in response to messages from the listeners, and informs the view when the color display needs to be changed.
BarListener	The controller contains three instances of the bar listener, one attached to each scroll bar. The listeners detect changes in the scroll bars and inform the model.
GenericWindow Listener	The controller contains one instance of the GenericWindowListener encountered earlier in the lesson. This listener closes the application's window when the user clicks the close box.

Design and Implementation of the ColorMeterView

The constructor performs these tasks:

■ Instantiates the model, passes a pointer back to the view, and initializes the color to pure red.

■ Instantiates the window objects and adds them to a grid bag layout.

■ Initializes the appearance of the view to match the model.

■ Attaches listeners to the scroll bars and to the window.

The method `public void update (Color color)` performs these tasks:

■ Is called by the model whenever the color changes.

■ Redisplays the color patch and the numbers beside the scroll bars to reflect the latest color.

```java
import java.awt.*;

public class ColorMeterView extends Frame{

    // Declare variables for the window objects.
    private Label       redLabel;
    private Label       greenLabel;
    private Label       blueLabel;
    private Scrollbar   redBar;
    private Scrollbar   greenBar;
    private Scrollbar   blueBar;
    private Label       redValue;
    private Label       greenValue;
    private Label       blueValue;
    private Canvas      colorCanvas;

    // Declare a variable for the model.
    private ColorMeterModel model;

    // Constructor.
    public ColorMeterView(){

        // Set the title.
        setTitle ("Color colorCanvas");

        // Instantiate the model.
        model = new ColorMeterModel (this, new Color (255,0,0));

        // Instantiate the window objects.
        redLabel    = new Label("Red");
        greenLabel  = new Label("Green");
        blueLabel   = new Label("Blue");
        redBar      = new Scrollbar(Scrollbar.HORIZONTAL, 0, 50, 0, 305);
        greenBar    = new Scrollbar(Scrollbar.HORIZONTAL, 0, 50, 0, 305);
        blueBar     = new Scrollbar(Scrollbar.HORIZONTAL, 0, 50, 0, 305);
        redValue    = new Label("    ");
        greenValue  = new Label("    ");
        blueValue   = new Label("    ");
        colorCanvas = (new Canvas());
        colorCanvas.setSize(100, 50);

        // Instantiate and set a grid bag layout.
        GridBagLayout layout = new GridBagLayout();
        setLayout(layout);

        // Add the window objects to the layout.
        //                              row,col,width,height
```

```
        addComponent(layout, redLabel    , 0, 0, 1, 1);
        addComponent(layout, greenLabel  , 1, 0, 1, 1);
        addComponent(layout, blueLabel   , 2, 0, 1, 1);
        addComponent(layout, redBar      , 0, 1, 1, 1);
        addComponent(layout, greenBar    , 1, 1, 1, 1);
        addComponent(layout, blueBar     , 2, 1, 1, 1);
        addComponent(layout, redValue    , 0, 2, 1, 1);
        addComponent(layout, greenValue  , 1, 2, 1, 1);
        addComponent(layout, blueValue   , 2, 2, 1, 1);
        addComponent(layout, colorCanvas , 3, 0, 3, 1);

        // Initialize the appearance of the view to match the model.
        redBar.setValue (255);
        greenBar.setValue (0);
        blueBar.setValue (0);
        update (new Color (255,0,0));

        // Add listeners to three scrollbars.
        redBar.addAdjustmentListener
            (new BarListener(model, ColorMeterModel.RED));
        greenBar.addAdjustmentListener
            (new BarListener(model, ColorMeterModel.GREEN));
        blueBar.addAdjustmentListener
            (new BarListener(model, ColorMeterModel.BLUE));

        // Add a listener to the window.
        addWindowListener(new GenericWindowListener());
    }

    // Add a component to the layout in the indicated row and column
    // with the indicated height and width.
    private void addComponent(GridBagLayout layout,
                        Component component,
                        int row, int col,
                        int width, int height){

        GridBagConstraints constraints = new GridBagConstraints();

        constraints.insets.bottom = 2;
        constraints.insets.top    = 2;
        constraints.insets.left   = 2;
        constraints.insets.right  = 2;

        constraints.gridx = col;
        constraints.gridy = row;
        constraints.gridwidth = width;
        constraints.gridheight = height;
        layout.setConstraints(component, constraints);
        add (component);
    }

    // The model calls this method whenever the model wants
    // to update the view. It updates the number to the right of
```

```
        // each scrollbar and repaints the canvas in the current color.
        public void update(Color color){
            redValue.setText("" + color.getRed());
            greenValue.setText("" + color.getGreen());
            blueValue.setText("" + color.getBlue());
            colorCanvas.setBackground(color);
            colorCanvas.repaint();
        }

        public static void main (String[] args){
            Frame frm = new ColorMeterView();
            frm.setSize (200, 200);
            frm.setVisible (true);
        }

    }
```

Design and Implementation of the `ColorMeterModel`

Define three constants (RED, GREEN, BLUE) to represent the three different components of a color. Two instance variables are needed:

1. `color`—indicates the current color.

2. `view`—points back to the view class, thus allowing the model to send messages to the view.

   The constructor performs the following tasks:

- Initializes the variable that points back to the view.

- Initializes the variable that holds the color.

   The method `public void changeColor(int componentToChange, int componentValue)` performs the following tasks:

- Is called by the scroll bar listeners.

- Has a first parameter that indicates the color component to be changed (red, blue, or green).

- Has a second parameter that indicates the component's new value.

- Sets the specified component to the value indicated and tells the view to update itself.

```
    import java.awt.*;

    public class ColorMeterModel{

        // Constants that define the three components of a color:
        // red, blue, green.
        public static final int RED = 0;
        public static final int GREEN = 1;
        public static final int BLUE = 2;
```

```
      private Color color;
      private ColorMeterView view;

      public ColorMeterModel(ColorMeterView vw, Color initialColor){
         view = vw;
         color = initialColor;
      }

      // Change one component of the color.
      // componentToChange -- indicates which component to change
      // (red, blue, or green).
      // componentValue -- indicates the new value of the component.
      public void changeColor(int componentType,
                              int componentValue){

         // Get the current component colors.
         int redValue = color.getRed();
         int greenValue = color.getGreen();
         int blueValue = color.getBlue();

         // Change the value of the indicated component.
         switch (componentToChange){
            case RED:
               redValue = componentValue;;
               break;
            case GREEN:
               greenValue = componentValue;
               break;
            case BLUE:
               blueValue = componentValue;
               break;
         }

         // Reset the meter's color.
         color = new Color(redValue, greenValue, blueValue);

         // Update the view to reflect the change in color.
         view.update (color);
      }
   }
```

Design and Implementation of the `BarListener`

The `BarListener` class implements the `AdjustmentListener` interface. A bar listener object maintains two instance variables, `model` and `colorOfBar`, to refer to the model and the color associated with the bar, respectively. When the user interacts with a scroll bar, an `AdjustmentEvent` occurs. This event is passed to the `adjustmentValueChanged` method, which is implemented here. The `adjustmentValueChanged` method

■ Extracts the integer value from the scroll bar's event.

■ Assigns it back to the scroll bar.

- Runs the application's `changeColor` method with this integer and the bar's color code as parameters.

```java
import java.awt.*;
import java.awt.event.*;

public class BarListener implements AdjustmentListener{

    private ColorMeterModel model;
    private int colorOfBar;

    public BarListener(ColorMeterModel cmmdl, int color){
        model = cmmdl;
        colorOfBar = color;
    }

    public void adjustmentValueChanged(AdjustmentEvent e){
        Scrollbar bar = (Scrollbar)e.getSource();
        int value = Math.min (255, e.getValue());
        bar.setValue (value);
        model.changeColor(colorOfBar, value);
    }
}
```

Applets and the AWT

We have seen how to convert stand-alone programs into applets when GBFrame and GBApplet are used. The conversion process follows the same pattern when the AWT is used. Here are a few points to remember:

1. The applet must import the package **java.applet** and must extend Java's `Applet` class.

2. Window objects are created and added to the interface in an `init()` method rather than in a constructor.

3. There is no `main` method.

4. Because applets are embedded in Web pages, the Web browser handles the applet's closing. Thus, there is no need for a `WindowListener`.

5. Like stand-alone applications, applets need listeners to detect and handle events in components.

6. Applets can be split between a view and a model in the same manner as before.

To illustrate the conversion process, here is the `FahrenheitToCentigrade` program from the beginning of the lesson rewritten as an applet:

```java
import java.awt.*;
import java.awt.event.*;
import java.applet.*;

public class ConversionWithAWT extends Applet
                        implements ActionListener{
```

```
    private Label     fahrenheitLabel;
    private TextField fahrenheitField;
    private Label     centigradeLabel;
    private TextField centigradeField;
    private Button    fahrenheitButton;
    private Button    centigradeButton;

    public void init(){
        fahrenheitLabel  = new Label ("Degrees Fahrenheit");
        fahrenheitField  = new TextField ("212", 6);  // 6 columns wide
        centigradeLabel  = new Label ("Degrees Centigrade");
        centigradeField  = new TextField ("100", 6);  // 6 columns wide
        fahrenheitButton = new Button ("Compute Fahrenheit");
        centigradeButton = new Button ("Compute Centigrade");

        FlowLayout layout = new FlowLayout();
        setLayout (layout);
        add (fahrenheitLabel);
        add (fahrenheitField);
        add (centigradeLabel);
        add (centigradeField);
        add (fahrenheitButton);
        add (centigradeButton);

        fahrenheitButton.addActionListener (this);
        centigradeButton.addActionListener (this);
    }

    public void actionPerformed (ActionEvent e){
        String str;
        int fahrenheit, centigrade;
        Button btn = (Button)e.getSource();

        if (btn == fahrenheitButton){
            str = centigradeField.getText().trim();
            centigrade = (new Integer (str)).intValue();
            fahrenheit = centigrade * 9 / 5 + 32;
            fahrenheitField.setText ("" + fahrenheit);
        }
        else{
            str = fahrenheitField.getText().trim();
            fahrenheit = (new Integer (str)).intValue();
            centigrade = (fahrenheit - 32) * 5 / 9;
            centigradeField.setText ("" + centigrade);
        }
    }
}
```

Summary

In this lesson, you learned:

■   Java's AWT was developed to handle GUIs. GUI components are subclasses of the Component class. The components include canvases, scroll bars, menus, and containers in addition to buttons, checkboxes, and other familiar window objects.

- Layout manager classes control the placement of objects in a window. Common layouts include border, flow, grid, grid bag, and card.

- The AWT includes components for handling many types of events associated with a GUI, such as mouse clicks, mouse movements, pressed keys, and so on. Events are ignored unless listeners are available to handle them.

- To create a dialog in a Java application or applet, use the AWT `Dialog` class.

- When creating a large, complicated program, use the MVC pattern.

LESSON 13 REVIEW QUESTIONS

FILL IN THE BLANKS

Complete each of the following statements by writing your answer in the blank provided.

1. The term AWT stands for _____.

2. The four major categories of classes that are used to construct GUI applications are_____, _____, _____, and _____.

3. Three examples of container classes are_____,_____, and _____.

4. The default layout of the `Frame` class is _____.

5. The default layout of the `Applet` class is _____.

6. The term MVC stands for _____.

WRITTEN QUESTIONS

Write your answers to the following questions.

1. What is a listener object? Describe how a listener object functions in a Java program that uses the AWT.

2. Describe how a dialog communicates with the application that uses it.

3. Explain the difference between a popup menu and a pull-down menu.

4. How does one set up a text field to ignore certain characters typed by the user?

1. The key listener for the Fahrenheit to centigrade program allows only digits to be typed in the text fields. Fix the program so that the key listener also allows the user to type the backspace key. **_Hint:_** The backspace character is represented as `'\b'` in Java.

2. Redo the Fahrenheit to centigrade application with AWT so that your program adheres to the MVC pattern. **_Hint:_** Divide the existing `ConversionWithAWT` class into two classes, `ConversionView` and `ConversionModel`. The model should maintain instance variables for degrees Fahrenheit and degrees centigrade. When the user clicks a button, the associated listener sends a message to the model to perform the requested conversion. The model then sends a message to the view to obtain the input data, performs the conversion, updates the instance variables, and sends another message to the view to update the interface with the results.

3. Redo the shapes-drawing program of Unit Review 3 using AWT.

4. Modify the shapes-drawing program of Project 3 so that the user can select the color from a dialog that displays a color meter.

5. Redo the tic-tac-toe applet of Lesson 12 using AWT. Use a grid layout to set up the 3-by-3 grid of buttons.

CRITICAL THINKING ACTIVITY

The purpose of **BreezyGUI** is to ease the writing of GUI-based programs in Java. In what ways does **BreezyGUI** achieve this goal? Why would anyone want to program with Java's AWT instead?

UNIT 4 REVIEW QUESTIONS

TRUE/FALSE

On a separate piece of paper, type True if the statement is true or False if it is not.

T   F   1. A stream of bytes from which data are read is called an input stream.

T   F   2. Java lets you read characters from a file one character at a time, one word at a time, or one line at a time.

T   F   3. A file dialog is a window that displays as the result of an event.

T   F   4. Hypertext and hypermedia are both ways to jump from page to page on the Web.

T   F   5. The HEAD markup tag designates the title that appears in the browser's window.

T   F   6. You can code six types of lists using HTML tags.

T   F   7. The .wav extension designates an inline image.

T   F   8. The AWT lets you write a program once and run it anywhere.

T   F   9. Listener objects tell buttons where the listener code is located.

T   F   10. The flow layout displays objects in the order in which they are added.

FILL IN THE BLANKS

On a separate piece of paper, type the information necessary to complete the following statements.

1. The set of classes used to connect a program to a file stream are defined in Java's _____ package.

2. A(n) _____ statement provides a way to locate and respond to run-time errors.

3. Sequences of characters separated by white space characters and processed as words are called _____.

4. A stream of bytes to which data are written is called a(n) _____.

5. The World Wide Web consists of two kinds of machines: _____ and
   _____.

6. HTML codes called _____ indicate the format of text elements or links to other nodes.

7. To convert a Java application to an applet, you must replace the name `GBFrame` with the name
   _____.

8. In the AWT, all of the GUI components are subclasses of an abstract class called
   _____.

9. A(n) _____ is a rectangular area within a window that can be painted independently of
   the rest of the window.

10. _____ objects are so called because they contain other window objects.

WRITTEN QUESTIONS

On a separate piece of paper, type the answers to the following questions or problems.

1. Assume that the data for a student have been saved in a binary file. These data include the
   student's ID number, name, and five grades. The types of data are positioned in the file as follows:

   ```
   <int> <String> <5 doubles>
   ```

   Write a Java code segment that opens a data input stream on this file and reads the student's data
   into the appropriate variables.

2. Describe how to convert an application written with **BreezyGUI** to an applet.

3. Explain how a Web browser accesses and runs an applet.

4. A programmer is designing an application that writes integer data from an array to a file. Which
   Java classes would be appropriate for this kind of output operation? Write a pseudocode algorithm
   that describes the task.

5. A Java application has a pull-down menu of colors. Describe how a programmer would convert
   this feature so that the program could run as a Java applet.

6. Explain the difference between an ordinary window object and a container object.

UNIT 4 APPLICATIONS

1. Merging the contents of two files is a common operation. Write a program that reads words from two
   text files. You may assume that the words in each input file are sorted in ascending order. Write all of
   these words to a third file, so that the contents of this file are also sorted in ascending order.

2. Add a command to the program of Application 1 that concatenates two files. This operation should place the results in a third file.

3. Convert the color meter application of the Lesson 13 Case Study to an applet. Test the program in a Web browser.

CRITICAL THINKING ACTIVITY

The programmer who does file I/O with arrays must deal with the problem of not knowing how many data objects need to be read during file input. Discuss this problem and propose a solution.

APPENDIX A

Java Resources and Environments

Because of Java's popularity as a programming language, Java resources are available from a number of vendors and from sites on the Internet. Windows, Macintosh, and UNIX platforms are available. Java environments vary from the simplest command prompt environment used throughout this text to integrated development applications that provide a Java compiler along with other tools to streamline creation of applications and applets.

This appendix covers the basics of working with some common Java environments. If you are using a Java application that is not discussed in this appendix, you can probably gather enough pointers from this appendix and your application's help files to use Java successfully.

Working with Sun's Java Development Kit

Sun Microsystems maintains an excellent Web site where programmers can find complete documentation for the Java API (Application Programming Interface) and download a free JDK (Java Development Kit).

Downloading JDK 1.1

To download the JDK 1.1, go to Sun's Java home page, located at **http://www.java.sun.com.** Click the *Products & APIs* hyperlink to go to the PRODUCTS & APIs page. Click the Product Quick Pick list arrow to display a list of products. Click the *Java Development Kit 1.1 Platform—JDK* choice and click the **Go** button. You then have a choice of versions to download. Windows users will probably want to click the *JDK 1.1 Win32 Release* hyperlink.

Be sure to select JDK 1.1 (**BreezyGUI** cannot be used with JDK 1.0). Note that at the time of this writing, the most current version of JDK 1.1 was JDK 1.1.6. The last digit might be higher by the time you read this book. You can also use JDK 1.2, if that version is available by the time you read this book.

The JAVA DEVELOPMENT KIT page gives specific instructions for downloading the current version of JDK software and documentation. Read the instructions on this and following Web pages to download the software and documentation.

Installing and Setting up the JDK

After downloading, install the JDK on your computer by running the installation program. You should print the **Readme** file for further reference. The installation will create a folder named JDK1.1.6 on your hard drive.

As part of the setup process, you might want to modify your computer's PATH statement. After a default installation, you must tell the computer exactly where to find the Java tools needed for a particular task. For example, to compile the Java file **GoodMorning.java,** you would have to type the following sequence at the MS-DOS prompt:

```
C:\jdk1.1.6\bin\javac GoodMorning.java
```

To avoid having to specify the path to the JDK1.1.6 folder each time you use a Java command, you can add the following line to your **autoexec.bat** file's PATH statement:

```
C:\jdk1.1.6\bin
```

After adding this information to the PATH statement, you can use a Java command at the current prompt without specifying any additional information.

Creating a Folder for Java Files

For best results using the programs in this book, create a folder on your hard drive to contain your Java files. Place in your Java files folder the **BreezyGUI** folder from CD-ROM (or from a disk your instructor gives you). You might want to create additional subfolders within your Java files folder to store the programs for each lesson in the book.

 **IMPORTANT:**

Your Java programs will not compile or run properly unless the **BreezyGUI** folder is in the same folder with your Java files.

Working with Java Files

Lesson 2 provides step-by-step instructions on how to type, save, compile, and run a Java program. Remember that a Java source file must have the same name as the class it contains and must end with the **.java** extension. Java class names and file names are case sensitive. If you receive a message indicating that a file could not be found, check that you have typed the file name correctly at the prompt. You can define more than one class in a source file, but the usual procedure is to have one source file for each class.

When running applets, both the HTML file and the Java application called in the file must be in the same folder.

Program files are provided to save time in typing Java programs. To open a program file in Notepad, click **File** and then **Open.** In the Open dialog box, locate the folder that contains the program file you want to open. You may need to specify that All Files be displayed to see the **.java** files. Click the file to select it, and then click the **Open** button.

Basic Operations

You type instructions at the MS-DOS prompt to use the Java tools. The operations you will use most often are summarized below.

COMPILING A PROGRAM

The basic syntax is `javac <filename>`, where `<filename>` is a Java source file name (ending in the .java extension). Java locates and compiles all of the files required by your program. Any syntax error messages are displayed in the command window, and a byte code (**.class**) file is generated for each class defined in your program.

RUNNING AN APPLICATION

The basic syntax is `java <filename>`, where `<filename>` is the name of the class that defines the `main` method of your program. Note that the **.class** extension must be omitted. Run-time error messages are displayed in the command window. To pass a parameter for the program, type it following the file name (e.g., `java RandomNumber 5`).

RUNNING AN APPLET

The basic syntax is `appletviewer <filename>`, where `<filename>` is the name of an HTML file that links to your applet. You can also view an applet in your Web browser by locating the **Open** command on the **File** menu and then using a browse button to find your HTML file.

Working with Microsoft Visual J++ 6.0

Microsoft's Visual J++ 6.0 is an integrated application that enables you to create Java programs and applets, compile them, debug them, and run them in one environment. The sections below give you the basic information you need to run the programs in this book in the Visual J++ 6.0 environment.

Storing J++ Projects

During installation, J++ 6.0 creates a folder called **Visual Studio Projects** in the **My Documents** folder (in Windows 95 and 98). However, you can create your own folder within this folder to hold your Java files. As you work through the lessons in this book, you may want to create subfolders for each lesson, to keep your Java files organized.

Setting Up a New Project

Visual J++ 6.0 requires you to create a new project to hold the files for a program. To start a new project, follow these steps:

Step 1. Launch Visual J++. The New Project dialog box automatically appears to ask you what kind of project you want to create (see Figure A-1). The default project is *Windows Application* and the default name of the new project is **Project1**. Rename the project and choose another location for it if desired. Click **Open** to open the new project.

FIGURE A-1
The New Project dialog box

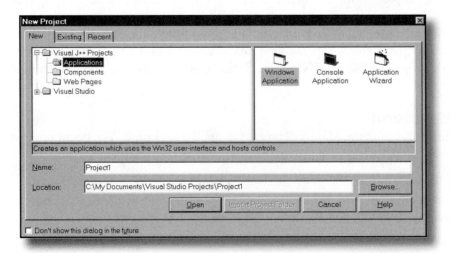

Step 2.   The design window opens, with information about the new project in the Project Explorer pane at the right side of the window. By default, Visual J++ places a form in the new project (Figure A-2). For the programs in this text, you will not need this form. To delete it, click the + button to the left of **Project1** in the Project Explorer pane. Right-click on the **Form1.java** form and select **Delete** from the shortcut menu. Click **Yes** when asked if you want to delete the form.

FIGURE A-2
The project has a default form

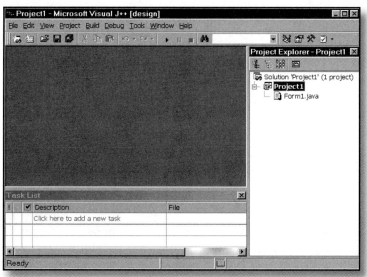

Creating or Opening a Source File

To create a new Java file, click **File** and then **New File.** In the New File dialog box, you have a choice whether to create a General file or a Visual J++ file. Click the file type you want and then click **Open.** The new file appears in the J++ window.

Run-Time Tip

> **When you create an application using the Java File option, you will notice that J++ colors some portions of the program you type. Comments are colored green, for example, and keywords are blue. J++ also automatically indents portions of your program.**

After you have finished typing a program, save it by clicking the **Save** command on the **File** menu. The file name should be the same as the name of the class contained in the program file. Make sure to type the **.java** extension at the end of the file name. The file will then be saved as a Miscellaneous File in your current project (Figure A-3).

The easiest way to add a file from another source to your project is to use Windows Explorer. Copy the Java file to the project folder in the **My Documents** folder. To run most programs in this text, you must also copy the **BreezyGUI** package folder to the project folder. When you return to J++ after copying files and folders this way, you will see that J++ has automatically updated the project with the new files. To edit a file that you have added in this way, double-click on its icon in the project pane. Figure A-4 shows such a project after we have added the file **FahrenheitToCentigrade.java** and the package **BreezyGUI.**

A file has been created and added to the project

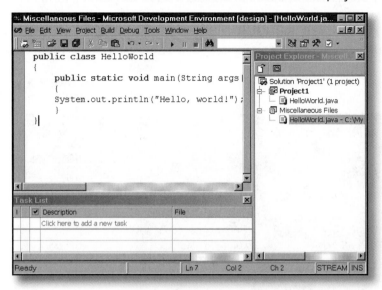

A new file and the **BreezyGUI** package have been added to the project

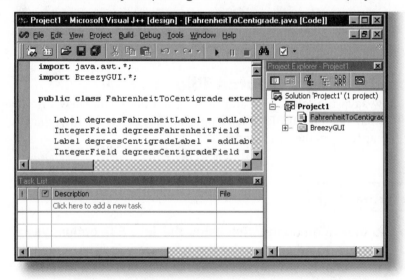

Compiling and Starting an Application

After you have created or copied the files necessary for the project, you are ready to run it. Follow these steps:

Step 1. Before you start the program, you must make sure J++ knows the name of the file that contains the `main` method. Click the **Project** menu and then **Project1 Properties.** (This menu entry will change its name based on the name of your current project.) The **Project1** Properties dialog box opens, as shown in Figure A-5. Click the **Apply** button to make sure J++ will use the file listed during the compiling process. To display your program in a command window similar to those shown elsewhere in this book, click the *Launch as a console application* check box. Click **OK**.

 **Run-Time Tip**

Non-GUI applications should be launched as terminal applications. GUI applications should be launched as terminal applications while they are under development, so you can view the run-time error messages and display debugging output in the terminal window. When a GUI application is ready for "release," you can turn the console application switch off and rebuild.

FIGURE A-5
Specify settings for running the program
in the Properties dialog box

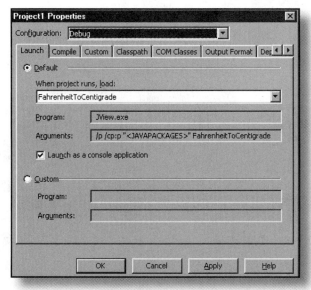

Step 2. Click the **Debug** menu and then **Start Without Debugging.** J++ compiles the application and displays any syntax error messages in the Task List pane at the bottom of the window. The following items will be created in your current project folder:

    a. A **.class** file. This is the byte code for your program.

    b. An **.exe** file. This is your program as a stand-alone application. You can launch it from the Explorer or run it as a DOS command.

    c. A **.vjp** file. This is your Visual J++ project file. You can launch this to re-open Visual J++ from the Explorer, or you can open it as an existing project from the Visual J++ **File** menu.

Step 3. If necessary, use the information in the Task List pane to locate and fix errors (a double-click on an error message sends the cursor to the offending code in the editor pane). Then click the **Start Without Debugging** command again.

Step 4. Java runs the program and displays the GUI window in the top left corner of the screen, as shown in Figure A-6. To end this program, click its close box. The **JVIEW** window will also close and return you to the application screen.

When you are finished with a program, remove all source files from the project and add new ones, or start a new project and repeat the steps above to create new programs.

Run-Time Tip

When you select a file in the project pane and delete it, Visual J++ not only removes the file from the project, but also deletes it from the folder (moves it to the recycle bin). To prevent the loss of valuable work, be sure to copy your program file to a safe place before removing it from a project, or create a new project for each new program.

FIGURE A-6
Results of running the program

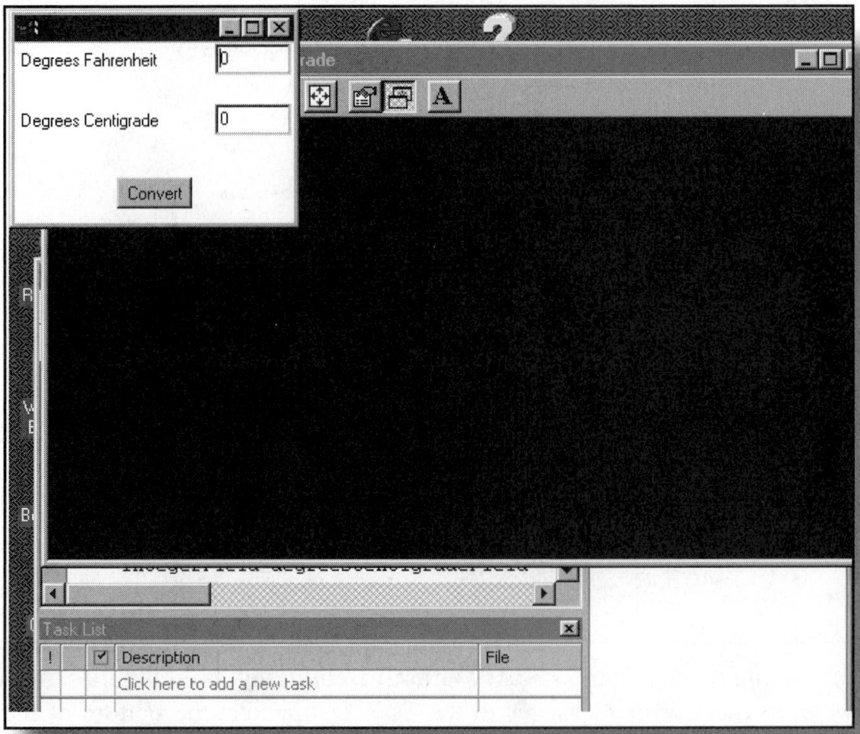

Passing a Parameter to a Program

Sometimes you need to pass a parameter or argument to a Java application when it is launched. You can pass a parameter to an application in Visual J++ by following these steps:

Step 1. Click **Project** and then **Projectx Properties.**
Step 2. Click the **Custom** option button in the dialog box.
Step 3. In the field labeled **Arguments** at the bottom of the dialog box, enter the parameter to the right of the existing parameters. Each parameter should be separated by at least one space. Figure A-7 shows the Properties dialog box after the user has entered a single parameter of 10 (the program **TestDataStreams.java** comes with Lesson 11).
Step 4. Click **Apply** (if necessary) and click **OK.**
Step 5. Run the program. To run the program with a different parameter, you must reopen the **Properties** dialog and edit the parameter.

Specifying a parameter to an application

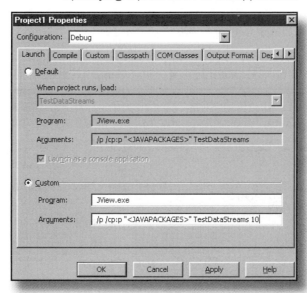

Creating and Running an Applet

An applet is a Java program that runs in an HTML document on a Web browser. You can create both the HTML document and the Java applet in Visual J++.

To create the HTML document, click **File** and then **New File.** Select the **New HTML Page** option. Visual J++ displays a workspace where you can create an HTML document. Click the **Source** tab at the bottom of the workspace to see sample HTML markup tags already in place (see Figure A-8). All you need to do is add text and any additional markup tags. The **QuickView** tab at the bottom of the workspace shows you a quick preview of how your document will look on a browser. When you save the HTML document, it will automatically store in your current project. Make sure the Java program you want to run as an applet is also stored in the project.

FIGURE A-8

Use the workspace to create an HTML document

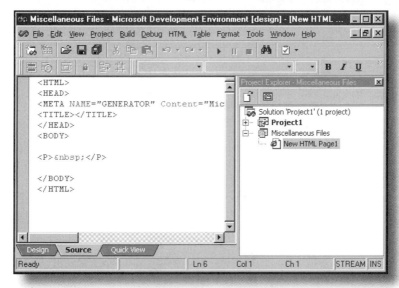

You can modify an existing application or create a new one for the applet. To convert an application, follow the instructions in Lesson 12. Make sure the applet has the same name as the class referenced in the HTML document.

To run the example Fahrenheit to centigrade applet in Lesson 12, follow these steps:

Step 1. Copy the files **FahrenheitToCentigrade.java** and **fahrtocent.html** from Lesson 12 to the project folder, and be sure that this folder also contains **BreezyGUI** (see Figure A-9).

FIGURE A-9
Copying an applet and its html file to a workspace

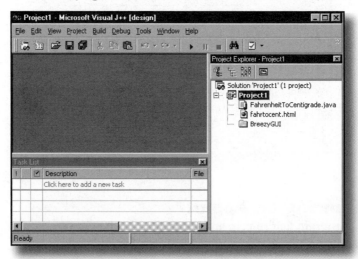

Step 2. Click **Project** and then choose **Projectx Properties**. You now can choose either **Fahrenheit-ToCentigrade** (the applet) or **fahrtocent.html** (the HTML file) as the file to load when the program runs (see Figure A-10). If you choose the applet file, the program runs in an appletviewer without the HTML text (see Figure A-11). If you choose the HTML file, the program runs in the Internet Explorer with the HTML text (see Figure A-12). Pull down the list and select one of these files.

FIGURE A-10
Selecting the file to load when running an applet

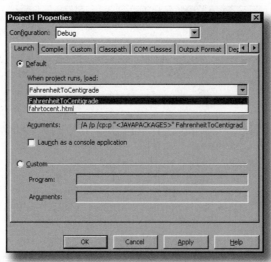

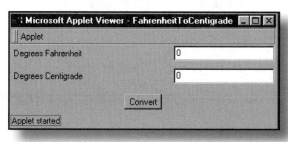

FIGURE A-11
Running a program in the appletviewer

FIGURE A-12
Running a program in the Internet Explorer

Step 3.   If you are running the program from the appletviewer, check the **Launch as Console Application** box.

Step 4.   Click **Apply** and click **OK.**

Step 5.   Run the program by clicking **Debug** and then choosing **Start Without Debugging.** If you are running **FahrenheitToCentigrade** in the appletviewer, you will see a warning dialog box and a warning message in the task list that the applet has defined no `init` method. If you are running **fahrtocent.html** in the Internet Explorer, you will see a warning dialog and a message that the main class file cannot be found. You can ignore these warnings by clicking **OK,** and the program will run in either case.

If you are just developing an applet, test it in the appletviewer until it behaves correctly. Then run its HTML document to test it together with its Web page.

Working with Borland JBuilder University Edition

Borland JBuilder University Edition is an integrated application that enables you to create Java programs and applets, compile them, debug them, and run them in one environment. The sections below give you the basic information you need to run the programs in this book in the JBuilder environment.

Storing JBuilder Projects

During installation, JBuilder creates a folder called **myprojects** in the **JBuilder** folder (in Windows 95 and 98). However, you can create your own folder within this folder to hold your Java files. As you work through the lessons in this book, you may want to create subfolders for each lesson, to keep your Java files organized.

Setting up a New Project

JBuilder requires you to create a new project to hold the files for a program. To start a new project, follow these steps:

Step 1.   Launch Jbuilder. Click the **File** menu on the menu bar and then choose **New Project** (see Figure A-13). The Project Wizard dialog will pop up (see Figure A-14). JBuilder specifies a path to the project file **untitled1.jpr** within the folder **untitled1.** You can change these names or just click **Finish** to save the project. Note that you can also enter documentation about the project, such as its title, your name, and a brief description.

FIGURE A-13
The JBuilder menu bar

FIGURE A-14
The Project Wizard dialog box

Step 2. The Project window opens, with the documentation about the new project in the Project Notes pane at the right side of the window (see Figure A-15). A list of the project files appears in the left pane. Note that the file icon **untitled1.html** appears beneath the file icon **untitled.jpr.** The **.html** file contains the documentation that was entered in the Project Wizard dialog. You use the **.jpr** file to reopen the project from the Explorer or from the JBuilder **File** menu.

FIGURE A-15
The Project window

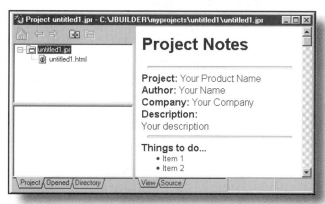

Step 3. JBuilder has also created the folder **c:\JBuilder\myprojects\untitled1.** You will put your current Java source program file in this folder. JBuilder has also created the folder **c:\JBuilder\myclasses.** When you compile a Java program, JBuilder will deposit the **.class** file here. You should now copy the **BreezyGUI** folder to the **myclasses** folder. Then JBuilder will be able to find **BreezyGUI** no matter which project folder you are working in.

Opening a Source File

In this example, we use the file **FahrenheitToCentigrade.java** from Lesson 2. Use Windows Explorer to copy this file to the current project folder. Then click the little folder labeled **+** above the left pane of the Project window. A dialog box opens on the available files in the project folder. In this example, you select the file **FahrenheitToCentigrade.java** and click **Open.** Figure A-16 shows the updated Project window. Note that a little folder labeled **-** has appeared above the left pane. Clicking this icon removes the selected file from the project (but does not delete it from the folder).

FIGURE A-16
The Project window after a file has been added to the project

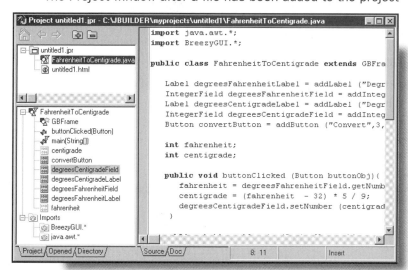

Compiling and Starting an Application

After you have added the files necessary for the project, you are ready to run it. Simply choose the menu option **Run "FahrenheitToCentigrade"** from the **Run** menu, or click the lightning bolt icon below the menu bar. If there are syntax errors, the error messages will appear in a pane at the bottom of the project window, and the line of code with the first error will be highlighted in the editor pane.

When you are finished with a program, remove all source files from the project and add new ones, or start a new project and repeat the steps above to create new programs.

Passing a Parameter to a Program

To pass a parameter to an application in JBuilder, follow these steps:

Step 1. Click **Run** and then choose **Parameters.** The Properties dialog box opens.
Step 2. Enter the parameters, separated by spaces, in the **Command Line Parameters** field. Figure A-17 shows this dialog box after the user has entered the parameter 10.

FIGURE A-17
Specifying a parameter to an application

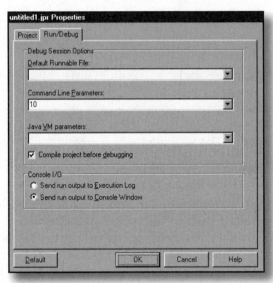

Step 3. Click OK.
Step 4. Run the program. To run the program with a different parameter, you must reopen the **Properties** dialog and edit the parameter.

Creating and Running an Applet

An applet is a Java program that runs in an HTML document on a Web browser. You can create both the HTML document and the Java applet in Jbuilder.

To create the HTML document, click **File** and then choose **New.** In the New dialog box (Figure A-18), double-click the HTML icon.

JBuilder adds an HTML file to the project and provides a view of it in the editor pane. You can toggle between **View** and **Source** to view and edit the HTML document (see Figure A-19). Make sure the Java program you want to run as an applet is also stored in the project.

FIGURE A-18
Choose the HTML icon

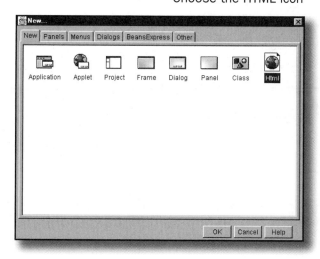

FIGURE A-19
The source code for an HTML file in the Project window

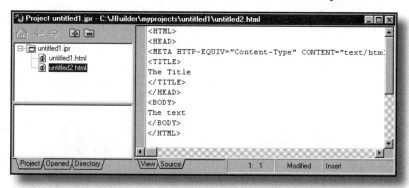

You can modify an existing application or create a new one for the applet. To convert an application, follow the instructions in Lesson 12. Make sure the applet has the same name as the class referenced in the HTML document.

To run the example Fahrenheit to centigrade applet in Lesson 12, follow these steps:

Step 1. Copy the files **FahrenheitToCentigrade.java** and **fahrtocent.html** from Lesson 12 to the project folder.

Step 2. Use the + button to add these two files to the project (see Figure A-20).

Step 3. Compile and run the program by selecting the lightning bolt or the menu option **Run Applet in "fahrtocent.html"** from the **Run** menu. The program runs in an appletviewer without the HTML text (see Figure A-21).

Run-Time Tip

If you are just developing an applet, test it in the appletviewer until it behaves correctly. Then launch its HTML document in the Windows Explorer to test it together with its Web page.

Adding an applet and its HTML file to a project

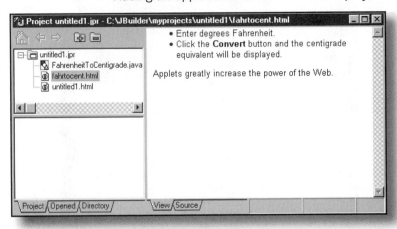

FIGURE A-21

Running a program in the appletviewer

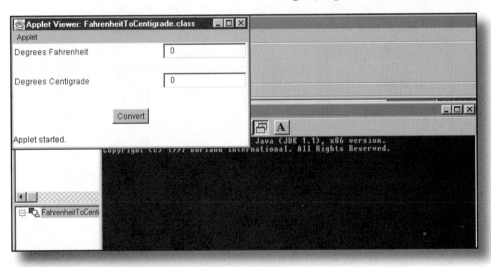

Creating a New Application or Applet

When you want to write a Java application or applet from scratch, perform the following steps:

Step 1. Click **File** and then choose **New.**

Step 2. Double-click the icon labeled **Frame** in the **New** dialog box. A **New Frame** dialog box opens to ask you for the name of the class (see Figure A-22). Edit the class name to the desired name, and click **OK.**

Step 3. Delete all of the code that JBuilder provides in the editor pane, and write the program that you want instead (see Figure A-23). Save the file by choosing **Save** on the **File** menu, and run the program.

FIGURE A-22
Creating a new Java program file

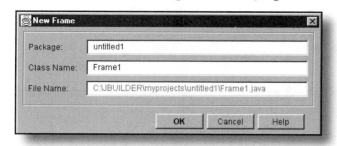

FIGURE A-23
Code to replace with the code for your program

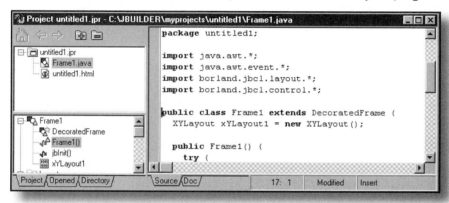

Working with Symantec Visual Café for Macintosh

Visual Café is an integrated application that enables you to create Java programs and applets, compile them, debug them, and run them in one environment. The sections below give you the basic information you need to run the programs in this book in the Visual Café environment.

Creating Folders for Java Files and Classes

You can create your own folders to hold your Java programs and classes. In Visual Café, classes are stored separately from programs. In the Finder, click **File** and then **New Folder** to create a new folder. As you work through the lessons in this book, you might want to create subfolders for each lesson, to keep your Java files organized.

Locating the BreezyGUI Package

In order for the programs in this book to compile and run correctly, you must place the **BreezyGUI** folder in the **classes** folder contained in the **(Java Libraries)** folder in the Visual Café folder (see Figure A-24).

Macintosh HD	
41 items, 233.2 MB available	
Name	**Date Modified**
▷ 🖿 System Folder	Mon, Jul 6, 1998, 9:14 AM
▽ 🖿 Visual Cafe 2.0 PDE	Thu, Jul 9, 1998, 11:40 AM
▷ 🖿 (Documentation)	Thu, Feb 26, 1998, 1:27 PM
▽ 🖿 (Java Libraries)	Thu, Jun 25, 1998, 9:28 AM
▷ 🖿 Class Cache	Mon, Jul 27, 1998, 12:38 PM
▽ 🖿 classes	Mon, Jul 27, 1998, 12:36 PM
▷ 🖿 BreezyGUI	Mon, Jul 27, 1998, 11:28 AM
▷ 🖿 java	Thu, Feb 26, 1998, 1:28 PM
▷ 🖿 symantec	Thu, Feb 26, 1998, 1:28 PM
🖿 Symantec Classes.zip	Tue, Nov 11, 1997, 4:11 PM
▷ 🖿 Debugger Support	Thu, Feb 26, 1998, 1:28 PM
🖿 Java 1.1 conversions	Thu, Oct 23, 1997, 9:17 PM
▷ 🖿 Project Template Additions	Thu, Feb 26, 1998, 1:28 PM

Setting up a New Project

Visual Café requires you to create a new project to hold the files for a program. To start a new project, follow these steps:

Step 1. In Visual Café, click **File** and then **New Project.** The New Project dialog box opens as shown in Figure A-25. Click **Empty Project** and click **Create.** Visual Café opens a new, untitled project on the desktop.

Step 2. Save the project in your Java files folder by clicking **File** and then **Save.** Type a name for the folder as shown in Figure A-26 and then click the **Save** button. A project does not have to have the same name as the Java files stored within it. You might store a source file called **FahrenheitToCentigrade.java,** for example, in a project named Fahrenheit Converter.

FIGURE A-25
The New Project dialog box

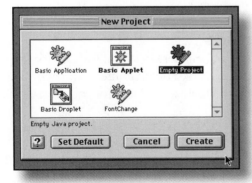

FIGURE A-26
Save the project in your Java files folder

Creating or Opening a Source File

You now have a project ready to store your source files. You can create a new source file by clicking **File** and then **New.** A new, untitled document appears. You can type code directly into this document. Visual Café automatically boldfaces keywords and colors other items such as labels and comments (Figure A-27) and positions braces and indents.

FIGURE A-27

A new source document in Visual Café

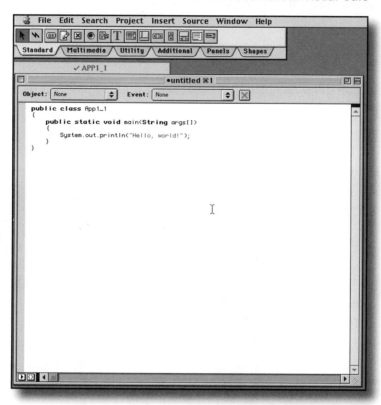

When you have finished typing the code, save the document in the same folder where you saved your project. Visual Café automatically names the file with the class name and the **.java** extension (see Figure A-28).

FIGURE A-28

Save the source file in the
same folder with the project

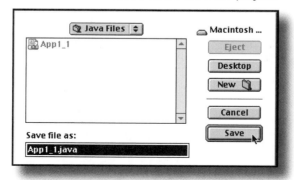

If you are opening a source file from another location, such as a CD-ROM or a floppy disk, click **File** and then **Open.** Locate the file, click to select it, and click the **Open** button. After you have opened the file, save it using **Save File as** to the folder containing your Java files.

Inserting Files into the Project

To compile and run a program, you must insert all the files relevant to that program into the project. To do this, follow these steps:

Step 1.   Click **Insert** and then **Files**. Select the file you want to add to the project and click the **Add** button (Figure A-29).

Step 2.   If you need to add additional files to the project, click each in turn, then the **Add** button. When finished, click the **Done** button.

Your project then shows that an object has been added to it (Figure A-30). You are now ready to compile and run the project.

FIGURE A-29
Add files to the project using this dialog box

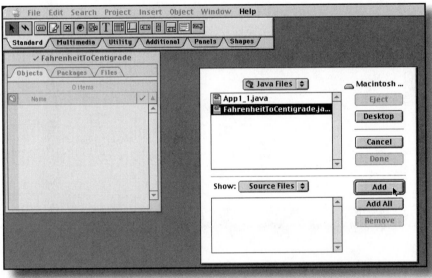

FIGURE A-30
An object has been added to the project

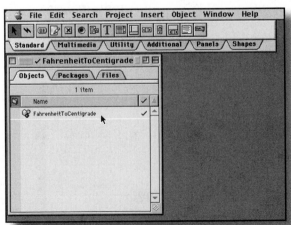

Compiling and Running the Project

Visual Café automates the process of compiling and running a project. But before you compile and run, you must specify a location for the **.class** file that will be generated during this process. Follow these steps to create a path for the output and to execute the program:

Step 1. With the project active on your desktop, click **Project** and then **Options.** The Project Options dialog box opens. Click the **Output** tab. Make sure the *.class directory* option button is selected. To specify the folder you created to store classes, click the **Set** button. Find your classes folder and click **Set** again. The **.class** directory text box should now display the name of the folder you created to hold your Java classes (see Figure A-31). Then click **Save.**

Step 2. To compile and run the project, click **Project** and then **Run.** Visual Café begins the compiling process, and if your program is error free, creates the appropriate output. Figure A-32 shows the result of a typical GUI application.

FIGURE A-31
Specify the location of your classes folder

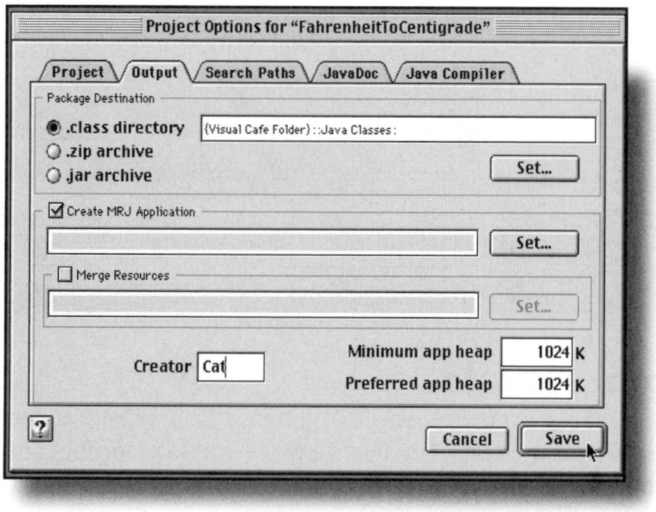

Project Options for "FahrenheitToCentigrade"

Project / Output / Search Paths / JavaDoc / Java Compiler

Package Destination
- ● **.class directory**   (Visual Cafe Folder)::Java Classes:
- ○ **.zip archive**
- ○ **.jar archive**   Set...

☑ Create MRJ Application   Set...

☐ Merge Resources   Set...

Creator Cat

Minimum app heap 1024 K
Preferred app heap 1024 K

?   Cancel   Save

FIGURE A-32
The GUI output of a project

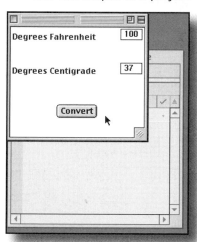

Degrees Fahrenheit   100

Degrees Centigrade   37

Convert

Passing a Parameter in Visual Café

To pass a parameter to a program, you click **Project** and then **Options** after you have added files to your project. The Project Options dialog box opens. Type the parameter in the Arguments to main ( ) text box, as shown in Figure A-33. Then click the **Save** button. Visual Café stores this information for the project so that you do not have to specify the parameter the next time you run the project.

FIGURE A-33
Passing a parameter to main( )

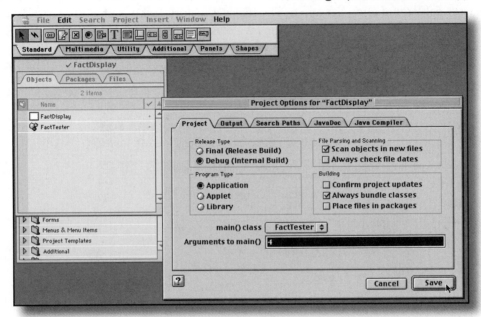

Working with Java Console

Mac versions of Java do not accept terminal input. Programs that result in terminal output use the Java Console window shown in Figure A-34. If your Java Console window appears and disappears very quickly, you can remedy the situation by "commenting out" any GBFrame.pause statement, as shown in Figure A-35. This should result in your Java Console appearing and remaining on the screen until you click the close box.

After you run a program that results in terminal output, the program may continue to run even after you click the close box. To force the program to quit running, press the Command, Option, Control, and Esc keys at the same time. Then click the Force Quit option.

FIGURE A-34
Output to the Java Console window

FIGURE A-35
Note that the GBFrame.pause statement
has been commented out

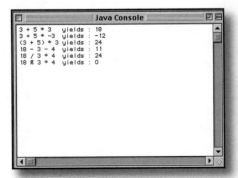

Creating and Running an Applet

An applet is a Java program that runs in an HTML document on a Web browser. You can create both the Java application and the HTML document in Visual Café.

To create the HTML document, click **File** and then **New.** A new document opens on your desktop. Type the HTML markup tags and the text that will appear on the Web page. Save the document to the folder containing your Java applications, using the **.html** extension. Visual Café colors the markup tags in your document after you have saved it (see Figure A-36).

FIGURE A-36
A completed HTML document

You can modify an existing application or create a new one for the applet. To convert an application, follow the instructions in Lesson 12. Make sure the application has the same name as the class inserted in the HTML document. Insert the HTML file in the application project just as you would any other source file.

Before running the applet, you must let Visual Café know that you wish to run the program as an applet rather than an application. To do this, access the Project Options dialog box (click **Project** and then **Options**). In the *Program Type* area, click the **Applet** option. The associated HTML file should appear in the *HTML file* list box. You can also specify a particular viewer, such as your Web browser, for the applet (Figure A-37). Click **Save** when finished.

FIGURE A-37
Check the options for viewing your applet before you run it

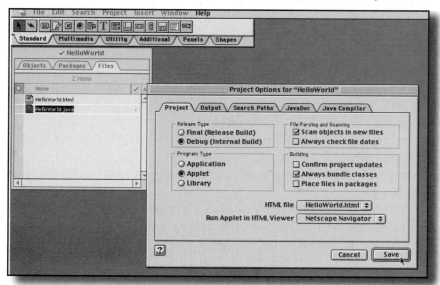

After you have specified the project settings, click **Project** and then **Run.** The applet will compile and run in the HTML document in the specified viewer (Figure A-38).

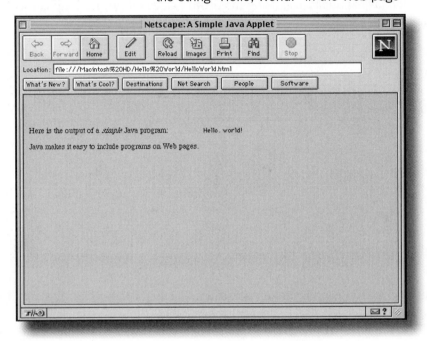

Java Support on the Web

There are many locations on the World Wide Web where you can find information on Java. Sun Microsystems maintains a number of very useful sites, including:

Sun Microsystem's top-level Java page (http://www.javasoft.com). This page contains news about events in the Java world and links to documentation, Java-related products, program examples, and free downloads of the JDK.

Products and APIs (http.//www.javasoft.com/products/index.html). This page allows you to select the version of JDK that matches your computer and to begin the download process. You can also download the documentation if you do not want to access it on the Web.

API user's guide (/http./www.javasoft.com/products/jdk/1.1/docs/api/API_users_guide.html). This page introduces you to the documentation for the Java API and describes the most effective ways to browse this documentation.

Package index (http://www.javasoft.com/products/jdk/1.1/docs/api/packages.html). This page has links to all of the Java packages.

Class hierarchy (http://www.javasoft.com/products/jdk/1.1/docs/api/tree.html). This page has links to the individual Java classes.

We suggest that you bookmark all of these links, and use the last two on a daily basis. You might even bookmark the links to the most commonly used packages, such as **java.lang** and **java.awt.** When you visit a package, you can browse all of the classes in that package. When you visit a class, you can browse all of the variables and methods defined in that class. There are numerous cross references to superclasses and related classes in a given package.

If you are using Microsoft's Visual J++, you can find specific information about the application at **http.//www.microsoft.com/visualj/.** This home page contains news about new releases and numerous links to product information, downloads, and documentation.

If you are using Symantec's Visual Café, you can find specific information about the application at **http.//www.café.symantec.com.** Here you will find information on product updates, product downloads, and product information.

Additional Resources

In addition to their Web resources, Sun Microsystem's Java development team has published a number of useful reference books on various features of Java programming. Here are a few:

Arnold and Gosling, *The Java Programming Language,* Second Edition (Addison-Wesley, 1998).

Gosling and Yellin, *The Java Application Programming Interface, Volume 1: Core Packages* (Addison-Wesley, 1996).

Gosling and Yellin, *The Java Application Programming Interface, Volume 2: Window Toolkit and Applets* (Addison-Wesley, 1996).

Gosling, Joy, and Steele, *The Java Language Specification* (Addison-Wesley, 1996).

Lea, *Concurrent Programming in Java: Design Principles and Patterns* (Addison-Wesley, 1997).

APPENDIX B

Reserved Words

The words in boldface are not discussed in this text. For a discussion of them, see the references mentioned in Appendix A.

abstract	double	import	private	**throws**
boolean	else	**inner**	protected	**transient**
break	extends	instanceOf	public	try
byte	final	int	**rest**	**var**
case	**finally**	interface	return	void
catch	float	long	short	**volatile**
char	for	**native**	static	while
class	**future**	new	super	
const	**generic**	null	switch	
continue	**goto**	operator	**synchronized**	
default	if	**outer**	this	
do	implements	**package**	**throw**	

Operator Precedence

The operators in boldface are not discussed in this text. For a discussion of them, see the references mentioned in Appendix A.

OPERATOR	FUNCTION	ASSOCIATION
( ) [ ] .	Parentheses Array subscript Object member selection	Left to right
++ -- + - ! ~ (type)	Increment Decrement Unary plus Unary minus Boolean negation **Bitwise negation** Type cast	Right to left
* / %	Multiplication Division Modulus	Left to right
+ -	Addition or concatenation Subtraction	Left to right
<< >> >>>	**Bitwise shift left** **Bitwise shift right** **Bitwise shift right, sign extension**	**Left to right**
< <= > >= instanceOf	Less than Less than or equal to Greater than Greater than or equal to Class membership	Left to right
== !=	Equal to Not equal to	Left to right
&	**Boolean AND (complete)** **Bitwise AND**	**Left to right**

(continued on next page)

OPERATOR	FUNCTION	ASSOCIATION
^	**Boolean exclusive OR** **Bitwise exclusive OR**	**Left to right**
¦	**Boolean OR (complete)** **Bitwise OR**	**Left to right**
&&	Boolean AND (partial)	Left to right
¦¦	Boolean OR (partial)	Left to right
?:	**Ternary conditional**	Right to left
=	Assign	Right to left
+=	Add and assign	
-=	Subtract and assign	
*=	Multiply and assign	
/=	Divide and assign	
%=	Modulo and assign	
<<=	**Shift left and assign**	
>>=	**Shift right and assign**	
>>>=	**Shift right, sign extension, and assign**	
&=	**Boolean or bitwise AND and assign**	
¦=	**Boolean or bitwise OR and assign**	
^=	**Boolean or bitwise exclusive OR and assign**	

APPENDIX D

ASCII Character Set

The table included here shows the ordering of the ASCII character set. The printable characters range from ASCII 33 to ASCII 126. The values from ASCII 0 to ASCII 32 and ASCII 127 are associated with white space characters, such as the horizontal tab (HT), or nonprinting control characters, such as the Escape key (Esc). The digits in the left column represent the leftmost digits of the ASCII code, and the digits in the top row are the rightmost digits in the ASCII code. Thus, the ASCII code of the character *R* at row 8, column 2, is 82.

	0	1	2	3	4	5	6	7	8	9
0	NUL	SOH	STX	ETX	EOT	ENQ	ACK	BEL	BS	HT
1	LF	VT	FF	CR	SO	SI	DLE	DC1	DC2	DC3
2	DC4	NAK	SYN	ETB	CAN	EM	SUB	ESC	FS	GS
3	RS	US	SP	!	"	#	$	%	&	`
4	(	)	*	+	,	–	.	/	0	1
5	2	3	4	5	6	7	8	9	:	;
6	<	=	>	?	@	A	B	C	D	E
7	F	G	H	I	J	K	L	M	N	O
8	P	Q	R	S	T	U	V	W	X	Y
9	Z	[	\	]	^	_	'	a	b	c
10	d	e	f	g	h	i	j	k	l	m
11	n	o	p	q	r	s	t	u	v	w
12	x	y	z	{	|	}	~	DEL		

APPENDIX E

Number Systems

When we make change at the store, we use the decimal (base 10) number system. The digits in this system are the characters 0 through 9. Computers represent all information in the binary (base 2) system. The digits in this system are the characters 0 and 1 only. Because binary numbers can be very long strings of 1s and 0s, programmers also use the octal (base 8) and hexadecimal (base 16) number systems, usually for low-level programming in assembly language. The octal digits range from 0 to 7, and the hexadecimal digits include the decimal digits and the letters A through F. These letters represent the numbers 10 through 15, respectively.

To identify the system being used, we can attach the base as a subscript to the number. For example, the following numbers represent the quantity 414 in the binary, octal, decimal, and hexadecimal systems:

414 in binary notation	110011110_2
414 in octal notation	636_8
414 in decimal notation	414_{10}
414 in hexadecimal notation	$19E_{16}$

Note that as the size of the base grows, either the number of digits or the digit in the largest position might get smaller.

Each number system uses positional notation to represent a number. The digit at each position in a number has a positional value. The positional value of a digit is determined by raising the base of the system to the power specified by the position. For an n-digit number, the positions (and exponents) are numbered 0 through $n - 1$, starting with the rightmost digit and moving to the left. For example, as Figure E-1 illustrates, the positional values of a three-digit decimal number are 100 (10^2), 10 (10^1), and 1 (10^0), moving from left to right in the number. The positional values of a three-digit binary number are 4 (2^2), 2 (2^1), and 1 (2^0).

FIGURE E-1

Base 10
Positional values | 100 | 10 | 1 |
Positions   2   1   0

Base 2
Positional values | 4 | 2 | 1 |
Positions   2   1   0

The quantity represented by a number in any system is determined by multiplying each digit (as a decimal number) by its positional value and adding the results. The following examples show how this is done for numbers in several systems:

414 base 10 =
$4 * 10^2 + 1 * 10^1 + 4 * 10^0 =$

$4 * 100 + 1 * 10 + 4 * 1 =$

$400 \quad + 10 \quad + 4 = 414$

110011110 base 2 =

$1 * 2^8 + 1 * 2^7 + 0 * 2^6 + 0 * 2^5 + 1 * 2^4 + 1 * 2^3 + 1 * 2^2 + 1 * 2^1 + 0 * 2^0 =$

$1 * 256 + 1 * 128 + 0 * 64 + 0 * 32 + 1 * 16 + 1 * 8 + 1 * 4 + 1 * 2 + 0 * 1 =$

$256 \quad + 128 \quad + 0 \quad + 0 \quad + 16 \quad + 8 \quad + 4 \quad + 2 \quad + 0 =$
414

636 base 8 =

$6 * 8^2 + 3 * 8^1 + 6 * 8^0 =$

$6 * 64 + 3 * 8 + 6 * 1 =$

$384 \quad + 24 \quad + 6 = 414$

19E base 16 =

$1 * 16^2 + 9 * 16^1 + E * 16^0 =$

$1 * 256 + 9 * 16 + 14 * 1 =$

$256 \quad + 144 \quad + 14 = 414$

Each of the above examples converts from the number in the given base to the corresponding decimal number. To convert a decimal number to a number in a given base, we use division and remainder rather than multiplication and addition. The process works as follows:

1. Find the largest power of the given base that divides into the decimal number.
2. The quotient becomes the digit at that power's position in the new number.
3. Repeat Steps 1 and 2 with the remainder, until the remainder is less than the number.
4. If the last remainder is greater than 0, the remainder becomes the last digit in the new number.
5. If you must skip a power of the base when performing Step 3, then put a 0 in that power's position in the new number.

To illustrate, let us convert the decimal number 327 to the equivalent binary number.

The highest power of 2 by which 327 is divisible is 256 or 2^8. Thus, we'll have a nine-digit binary number, with a 1 in position 8 (Figure E-2).

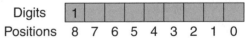

The remainder of the first division is 71. The highest power of 2 by which 71 is divisible is 64 (2^6). Thus, we have skipped 128 (2^7), so we write a 0 in position 7 and a 1 in position 6 (Figure E-3).

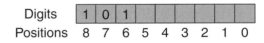

The remainder of the second division is 7. Thus, as you can see, we skip 3 more powers of 2— 32, 16, and 8—on the next division, in order to use 4. So, we place 0s at positions 5, 4, and 3, and a 1 at position 2 in the new number (Figure E-4).

FIGURE E-2

Digits	1								
Positions	8	7	6	5	4	3	2	1	0

FIGURE E-3

Digits	1	0	1						
Positions	8	7	6	5	4	3	2	1	0

FIGURE E-4

Digits	1	0	1	0	0	0	1		
Positions	8	7	6	5	4	3	2	1	0

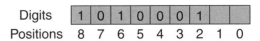

The remainder of the third division is 3. This is divisible by the next power of 2, 2, so we put a 1 at position 1 in the new number. The remainder of the last division, 1, goes in position 0 (Figure E-5).

One reason that programmers prefer to use octal or hexadecimal notation instead of binary notation is that octal and hexadecimal are more expressive (one can say more with less). Another reason is that it is very easy to convert an octal number or a hexadecimal number to the corresponding binary number. To convert octal to binary, assume that each digit in the octal number represents three digits in the corresponding binary number. Then start with the rightmost octal digit and write down the corresponding binary digits, padding these to the left with 0s to the count of three, if necessary. Proceed in this manner until all of the octal digits have been converted. Figure E-6 shows such conversions.

The conversion of hexadecimal numbers to binary numbers works in a similar way, except that each hexadecimal digit translates to four binary digits.

Digits	1	0	1	0	0	0	1	1	1
Positions	8	7	6	5	4	3	2	1	0

Octal	547	372
Binary	101 100 111	11 111 010

Java Exception Handling

Java divides run-time errors into two broad categories: errors and exceptions. Errors are serious run-time problems that usually should not be handled by the programmer. For example, if a method gets stuck in an infinite recursion, as described in Lesson 5, Java will throw a StackOverflowError. Java defines a separate class for each type of error. You can browse through these in Sun Microsystem's Web site, as described in Appendix A, starting with the class Error in the package **java.lang.**

Exceptions come in two varieties: those that Java requires the programmer to handle, such as IOException, and those that the programmer may or may not handle, such as ArithmeticException and ArrayIndexOutOfBoundsException. To explore Java's Exception class hierarchy on Sun's Web site, select the desired package in the package index and scroll to the bottom of the page. Most of the exception classes are defined in **java.lang,** but several important ones are also defined in **java.io** and **java.util.**

Lesson 11 showed how to use the try-catch statement to handle exceptions associated with file streams. The next code segments show how one might handle exceptions in the cases of division and array subscripting:

```
// Catch an attempt to divide by zero

try{
   quotient = dividend / divisor;
   System.out.println("Successful division");
}
catch (ArithmeticException e){
   System.out.println("Error1: " + e.toString());
}
```

```
// Catch an attempt to use an array index that is out of range

try{
   a[x] = 0;
   System.out.println("Successful subscripting");
}
catch (ArrayIndexOutOfBoundsException e){
   System.out.println("Error2: " + e.toString());
}
```

When Java detects an error and throws an exception, control is immediately transferred from the offending instruction in the try statement to the catch statement. Thus, the output of the first message would be skipped if an exception occurs in either of the above code segments. If the try statement completes successfully, the catch statement is not executed.

A `try` statement can be followed by more than one `catch` statement. For example, the next code segment combines the exception handling of the previous two segments:

```
// Catch an attempt to divide by zero and to use an array index
// that is out of bounds

try{
   quotient = dividend / divisor;
   System.out.println("Successful division");
   a[x] = quotient;
   System.out.println("Successful subscripting");
 }
catch (ArithmeticException e){
   System.out.println("Error1: " + e.toString());
}
catch (ArrayIndexOutOfBoundsException e){
   System.out.println("Error2: " + e.toString());
}
```

The same two exceptions are possible in this example, but Java will get to throw only one of them. When this occurs, control shifts to the first `catch` statement following the `try` statement. If the class of the exception thrown is the same as or is a subclass of the class of that `catch` statement's parameter, then the code for the `catch` statement executes. Otherwise, Java compares the exception thrown to the parameter of the next `catch` statement, and so on.

It is possible (and often desirable) to define new kinds of exceptions that can be thrown by methods in user-defined classes. The rules for doing this are beyond the scope of this text, but can be found on Sun's Web site and in several of the books listed in Appendix A.

Java Packages

A Java package is a name that stands for a set of related classes. For example, the package **java.io** stands for all of the Java file stream classes. Exceptions (discussed in Lesson 11) and interfaces (discussed in Lesson 13) can also be parts of a package. You can browse Java's packages by following the procedure described in Appendix A.

The package **java.lang** contains many commonly used classes, such as `Math` and `String`. This package is implicitly imported into every Java program file, so no `import` statement is required. To use any other package, such as **java.io**, in a program file, the programmer must explicitly import the package with an `import` statement.

The program examples in this text import all of the classes in a given package, using the form

```
import <package name>.*;
```

It is also possible to import selected classes from a given package and omit others. For example, the following line would import just the `Hashtable` class from the **java.util** package, and omit the others:

```
import java.util.Hashtable;
```

This statement has the effect of making the `Hashtable` class visible to the program file, but leaves the rest of the classes in the **java.util** package invisible.

It is possible (and desirable) to create packages of related classes that you have designed and implemented. For example, one might put the `Student` class and the `StudentTestScoresModel` class discussed in Lesson 8 into a single package called **StudentTestScores**. The rules for doing this are beyond the scope of this text, but can be found on Sun's Web site and in several of the books listed in Appendix A.

APPENDIX H

BreezyGUI

Programs that use **BreezyGUI** should import the package as follows:

```
import BreezyGUI.*;
```

To use **BreezyGUI** in a Java application, define the application class as an extension of the class GBFrame.

BreezyGUI provides the following features:

1. A grid bag layout and methods for creating and positioning window objects in it. The row and col parameters specify a row and a column in the layout's grid (counting from 1). The width and height parameters specify the number of columns and rows through which a window object extends.

2. A set of abstract methods for handling typical events, such as button selections, menu item selections, list item selections, and mouse events. The programmer overrides these methods for use in particular applications.

3. A set of specialized data entry field classes for integers and floating-point numbers.

4. A method for displaying message boxes.

5. A class for formatting strings with center, left, or right justification.

To use **BreezyGUI** in a Java applet, define the applet class as an extension of GBApplet, omit the method main, and define an init method instead of a constructor method. GBApplet provides the same functionality as above, but without menus. To use **BreezyGUI** in a Java dialog, define the dialog class as an extension of GBDialog.

Method Specifications for Classes GBFrame, GBApplet, and GBDialog

Methods That Add Window Objects to a Window

Label addLabel(String text, int row, int col, int width, int height)

> **Action:** Creates a new label with the given text, places the label in the framework at the given location, and returns the label.
>
> **Example:** Label radiusLabel = addLabel("Radius", 1, 1, 1, 1);

Button addButton(String label, int row, int col, int width, int height)

> **Action:** Creates a new button with the given label, places the button in the framework at the given location, and returns the button.

Example: `Button calculateButton = addButton("Calculate", 1, 1, 1, 1);`

`IntegerField addIntegerField(int number, int row, int col, int width, int height)`

> **Action:** Creates a new integer field with the given number, places the integer field in the framework at the given location, and returns the integer field.
>
> **Example:** `IntegerField radiusField = addIntegerField(0, 1, 1, 2, 1);`

`DoubleField addDoubleField(double number, int row, int col, int width, int height)`

> **Action:** Creates a new double field with the given number, places the double field in the framework at the given location, and returns the double field.
>
> **Example:** `DoubleField areaField = addDoubleField(0.0, 1, 1, 2, 1);`

`TextField addTextField(String text, int row, int col, int width, int height)`

> **Action:** Creates a new text field with the given text, places the text field in the framework at the given location, and returns the text field.
>
> **Example:** `TextField nameField = addTextField("Sandy", 1, 1, 3, 1);`

`TextArea addTextArea(String text, int row, int col, int width, int height)`

> **Action:** Creates a new text area with the given text, places the text area in the framework at the given location, and returns the text area.
>
> **Example:** `TextArea resultArea = addTextArea("", 1, 1, 5, 2);`

`List addList(int row, int col, int width, int height)`

> **Action:** Creates a new list, places the list in the framework at the given location, and returns the list.
>
> **Example:** `List nameList = addList(1, 1, 5, 1);`

`Checkbox addCheckbox(String text, int row, int col, int width, int height)`

> **Action:** Creates a new checkbox with the given text, places the checkbox in the framework at the given location, and returns the checkbox.
>
> **Example:** `Checkbox marriedBox = addCheckbox ("Married", 1, 1, 1, 1);`

`MenuItem addMenuItem(String menuLabel, String itemLabel)`

> **Action:** Creates a menu with the specified label if one does not exist, creates a menu item with the specified label, adds the menu item to the menu, and returns the menu item. *Note:* Not available for `GBApplet` and `GBDialog`.
>
> **Example:** `MenuItem saveFileItem = addmenuItem("File", "Save");`

Methods That Display Message Boxes

`void messageBox(String message)`

> **Action:** Displays a message box with the specified string.

Example: `messageBox("Computation completed.");`

`void messageBox(Double number)`

    Action: Displays a message box with the specified number.

    Example: `messageBox(3.14);`

`void messageBox(Object obj)`

    Action: Displays a message box with the string representation of the object.

    Example: `messageBox(newStudent());`

Methods for Handling Events in Window Objects

`void buttonClicked(Button buttonObj)`

    Action: The framework invokes this method when a button is selected. The application should override this method to take the appropriate action. The parameter is the button where the event occurred.

`void listDoubleClicked(List listObj, String itemClicked)`

    Action: The framework invokes this method when a list item is double-clicked. The application should override this method to take the appropriate action. The parameters are the list and the list item where the event occurred. *Note:* This method is invoked *after* the method `listItemSelected` (see below).

`void listItemSelected(List listObj)`

    Action: The framework invokes this method when a list item is selected with a single-click or a double-click. The application may or may not override this method to take the appropriate action. The parameter is the list in which the item was selected. The programmer can use the `List` methods `getSelectedIndex()` and `getItem(int)` to determine the selected item.

`void menuItemSelected(MenuItem mI)`

    Action: The framework invokes this method when a menu item is selected. The application should override this method to take the appropriate action. The parameter is the menu item where the event occurred. *Note:* Not available for `GBApplet` and `GBDialog`.

`void mouseClicked(int x, int y)`

    Action: The framework invokes this method when the mouse is clicked. The application should override this method to take the appropriate action. The parameters represent the window coordinates of the mouse when the event occurred.

`void mousePressed(int x, int y)`

    Action: The framework invokes this method when the mouse is pressed. The application should override this method to take the appropriate action. The parameters represent the window coordinates of the mouse when the event occurred.

```
void mouseReleased(int x, int y)
```

Action: The framework invokes this method when the mouse is released. The application should override this method to take the appropriate action. The parameters represent the window coordinates of the mouse when the event occurred.

```
void mouseMoved(int x, int y)
```

Action: The framework invokes this method when the mouse is moved. The application should override this method to take the appropriate action. The parameters represent the window coordinates of the mouse when the event occurred.

```
void mouseDragged(int x, int y)
```

Action: The framework invokes this method when the mouse is dragged. The application should override this method to take the appropriate action. The parameters represent the window coordinates of the mouse when the event occurred.

Method Specification for Class `GBDialog`

```
GBDialog(Frame f)
```

Action: This is the constructor. Its use is required in the constructor of a `GBDialog` subclass and is invoked by calling `super`. The constructor's parameter is the parent frame of the dialog. When the dialog is used by an application, the parent frame is a reference to the application. When the dialog is used by an applet or by another dialog, the parent frame is an anonymous frame.

Example: `super(this);`

```
String getDlgCloseIndicator()
```

Action: Returns the dialog's closing indicator. The value of this indicator is `"Cancel"` by default.

Example: `String indicator = theDialog.getDlgCloseIndicator();`

```
Void setDlgCloseIndicator(String s)
```

Action: Sets the dialog's closing indicator to the given string.

Example: `setDlgCloseIndicator("OK");`

Method Specifications for Class `Format`

The class `Format` allows a programmer to center, left justify, or right justify data within a number of columns.

```
static String justify(char justification, String text, int width)
static String justify(char justification, char ch, int width)
static String justify(char justification, long number, int width)
static String justify(char justification, double number, int width, int precision)
```

Action: Formats and returns the string representation of the given data, where justification is `'l'`, `'r'`, or `'c'`. The data are centered, left justified, or right justified within the given width.

Examples:
```
String strOutput  = Format.justify('r', "Hi there!", 34);
String charOutput = Format.justify('c', 'A', 10);
String intOutput  = Format.justify('l', 21, 80);
String dollars    = Format.justify('r', 3.1416, 10, 2);
```

Method Specifications for Class `IntegerField`

```
int getNumber()
```

Action: Returns the integer currently stored in the integer field, or 0 if the integer is malformed.

Example: `int radius = radiusField.getNumber();`

```
void setNumber(int number)
```

Action: Displays the specified number in the integer field.

Example: `radiusField.setNumber(2316);`

```
boolean isValid()
```

Action: Returns true if the integer in the field is well formed, and false otherwise.

Example: `if (radiusField.isValid())`

Method Specifications for Class `DoubleField`

```
double getNumber()
```

Action: Returns the floating-point number currently stored in the double field, or 0 if the number is malformed.

Example: `double velocity = velocityField.getNumber();`

```
void setNumber(double number)
```

Action: Displays the specified number in the double field.

Example: `areaField.setNumber(527.32);`

```
boolean isValid()
```

Action: Returns true if the floating-point number in the field is well formed, and false otherwise.

Example: `if (velocityField.isValid())`

```
void setPrecision(double number)
```

Action: Sets the number of digits to be displayed after the decimal point in the double field.

Example: `salaryField.setPrecision(2);`

```
int getPrecision()
```

Action: Returns number of digits to be displayed after the decimal point in the double field.

Example: `System.out.println("Precision = " + salaryField.getPrecision());`

GLOSSARY

A

Abstract   Simplified or partial hiding detail.

Abstract Class   A class that defines attributes and methods for subclasses but is never instantiated.

Abstract Data Type (ADT)   An ADT consists of a class of objects, a defined set of properties of those objects, and a set of operations for processing the objects.

Abstract Method   A method that is specified but not implemented in an abstract class. The subclasses must implement this method.

Abstract Windowing Toolkit (AWT)   The Java package that contains the definitions of all the classes used to set up graphical user interfaces.

Accessor   A method used to examine an attribute of an object without changing it.

Actual Parameter   A variable or expression contained in a method call and passed to that method. *See also* **Formal Parameter**.

Adapter Class   A Java class that allows another class to implement an interface class without implementing all of its methods. *See also* **Interface Class.**

Address   Often called address of a memory location, this is an integer value that the computer can use to reference a location. *See also* **Value.**

Algorithm   A finite sequence of effective statements that, when applied to a problem, will solve it.

Alias   A situation in which two or more names in a program can refer to the same memory location. An alias can cause subtle side effects.

Analysis   The phase of the software life cycle in which the programmer describes what the program will do.

Applet   A Java program that can be downloaded and run on a Web browser.

Application Software   Programs designed for a specific use.

Argument   A value or expression passed in a method call.

Arithmetic Expression   A sequence of operands and operators that describes the calculation of a numeric value.

Arithmetic/Logic Unit (ALU)   The part of the central processing unit (CPU) that performs arithmetic operations and evaluates expressions.

Arithmetic Overflow   A situation that arises when the computer's memory cannot represent the number resulting from an arithmetic operation.

Array   A data structure whose elements are accessed by means of index positions.

Array Index   The relative position of the components of an array.

Artificial Intelligence (AI)   A study of human behavior that uses computer models, or the effort to develop machines that perform tasks that require human expertise.

ASCII Character Set   The American Standard Code for Information Interchange ordering for a character set. The ASCII character set is listed in Appendix D.

Assembler   A computer program that translates programs written in assembly language to the equivalent programs in machine language.

Assembly Language   A computer language that allows the programmer to express operations and memory addresses with mnemonic symbols.

Assignment Statement   A method of putting values into memory locations.

Associative Link A means of recognizing and accessing items in a network structure, such as the World Wide Web.

Attribute A property that a computational object models, such as the balance in a bank account.

B

Behavior The set of actions that a class of objects supports.

Binary Digit A digit, either 0 or 1, in the binary number system. Program instructions are stored in memory using a sequence of binary digits. *See also* **Bit.**

Bit A binary digit.

Black Box A metaphor for a chunk of code or a computational object that hides its inner workings from its users.

Block An area of program text, enclosed in Java by the symbols {}, that contains statements and data declarations.

Boolean Expression An expression whose value is either true or false. *See also* **Compound Boolean Expression** and **Simple Boolean Expression.**

Border Layout A Java layout class that allows the programmer to place window objects in five areas (north, south, west, east, and center) of a window. Border layout is the default layout for Java applications.

Bottom-Up Implementation A method of coding a program that starts with lower-level modules and a test driver module.

Buffer A block of memory into which data are placed for transmission to a program, usually with file or string processing.

Button A window object that allows the user to select an action by clicking a mouse.

Byte A sequence of bits used to encode a character in memory. *See also* **Word.**

Byte Code The kind of object code generated by a Java compiler and interpreted by a Java virtual machine. Byte code is platform independent.

C

Call Any reference to a method by an executable statement. Also referred to as **Invoke.**

Call Stack The trace of method calls that appears when Java throws an exception during program execution.

Canvas A Java window object used to draw images.

Card Layout A Java layout class that allows the programmer to manipulate the window as a stack of cards.

Cartesian Coordinate System The system used to describe points in a plane in geometry.

Cast An operator that is used to convert a value of one type to a value of a different type (e.g., `double` to `int`).

Central Processing Unit (CPU) A major hardware component that consists of the arithmetic/logic unit (ALU) and the control unit.

Character Set The list of characters available for data and program statements.

Checkbox A window object that allows the user to check a labeled box.

Child A class that inherits features and behavior from its parent class.

Choice List A window object that allows the user to select from a pull-down list of options.

Class A description of the attributes and behavior of a set of computational objects.

Class Constant A constant that is visible to all instances of a class and, if public, is accessed by specifying the class name. For example, `Math.PI` is a class constant.

Class Constructor A method used to create and initialize an instance of a class.

Class Method A method that is invoked when a message is sent to a class. For example, `Math.sqrt` is a class method. *See also* **Message.**

Class Variable   A variable that is visible to all instances of a class and, if public, is accessed by specifying the class name.

Client   A computational object that receives a service from another computational object.

Client/Server Relationship   A means of describing the organization of computing resources in which one resource provides a service to another resource.

Coding   The process of writing executable statements that are part of a program to solve a problem. *See also* **Implementation.**

Cohesive Method   A method designed to accomplish a single task.

Comment   A nonexecutable statement used to make a program more readable.

Compiler   A computer program that automatically converts instructions in a high-level language to machine language.

Components   *See* **window object.**

Compound Boolean Expression   Refers to the complete expression when logical connectives and negation are used to generate Boolean values. *See also* **Boolean Expression** and **Simple Boolean Expression.**

Compound Statement   Uses the symbols { and } to group several statements and data declarations as a unit. *See also* **Block.**

Concatenation   An operation in which the contents of one data structure are placed after the contents of another data structure.

Concrete Class   A class that can be instantiated. *See also* **Abstract Class.**

Conditional Statement   *See* **Selection Statement.**

Conjunction   The connection of two Boolean expressions using the logical operator && (AND), returning false if at least one of the expressions is false, or true if both expressions are true.

Constant   A symbol whose value cannot be changed.

Contained Class   A class that is used to define a data object within another class.

Container   A Java class that allows the programmer to group window objects for placement in a window.

Control Loop   A statement that allows the computer to execute a set of statements repeatedly.

Control Structure   A structure that controls the flow of execution of program statements.

Control Unit   The part of the central processing unit that controls the operation of the rest of the computer.

Coordinate System   A grid that allows a programmer to specify positions of points in a plane or of pixels on a computer screen.

Cryptanalysis   A set of methods for decoding information that has been hidden in codes.

Cryptography   The study of methods for encoding information to keep it hidden.

D

Data   The particular characters that are used to represent information in a form suitable for storage, processing, and communication.

Data Input Stream   A Java class that supports the input of data from a binary file.

Data Output Stream   A Java class that supports the output of data to a binary file.

Data Type   A formal description of the set of values that a variable can have.

Data Validation   The process of examining data prior to their use in a program.

Debugging   The process of eliminating errors or "bugs" from a program.

Declaration Statement   A statement that introduces a variable and its data type for the first time in a program.

Decrement   To decrease the value of a variable.

Deep Copying   The process whereby all of the internal components of an object are completely copied.

Default Constructor   A method that Java provides for creating objects of a class. The programmer can override this method to do extra things.

Definition List   An HTML structure that allows a user to display a keyed list on a Web page.

Design   The phase of the software life cycle in which the programmer describes how the program will accomplish its tasks.

Design Error   An error such that a program runs, but unexpected results are produced. Also referred to as a logic error. *See also* **Run-Time Error** and **Syntax Error.**

Dialog   A type of window that pops up to display information or receive it from the user.

Disjunction   The connection of two Boolean expressions using the logical operator ¦¦ (OR), returning True if at least one of the expressions is True, or False if they are both False.

Divide-and-Conquer Algorithms   A class of algorithms that solves problems by repeatedly dividing them into simpler problems. *See also* **Recursion.**

`double`   A Java data type used to represent numbers with a decimal point.

`do-while Loop`   A post-test loop examining a Boolean expression after causing a statement to be executed. *See also* `for` **Loop**, **Loops,** and `while` **Loop.**

Driver   A method that is used to test other methods.

E

Element   A data value that is contained in a larger structure such as an array.

Empty Statement   A semicolon used to indicate that no action is to be taken. Also referred to as a **Null Statement.**

Encapsulation   The process of hiding and restricting access to the implementation details of a data structure.

End-of-File Marker   A special marker inserted by the machine to indicate the end of the data file.

End-of-Line Character   A special character (\n) used to indicate the end of a line of characters in a string or a file stream.

Entrance-Controlled Loop   *See* **Pretest Loop.**

Event   An occurrence, such as a button click or a mouse motion, that can be detected and processed by a program.

Event-Driven Loop   A process, usually hidden in the operating system, that waits for an event, notifies a program that an event has occurred, and returns to wait for more events.

Exception   An abnormal state or error that occurs during run time and is signaled by the operating system.

Exception-Driven Loop   The use of exceptions to implement a normal loop, usually for file input.

Exchange Sort   A sorting algorithm that sorts the components of an array in either ascending or descending order. This process puts the smallest or largest element in the top position and repeats the process on the remaining array components.

Exit-Controlled Loop   See **Post-Test Loop.**

Expanding Capabilities Implementation   A coding strategy that begins with a running but incomplete program and gradually adds features until the program is complete.

Extension   The process whereby a programmer builds a new class using the features and behavior of an existing class.

External Image   An image displayed when the user selects a link on a Web page.

F

Fibonacci Numbers   A series of numbers generated by taking the sum of the previous two numbers in the series. The series begins with the numbers 1 and 2.

File   A data structure that resides on a secondary storage medium.

File Input Stream   A Java class that is used to connect a program to a file for input.

File Output Stream   A Java class that is used to connect a program to a file for output.

Finality   The use of the keyword `final` to specify that a method cannot be implemented by a subclass.

Final Method   A method that cannot be implemented by a subclass.

Fixed Point   A method of writing decimal numbers where the decimal is placed where it belongs in the number. *See also* **Floating Point.**

Floating Point   A method for writing numbers in scientific notation to accommodate numbers that may have very large or very small values. *See also* **Fixed Point**.

Flowchart   A diagram that displays the flow of control of a program. *See also* **Control Structure.**

Flow of Control   A description of how a program executes, using a diagram that depicts its branches and loops.

Font   The kind of type set used for text, such as Courier and Times Roman.

`for` Loop   A structured loop consisting of an initializer expression, a termination expression, an update expression, and a statement.

Formal Parameter   A name, introduced in a method definition, that is replaced by an actual parameter when the method is called.

Frame   A Java class that defines the window for an application. *See also* **Application Software.**

Function Applications   Function calls, in which parameters are evaluated and passed to functions for processing.

Function-Oriented Programming   A method of programming in which programs are composed of functions that do not reference global variables.

G

Garbage Collection   The automatic process of reclaiming memory when the data of a program no longer need it.

Global Identifier   A name that can be used by all of the methods of a class.

Global Variable   *See* **Global Identifier.**

Graphical User Interface (GUI)   A means of communication between human beings and computers that uses a pointing device for input and a bitmapped screen for output. The bitmap displays images of windows and window objects such as buttons, text fields, and pull-down menus. The user interacts with the interface by using the mouse to manipulate the window objects directly. *See also* **Window Object.**

Graphics Context   The object that stores information about images that are displayed in a window or window object.

Grid Bag Layout   A Java layout class that allows the user to place window objects in a two-dimensional grid in the window and to have control over how the window objects occupy the cells in that grid.

Grid Layout   A Java layout class that allows the user to place window objects in a two-dimensional grid in the window.

H

Hacking   A style of computer programming that uses clever methods to solve difficult programs with little apparent effort, usually to impress peer programmers.

Hardware   The actual computing machine and its support devices.

Hierarchy   The organization of classes in which each class inherits features and attributes from a parent class. *See also* **Child** and **Parent.**

High Cohesion   The property of a method so that it performs a single, well-defined task.

High-Level Language   Any programming language that uses words and symbols to make it relatively easy to read and write a program. *See also* **Assembly Language** and **Machine Language.**

Hyperlink   A connection that allows the user to move from one chunk of information to another in a hypertext. *See also* **Hypertext.**

Hypermedia A data structure that allows the user to access different kinds of information (text, images, sound, video, applications) by traversing links.

Hypertext A data structure that allows the user to access different chunks of text by traversing links.

Hypertext Markup Language (HTML) A programming language that allows the user to create pages for the World Wide Web.

Hypertext Transport Protocol (HTTP) The scheme used to provide addresses for pages on the World Wide Web.

I

Identity The property of an object that it is the same thing at different points in time, even though the values of its attributes might change.

if-else Statement A selection statement that allows a program to perform alternative actions based on a condition.

Implementation The phase of the software life cycle in which the program is coded in a programming language.

Increment The process of increasing a number by 1.

Index *See* **Array Index.**

Infinite Loop A loop in which the controlling condition is not changed in such a manner to allow the loop to terminate.

Information Hiding A condition in which the user of a module does not know the details of how it is implemented, and the implementer of a module does not know the details of how it is used.

Inheritance The process by which a subclass class can reuse attributes and behavior defined in a superclass. *See also* **Subclass** and **Superclass.**

Initializer List A means of expressing a set of data that can be assigned to the cells of an array in one statement.

Inline Image An image that is loaded when the user accesses a Web page.

Input Device A device that provides information to the computer. Typical devices are a mouse, keyboard, disk drive, microphone, and network port. *See also* **I/O Device** and **Output Device.**

Instance A computational object bearing the attributes and behavior specified by a class.

Instance Method A method that is called when a message is sent to an instance of a class. *See also* **Message.**

Instance Variable Storage for data in an instance of a class.

Instantiation The process of creating a new object or instance of a class.

Integer A data type that allows a programmer to represent whole numbers.

Integer Overflow A condition in which an integer value is too large to be stored in the computer's memory.

Interface A formal statement of how communication occurs between the user of a module (class or method) and its implementer.

Interface Class A Java class that simply specifies the methods to be implemented by another class. A class that implements several interface classes can thus adopt the behavior of several classes.

Interpreter A computer program that decodes and executes the instructions of another computer program.

Invoke *See* **Call.**

I/O Device Any device that allows information to be transmitted to or from a computer. *See also* **Input Device** and **Output Device.**

Item *See* **Element.**

J

Justification The process of aligning text to the left, the center, or the right within a given number of columns.

K

Key Field   A privileged data value that is used when one object is compared to another.

Keywords   *See* **Reserved Words.**

L

Library   A collection of methods and data organized to perform a set of related tasks. *See also* **Class** and **Package.**

Lifetime   The time during which a data object or method call exists.

Listener   A Java class that detects and responds to events.

Literal   An element of a language that expresses itself, such as 34 or "Hi there."

Loader   A system software tool that places program instructions and data into the appropriate memory locations before program startup.

Local Identifier   A name whose value is visible only within a method or a nested block.

Local Variable   *See* **Local Identifier.**

Logic Error   *See* **Design Error.**

Logical Operator   Either logical connective (&&, ¦¦) or negation (!).

Long   A Java data type used to represent large integers.

Loops   Program statements that cause a process to be repeated. *See also* `for` **Loop,** `do-while` **Loop,** and `while` **Loop.**

Low Cohesion   The property of a method such that it performs several tasks that are not closely related.

M

Machine Language   The language used directly by the computer in all its calculations and processing.

Main (Primary) Memory   Memory contained in the computer. *See also* **Memory** and **Secondary Memory.**

Mantissa/Exponent Notation   A notation used to express floating-point numbers.

Markup Tag   A syntactic form in the hypertext markup language used to create different elements displayed on a Web page.

Megabyte   Shorthand for approximately one million bytes.

Memex   A fictional machine, described by Vannevar Bush in 1945, that would allow users to perform many of the tasks that they now perform with the World Wide Web.

Memory   The ordered sequence of storage cells that can be accessed by address. Instructions and variables of an executing program are temporarily held here. *See also* **Main Memory** and **Secondary Memory.**

Menu Item   A window object that displays as an option in a pull-down menu or popup menu.

Message   A symbol used by a client to ask an object to perform a service. *See also* **Method.**

Message Box   A window object that pops up to display text and that can be closed by clicking an **OK** button.

Method   A chunk of code that can be treated as a unit and invoked by name. A method is called when a message is sent to an object. *See also* **Class Method** and **Instance Method.**

Method Heading   The portion of a method implementation containing the function's name, parameter declarations, and return type.

Mixed-Mode Arithmetic   Expressions containing data of different types; the values of these expressions will be of either type, depending on the rules for evaluating them.

Modal   A state in which the computer user cannot exit without explicitly signaling the computer, usually with an "Accept" or "Cancel" option.

Model/View/Controller Pattern (MVC Pattern)   A design plan in which the roles and responsibilities of the system are cleanly divided among data management (model), user interface display (view), and user event handling (controller) tasks.

Modem A device that connects a computer to a telephone system to transmit data.

Module An independent unit that is part of a larger development. A module can be a method or a class (set of methods and related data).

Module Specifications In the case of a method, a description of data received, information returned, and task performed by a module. In the case of a class, a description of the attributes and behavior.

Multidimensional Array An array that has two or more dimensions.

Mutator A method used to change the value of an attribute of an object.

N

Negation The use of the logical operator ! (NOT) with a Boolean expression, returning True if the expression is False, and False if the expression is True.

Nested `if` Statement A selection statement used within another selection statement.

Nested Loop A loop as one of the statements in the body of another loop.

Network A collection of resources that are linked together for communication.

Neural Net A computational object that is capable of learning a set of rules for performing tasks such as character recognition.

Newline Character A special character, denoted by \n, that is used to move text output to the next line on the screen.

Null Pointer Exception A run-time error that occurs when a program attempts to reference an object by means of a variable whose value happens to be null. *See also* **Null Value.**

Null Statement *See* **Empty Statement.**

Null Value A special value that indicates that no object can be accessed.

O

Object A collection of data and operations, in which the data can be accessed and modified only by means of the operations.

Object Code *See* **Object Program.**

Object-Oriented Programming The construction of software systems that use objects.

Object Program The machine code version of the source program.

Off-By-One Error Usually seen with loops, this error shows up as a result that is one less or one greater than the expected value.

One-Dimensional Array An array in which each data item is accessed by specifying a single index.

Opcode A symbol in assembly language or machine language that denotes a type of computer instruction, such as addition or subtraction.

Operating System A large program that allows the user to communicate with the hardware and performs various management tasks.

Ordinal Data Type A data type ordered in some association with the integers. Each integer is the ordinal of an associated value of the data type.

Origin The point (0,0) in a coordinate system.

Output Device A device that allows you to see the results of a program. Typically it is a monitor, printer, speaker, or network port. *See also* **Input Device** and **I/O Device.**

Overflow In arithmetic operations, a value may be too large for the computer's memory location. A meaningless value may be assigned or an error message may result.

Overloading The process of using the same operator symbol or identifier to refer to many different functions. *See also* **Polymorphism.**

Overriding The process of reimplementing a method already implemented in a superclass.

P

Package   A group of related classes in a named directory.

Paint Mode   The state of a Java program in which images are drawn by replacing the existing pixel values on the screen.

Panel   A window object whose purpose is to contain other window objects.

Parallel Arrays   Arrays of the same length but with different component data types.

Parameter   *See* **Argument**.

Parameter List   A list of parameters. An actual parameter list is contained in a method call. A formal parameter list is contained in a method heading.

Parent   The immediate superclass of a class.

Pattern   A typical way of doing things that has proved useful. *See also* **Model/View/Controller Pattern.**

Peripheral Memory   *See* **Secondary Memory** and **Memory.**

Persistence   The property of a data model that allows it to survive different runs of an application. *See also* **Serialization.**

Pixel   A picture element or dot of color used to display images on a computer screen.

Pointer   A reference to an object that allows one to access it.

Polymorphism   The property of one operator symbol or method identifier having many meanings. *See also* **Overloading.**

Popup Menu   A window object that allows the user to pop the menu up and select from a list of menu items. *See also* **Menu Item.**

Portable   Able to be transferred to different applications or computers without changes.

Postcondition   A statement of what is true after a certain action is taken.

Post-Test Loop   A loop where the control condition is tested after the loop is executed. A `do-`while loop is a post-test loop. Also referred to as an **Exit-Controlled Loop.**

Precedence   The ranking of operators that tells the computer the order in which to perform operations in an expression.

Precondition   A statement of what is true before a certain action is taken.

Pretest Loop   A loop where the control condition is tested before the loop is executed. A `while` Loop is a pretest loop. Also referred to as an **Entrance-Controlled Loop.**

Primary Memory   *See* **Main Memory** and **Memory.**

Primitive Data Type   A data type such as `char`, `int`, `double`, or `boolean`, whose values are stored directly in variables of that type. Primitive data types are always passed by value when they are parameters in Java, and copied during assignment statements.

Print Stream   A Java class that sends text output to the terminal window.

Private Method   A method that is accessible only within the scope of a class definition.

Private Variable   A variable that is accessible only within the scope of a class definition.

Procedural Programming   A style of programming that decomposes a program into a set of methods or procedures.

Production Rules   Conditional statements that are used in programs in artificial intelligence.

Program   A set of instructions that tells the machine (the hardware) what to do.

Program Walk-Through   The process of carefully following, using pencil and paper, steps the computer uses to solve the problem given in a program. Also referred to as a **Trace.**

Programming Language   Formal language that computer scientists use to give instructions to the computer.

Protected Variable   A variable that is accessible only within the scope of a class definition or within the class definition of a subclass.

Pseudocode A stylized half-English, half-code language written in English but suggesting Java code.

Public Method A method that is accessible to any program component that uses the class.

Public Variable A variable that is accessible to any program component that uses the class.

Pull-Down Menu A window object that allows the user to pull down and select from a list of menu items. *See also* **Menu Item.**

R

Radio Button A type of checkbox that appears in a group, permitting the user to select only one checkbox in the group. *See also* **Checkbox.**

Range Bound Error The situation that occurs when an attempt is made to use an array index value that is less than 0 or greater than or equal to the size of the array.

Recursion The process of a subprogram calling itself. A clearly defined stopping state must exist. Any recursive subprogram can be rewritten using iteration.

Recursive Method A method that calls itself.

Recursive Step A step in the recursive process that solves a similar problem of smaller size and eventually leads to a termination of the process.

Recursive Subprogram *See* **Recursion.**

Reference Type A data type such as `array`, `String`, or any other Java class, whose instances are not stored directly in variables of that type. References or pointers to these objects are stored instead. References to objects are passed when they are parameters in Java, and just the references, not the objects, are copied during assignment statements.

Refreshable Image An image that is redisplayed when the user resizes or minimizes a window.

Relational Operator An operator used for comparison of data items of the same type.

Reliability The property of a program such that it solves the problems originally specified by its users.

Repetition *See* **Loops.**

Reserved Words Words that have predefined meanings that cannot be changed. A list of reserved words for Java is given in Appendix B.

Return Type The type of value returned by a method.

Robot A machine that performs many of the tasks that humans can perform.

Robust The state in which a program is protected against most possible crashes from bad data and unexpected values.

Root The topmost class in a hierarchy; a root has no parent class. *See also* **Hierarchy.**

Run-Time Error An error detected when, after compilation is completed, an error message results instead of the correct output. *See also* **Design Error**, **Exception,** and **Syntax Error.**

S

Scanning The process of picking words or tokens out of a stream of characters.

Scope The largest block in which the variable is available.

Scroll Bar A window object that allows the user to select a value from a continuous range.

Scrolling List A window object that displays a selectable list of strings.

Secondary Memory An auxiliary device for memory, usually a disk or magnetic tape. *See also* **Main Memory** and **Memory.**

Secondary Storage Device A device that is capable of storing data permanently. *See also* **Secondary Memory.**

Selection The process by which a method or a variable of an instance or a class is accessed.

Selection Statement A control statement that selects some particular logical path based on the value of an expression. Also referred to as a **Conditional Statement.**

Self-Documenting Code   Code that is written using descriptive identifiers.

Semantics   The rules for interpreting the meaning of a program in a language.

Serialization   A mechanism that maintains the persistence of objects in a data model. *See also* **Persistence.**

Server   A computational object that provides a service to another computational object.

Short   A Java data type used to represent small integers.

Short-Circuit Evaluation   The process whereby a compound Boolean expression halts evaluation and returns the value of the first subexpression that evaluates to true, in the case of ¦¦, or false, in the case of **&&.**

Side Effect   A change in a variable that is the result of some action taken in a program, usually from within a method.

Simple Boolean Expression   An expression in which two numbers or variable values are compared using a single relational operator. *See also* **Boolean Expression** and **Compound Boolean Expression.**

Softbot   A program that is capable of performing many tasks performed by humans, such as filtering out unwanted e-mail.

Software   Programs that make the machine (the hardware) do something, such as word processing, database management, or games.

Software Engineering   The process of developing and maintaining large software systems.

Software Life Cycle   The process of development, maintenance, and demise of a software system. Phases include analysis, design, coding, testing/verification, maintenance, and obsolescence.

Software Reuse   The process of building and maintaining software systems out of existing software components.

Source Program   A program written by a programmer.

Stand-Alone Program   A Java program that runs directly on a computer, without the aid of a Web browser. Also known as an **Application.**

State   The set of all the values of the variables of a program at any point during its execution.

Statement   A unit of program code that performs a task.

Stepwise Refinement   The process of repeatedly subdividing tasks into subtasks until each subtask is easily accomplished. *See also* **Structured Programming** and **Top-Down Implementation.**

Stopping State   The well-defined termination of a recursive process.

Stream   A channel in which data are passed from sender to receiver.

Stream Tokenizer   A Java class that allows the programmer to input text from a file one word at a time.

String   An abbreviated name for a string literal.

String Literal   One or more characters, enclosed in double quotes, used as a constant in a program.

Structure Chart   A graphic method of indicating the relationship between modules when designing the solution to a problem.

Structured Programming   Programming that parallels a solution to a problem achieved by top-down implementation. *See also* **Stepwise Refinement** and **Top-Down Implementation.**

Stub Programming   The process of using incomplete functions to test data transmission among them.

Subclass   A class that inherits attributes and behavior from another class.

Subscript   *See* **Array Index** or **Loop Index.**

Substring   A string that represents a segment of another string.

Superclass The class from which a subclass class inherits attributes and behavior. *See also* **Subclass** and **Inheritance.**

Syntax The rules for constructing well-formed programs in a language.

Syntax Error An error in spelling, punctuation, or placement of certain key symbols in a program. *See also* **Design Error** and **Run-Time Error.**

System Software The programs that allow users to write and execute other programs, including operating systems such as Windows and MacOS.

T

Tail-Recursive The property that a recursive algorithm has of performing no work after each recursive step. *See also* **Recursion.**

Text Area A window object that provides a scrollable region within which the user can view or enter several lines of text.

Text Field A window object in which the user can view or enter a single line of text.

Text File A file whose data consist of characters and that normally can be viewed with a text editor.

Thread A computational process that can execute concurrently with other processes.

Token An individual word or symbol.

Top-Down Design A method of design whereby you describe how a task is performed in terms of subtasks. *See also* **Top-Down Implementation.**

Top-Down Implementation A method for coding whereby the user starts with a top-level task and implements subtasks. Each subtask is then subdivided into smaller subtasks. This process is repeated until each remaining subtask is easily coded. *See also* **Stepwise Refinement** and **Structured Programming.**

Trace *See* **Program Walk-Through.**

Transient Image An image that is lost when the user resizes or minimizes a window.

Truth Table A means of listing all of the possible values of a Boolean expression.

Two-Dimensional Array An array in which each data item is accessed by specifying a pair of indices.

Type *See* **Data Type.**

Type Promotion The process of converting a less inclusive data type, such as `int`, to a more inclusive data type, such as `double`.

U

Unicode A character set that uses 16 bits to represent more than 65,000 possible characters. These include the ASCII character set as well as symbols and ideograms in many international languages. *See also* **ASCII Character Set.**

Uniform Resource Locator (URL) The address of a page on the World WideWeb.

User-Defined Class A new data type introduced and defined by the programmer.

User-Defined Method A new function introduced and defined by the programmer.

User Requirements Phase The part of the software development life cycle in which the user's request, as interpreted by the programmer, is written out in detail.

V

Value A data item that is stored in a memory location.

Variable A memory location, referenced by an identifier, whose value can be changed during a program.

Virtual Machine A software tool that behaves like a high-level computer.

Virus A computer program that is capable of being attached to another program, copying itself to a disk or to memory, and causing possible harm to data on the host computer.

Visibility Modifier A symbol (`public`, `protected`, or `private`) that specifies the kind of access that clients have to a server's data and methods.

Void Method A method that returns no value.

W

Waterfall Model A series of steps in which a software system trickles down, from analysis to design to implementation. *See also* **Software Life Cycle.**

`while` **Loop** A pretest loop that examines a Boolean expression before causing a statement to be executed.

Window A rectangular area of a computer screen that can contain window objects. Windows typically can be resized, minimized, zoomed, or closed. *See also* **Frame.**

Window Object A computational object that displays an image, such as a button or a text field, in a window, and supports interaction with the user.

Word A unit of memory consisting of 1 or more bytes. Words can be addressed.

X

XOR Mode The state of a Java program in which images are drawn by saving the existing pixel values on the screen so that they can subsequently be restored.

INDEX

H

I